FACING THE CHALLENGE OF DEMOCRACY

FACING THE CHALLENGE OF DEMOCRACY

EXPLORATIONS IN THE ANALYSIS OF PUBLIC OPINION AND POLITICAL PARTICIPATION

EDITED BY

Paul M. Sniderman and
Benjamin Highton

PRINCETON UNIVERSITY PRESS   PRINCETON AND OXFORD

Library of Congress Cataloging-in-Publication Data

Facing the challenge of democracy : explorations in the analysis of public opinion and political participation / edited by Paul M. Sniderman and Benjamin Highton.

   p. cm.

Includes bibliographical references and index.

ISBN 978-0-691-15110-6 (hardback : alk. paper) —

ISBN 978-0-691-15111-3 (pbk. : alk. paper)   1. Political participation—United States.

2. Public opinion—United States. 3. United States—Politics and government—1989–

I. Sniderman, Paul M.   II. Highton, Benjamin.

  JK1764.F33 2011

  323'.0420973—dc22

2011002780

British Library Cataloging-in-Publication Data is available

With as much respect as affection, this book is dedicated to

Barbara Kaye Wolfinger

Contents

ALL BUT ONE OF THE SCHOLARS THAT WE INVITED to contribute to this book immediately accepted; all made the deadline for the review of the manuscript by external referees; all did the additional work that we asked of them; all made or beat the deadline for submission of the final version of their chapters—all right, one was three days late.

This is not the customary experience for a collaborative work, it hardly needs saying. Why did virtually everyone accept our invitation? Why did all do all what we asked of them? The only reason that we can come up with is the same reason that motivated us to do the book: a desire to honor Raymond Wolfinger.

For all who are familiar with his work, it is obvious why. His work—all his work—is authoritative, displaying three qualities. He has guillotine logic in deducing empirical implications of others' arguments. He has a rare power of imagination in thinking up empirical tests. And he is ruthless in putting his own views to the test. Richard Feynman defined a scientist as one who tries to prove himself wrong. By that standard, Ray Wolfinger is a genuine scientist.

There is another characteristic that we have heard attributed to Ray's work—that it is atheoretical. There is a sense in which we think that is right. He is offended by what Frederick Maitland, a legal historian of genius, described as "glittering generalizations." And he is offended for the same reason as Maitland: because of their combination of pretentiousness and imprecision. On the other hand, having invested a good deal of time in a close reading of all—or nearly all—of his work, from the earliest to the latest, we will tell you that his work is theoretical, right to its core, and in exactly one of the senses in which the word "theoretical" does real work in the social sciences.

Here is an example of what we have in mind. Robert Merton characterized political machines as serving an integrative function for immigrants by distributing resources to them in exchange for their votes. Wolfinger makes a stabbingly smart observation. Political machines are not in the business of handing out resources. They give big rewards to their leaders and chicken feed to the rest. This is the kind of observation that only a person who knows firsthand how things work in politics would make. When we say how "things" work, we mean political institutions all in all—political machines yes, but also Congress and parties and voting regimes, because he has made lasting contributions in all these fields.

And then there is another quality that distinguishes Ray's work. It has an aesthetic quality—precision, drive, economy of expression, and above all, lucidity. The writing is so direct, transparent, and spot on, that it appears just obviously right—what everyone should have seen and understood—except that no one had. We thought hard about how to convey the aesthetic style of Ray's work, for a long time without success—until we remembered a story told of someone who asked Jonathan Swift how he wrote with so singular a style. Swift replied: "It is easy. Just put the right word in the right place." And that, in our view, is what Ray Wolfinger has done. He has put just the right words in just the right places.

P.M.S. and B.H.

Acknowledgments

OUR LARGEST DEBT IS TO the contributors to this book. We could not have asked more of them, above all, in sticking to the schedule whatever else was happening in their lives. They could not have done more for us, not only in sticking to it, but above all, in the effort that they put into their contributions. Our expression of gratitude to them is not ritualistic. It is heartfelt.

Behind the scenes, two people played an indispensable role in coordinating and facilitating all that was necessary to put together this book—Jackie Sargent, Administrator of the Department of Political Science at Stanford, and Eliana Vasquez, Faculty Support Administrator. They make going to work a pleasure. In addition, Matthew Pietryka provided valuable assistance in helping us prepare the manuscript. We also are grateful for the support of the National Science Foundation (SES–0842677) and Institute for Research in the Social Sciences.

Willing hearts but empty pockets is a guarantee of frustration and failure. But even with willing hearts and the helping hands of colleagues, we would not have crossed the goal line—indeed, we would not have even got on the field—without our editor, Chuck Myers. He set the bar high. But all the help that one could hope for when publishing a book, he provided, and all the misadventures that one should fear when attempting to put a book together, he prevented.

There is one last person we should like to acknowledge, Barbara Kaye Wolfinger, for two distinct reasons. One is her partnership with the person this book honors. Whether he would have achieved all that he has without her is a hypothesis that we do not know how to test. But we are willing to bet our children and grandchildren's educational trust funds on its validity. The other reason to acknowledge her is the part that she has played in our lives. For both these reasons, we dedicate this book to her and whatever monies that it should earn to the organization that she has served—as President, Vice President, Board Director, and, not least, volunteer on the hotline—first known as Suicide Prevention, and now because of the broader umbrella of support it provides—Crisis Support Services, Alameda County, California.

Contributors

John H. Aldrich (PhD, Rochester) is the Pfizer-Pratt University Professor of Political Science at Duke University. He specializes in American politics and behavior, formal theory, and methodology. He has authored or coauthored *Why Parties*, *Before the Convention*, and a series of books on elections, the most recent of which is *Change and Continuity in the 2008 Elections*, among others. He is a Fellow of the American Academy of Arts and Sciences.

Stephen Ansolabehere is Professor of Government at Harvard University. He is author of *The Media Game* (1993), *Going Negative* (1996), and *The End of Inequality* (2008), and numerous articles on politics, law, and elections. He directed the Caltech/MIT Voting Technology Project in the aftermath of the 2000 election recount.

Edward G. Carmines (PhD, SUNY-Buffalo) is Warner O. Chapman Professor of Political Science and Rudy Professor at Indiana University. He is also the Research Director at the Center on Congress and Director of the Center on American Politics at Indiana University. Professor Carmines has published research on public opinion, political behavior, and research methodology in the top journals of the discipline including the *American Political Science Review*, *American Journal of Political Science*, and *The Journal of Politics*. Two of his seven books, *Issue Evolution* (with James A. Stimson) and *Reaching Beyond Race* (with Paul Sniderman), have won the American Political Science Association's Kammerer Award for Best Book in the Field of U.S. National Policy. Carmines was a Fellow at the Center for Advanced Study in the Behavioral Sciences at Stanford University in 2000–2001 and was a Fellow at the Center for the Study of Democratic Politics at Princeton University in 2006–2007.

Jack Citrin is Heller Professor of Political Science and Director of the Institute of Governmental Relations at the University of California, Berkeley. His research interests have centered on political trust and legitimacy, direct democracy, the tax revolt, immigration and language politics, and, most recently, the future of national identity in the United States and Europe. His books include *Tax Revolt: Something for Nothing in California*; *How Race, Ethnicity and Immigration Are Transforming the American Electorate*; the monograph *The Politics of Disaffection among American and British Youth*; the forthcoming (with David Sears) *American Identity and the Politics of Multiculturalism*; as well as many articles and book chapters on these themes.

Susanna Dilliplane (MA, University of Pennsylvania) is a doctoral candidate at the Annenberg School for Communication, University of Pennsylvania. Her research focuses on political communication, its effects on political attitudes and behaviors, and the implications of expanded news and information choices.

Christopher Ellis is an Assistant Professor of Political Science at Bucknell University. His research interests include public opinion, political representation, and mass-elite linkages in public policymaking. He earned his PhD from the University of North Carolina–Chapel Hill.

Michael J. Ensley (PhD, Duke University) is an Assistant Professor of Political Science at Kent State University. Professor Ensley's research uses advanced statistical methods to analyze how candidates for and members of the U.S. Congress respond to the competing demands of citizens, activists, interests groups, and political parties. He has published articles in the *American Journal of Political Science, Public Choice, Political Analysis,* and *American Politics Research.* Ensley is the 1998–2001 recipient of the National Science Foundation Graduate Fellowship and the 2001–2002 National Election Studies Fellowship.

Melanie Freeze is a doctoral candidate in the Department of Political Science at Duke University. Her current research focuses on the influence of partisan identities on information processing under conditions of threat. She also is interested in the source, message, and recipient components of political persuasion in the context of campaigns and elections.

Donald P. Green is A. Whitney Griswold Professor of Political Science at Yale University, where he has taught since 1989. His research interests in political science span a wide array of topics: voting behavior, partisanship, campaign finance, prejudice, and hate crime. His coauthored books include *Pathologies of Rational Choice Theory: A Critique of Applications in Political Science* (Yale University Press, 1994), *Partisan Hearts and Minds: Political Parties and the Social Identities of Voters* (Yale University Press, 2002), and *Get Out the Vote: How to Increase Voter Turnout* (Brookings Institution Press, 2008).

Eitan Hersh is an Assistant Professor of Political Science at Yale University. He specializes in the study of campaign strategy, voting behavior, election administration, and information technology and politics. His dissertation, *Information-Based Candidate Strategy,* offers a theory of voter mobilization that emphasizes the role of personal data in shaping electoral coalitions.

Benjamin Highton is an Associate Professor in the Political Science Department at the University of California, Davis. He specializes in the study of elections, public opinion, and voting behavior. His research has been supported by grants from the Ford, Carnegie, and CIRCLE foundations. Before joining the faculty at UC Davis, he was an American Political Science Association Congressional Fellow and worked for Senator Paul Wellstone.

Simon Jackman codirects the Stanford Center for American Democracy and is one of the principal investigators of the American National Election Studies, 2010–2013. His research centers on American electoral politics, public opinion, democratic representation, and the art and science of survey research. In recent years, his research has investigated the Internet as a platform for survey research, to better track the evolution of public opinion and produce more politically relevant assessments of American political attitudes. In 2007–2008, Jackman and Lynn Vavreck were the principal investigators of the Cooperative Campaign Analysis Project, an Internet-based, six-wave, longitudinal study of the American electorate leading up to the 2008 presidential election. In 2009, he published a statistics text, *Bayesian Analysis for the Social Sciences*. Jackman is also an Associate Editor of *Annual Reviews of Political Science* and *Political Analysis*.

Gary C. Jacobson is Distinguished Professor of Political Science at the University of California, San Diego, where he has taught since 1979. He received his AB from Stanford in 1966 and his PhD from Yale in 1972. He specializes in the study of U.S. elections, parties, interest groups, public opinion, and Congress. He is the author of *Money in Congressional Elections, The Politics of Congressional Elections*, and *The Electoral Origins of Divided Government* and coauthor of *Strategy and Choice in Congressional Elections* and *The Logic of American Politics*, as well as more than 80 research articles. His most recent book is *A Divider, Not a Uniter: George W. Bush and the American People*. Jacobson has served on the Board of Overseers of National Election Studies (1985–1993), the Council of the American Political Science Association (1993–1994), the APSA's Committee on Research Support, as Treasurer of the APSA (1996–1997) and as chair of the APSA's Elections Review Committee (2001–2002). He has been a fellow at the Center for Advanced Study in the Behavioral Sciences and is a fellow of the American Academy of Arts and Sciences.

Matthew R. Knee (MA, MPhil, Yale University) is a doctoral candidate in the Yale University Department of Political Science. His research focuses on electoral mobilization, election law, ethnic and religious political organizing, and experimental and quasi-experimental methods in political science.

Jonathan Krasno is an Associate Professor of Political Science at Binghamton University. His research focuses on public opinion, congressional elections, campaigns, and campaign financing. He is author of *Challengers, Competition, and Reelection* (Yale University Press, 1994), *Buying Time* (Brennan Center, 2000), and articles in *American Journal of Political Science*, *Journal of Politics*, and elsewhere. In addition to his scholarly interests, Krasno has been an active participant in ongoing debate over campaign finance reform, most notably serving as an expert witness in federal trials in California, Colorado, Louisiana, Missouri, and Washington, DC.

Arthur Lupia is the Hal R. Varian Collegiate Professor of Political Science at the University of Michigan. He cofounded TESS (Time Shared Experiments in the Social Sciences) and served as a Principal Investigator of the American National Election Studies from 2005 to 2009. His research topics include civic competence, political persuasion, delegation and accountability, and political coalitions. His books include *The Democratic Dilemma: Can Citizens Learn What They Need to Know?* (1998), *Elements of Reason: Cognition, Choice, and the Bounds of Rationality* (2000), and *The Cambridge Handbook of Experimental Political Science* (2011).

David B. Magleby, Distinguished Professor of Political Science, Senior Research Fellow at the Center for the Study of Elections and Democracy, and Dean of the College of Family, Home and Social Sciences at Brigham Young University, has published books and articles on direct democracy, voting behavior, and campaign finance. He is also coauthor of *Government by the People,* an American government textbook. He received his BA from the University of Utah and his PhD from the University of California, Berkeley. He has been a Fulbright Scholar at Oxford University and a past president of Pi Sigma Alpha, the national political science honor society.

Eric McGhee is a Research Fellow at the Public Policy Institute of California (PPIC), where his work focuses on political reform, legislative behavior, elections, and public opinion. Before joining PPIC, he was an Assistant Professor of Political Science at the University of Oregon, and before that he was an APSA Congressional Fellow in the office of Rep. Adam Schiff. He received his PhD in political science in 2003 from the University of California, Berkeley.

Diana Mutz is Samuel A. Stouffer Professor of Political Science and Communication at the University of Pennsylvania. She is the author of two award-winning books, *Hearing the Other Side: Deliberative versus Participatory Democracy* (2006) and *Impersonal Influence* (1998), as well as many research articles on political communication in American politics.

She also serves as Director of the Institute for the Study of Citizens and Politics at the Annenberg Public Policy Center.

Candice J. Nelson is an Associate Professor of Government at American University (AU) and Director of AU's Campaign Management Institute. She is the coauthor of *Vital Signs: Perspectives on the Health of American Campaigning* (Brookings Institution, 2005), *The Myth of the Independent Voter* (University of California, 1992), and *The Money Chase: Congressional Campaign Finance Reform* (Brookings Institution, 1990). She is the coeditor of *Campaigns and Elections American Style* (Westview Press, 1995, 2004, 2009), *Shades of Gray: Perspectives on Campaign Ethics* (Brookings Institution, 2002), *Campaign Warriors: Political Consultants in Elections* (Brookings Institution, 2000), and *Crowded Airwaves: Campaign Advertising in Elections* (Brookings Institution, 2000). She received her PhD at the University of California at Berkeley.

Benjamin I. Page is the Gordon Scott Fulcher Professor of Decision Making, Professor of Political Science, and Faculty Associate, Institute of Policy Research, Northwestern University. He holds a JD from Harvard Law School and a PhD in political science from Stanford and has done postdoctoral work in economics at MIT and Harvard. His interests include public opinion and policy making, political economy, the mass media, and U.S. foreign policy. His most recent books are *Living with the Dragon: How the American Public Views the Rise of China* (Columbia University Press, 2010, with Tao Xie) and *Class War? What Americans Really Think about Economic Inequality* (University of Chicago Press, 2009, with L. Jacobs). Other books include *The Foreign Policy Disconnect* (University of Chicago Press, 2006, with M. Bouton; winner of the APSA's Kammerer Award for the best book on U.S. national policy); *The Rational Public* (University of Chicago Press, 1992, with R. Shapiro; winner of the APSA's Converse Award for a book of enduring significance on public opinion); *Who Deliberates? Mass Media in Modern Democracy* (University of Chicago Press, 1996); *What Government Can Do: Dealing with Poverty and Inequality* (University of Chicago Press, 2000, with J. Simmons); and *Who Gets What from Government* (University of California Press, 1983; winner of the Policy Studies Organization Best Book Award). He has been a Fellow at the Center for Advanced Study in the Behavioral Sciences and at the Hoover Institution and is a member of the American Academy of Arts and Sciences.

Kathryn Pearson (PhD, UC Berkeley) is an Assistant Professor of Political Science at the University of Minnesota. She specializes in American politics; her research focuses on the U.S. Congress, congressional elections, and women and politics and has recently appeared in *The Journal of Politics*,

Legislative Studies Quarterly, and *Perspectives on Politics*. She is currently working on a book, *Party Discipline in the House of Representatives*.

Eric Schickler is the Jeffrey and Ashley McDermott Professor of Political Science at the University of California, Berkeley. He is the author of *Disjointed Pluralism: Institutional Innovation and the Development of the U.S. Congress* (Princeton University Press, 2001), *Partisan Hearts and Minds* (coauthored with Donald Green and Bradley Palmquist), and *Filibuster: Obstruction and Lawmaking in the U.S. Senate* (coauthored with Gregory Wawro; Princeton University Press, 2006). He has authored or coauthored articles in the *American Political Science Review*, *American Journal of Political Science*, *Journal of Politics*, *Legislative Studies Quarterly*, *Comparative Political Studies*, *Polity*, *Public Opinion Quarterly*, and *Studies in American Political Development*.

John Sides is a Professor in the Department of Political Science at George Washington University. He studies political behavior in American and comparative politics. His current research focuses on political campaigns, the effects of factual information on public opinion, citizenship laws and national identity, and measurement equivalence. His work has appeared in the *American Political Science Review*, *American Journal of Political Science*, *American Politics Research*, *British Journal of Political Science*, *Journal of Politics*, *Political Communication*, *Political Studies*, *Presidential Studies Quarterly*, and *Legislative Studies Quarterly*.

Paul M. Sniderman is the Fairleigh S. Dickinson Jr. Professor of Public Policy at Stanford. His research concentrates on the analysis of political reasoning and commitment to democratic values. His most recent book is *When Ways of Life Collide*. He is a Fellow of the American Academy of Arts and Sciences and of the Association for the Advancement of Science.

James A. Stimson is the Raymond Dawson Distinguished Bicentennial Professor of Political Science at the University of North Carolina at Chapel Hill. Stimson is former President of the Midwest Political Science Association and Treasurer of the American Political Science Association. He has authored or coauthored six books and is a Fellow at the American Academy of Arts and Sciences, a Fellow at the Center for Advanced Study in the Behavioral Sciences (1994–1995), and a Guggenheim Fellow (2006–2007). He has won the Heinz Eulau and Gladys Kammerer Awards of the American Political Science Association, the Chastain Award of the Southern Political Science Association, and the Pi Sigma Alpha Award of the Midwest Political Science Association. Former Editor of *Political Analysis*, he has served on the editorial boards of *American Journal of Political Science*, *Journal of Politics*, *Political Methodology*, *Public Opinion Quarterly*, and *American Politics Quarterly*.

Lynn Vavreck is an Associate Professor of Political Science at the University of California, Los Angeles. She is the author of *The Message Matters: The Economy and Presidential Campaigns*, and coeditor (with Larry Bartels) of *Campaign Reform: Insights and Evidence*. In 2007, she fielded the Cooperative Campaign Analysis Project with co–Principal Investigator Simon Jackman. She sits on the Advisory Board to the British Election Study and the American National Election Study's Board of Overseers.

Michael W. Wagner (PhD, Indiana University) is an Assistant Professor of Political Science at the University of Nebraska–Lincoln (UNL). Wagner's research generally focuses on the interplay between political elites and the public, with most of his research examining questions of political communication, partisanship, and biology and politics. He is published in the *Annual Review of Political Science, Political Research Quarterly, American Politics Research*, and in many other academic journals and edited volumes. He was Project Director for the 2006 Congressional Election Study conducted by the Center on Congress. Wagner was named UNL's 2009 Outstanding Educator of the Year. He is the recipient of grants from the National Science Foundation and the Dirksen Congressional Center.

Mark C. Westlye (PhD, UC Berkeley) is the author of *Senate Elections and Campaign Intensity* (1991). He recently retired from the Office of the President of the University of California, where he directed academic personnel policy for graduate student employees and postdoctoral scholars and developed programs to assist promising undergraduates in moving into graduate study.

Tao Xie is an Associate Professor at the American Studies Center, Beijing Foreign Studies University. He holds a PhD in political science from Northwestern University (2007). His research interests include Congress, public opinion, and Sino-U.S. relations. He has published two books, *U.S.-China Relations: China Policy on Capitol Hill* (Routledge, 2009) and *Living with the Dragon: How the American Public Views the Rise of China* (Columbia Univeristy Press, 2010, coauthored with Benjamin I. Page).

FACING THE CHALLENGE OF DEMOCRACY

Introduction

Facing the Challenge of Democracy

Paul M. Sniderman and Benjamin Highton

IN POLITICS, SKEPTICS OUTBID CYNICS. A cynic questions whether people will do the right thing even though they know the right reason to do it. A skeptic doubts that they know the right reason and in any case questions whether they have the competence to do the right thing when it comes to politics.

Skeptics far outnumber cynics in the debate over whether ordinary citizens are capable of discharging the duties of citizenship. A long parade of studies has shown that citizens fail minimally challenging tests of knowledge of public affairs and institutions.[1] A still deeper vein of skepticism contends that citizens tend to make a muddle of things when reasoning about politics. We have too few fingers on our hands and toes on our feet to count the number of studies showing that citizens vote for candidates and parties committed to policies that will make them worse off rather than better off; or hold contradictory preferences, clamoring for lower taxes, for example, while demanding more government spending for social services; or are embarrassingly susceptible to errors and biases in their reasoning; or make political choices for comically irrelevant reasons—most notoriously, punishing incumbents for shark attacks at tourist beaches. (And so on.)[2] Naturally, a barrage of counterarguments has been mounted. Ignorance of politics is rational, Downs famously argues.[3] Or others (including Downs) contend that even knowing as little about politics as citizens do, they nonetheless can reason efficiently through the use of judgmental shortcuts.[4] And still others have argued that even if most citizens make a muddle of things, elections are decided by changes at the margin, and at the margin, choices are informed.[5] (And so on.)

What is this tug-of-war between camps with opposing judgments of citizen competence about? It is, most fundamentally, about the capacity of citizens to make politically coherent choices. One way to gain traction in this tug-of-war—not the only way, to be sure, but all the same a pivotal one—is to understand as deeply as possible the properties of political preferences of ordinary citizens. Accordingly, the studies here fall in three sections. Part I focuses on the political logic of preference consistency; part II on the most prominent feature of political preferences in contemporary politics—polarization; part III on the relationship between policy preferences and electoral representation.

Part I: The Political Logic of Preference Consistency

We begin with a definition. By a "preference," we mean a disposition to respond consistently, either negatively or positively, to a focal object.[6] Political preferences are variously denominated, running (in order of generality of scope) from ideological orientation, basic values, partisanship, policy preferences, to electoral choices. In promoting political consistency to a top-of-the-list item on our research agenda, some may suspect that we are writing tongue-in-cheek, since consistency in political preferences is precisely what ordinary citizens supposedly lack.[7] So we want to begin with a paradox: in politics, citizens must sometimes make inconsistent choices in order, ultimately, to have made a consistent one.

The logic of this paradox is set out in chapter 1. This chapter, by Lupia, makes two distinct contributions, one having to do with the measurement of preferences, the other having to do with the theory of choice. On the first front, Lupia brings out how the preferences of citizens may appear fickle and incoherent because of measurement error. Lupia does this, we are pleased to say, not by issuing the customary hortatory injunction to improve measurement, but by putting on the table specific improvements in widely used measures in public opinion research. All the same, we want to concentrate on the second front, his argument on the theory of political choice, since it is wide in its application and deep in its implications.

The dominant approach in the study of political choice, Lupia observes, is "institution free." Consider the paradigmatic example of this approach—the canonical Downsian model of rational choice. In this model, rationality requires voters consistently—indeed, invariantly—to choose the candidate whose position is closest to theirs. But, Lupia argues, making the "correct" choice is not so straightforward; political choices are institution-dependent. Consider governments made up of party coalitions. A moderate may more closely realize her preferences by voting, not for her moderate party, but instead for an extreme one, and by "overshooting" her true preference, pull the overall coalition closer to it.[8] Hence the paradox: to wind up with a consistent choice, it sometimes is necessary to deviate along the way. This is not a matter of being inconsistent. It is a textbook case of being strategic.

But are we begging the question, presupposing that citizens' political preferences are politically coherent rather than demonstrating it? Yes, there are strategic choices in politics, and therefore the appearance of preference inconsistency may be explained away. But why take inconsistency as the starting point, as though it (or the appearance of it) is the characteristic state of affairs? There actually are two questions here that are being asked at the same time. Is it the case that citizens put their preferences together coherently? And, supposing that they do, how do they do it? But although the two questions are distinct, the fate of the first is tied to that of the second. Against a background of thirty years and more of conflicting results, no merely empirical analysis can constitute dispositive evidence. We will not be persuaded that citizens make coherent political choices until we have good ideas how they can pull it off.

Good ideas, we say, because we have a deep-in-the-bones conviction that there is no single sovereign theory of political reasoning equally applicable to all regardless of who or what in politics we may be concerned to understand. But we are persuaded that making the empirical case for preference consistency depends on coming up with new ideas about how citizens can pull this off. One such new idea is Page and Xie's provocative theory of "purposive belief systems." Their theory is provocative on two grounds. The first has to do with intellectual strategy. Contrary to the drunk who looks for his keys not where he lost them, next to his car, but a half block away "cause that's where the light is," Page and Xie look where the light is dim. They examine preferences where we, at any rate, would be least likely to expect consistency—the domain of foreign policy preferences, in particular, American public opinion toward China. There, of all places, they apply their theory of purposive belief systems.[9] Schematically, the theory is built around three classes of constructs—values, goals, and threats. Taking account of the interplay on the three, they summarize the evidence as suggesting that citizens "tend to think sensibly about politics, instrumentally deriving their policy preferences from values they hold, threats they perceive, and goals they embrace."

Their theory of purposive belief systems is provocative on another ground. Earlier, Page (with Shapiro) mounted arguably the most theoretically grounded critique of the consensus view of citizens as empty-headed (the nonattitudes problem), or muddle-headed (the lack of constraint problem), or both.[10] Leveraging Condorcet's theorem, their argument granted that the policy preferences of individuals had a large component of randomness. But taken as a whole, these random errors tend to cancel each other out, they argued. The result is that the collective opinion of the public tends to be "real, stable, and sensible,"[11] even though the opinions of (many of) the individuals who make up the public are not. This, roughly, is the so-called miracle of aggregation. In contrast, in their theory of purposive belief systems, Page and Xie advance a striking conjecture:

"[Mere] aggregation, alone, will not do it; as a leading political scientist once pointed out, 'a thousand times nothing is still nothing.' "[12] Coherence in the public as a whole, Page and Xie now propose, is grounded in the coherence of indivduals' preferences. In their words,

> empirical relationships among logically connected values, interests, beliefs, and policy preferences are apparently strong enough so that, if and when most Americans agree on centrally relevant values and beliefs, majorities of Americans will come to favor a set of policies that coherently and consistently reflect those values and beliefs. . . . The aggregation of individual opinions can indeed dispose of offsetting random errors, but it will reveal something coherent at the collective level only if certain coherent tendencies are shared in the minds of individuals. We believe that we have uncovered such tendencies.[13]

There are not many examples of political scientists rethinking career-defining ideas. This is one.

To this point, we have been proceeding as though the meaning of a preference is obvious: preferences are "tastes." A liberal is a liberal just to the degree that he has a consistent taste for liberal policies; an isolationist is an isolationist just to the degree that she has a consistent taste for isolationist policies. Most often, indeed, very nearly always, this is the right way—or at least a satisfactory way—to think of preferences both theoretically and operationally. But it is not the only way. In their analysis of "cosmopolitanism," Jackman and Vavreck bring out a different way to think about—and measure—preferences.

Preferences may be conceived as "exercise dispositions." An exercise disposition is a tendency to perform certain acts. This is the way that they conceive of cosmopolitanism; hence the aptness of Appiah's analogy to conversation in bringing out the meaning of cosmopolitanism.[14] It also is the key to their measurement strategy: determine what people have done (or not done) rather than what they like (or dislike). To be sure, Jackman and Vavreck treat cosmopolitanism as a hybrid, sometimes speaking of it as though it consists in the exercise of faculties, sometimes as though it involves a set of distinctive tastes. This is not unreasonable since the activities that being cosmopolitan involves and the tastes that are acquired as a consequence of these activities are entangled. But it is by virtue of treating what people do, not what they say they like, that Jackman and Vavvreck make an advance both conceptually and operationally. And the result? A breakthrough in the study of race and contemporary American politics.

Why do we describe their uncovering a connection between being cosmopolitan and voting for Obama as a breakthrough? Not because cosmopolitanism is the key to understanding Obama's victory. It hardly swept him to the Democratic Party nomination and then to the White

House. What Jackman and Vavreck have done is provide a showcase example of the value of looking at the politics of race with fresh eyes. An enormous effort has been invested over the last forty years in undergirding claims that racism remains a dominating force in American politics.[15] Yet, as one political scientist pungently remarked, "But the black guy won." Obama's victory is not a demonstration that racism has shriveled up. Prejudice remains an influence in American life and politics. But Obama's victory does suggest that the accounts now on the table that have insisted that prejudice still has a tight grip on the minds of white Americans have neglected countervailing factors. Hence the importance of Jackman and Vavreck's imaginative idea to add cosmopolitanism to the list of the usual suspects in the analysis of racism—and, we suspect, to the broader analysis of political choice.

The economy of discovery in political science is instructive. Simple insights tend to give bigger payoffs than complex formulations. Mutz and Dilliplane's study is a trophy illustration of this maxim. Political campaigns are increasingly seen as political events that shape—or at least have the potential to shape—political preferences in a host of ways. Mutz and Dilliplane provide a high-octane example of asymmetric responses of the citizenry to campaign events. The question they ask is, what difference did McCain's choice of Sarah Palin as a running mate make? This question, they also make plain, actually is a bundle of questions. The one at the center of their analysis is what effect did Palin's selection have on voters' perceptions of McCain?

To answer that question, Mutz and Dilliplane make two clever moves. First, they calculate separately the effects of increasing and of decreasing ideological distance between McCain's (perceived) ideological location and the voter's. Second, they calculate the effects of these two changes separately for Democrats, independents, and Republicans and liberals, moderates, and conservatives. Consistent with common sense, McCain's choice of Palin operated as a signal. Voters perceived McCain to be more conservative as a consequence of his choice. More interesting by far, and consistent with Mutz and Dilliplane's reasoning, the effect varied with voters' partisanship and ideological orientation. As they write, "the shift *toward* their own views that those on the right perceived in McCain was more sizable than the shift *away* perceived by those on the left and in the middle."[16]

Mutz and Dilliplane take pains to show that McCain made no net gain by his selection of Palin. But as a matter of theory, their bringing to light the asymmetric effects of candidate behavior opens the door to a richer analysis of candidate strategy. Indeed, at the limit, it removes the tension between making strident appeals to mobilize the base and making moderate ones to appeal to the median voter.

To this point, our focus has been preference consistency. But it would be folly to ignore inconsistency. Hence the importance of Ellis and Stimson's contribution. They bring inconsistency front-and-center—an inconsistency, moreover, with in-your-face strategic implications. In their words, "when asked about specific government programs and specific social goals, the American public generally wants the government to do more, spend more, and redistribute more. But at the same time, citizens are considerably more likely to identify themselves as conservatives than as liberals."[17]

The time-honored explanation why a substantial number think their outlook on politics is conservative when, in fact, their policy preferences are liberal is that ordinary citizens make a muddle of political ideas. Ellis and Stimson set out on a different explanatory route. They make a strikingly original contribution by uncovering the roots of this clash of symbolic and operational ideologies.[18] It does not arise out of a fit of absent-mindedness or impulsiveness or erratic reasoning. Ellis and Stimson show that there are systematic causes of why some people choose both the conservative label and liberal policy preferences. One, perhaps the most important one, is that the term "conservative" strikes in many people's minds a religious chord. When they are asked about their outlook on the world, they think of their religious outlook, and in this context, they see themselves as conservative. Again, in Ellis and Stimson's words, "When asked to choose a political ideology, they draw upon the only connotation of 'conservatism' with which they have a deep understanding—religious conservatism, regardless of the term's implications for real political conflict."[19] That is one part of the explanation of the contradiction. Another is the greater esteem in which the term "conservative" is held than "liberal" in the American political culture. Hence the asymmetry between right and left in American politics. On the one side, conservative elites emphasize their "conservatism" but do not advertise their conservative policies. On the other side, elite liberals appeal for support on the basis of their policies, but shrink from criticizing conservatism in and of itself. The result is a dominant media message that favors conservatism, and people who form their ideological identification on the basis of the dominant frames presented by the media become "conservative."

Ellis and Stimson's discoveries have major implications for politics a good distance beyond the mission of this book. They offer a new depiction of the "median voter" as a "conflicted conservative," which we would argue goes a long way toward explaining the nature of political rhetoric and political appeals in national campaigns. The discovery of conflicted conservatives also points to a deep asymmetry in American politics. Contrary to the received wisdom that sees the right as cohesive and the left as divided, it is the left that is cohesive, both supporting liberal policies and understanding its outlook to be liberal, and it is the right that is divided, with many supporting the policies of the left while nonetheless thinking their outlook to be conservative. The implication is that there is a reservoir of support for liberal policies that can be strategically tapped by focusing political discourse at the "operational" rather than the "symbolic" level dimensions of ideology.

For the problem before us, which is to wrestle out a deeper understanding of preference consistency, Ellis and Stimson's discovery of conflicted conservatives suggests the worth of distinguishing two types of inconsistency. One is the kind that most researchers have had in mind when referring to lack of constraint in mass belief systems: political ideas minimally related one to another. We will call this type of consistency "slack," since there is at least the possibility of people pulling their ideas about politics together. Ellis and Stimson's conflicted conservatives represent an altogether different kind of inconsistency. One point is this. They wind up holding inconsistent preferences, but not flatly contradictory ones, since they are at different levels of abstraction, one symbolic and the other operational. That the preferences in play are at different levels of abstraction is not inconsequential, since it provides a clue to how people can hold them simultaneously without feeling a sense of inconsistency. This is not an inconsequential point, but it is not the one that we want to highlight. Conflicted conservatives wind up holding preferences at odds with one another, not because they are indifferent to consistency, but precisely because they are motivated to achieve it. The difficulty is that they are motivated to achieve consistency with respect to two sets of considerations, social welfare policy and religious convictions, that are at odds with one another politically. This type of inconsistency we call "motivated." It is genuine inconsistency—we do not want to suggest otherwise—but paradoxically it is inconsistency that is a product of striving for consistency within domains of life. And it is a characteristic of political thinking precisely because politics is distinctively the arena in which the conflicting claims of different domains of life—religious, economic, familial, among others—collide head-on with one another. To put the point summarily, preference consistency in politics needs to be understood against the inescapability of value conflict in politics.

Part II: Polarization and the Party System

Part II explores a signature characteristic of policy preferences in contemporary American politics—"polarization." That the positions of party elites have become polarized, no one doubts. But how voters have reacted to elite polarization—that is a matter under active investigation. One line of research has to do directly with preference consistency. It is consensually agreed that party identification and policy preferences are far more consistently aligned now than a generation ago,[20] though whether ordinary citizens have paralleled partisan elites in becoming less centrist and more extreme in their political views is hotly contested, and seems likely to remain so for a good while.[21]

Through a clever use of underutilized data, Jacobson analyzes voters' reactions to the polarization of elite position taking. Pooling the results from 650 state-level surveys in 2005 and 2006, he measures overall and partisan differences in approval of the president and senators and then sets about understanding their causes. He finds that state-level approval of President Bush followed predictable patterns. Bush had higher levels of approval in more Republican and more conservative states. What would you expect other than partisan scorecards, you might reply. But, Jacobson shows, partisans do not keep similar partisan scorecards for their senators, and who would have predicted that? Party polarization, defined as the difference in approval between Democrats and Republicans, is almost twice as large for the president as for senators. The reason: senators far more often succeed at gaining the approval of partisans of the other party (on average 42 percent). In contrast, President Bush failed in that regard with an average of just 13 percent in the state polls.

On the surface, partisans appear to be treating the president as a special case, evaluating him on a markedly more partisan and polarized basis than they do senators. Surface impressions are just that, superficial. Senatorial approval is higher and party polarization in approval is lower, Jacobson demonstrates, when senators are more moderate in their position taking. This findings brings forward some of the complexity so subtly sewn into the idea of preference consistency as ordinarily to escape notice. Initial appearances to the contrary notwithstanding, voters are being quite consistent, evaluating the president and senators on the same basis, with partisans from the other party punishing incumbents for policy extremism in both cases. Some expressions of preferences, which appear to be inconsistent, are the product of consistent adherence to a common underlying decision rule.

There is a deeper political lesson to draw from Jacobson's demonstration of a correlation between senatorial position-taking and cross-party approval. We say a deeper lesson, because it brings out of the shadows a strategic puzzle. As Jacobson observes, if senators wanted to maximize their approval ratings, then ideological moderation is the obvious strategy. But he demonstrates that a fair number of senators, who would benefit from this strategy, eschew it. Why do they not act in their electoral self-interest? Because, Jacobson suggests, senators' policy preferences trump electoral consideration unless their survival is at stake. In his words, "most senators prefer to support their party and its positions because they are themselves partisans and ideologues . . . and so act as such unless moderation is a condition of political survival."[22]

One reading of Jacobson's contribution is that it adds one more brick to the rising wall of evidence of a disconnect between partisan elites and the voters: elected representatives thumbing their noses, declining to adjust their positions to the voters', unless their back is to the wall. All the more reason, then, to study Aldrich and Freeze's contribution. Politicians and voters are connected, they argue, just so far as they share a common framework for interpreting, evaluating, and responding to policy proposals. Some voters care deeply about a specific policy, and are guided by their views on it alone. It is not obvious, to say the least, how representation issue-by-issue-by-issue can work in liberal democracy. An overarching framework, organizing and incorporating the issues being contested, is necessary—a framework, moreover, that is readily intelligible and repetitively communicated.

What is that framework? The left-right dimension, Aldrich and Freeze propose. This suggestion cannot fail to bring a smile to the lips of public opinion researchers of a certain age. The claim that the electorate was incapable of understanding and deploying a left-right ideological dimension was considered a golden nugget of scientific truth not so long ago. But the wheel turns, and there now is a shelf full of studies demonstrating that the public organizes its preferences along left-right lines on two policy agendas—social welfare issues and traditional social values.[23] They may not be able to define liberalism or conservatism as political philosophies. All the same, large numbers hold coherent ideological views, taking consistent liberal or conservative positions on issues on the same policy agendas. Aldrich and Freeze then point to a specific mechanism facilitating a connection between elite and voter preferences—the policy reputations of the parties. They make the case that the parties' policy reputations now have a relatively clearer meaning with regard to their location on an underlying left-right dimension. In pointing up the role of the parties' policy reputations as a communicative mechanism, Aldrich and Freeze strikingly reorient the disconnect argument. In its most common form, the disconnect argument holds that partisan elites are more polarized, *in the sense* that they bunch up at the extremes of the liberal-conservative policy dimension; while voters' preferences are not polarized, *in the sense* that they tend primarily to take moderate positions on the left-right dimension. Grant this. Aldrich and Freeze's deep point is that both are thinking about politics in the same framework. And so far as they are, voters can participate in policy debate on the same terms as politicians and, thanks to the signaling role of parties' policy reputations, keep track of the political thrust of competing politicians' policy proposals.

Keeping track of politicians' policy proposals and keeping control of them is not the same thing, to be sure. Assume that politicians and voters share a common framework for understanding and evaluating policy proposals. That still leaves open—indeed, in some respects makes still more puzzling—the question of why politicians do not move toward the center. Why not close the gap between their (relatively) extreme positions and voters' (relatively) moderate ones? Aldrich and Freeze are uncomfortable with simply assuming that politicians take the policy positions they do because they believe what they believe. Why then do they believe what they believe, one surely is entitled to ask. To say that they believe because they believe seems grasping at thin air. Aldrich and Freeze recognize that other factors surely are at work—interest groups, to cite the most obvious example. Still, they feel it necessary to push further in search of an answer. The result: they go on to make their second—and quite powerful—insight. They look at the extent to which various strata of activists are polarized in their policy preferences. In the process, they call attention to a group of party activists that has flown under the radar screen in previous studies of party polarization: large donors to presidential candidates. Consistent with previous research, they discover a trend toward growing polarization among political activists in general. But ideological polarization, they demonstrate, has grown faster between Democrats and Republicans who give substantial presidential campaign donations, and is now larger than the degree of ideological polarization of any other activist group. Of course, more work is necessary. But Aldrich and Freeze's proposal that political candidates are responding to substantial contributors strikes us as an elegantly economical (if dispiriting) finding.

Krasno follows up on a finding of Jacobson's from the first chapter of this section: the provocative observation that candidates do not optimize. Krasno's focus is political parties, though, not individual candidates, and his story is one of ironies. Candidates need money, and as a result of court decisions, political parties have no limits on the amount of money that they can spend on candidates' behalf and a free hand (or nearly so) in choosing which candidates to spend it on. This is an era of increasing party, not candidate, dominance, it would seem to follow.

No, Krasno replies. In his account, campaigns were and remain candidate-centered, not party-centered, because candidates and parties have different interests at the end of the day. True, money plays a more important role now than in earlier eras. True also that parties help raise and spend vast sums of money. But because of the electoral logic of competition, argues Krasno, they are investors who do not invest in their own interest as organizations. Instead, they invest where the marginal utility of their dollars is highest. In his words, "parties try to decide whom to help by determining where their help is likeliest to do the most good. That is, they try to play in the closest contests where their support might make the difference between victory and defeat for their candidate."[24] And the consequence of this strategy, Krasno contends, is that the most valuable resource that the national parties can provide—namely, money—is funneled into an ever smaller number of candidates and campaigns. Hence the paradox: the parties have the resource that candidates most want but thanks to the logic of electoral competition, what should give them a command presence as national organizations reduces them to a helpmate's role in the service of individual candidates.

Running through all these analyses is a common theme: the minimizing of electoral responsiveness in contemporary politics. Jacobson points to senators who could gain from taking more moderate positions, but choose not to do so. Aldrich and Freeze make a case for large contributors being a driver of polarization of partisan elites, which points to a positive explanation of why representatives are taking more extreme positions than their voters. Krasno makes a case that the national parties must put the interests of a relatively small number of candidates before their own interest in representing the views of the voters who identify with them. In short, all three are stories of a disconnect between voters and their representatives, not because of the limitations of ordinary citizens, but because of the dynamics of elite politics.

Supposing, on another line of argument, that there is a disconnect between partisan elites and voters, how, one wants to ask, does it play itself out in electoral politics? McGhee and Pearson provide one answer, one that develops the idea of polarization in an intriguing way, as it seems to us. All agree that party polarization in the electorate has increased, at any rate defined as consistency between voters' party identification and the party of the candidate they vote for.[25] McGhee and Pearson's contribution is to explore the micro-foundations of this aspect of polarization—or as many would prefer to say, "sorting."[26] Partisan sorting refers to the proportion of Democrats and Republicans who take their party's side on a political choice. It explicitly does not make the further presumption that the positions voters now take are more polarized—that is, less moderate—than the ones they earlier took.

According to McGhee and Pearson's story, the key to the electoral dynamics of polarization is the reactions of voters' of the other party to the incumbent. They now are far more likely to dislike the incumbent than they used to be, and hence are less likely to defect from their party and vote for the candidate of the other party than they used to be. The result: a more polarized (i.e., party-consistent) electorate. This is a neatly partisan explanation of a self-evidently partisan phenomenon—namely, polarization. Also, it appears to be yet more evidence in favor of a party-centered interpretation of contemporary politics. But in an unexpected twist—unexpected by us, certainly—McGhee and Pearson dissent. If this change has been driven by voters' reactions to parties, they argue, then the ideological distance between challenger partisans and the opposing parties will have increased. Instead, McGhee and Pearson find that the ideological distance between a challenger partisan and the incumbent is much more important than the ideological distance between a challenger partisan and the incumbent's party. This finding, which complements those in Jacobson's essay, implies that incumbents, and candidates for elective office more generally, are not prisoners of the ideological reputations of their parties. This is an intriguing candidate explanation for the disconnect between politicians' and voters' preferences, though it remains to be determined whether candidates can take more extreme positions just because the parties' policy reputations are now so distinct.

Implicit to this point has been the definition of a partisan. The next chapter tackles this issue head on. By way of context, it is consensually agreed that seeing oneself as attached to one of the two parties goes along with other desirable characteristics for citizens to have. Compared to those who identify with one or the other of the major parties, independents tend to be less knowledgeable about politics, less interested, less politically aware, more likely to use the parties as a way of understanding the ideological meaning of the political alternatives on offer, and more susceptible to campaign manipulation. All this is well-established. What causes what is another matter. For that matter, being more knowledgeable about politics is not the same thing as being knowledgeable. Still and all, more voters identifying themselves with one of the political parties seems to be a better state of affairs than fewer doing so.

It is against this background that the concern over the increasing numbers of Americans who identify themselves as political independents needs to be understood. Magleby, Nelson, and Westlye tote up the evidence indicating that the proportion of independents in the electorate has significantly increased over the last generation and tick off the adverse implications that leading researchers have drawn. Yet one more illustration, it would seem, that as short of the mark as citizens have fallen in the past, they can fall still shorter.

Magleby and his colleagues do an excellent job in laying out the case for the prosecution. Why do we say an excellent job? Because they have tried to make the best case that the number of independents in the electorate has shot up, presenting the studies that come to this conclusion in clear and compelling terms, even though their own view is quite the opposite.

Here, words can so easily mislead. The canonical procedure in measuring party identification is, first, to ask citizens whether they identify with one of the parties or see themselves as an independent. Then, if they see themselves as a Democrat or a Republican, they are asked whether they see themselves as a strong Democrat or Republican. Alternatively, if they identify themselves as an independent, they are asked whether they feel closer to one of the parties or not. We have then strong partisans, weak partisans, leaners (or partisan independents), and pure independents.

In a series of publications,[27] Wolfinger and his students showed that from the 1950s through the 1980s, "leaners" were more like partisans—and more like strong partisans than weak ones in many ways—than pure independents, including being more interested and knowledgeable about politics. They said that they were independents. In fact, they were partisans.

That was the way things were then. But how are they now after several decades of increasing elite party polarization? Putting to use a sliver of the empirical results at their finger tips, Magleby, Nelson, and Westlye show that the apparent surge in the numbers of "independents" is a double illusion. The proportion who are pure independents is the same now as a half century ago, and partisan independents are as engaged in politics and as loyal to their party in the voting as strong partisans and significantly more so than weak partisans. Imperfect as they are, ordinary citizens are not more so now than they were.

Part III: Participation and Representation

The idea of a disconnect between politicians' and voters' preferences has popped up like a jack-in-the box, albeit in diverse forms. All the same, we would like to approach it from yet one more direction.

Some paradoxes are puzzles, which is a very good thing, since puzzles have solutions. A classic example of an electoral paradox that also is a puzzle has to do with turnout levels in elections and the electoral representation of preferences. The wealthy are far more likely to vote than the poor and also differ in how they vote and what policies they prefer. These undisputed facts produce a widespread belief "that if everybody in this country voted, the Democrats would be in for the next 100 years."[28] Yet, political scientists who study the question tend to disagree.

Election commentators rely on the conventional wisdom because it appears to be a self-evident truth, akin to other self-evident truths that flirt with tautology—e.g., bad weather lowers turnout. In their pioneering work, however, Wolfinger and colleagues have presented striking evidence of the similarity of preferences of voters and nonvoters.[29] And when we say "similarity of preferences," we are referring to preferences over policies and values that drive contemporary politics. This includes the most fundamental political orientation, party identification, but also a host of others, including candidate preferences, policy preferences, and policy priorities. Moreover, Wolfinger and his colleagues report that similarity of preferences of voters and nonvoters is robust under alternative counterfactuals—a relaxation of registration requirements, for example, or a projection of universal (100%) turnout.

To say that the findings of Wolfinger and his colleagues have proven provocative is in the same league as describing an explosion as a substantial noise. A long-standing critique of American democracy is that turnout is low relative to other democracies. Since the well-off are more likely to vote than the poor, it follows that the American party system is biased in favor of the well-off. This critique is, for some, a self-evident truth. Hence the importance of the two studies on turnout and representation, one by Ansolabehere and Hersh, the other by Sides, Schickler, and Citrin. Each approaches the problem from a different methodological route. So it is all the more striking that the substantive conclusions of each reinforce those of the other.

Ansolabehere and Hersh introduce methodological innovations on three fronts. For one, theirs is the first national study since 1990 to validate claims to have voted, which they accomplish through an ingenious "fuzzy matching" technique comparing reported voting with digitized voter databases. For another, previous estimates of turnout bias have conflated two factors: the degree of difference between voters and reported nonvoters on relevant dimensions (e.g., education) and the distributions of relevant dimension. Ansolabehere and Hersh provide separate estimates of the two. And for yet another, they match validated voters and nonvoters not only on demographic attributes, as previous studies have done,[30] but also on attitudinal variables as well, surely the heart of the matter.

Their methodological advances pay off. Eliminate the counterfeit voters, and the difference between those who go the polls and those who stay home shrinks further. This is true at the individual level and in the aggregate as well. Moreover, at the state level, the apparent conservative bias among voters is cut down considerably, oftentimes evaporating completely. And consistent with all of the preceding, simulating election results under full turnout shows only modest—if any—expected differences in outcomes under full turnout compared to actual election results.

Analyzing the same problem, Sides, Schickler, and Citrin take their own trail-blazing route in their analysis of state-level exits polls and the November Voter Supplement of the Current Population Survey. They make discoveries on three fronts. First, a handful of states aside, they show that the partisan differential (which gauges the extent to which the Democratic Party is disadvantaged) is minimally responsive to variation in turnout levels state by state. Second, and fascinatingly, they wring the actual political significance out of their statistical estimates of partisan differential, identifying the outcomes of actual elections it influenced. Finally, instead of calling it a day's work after calculating partisan differentials state by state, they identify factors explaining why partisan differential is persistently higher in some states than in others.

And what do they learn? Most importantly, even under favorable assumptions, differences between the preferences of voters and nonvoters are quite modest, averaging between just one and three percentage points. In a word, even if every legally eligible voter found her way to the voting booth, electoral outcomes would rarely change. What does this mean politically? Presidential and senatorial elections are statewide contests. Losing a state by one percent or by ten times that number costs a senatorial candidate the election and a presidential candidate a block of electoral votes. Across the 200 state-level presidential outcomes from 1992–2004, less than 10 percent switch from one party winning to the other. An even smaller number of Senate outcomes would change (3 percent) due to the less competitive nature of those elections. While not many outcomes would change under full turnout, Sides, Schickler, and Citrin do find that the variation in preferences between voters and nonvoters is systematic, arising largely as the result of variation in state-level differences rather than differences across time or election type.

Before moving on, we want to make a parenthetical comment. Here we have two teams of researchers, applying different methodological techniques to different data sets. Yet, the findings of one lead to the same broad conclusions as the findings of the other. Could this be an indication of the maturation of political science? On a related but slightly different note, the findings of both broadly support those first reported by Wolfinger and his colleagues. Yet, in pointing this out, the reports of both teams of researchers are marked by an odd tone—odd, that is, in the sense of unusual, not in the sense of off the mark. In our experience, the spirit of most political science research is adversarial. The aim is to demonstrate that what previous research had supposedly established, it hadn't established at all; indeed, a fair number of times, it had got the truth of the matter the wrong way round. In contrast, the spirit of these two studies is collegial rather than adversarial. And if someone were to wag his finger and ask, What have we learned when we have learned that what we thought was so, is so? We would turn and ask them, Can you not see how they have deepened our understanding?

A more favorable ratio of collegial- to adversarial-style research is a key to progress in the social sciences, we have become persuaded. This gets things just the wrong way about, one might reply. Style is a function of substance when the findings of a study are additions to—but consistent with—previous research, and a collegial style naturally follows; when they are at odds with previous research, an adversarial style (the "conventional wisdom" is X, but the truth is non-X) is only to be expected. For this reason, though not only for this reason, this section on election turnout includes Knee and Green's analysis of the effects of registration laws on voter turnout.

The basic argument underlying previous research runs as follows. To be allowed to vote requires first registering to vote, and registration requirements impose nontrivial costs. Relaxing registration requirements—for example, by coordinating voting registration with registration requirements for high-value benefits (e.g., a driver's license)—should increase voting turnout. So Wolfinger and Rosenstone found.[31] So also did many, though not quite all, subsequent researchers.

Reexamining the problem, Knee and Green lay out a quartet of statistical models, examining and applying them in turn. One is tempted to say that the models are examined in order of increasing complexity, and in a strictly computational sense that is correct. But to think of the progression of models as running from simple to complex gets their analytical enterprise the wrong way round. What it is about is identifying potentially misleading assumptions and then eliminating them one by one. And the result? Knee and Green's results indicate that the apparent influences of Election Day registration and registration closing dates—the two registration laws commonly believed to be most efficacious at improving turnout—are reduced substantially, as is confidence that there are any effects at all. Their findings raise doubt about the view that turnout in America is comparatively low due to high registration costs and suggest that past and possible future institutional reforms are limited in their ability to improve participation rates in the United States. Once more, however, we want to take the liberty of appending a parenthetical comment—actually, in this case, two comments. The first is that this chapter, like the two before it, dramatizes the increase in substantive depth of understanding thanks to progress in statistical modeling. The second comment is that although the findings of this chapter call into question the findings of some analyses of Wolfinger and his colleagues, there is nothing adversarial in its presentation of the question, summary of previous research, or statistical analyses. Quite the contrary: like the two chapters that precede it, it is a model of the collegial style.

There is a final substantive question. Part II focuses on the effect of the polarization of partisan elites on policy preferences and electoral choices of the public. Part III concentrates on political participation in the form of electoral turnout. The analysis of Carmines, Ensley, and Wagner hooks together these two concerns, investigating what effect, if any, the polarization of partisan elites has had, not on the preferences of ordinary citizens but on their behavior.

In responding to this question, since Zaller worked out his theory of public opinion,[32] most follow the now well-trodden route—to demonstrate the extent to which responsiveness to elite signals is conditional on political sophistication. The more politically aware and attentive are more responsive to elite cues. Carmines, Ensley, and Wagner, however, go off the beaten path, bringing out the extent to which responsiveness to partisan elites is conditional on the *structure* of policy preferences.

As we have noted, preferences across the array of policies that the parties now contest form a two-dimensional pattern. One dimension, the so-called social welfare agenda, consists of preferences on the extent to which (and to a lesser extent, the ways in which) government should intervene to assist those who are disadvantaged. The other dimension, the so-called traditional values agenda, consists of policy preferences on highly charged issues like abortion and gay rights. At the level of elite politics, these two dimensions reduce to one overall liberalism-conservatism dimension.[33] At the level of the electorate as a whole, they tend to be orthogonal.

Carmines and his colleagues take advantage of this orthogonality in a theoretically ingenious way. Their hypothesis, roughly, is that voters who share the outlook of their party are the most responsive to the polarization of partisan elites, and therefore the most likely to take a more active role in party politics as the ideological clash between the parties has intensified. We say that this is, roughly, their hypothesis, because they are among the first to get theoretical leverage out of the discrepancy between the one-dimensional structure of elite policy preferences and the two-dimensional structure of voters' policy preferences. Just so far as elite policy preferences are unidimensional, those who are conservative (liberal) on the social welfare dimension will be conservative (liberal) on the traditional values agenda. Call this pattern—conservative-conservative, liberal-liberal—the elite template. In contrast, just so far as the two policy agendas are orthogonal in the electorate as a whole, the off-diagonals— as well as the main diagonal—will be densely populated. Trading on this, Carmines and colleagues come up with an elegantly simple prediction: citizens who have moved from the off-diagonals to the main diagonal— that is, brought their positions into conformity with the template of party elites—will show an increase in participation. Those who remain on the off-diagonals, as well as those already on the main diagonal, have no new stimulus to increased participation. And so Carmines, Ensley, and Wagner find, not with respect to the vote, not surprisingly since voting tends to be a routinized affair, but with respect to more ego-involving forms of participation, among them, attending a rally or trying to influence others' votes.

A Codicil

When soliciting and organizing the studies for this volume, we had two goals in mind. First, we wanted each study to stand, on its own, interesting in its own right, providing new insight into the study of mass American politics. Second—and more important—we have aimed at assembling a collection of studies that, taken together, yields a portrait of how citizens face the challenges of democracy. Although we are far from supposing that the case against skepticism has been won, we are of the view that the contributions to the volume make a case for agnosticism.

Notes

1. The definitive work on the topic remains Delli Carpini and Keeter (1996). The title of Shenkman's (2008) recent book—*Just How Stupid Are We? Facing the Truth about the American Voter*—bluntly conveys the point.

2. The early Columbia studies (Lazarsfeld et al. 1948; Berelson et al. 1954) of voting behavior laid the empirical foundation for Converse's (1964) seminal work from which most research in this vein follows. Some noteworthy recent studies include Bartels (2005); Todorov et al. (2005); and Achen and Bartels (2006). Kuklinski and his collaborators do an excellent job of synthesizing the research on how the way in which citizens process information often leads them astray (Kuklinski and Quirk 2000, 2001; Kuklinski and Peyton 2007).

3. Downs (1957).

4. See, for example, Popkin (1991); Lupia (1994); Lupia and McCubbins (1998); and Lupia, McCubbins, and Popkin (2000).

5. V. O. Key famously made this argument. It subsequently became the premise in a radically new approach to the study of mass opinion, elections, and public policy, *The Macro Polity* (Erikson et al. 2002).

6. Campbell (1963).

7. The two canonical expressions of this perspective are Converse (1964) and Zaller (1992), though it is worth remarking that ideology, the most broad-gauged consistency construct in political analysis, is at the center of the second part of Zaller's analysis.

8. Kedar (2005, 2010).

9. Page with Bouton (2006).

10. Page and Shapiro (1992).

11. Page and Shapiro (1992), p. 1.

12. Page and Xie, this volume.

13. Page and Xie, this volume.

14. Appiah (2006).

15. The other principal current of research—that racial politics has become to a large degree part of the long-standing conflict between liberalism and conservatism—is one that one of us is associated with. So we shall only note it, not comment on it.

16. Mutz and Dilliplane, this volume.

17. Ellis and Stimson, this volume.

18. Why do we say strikingly original? Because, until their analysis, the contradiction between symbolic and operational ideologies had been simply written off as yet one more illustration of the muddled thinking of ordinary citizens.

19. Ellis and Stimson, this volume.

20. Levendusky (2009).

21. See the ongoing debate between Fiorina and Abramowitz, most recently Fiorina et al. (2008) and Abramowitz and Saunders (2008).

22. Jacobson, this volume.

23. Among the best recent studies are Ansolabehere et al. (2008) and Layman and Carsey (2002).

24. Krasno, this volume.

25. See especially Bartels (2000).

26. Fiorina and his collaborators have developed the idea of sorting extensively. A recent summary of their claims is Fiorina and Abrams (2008). See also Levendusky (2009).

27. Keith et al. (1977, 1986, 1992).

28. "Interview with John Kenneth Galbraith," *California Monthly*, February 1986, p. 11.

29. Rosenstone and Wolfinger (1978); Wolfinger and Rosenstone (1980); Highton and Wolfinger (2001).

30. The highest quality data sets are the Current Population Surveys, which do not ask about political attitudes as a matter of law.

31. Rosenstone and Wolfinger (1978); Wolfinger and Rosenstone (1980).

32. Zaller (1992).

33. The most extensive work is that of McCarty, Poole, and Rosenthal (Poole and Rosenthal 1997; McCarty, Poole, and Rosenthal 1997, 2006).

Part I

THE POLITICAL LOGIC OF PREFERENCE CONSISTENCY

I

How Do Political Scientists Know What Citizens Want?

AN ESSAY ON THEORY AND MEASUREMENT

Arthur Lupia

DEMOCRATIC GOVERNANCE HAS MANY VIRTUES. While scholars disagree about what these virtues are, there is a consensus that some virtues arise from the relationship between *what governments do* and *what citizens want*. It is no surprise, then, that many arguments about democratic governance's normative attributes are built upon claims about what citizens want.

The dependence of normative arguments on claims about citizen preferences is apparent in research on governmental responsiveness. A government's ability to achieve various normative goals depends on its knowledge of, and responsiveness to, citizen preferences.[1] Valid preference measurements can help analysts defend claims about the extent to which governments are responsive. Of course, governmental responsiveness to what citizens want can also have detrimental consequences.[2] Scholars who focus on such pathologies nevertheless recognize that governmental legitimacy and citizens' preferences are not independent. As Riker (1965) famously argued, "the essential democratic institution is the ballot box and all that goes with it."[3] Hence, claims about what citizens want are relevant to a wide range of questions about what government does.

The dependence of normative arguments on claims about what citizens want is also apparent in citizen competence debates. While it is well known that many citizens are unable to answer factual questions that scholars and journalists find important,[4] the normative implications of such inabilities are less well understood. Some pundits argue that citizens are so ignorant of basic political and economic concepts that governments should simply ignore what citizens want. More constructive researchers seek to clarify when and how citizens' inabilities to answer survey questions affect their preferences. Such research is conducted in different ways. Some scholars use surveys to solicit information about what citizens want.[5] Others theorize about what citizens *should* want.[6] Still others integrate both activities—they collect data on what citizens say they want and evaluate it with respect to assumptions about what citizens should want.[7]

The range of examples described above shows how arguments about democracy's normative virtues depend on the validity of claims about what citizens want. As many scholarly claims about preferences come from survey data, many scholarly findings also depend on the accuracy of survey-based preference measurements. In this essay, I examine how many political scientists conceptualize and measure what citizens want. I then contend that we can improve our current conceptualization and measurement of citizen preferences.

Progress can come from paying greater attention to how two factors, institutions and cognition, affect preferences. Institutions matter because they moderate the relationship between citizens' thoughts and government's actions. In examining the effect of institutions, I argue that many scholarly claims about what citizens *should* want ignore the moderating effect of institutions. For example, when scholars estimate "the vote for U.S. president that a voter would have cast if more enlightened," they often base their assessment on the assumption that a voter should prefer the candidate whose policy preferences are closest to his or her own. I draw from a number of recent and emerging studies to show how such institution-free estimates can produce invalid claims about what citizens should want.[8] For if a particular officeholder does not have dictatorial powers, then a citizen's optimal representative can be one whose preferences are quite different from his or her own. Understanding how institutional factors connect citizen preferences to governmental actions can help scholars defend more reliable claims about what citizens should want.

Greater attention to how citizens think can yield parallel improvements in preference measurement. Cognition matters because the frequency and content of a person's political thoughts influences how he or she comes to have, and express, particular preferences. Some scholars have fruitfully leveraged attention to cognition to clarify which survey-based measures of citizen preferences best reflect the preferences that people would have if they thought differently about politics.[9] Parallel endeavors are also changing how surveys measure preferences. To demonstrate such effects, I focus on question wording changes contained in the 2008 American National Election Studies (ANES). The content of these changes follows from evolving theories of optimal questionnaire design that themselves are well-informed by research on how people think.[10] I argue that asking questions in ways that better reflect *how citizens think* produces preference measures that better reflect what citizens want.

Greater attention to institutions and cognition can help scholars improve what they know about what citizens want. Today, it is common for scholars to treat preferences as "institution-free traits," where by "trait," I mean a habitual pattern of thought that is stable across time. I argue, however, that many of the most-scrutinized citizen preferences are neither institution-free nor measured well by badly worded questions. Greater attention to institutions and cognition can help scholars base arguments about democracy's normative virtues on increasingly reliable and credible claims about what citizens want.

Institutions and Which Candidates Citizens Should Prefer

Normative arguments about democracy often build from claims about what citizens should want. Because many social issues are complex, and because ample evidence suggests that many citizens spend little time thinking about such issues, it is widely presumed that what many citizens say they want is different from what they should want. The idea is that if citizens were to think more deeply about politics, they would have different preferences. Such claims are often made by persons who themselves spend significant time thinking about particular issues and are typically followed by a pronouncement or estimate of what preferences citizens ought to have.[11]

Such pronouncements are often defended by comparing a manifestation of citizen preferences, such as voting behavior or survey evidence, to some arguably objective standard of what these citizens should want. Poor voters who vote Republican, for example, are thought to be voting contrary to their own interests by writers who believe that Democratic legislators are better for the poor. More generally, it is widely presumed that citizens should prefer to elect politicians whose preferences are closest to their own and that citizens who do not do so are mistaken.

I contend that many such views are naïve when stated as *institution-free* generalities. To make this argument compactly will require a few simplifying assumptions. The first simplification is that we accept as potentially valuable the idea that there is normative virtue in decision-making processes that cause convergence between citizen preferences and the consequences of governmental actions. The second simplifying assumption is that, for the moment, we can dispense with concerns about utility aggregation (i.e., how policies that benefit one person may harm others). I make these assumptions in order to start my argument by evaluating a scenario where we can compare the preferences of one arbitrarily selected citizen to the consequences of the governmental actions that affect her. I use this exercise to provide an initial answer to the question, "Under what conditions should this citizen prefer to elect a candidate for office whose policy preferences are as close as possible to her own?" At the end of this section, I will show that relaxing these assumptions only further decreases the validity of claims that citizens should always prefer politicians whose policy preferences are closest to their own.[12]

To make matters concrete, let's start with the case of a lone voter who is given the opportunity to cast a single vote that determines which of two political parties will have complete control over all aspects of government for the rest of time. For simplicity, let's assume that it is common knowledge that everyone in society agrees that when evaluating the actions of government, only the lone voter's well-being matters. So, as indicated in our discussion of simplifications earlier, the voter need not concern herself with how her choice affects anyone except herself. Suppose, moreover, that one of the two parties is actually better for the voter because its actions will enhance her well-being more than the other. We call this party "the correct party" and call the other "the incorrect party." In this case, what the voter should want is easy to determine. She should prefer the correct party.[13] This scenario supports the claim that citizens should always prefer to elect politicians whose preferences are closest to their own.

Is this claim true generally? To see why it is not, let us now focus on institutional factors that connect a lone voter's decision with the governmental actions that affect her. A government consists of many elected and appointed offices. Political institutions are structured to induce delegation and coalition building among these actors. Such efforts affect the correspondence between what any single voter prefers and the actions of government that ultimately affect the voter's well-being.

To begin to incorporate such institutional factors into the previous example, suppose that instead of casting a single vote that determines which of two political parties will have complete control over all aspects of government for the rest of time, the lone voter will now simply determine the identity of a single member of a large legislative assembly. Even though the lone voter can determine her representative's identity, her choice does not determine the actions of government. Instead, the relationship between the voter's expressed preference and the governmental actions that affect her will depend on how her representative works with other members of the legislature.

The representative will make two important decisions: *with whom to coalesce* and *to whom to delegate*. Political science has examined these topics extensively.[14] A common lesson in these literatures is that the institutional context affects who coalesces with whom, who delegates to whom, and the consequences of such endeavors. In what follows, I briefly describe relevant coalition and delegation dynamics. I then use these lessons to clarify how scholars can use such dynamics to make more reliable claims about what citizens, such as the lone voter, should want.

Coalescence

The lone voter's representative is but one member of a legislative body with dozens or hundreds of other members. In legislatures around the world, legislators are usually required to obtain majority or supermajority support for an idea to become a law. Hence, to legislate, individual members of a legislature have to forge agreements with one another. But if there is sufficient preference diversity within a legislature, many of these agreements will require compromise. To achieve a desired objective A, the lone voter's representative may have to give up something he wants (i.e., desired objective B) to achieve a result that, while not exactly B, is also desirable. The agreements forged from these negotiations will turn not only on the policy preferences of the lone voter or her representative, but also on the allocation of bargaining skills and powers among legislators.

Bargaining skill and power allocations within a legislature derive from several sources. One source is other legislators' preferences. If the lone voter's representative prefers X to Y and if all other legislators prefer Y to X, the deck will be stacked against the lone voter's preference affecting government actions. In contrast, if all but one of the other legislators agree that X is preferred to Y, then government action is more likely to be consistent with the lone voter's preferences.

Another factor is legislators' abilities to articulate certain types of arguments at certain times—as well as their abilities to express patience or indignation at appropriate moments. Patience is particularly important. A legislator who needs a particular decision to be made now (perhaps because he is in a tight election) may be more willing to compromise than a legislator who is unaffected by the lack of a speedy decision. In bargaining, patience is often power.[15]

The distribution of bargaining power within a legislature is not simply a product of the life histories and DNAs of individual legislators. Power distributions are also affected by institutional rules. Rules that affect how many votes are needed to reach a decision, what happens if a decision cannot be reached, and so on will affect legislators' relative bargaining power.[16] These rules can also affect who has the ability to be patient, which, as suggested earlier, can affect the allocation of bargaining power.

Hence, attributes of other legislators and institutional factors over which the lone voter has no control are likely to sway legislative decisions in ways that affect the relationship between the candidate she chooses on Election Day and the policy consequences of that act. Such bargaining dynamics can limit, or even eliminate, any influence that the lone voter's representative may have in the legislature. So to draw a conclusion about the type of candidate that the lone voter should prefer, we need to consider the relationship between the options in front of her and their correspondence to policy outcomes.

But there is more to this relationship that we have not yet discussed.

At the time of an election, even the most learned legislative expert will be uncertain about what issues will come up during the legislative session and how the legislature will resolve such issues. Although many experts can name bills or issues that will definitely be raised, they cannot anticipate all of the crises that will unexpectedly arise. These new problems need not cut across traditional partisan or ideological lines. They may split the parties or unify former adversaries. These new schisms or alliances may have spillover effects—they may make it more difficult, or easier, respectively, for legislators to coalesce on formerly simple issues. Hence, the evolution of legislative alliances can further affect the relationship between the lone voter's choice and the actions of government.

Understanding this much about the coalitional nature of legislative decision making is sufficient to demonstrate why the lone voter should not always prefer the candidate whose policy preferences are closest to her own. To clarify conditions under which a voter would not want to prefer the closest candidate, suppose that the lone voter holds a moderate position on the one policy issue about which she cares most. If this issue is sufficiently important to her, it might seem reasonable to conclude that the voter would best be represented by a moderate who shares her views. If, however, moderates compromise in ways that extremists do not, then being represented by a moderate may lead to a suboptimal outcome for the voter.

Specifically, suppose that the lone voter most prefers policy outcome S. To the extent that a policy other than S will be passed, she prefers that the policy be as close to S as possible. Let ~S denote a different policy outcome that some other voters desire.

Assume that bargaining power is distributed among the legislators in a manner that leads them to conclude that the best outcome they can achieve is one that splits the difference between the preferred policy position of the lone voter's representative and ~S. If a moderate represents the lone voter in this case, splitting the difference will lead to a policy outcome halfway between S and ~S. If, however, the lone voter were to choose someone whose preferences are more extreme than her own in a particular direction (i.e., suppose that there exists a legislator whose most preferred outcome is Z and that Z is such that S is halfway between ~S and Z), and if such a representative agreed to split the difference with supporters of outcome ~S, then the lone voter ought to prefer to be represented by the extremist.

Empirical studies of voting patterns in several countries suggest that many voters take such dynamics into account when choosing representatives. As Kedar (2005, 2010) shows, in electoral systems where voters can use extreme candidates or parties to bring policy outcomes closer to ones they prefer, a significant number of them vote for extremists. Empirical and theoretical work on the U.S. Congress similarly suggests that such factors influence when rank-and-file legislators choose to change how they allocate power among one another.[17]

Of course, if the lone voter's representative is a member of a normal legislature, he will consider more than one issue during his term of office.

It may be that some of the issues will be like the one just described—cases where the lone voter is better represented by someone whose preferences are more extreme than her own. Other issues may be of a kind where the bargaining dynamics are different and the lone voter would be most effectively represented by someone who shares her preferences. What kind of candidate should a voter prefer in such instances?

To answer this question, analysts need to make an argument about how to weight the relative importance of various issues to the voter. Implicit in many such arguments made by scholars today are moral and ethical judgments about which there is little evidence and even less consensus. An implication for current scholarship is a reduction in credibility of claims by people who are quick to judge citizens' preferences as unenlightened or inconsistent because those preferences vary from analysts' own preconceived and institution-free conjectures about what citizens should want.

For example, when poor voters in the United States are castigated for voting Republican, the claim is typically built on the assumption that Democrats pursue policies such as social programs and progressive taxation that can provide poor people with benefits. But if at least some among the poor care about factors instead of, or in addition to, their economic plight, then it may be wrong to conclude that all poor voters should prefer Democrats. To cite just one example, for those among the poor who are deeply religious, who hail from religious traditions that hold the sanctity of human life as the paramount value, and who see abortion as contradicting that value, drawing a conclusion about what candidate or political party the voter should prefer based simply on economic factors is presumptive of many important moral and ethical questions. Therefore, even if we were to agree that such voters should prefer policies that help the poor economically as well as policies that limit the number of abortions, questions about which candidates or parties a voter should prefer would remain more difficult to answer when there are no candidates who take or oppose both positions.

Recognizing that representatives grapple with multiple issues makes proffering claims about which candidates citizens should prefer more difficult. But it does not make such claims impossible to defend. A way to make more credible and reliable claims about what citizens should want is to pay greater attention to factors that connect a voter's preferences to the outcomes that she experiences. This means paying attention to the electoral and legislative institutions that convert preferences to policies. Focusing on the institutional aspects of what citizens should want will not always produce a "point estimate" of what candidates voters should prefer, but this approach can help us more effectively sort claims that are consistent with the objective of achieving policy outcomes that the voter prefers from claims that will not lead to that outcome. Such an approach, when integrated with clearly stated arguments about the types of issue-to-issue trade-offs that voters ought to make, can lead to more precise and defensible statements about why specific kinds of voters should have certain kinds of preferences.

To this point in the argument, I have focused on legislatures as an intervening factor in the relationship between what voters want and what governments do. So it may be tempting to conclude that this argument holds only for citizen preferences in the context of representative legislatures. Indeed, one could argue that a choice of executive, such as a president who alone controls his branch of government, is one where the lone voter would surely want a person who shares her preferences. But this too is not the case.

To see why, note that if the executive is effectively a dictator—as is the case in some nations—then the conclusion is valid. If, however, making legislation requires the approval of the executive and other major actors, such as a legislature, then bargaining dynamics of the type described earlier come back into play. Consider, for example, a voter who has a choice between two presidential candidates, C and D. Candidate C shares the voter's preferences over policy outcomes. However, it is also known that candidate C is all too willing to compromise with those who disagree with him. Candidate D, in contrast, has policy preferences that are somewhat different from those of the voter but has personal circumstances that give him the power to bring other legislators around to his point of view. If the goal is to obtain policy outcomes that are best for the voter, the voter need not always prefer candidates like C.

In general, citizens do not have an opportunity to choose specific options from large and complex sets of possible policy outcomes. Instead, they choose, from a small and discrete set, candidates for representative or executive positions who must subsequently coalesce with others in order to make policy. As a result, considering how institutions convert expressed party or candidate preferences to policy outcomes can help us better understand which candidates or parties citizens should prefer.

Delegation

Legislative interactions are not the only factors that affect relationships between citizen preferences and policy outcomes. After a legislative agreement is struck, someone must implement it. Legislatures typically delegate such tasks to bureaucrats, many of who are employed in administrative agencies. Bureaucrats vary in their expertise and personal policy preferences. Some carry out the laws exactly as they are written. Others do not.[18] Understanding the conditions under which delegation produces such different outcomes can further clarify what kind of representative a voter should want.

A substantial scholarly literature examines the consequences of delegation.[19] It begins with the premise that bureaucrats and other government employees need not do what legislators tell them to do. In some cases, the interpretative discretion available to bureaucrats is a result of vaguely worded legislation. In other cases, bureaucrats purposefully reject legislative mandates.

This literature's main lesson is that institutional rules and the distribution of information plays a big role in determining the extent to which those to whom power is delegated (i.e., agents) act in accordance with the preferences of those who delegate (i.e., principals). Principals who have access to effective ways of learning about agents' actions (such as formal hearings or places for interest groups to report on agent activities—i.e., the "fire alarm oversight" approach of McCubbins and Schwartz [1984]) and who have means of sanctioning wayward agents find delegation more rewarding than do principals who lack these advantages.

This literature's insights are often cast aside when scholars argue that voters should prefer legislators whose preferences mirror their own. If it is best that the actions of government lead to policy outcomes that are as close as possible to what is best for a lone voter, then the kinds of parties or candidates that the lone voter should prefer depend not just on the bargaining dynamics described earlier but also on the dynamics of delegation. When we can expect bureaucrats to faithfully execute legislative instructions, attention to the correspondence between voter and candidate policy preferences and to legislative bargaining dynamics will often be sufficient to inform claims about what the lone voter should prefer. In cases where bureaucrats run amok, however, the question of which candidates the voter should prefer will depend on just how they run amok. If the lone voter is a moderate, and it is well known that the bureaucracy is controlled by extreme leftists, she may be better-served by electing those legislators who have the best chance of containing extreme leftists in the bureaucracy—even if those legislators' own policy preferences are not identical to her own.

Implications

Given the large set of interactions that connect individuals' political choices to the actions of government, we must conclude that dynamics of legislative coalescence and delegation are relevant to assessments of which candidates citizens should prefer. While the sequence of negotiations that affect delegation and coalescence may seem convoluted, literatures on these topics reveal a constructive logic from which greater clarity can emerge.

One implication of these literatures is that claims about what citizens should want should be derived differently in different countries. To see why, consider that countries have electoral and legislative systems that induce political parties to share legislative power in different ways. In the modal parliamentary democracy, for example, electoral systems produce coalition government. Coalition governments arise because no party obtains a majority of seats—the fraction required to legislate. In such cases, while elections determine how many seats in the legislature each political party will occupy, post-electoral negotiations determine who becomes (and hence the preferences of) the prime minister and who holds other positions of power.

So even if you are a voter who casts the decisive vote with respect to a single member of Parliament, the connection between your vote and the actions of government need not be direct and may vary from country to country. The relative bargaining power of various parties and cabinet ministers will influence how the preferences of any given voter influence governmental actions. Hence, evaluating citizen preferences in such systems should be done differently in systems that produce coalition governments than in countries that produce single-party majority governments. If we could agree, for example, that bureaucrats in a particular single-party government were highly responsive to the desires of the ruling party, then one could argue that what voters in that country should want is to elect the party whose preferences are closest to their own. Across the democratic world, however, such circumstances are rare. Hence, greater attention to institutions may increase the reliability of claims about which parties voters should prefer. As Kedar (2010) argues, if what really matters are policy outcomes, then claims about which parties and candidates a voter should prefer gain credibility when they are informed by the institutional processes that convert what voters want to what governments do.

Before closing this section, I would like to return to the two simplifying assumptions that I made at the outset. I shall argue that relaxing these assumptions only raises further doubts about the credibility of institution-free claims about what citizens should want. Suppose now that the lone voter is a member of society in which preferences besides her own are relevant. In such circumstances, the question of what citizens should want becomes bound with dynamics of preference aggregation. The scholarly study of preference aggregation, as it occurs in work on social choice theory, alerts us to the notion that normative claims about what citizens should want when individual preferences are sufficiently diverse require that we engage in interpersonal comparisons of utility.[20] While people who make claims about what citizens should want rarely use the language of utility comparisons when making their arguments, they often rely on a logical manifestation of the factor—a proposed weighting of salience or importance across political objects or object attributes.

For example, in assessments of how governments should act with respect to the issue of abortion, some weigh the plight of the pregnant woman heavily, while others emphasize the well-being of the unborn child. For this and other political issues, learned observers are likely to disagree on what weighting schemes citizens should employ.

A government's decision to spend money on health care rather than defense (or vice versa) leads to outcomes that leave some people better off and others worse off than other choices it can make. Choosing to set tax rates at one level and not another does the same. Choosing to stay within a budget or to run a deficit (i.e., choosing to spend money now for which people in the future will have to pay) does the same. Public policy affects people in different ways, and the decision to choose one policy over another implies an interpersonal comparison of utility.

Not everyone likes to think of policy in this way. Advocates of certain programs like to direct people's attention to the benefits of their program and to what would happen if the program is not supported at a particular level. They are less apt to specify the costs in other sectors that their preferred program imposes. By being vague about the opportunity costs, such costs can seem less important or even become temporarily invisible. But every such claim, when made in most political domains, implies a decision to privilege some issues at the expense of others.

So, when preference diversity is present, claims about what any individual citizen should want has interpersonal utility implications. Therefore, if someone is making a claim about what a particular citizen should want, they are also implicitly arguing for the primacy of a particular way of thinking about which issues and whose interests are more important than others. In many instances, people who are making claims about what preferences others should have are unaware of these factors or are unconcerned about them (i.e., they have already determined that they know which weighting scheme is best for others). If scholars who study citizen preferences pay greater attention to the institutional factors listed earlier, the interpersonal utility arguments that are nested within claims about what citizens should want will be easier for others to see and evaluate. When that happens, we can better evaluate the validity of such claims with respect to particular normative or material foundations.

Cognition and Preference Measurement on Surveys

As the previous section shows, many claims about what citizens should want are of questionable validity because they ignore the institutional context to which such preferences apply. We now turn to questions of how what citizens want is measured. Surveys are a common source of such measures. How credible are extant survey measures of citizen preferences? In this section, I argue that many survey-based claims about what citizens should want are of questionable validity because they ignore the cognitive context from which preferences emerge. Ignoring this context yields badly worded questions and produces data that reveals very little about what citizens do or should want. In what follows, I review cognitive underpinnings of citizen preferences, their implications for measurement, and tips for writing more effective questions.

A "preference" is a comparative evaluation of (i.e., a ranking over) a set of objects.[21] A preference serves as a cognitive marker that reminds people how to interact with various aspects of their environment. Preferences are stored in memory and drawn upon when people make conscious decisions. When people say that they prefer Lincoln to Douglass, for example, they identify an aspect of their environment (e.g., Lincoln) that, in their mind, provides them with greater pleasure or benefits than other environmental aspects (e.g., Douglass).

Many social scientists assume that preferences form through a memory-based process.[22] The idea behind a memory-based model is that people base their evaluations on information that they retrieve from memory. For example, when called upon to evaluate an object, people canvass their memories for information about object attributes and use what they find to form preferences.

The means and extensiveness of such memory-based canvassing is the subject of continuing scientific inquiry. One set of arguments focuses on comprehensive memory-based models, in which an individual recalls all relevant information and integrates it into an overall evaluation. For example, when an individual receives information about a candidate (e.g., the candidate's issue positions), she files it away in long-term memory. Later, she retrieves from long-term memory the candidate's issue positions on a host of issues, weights the information according to its importance or relevance, and finally integrates it into an overall evaluation.[23]

An important aspect of such models is that they assume that people engage in an enormous amount of computation. This aspect contrasts with the widely held view of many citizens as having neither the motivation nor the ability to engage in an exhaustive memory search and weighting of evidence. Some scholars have attempted to rectify this apparent contradiction by offering alternative memory-based models that assume less computation.

Accessibility models, for example, portray people as basing preferences on small sets of considerations. In these models, accessibility refers to the likelihood that a given consideration (or construct) will be retrieved from memory when forming a preference.[24] A large literature shows that people base many judgments on the considerations that are most accessible in memory.[25] For example, if economic considerations happen to be accessible in a voter's mind, she will base her candidate preference on economic considerations; if, instead, foreign affairs considerations are accessible, then the voter will base her preference on foreign affairs considerations.

The implications of such research for what scholars understand about what citizens want are many. Druckman and Lupia (2000) provide a broad overview of these implications for contemporary notions of preference formation and change. Here, I shall pursue a different set of implications. My goal in the remainder of this section is to clarify how greater attention to cognition can improve preference-related measurement and inference on surveys. Hence, I will focus on two recent examples of how scholars have used such attention to cognition to improve the use or construction of preference-related survey questions.

The first example comes from experimental work by Mathieu Turgeon. Turgeon (2009) begins with the premise that many people perceive preference-related survey claims to represent the views of all citizens. Yet, citizens vary in the extent to which they have well-formed preferences and the extent to which they are able to articulate those preferences to survey interviewers. As a result, Turgeon argues, surveys may provide a skewed view of what citizens want.

To determine the extent of such skew, Turgeon designed and implemented a series of survey experiments in Brazil and the United States. Control group respondents were asked preference-related questions (i.e., attitude questions) as they would be in a conventional survey. This means that the questions are asked and answered in quick succession. Treatment group participants are asked the same questions in a different way. They are asked to stop and think, typically for thirty seconds, before answering questions.

Asking survey respondents to stop and think has significant results for important segments of the population. In both Brazil and the United States, the aggregate effect of the intervention is to reduce the skew of item nonresponse (i.e., the types of people who do not provide substantive answers to the questions). Of course, there are some respondents who have so little information about politics that providing them with an opportunity to think about their responses produces no significant changes in how they answer questions. But for citizens who know a bit more, the opportunity to stop and think leads them to express preferences that their counterparts in the control group did not. Hence, asking survey respondents to stop and think about their responses reduces the skew in the aggregate reports of attitudes by leading more respondents to provide meaningful answers to the questions. At the same time that asking people to "stop and think" before responding reduces the number of less-informed people who do not provide meaningful answers to survey questions, it also appears to make some highly informed people more hesitant to offer opinions. Stopping and thinking may remind these individuals to remember that they have mixed feelings about certain issues. In both Brazil and the United States, the scale and magnitude of such inhibitory effects is far less than the increase in responses offered among less-informed respondents. Hence, the overall effect of the stimulus is to significantly reduce the extent to which aggregate survey responses overemphasize the views of well-informed people.

Turgeon's work shows how seemingly innocuous features of conventional survey interviewing processes—in this case, the rapid-fire aspect of the typical interview—generates a chasm between a common inference drawn from surveys (represents the aggregate views of the population) and the underlying reality (only certain types of people answer the questions). A means for closing the chasm further is to integrate knowledge of how people form and express attitudes into our design of, and assumptions about, what happens during a survey interview.

Prior and Lupia (2008) use research on memory storage as the basis for a series of experiments in which changes to the typical survey interview process produces variations in respondent opportunities to think about their answers and their motivation for thinking at all (e.g, in some treatments, subjects are paid for answering political knowledge questions correctly). Prior and Lupia identify incentives and opportunities that lead to improved measures of knowledge-related variables. For example, simply telling respondents that you will pay them $1 for every question that they answer correctly yields significant increases in the number of correct answers observed. Given that incentives and opportunities also affect a survey respondent's willingness and ability to express certain kinds of preferences, it stands to reason that analogous experimentation can both clarify the extent to which existing survey environments yield reliable preference measurements and provide data about particular variations to the conduct of surveys that could improve measurement validity.

The second example comes from the American National Election Studies (ANES). Many scholars use election surveys to measure and make inferences about what citizens want. It is also true that survey questions designed with preference measurement in mind can be worded in various ways. Many scholars recognize that not all question wordings leverage what psychologists and survey researchers have learned about how what citizens want relates to what they say to survey interviewers.

As interest in the use of surveys to measure preferences has evolved, so has interest in improving question wording. In 2008, the ANES pursued a comprehensive effort to ensure that its question wordings were consistent with best practices in question wording as practiced within the survey research community. These "best practices" have been heavily influenced by scholarship on the psychology of the survey response.[26] Among the important lessons produced by these inquiries are what I call "clarity of purpose" and "universality of meaning."

By "clarity of purpose," I mean the consequence of a set of practices that, to the greatest extent possible, makes the meaning of all words in a question clear to the respondent. A common violation of clarity of purpose comes from survey questions that are "double-barreled." A double-barreled question is one that mentions multiple issues in a single question. As Weisberg, Krosnick, and Bowen (1996) describe with respect to the question "Do you favor reducing American use of gasoline by increasing our taxes on foreign oil?"

> There are two issues here: One is whether to reduce gasoline consumption, and the other is whether to use taxes on foreign oil as a means of accomplishing that end. Some respondents may say no to the question because they do not believe consumption should be reduced; others might say no because they believe some other means of reducing consumption should be used. Asking two questions would be better: (a) "Do you think that American use of gasoline should be reduced?" If the person answers yes, ask, (b) "Do you favor or oppose a tax on foreign oil as a way to cut gasoline use?"[27]

By revising double-barreled questions so that each question pertains to one and only one issue, we should obtain more valid measures of what citizens want.

Another threat to measurement validity comes from violations of universality of meaning. By "universality," I mean that all respondents share, to the greatest extent possible, identical conceptions of what they are being asked to do. Examples of questions that violate universality are those that employ scholarly jargon or other words that are likely to be understood differently by different parts of the population. As Holbrook et al. (2007) argue:

> [q]uestions are often laden with social science jargon. . . . Because survey researchers are usually well educated, they may find such questions to be easily understandable. It is rare indeed to hear of a questionnaire designer calculating the reading difficulty level of a question or using a dictionary or thesaurus to find synonyms that are simpler and easier to understand.[28]

Violations of universality matter for several reasons. In the context of attempting to understand what citizens want, reductions in interrespondent comparability reduce measurement validity. Most scholars who use survey data to explain citizen preferences do not seek to support specific descriptions of every individual respondent. Rather, they seek to support claims about what groups of citizens want. To derive such estimates, the typical practice is to assume that respondents' answers to specific questions are comparable. In other words, survey analysts who use a specific question to generate a preference measure commonly assume that all people who answered the question were asked exactly the same question and understood it in the same way. Analysts do not base estimates of what citizens want on, say, abortion, by asking some respondents whether they favor or oppose abortion in particular circumstances and asking others whether they favor or oppose a continuation of the morning's weather. They know that such noncomparability would undermine the validity of the statistic as a measure of abortion views. But I contend that many analysts, by ignoring violations of universality, do something that is not all that different from attempting to draw inferences about abortion preferences using questions that are not identical.

Specifically, violations of universality reduce comparability when respondents understand a given question in different ways. The inclusion of jargon in the question wording can limit comparability. If some respondents understand the jargon and others do not, the likelihood of nonidentical readings of the questions can increase. Another common threat to comparability is questions with nonlabeled response options. Perhaps the best known source of such threats in the study of what citizens want are questions that attempt to measure preferences by asking respondents to place themselves on a numbered scale. Such questions will often define a response of "1" as what a respondent should choose if they are very much against a particular policy and a number such as "7" as what they should choose if they are very much in favor of the policy. Interior values such as 2 or 6 are not given explicit labels. Many scholars simply insert such numbered responses into their statistical analyses without considering the extent to which respondents interpret nonlabeled response options identically. If respondents differ sufficiently in how they interpret the nonlabeled responses, the threats to measurement validity and inferential reliability from treating such responses as if they satisfy universality differ only in degree, not in kind, from the abortion–weather example described earlier.

In the review of previous ANES Time Series questionnaires, Jon Krosnick and I (the 2008 principal investigators [PIs]) found a number of long-standing questions that used nonlabeled response options. In such cases, we introduced a new version of the question that did not have this attribute. In some of these cases, the new version of the question used a branching method.[29] This method first asked respondents whether they support or oppose a particular policy. A second question then branched out in different directions by asking whether the respondent's initial opinion was weak or strong. The version of the second question that the respondent received depended on his or her initial answer. To help scholars compare the question's old and new versions, we administered each version to half of the 2008 ANES respondent sample. Table 1-1 contains a list of such questions with the old versions listed in on the left and the new versions listed on the right.

The questionnaire design literature leads us to believe that the new questions will provide more valid measures of what citizens want on a range of important topics. Consider, for example, the first question listed in table 1-1. It is a long-standing ANES question and reads as follows:

> Please look at page 8 of the booklet. Some people think the government should provide fewer services even in areas such as health and education in order to reduce spending. Suppose these people are at one end of a scale, at point 1. Other people feel it is important for the government to provide many more services even if it means an increase in spending. Suppose these people are at the other end, at point 7. And, of course, some other people have opinions somewhere in between, at points 2, 3, 4, 5 or 6.
>
> Where would you place YOURSELF on this scale, or haven't you thought much about this?

Respondents answer this question while looking in a booklet that offers the following response options:

1. Govt should provide many fewer services
2.
3.
4.
5.
6.
7. Govt should provide many more services

As indicated in the question, responses 1 and 7 have labels. Responses 2 through 6 do not. Respondents are first asked this question about themselves and then asked parallel versions about the preferences of the major party presidential candidates. Given the presence of the nonlabeled response options, it is likely that responses to this question violate the universality of meaning assumption that many survey analysts simply treat as true.

Table 1-1. Examples of Changes to ANES Preference Questions

Old version	New version
Please look at page 8 of the booklet. Some people think the government should provide fewer services even in areas such as health and education in order to reduce spending. Suppose these people are at one end of a scale, at point 1. Other people feel it is important for the government to provide many more services even if it means an increase in spending. Suppose these people are at the other end, at point 7. And, of course, some other people have opinions somewhere in between, at points 2, 3, 4, 5 or 6.	"Do you think the government should provide MORE services than it does now, FEWER services than it does now, or ABOUT THE SAME NUMBER of services as it does now?"
	Depending on how the respondent answers this question, a second question follows.
Where would you place YOURSELF on this scale, or haven't you thought much about this?	[If the respondent answered MORE to the first question] "Do you think that the government should provide A LOT more services, SOMEWHAT more services, or SLIGHTLY more services than it does now?"
1. Govt should provide many fewer services 2. 3. 4. 5. 6. 7. Govt should provide many more services	[If the respondent answered FEWER to the first question] "Do you think that the government should provide A LOT fewer services, SOMEWHAT fewer services, or SLIGHTLY fewer services than it does now?"
Please look at page 9 of the booklet. Some people believe that we should spend much less money for defense. Suppose these people are at one end of a scale, at point 1. Others feel that defense spending should be greatly increased. Suppose these people are at the other end, at point 7. And, of course, some other people have opinions somewhere in between, at points 2, 3, 4, 5 or 6.	Do you think that the government should spend MORE on national defense, LESS on national defense, or ABOUT THE SAME on national defense as it does now?
	[If MORE] Do you think that the government should spend A LOT more, SOMEWHAT more, or SLIGHTLY more than it does now?
Where would you place YOURSELF on this scale, or haven't you thought much about this? . . .	[If LESS] Do you think that the government should spend A LOT less, SOMEWHAT less, or SLIGHTLY less than it does now?

Table 1-1. (*continued*)

Old version	New version
Please look at page 10 of the booklet. There is much concern about the rapid rise in medical and hospital costs. Some people feel there should be a government insurance plan which would cover all medical and hospital expenses for everyone. Suppose these people are at one end of a scale, at point 1. Others feel that all medical expenses should be paid by individuals through private insurance plans like Blue Cross or other company paid plans. Suppose these people are at the other end, at point 7. And, of course, some other people have opinions somewhere in between, at points 2, 3, 4, 5, or 6. . . . Where would you place YOURSELF on this scale, or haven't you thought much about this? . . .	Do you FAVOR, OPPOSE, or NEITHER FAVOR NOR OPPOSE the U.S. government paying for all necessary medical care for all Americans? [If FAVOR] Do you favor that A GREAT DEAL, MODERATELY, or A LITTLE? [If OPPOSE] Do you oppose that A GREAT DEAL, MODERATELY, or A LITTLE?

The new version of the question begins as follows:

Do you think the government should provide MORE services than it does now, FEWER services than it does now, or ABOUT THE SAME NUMBER of services as it does now?

Depending on how the respondent answers this question, a second question follows:

[If the respondent answered MORE to the first question] Do you think that the government should provide A LOT more services, SOMEWHAT more services, or SLIGHTLY more services than it does now?

[If the respondent answered FEWER to the first question] Do you think that the government should provide A LOT fewer services, SOMEWHAT fewer services, or SLIGHTLY fewer services than it does now?

This new version offers respondents the opportunity to choose from among responses that are simple and straightforward. Scholars who want to represent respondent preferences on this issue can use answers to the two questions to produce a seven-point scale if they want, where the seven points refer to "a lot more," "somewhat more," "slightly more," "about the same number," "slightly fewer," "somewhat fewer," and "a lot fewer."

The meaning of individual components of such scales is far less ambiguous than in the question's traditional version.

The new version also removes the double-barreled attribute from the original question by simply focusing on the number of government services. The old version asks respondents to choose between "providing fewer services and reducing spending" and "providing services while increasing spending." Respondents who want more services, however, may not want greater spending. Perhaps they support deficit financing of such services, or perhaps they believe that government is inefficient and that government can provide more services at a lower cost if it is properly motivated. Regardless of whether analysts think such preferences are reasonable or unreasonable, and leaving aside the trouble with the nonlabeled response options described earlier, it would be difficult to argue that the old version of the question optimally measures a respondent's preference for government services.

That said, some people have argued that the old questions should be retained because they have valid statistical properties—specifically, answers to these questions when combined into an index create scales that appear to be meaningful. In other words, there does appear to be some consistency in how people answer various questions of this kind (e.g., people who respond "3" to one question with nonlabeled response options tend to choose similar answers to one another on other nonlabeled response options). Many scholars in a range of academic fields, however, have pointed out the error in such arguments. For example, Gould (1996) maintains that "the key error of factor analysis lies in reification, or the conversion of abstractions into putative real entities."[30] In particular, he shows the flaws in attributing too much to the first principal component in a factor analysis—the same type of statistic referred to earlier upon which scholars want to base validity claims:

> The first principal component is a mathematical abstraction that can be calculated for any matrix of correlation coefficients; it is not a "thing" with physical reality. Factorists have often fallen prey to a temptation for *reification*—for awarding *physical meaning* to all strong principal components. Sometimes this is justified; I believe that I can make a good case for interpreting my first pelycosaurian axis as a size factor. But such a claim can never arise from the mathematics alone, only from additional knowledge of the physical nature of the measures themselves. For nonsensical systems of correlation have principal components as well, and they may resolve more information than meaningful components do in other systems. A factor analysis for a five-by-five correlation matrix of my age, the population of Mexico, the price of Swiss cheese, my pet turtles' weight, and the average distance between galaxies during the past ten years will yield a strong first principal component. This component—since all the correlations are so strongly positive—will probably resolve as high a per-

centage of information as the first axis in my study of pelycosaurs. It will also have no enlightening physical meaning whatsoever.[31]

In other words, the validity of a scale depends on additional knowledge of individual components of the indices themselves. In such cases, the literature on optimal questionnaire design continues to reveal the fallacy in the claim that it is more valid to assume that all respondents mean consistently different things by numbers such as 3 and 5 in a nonlabeled scale than it is to assume that all respondents consistently understand the meanings of simple labels such as "more" and "fewer."

Changes such those described earlier and in table 1-1 show that by leveraging insights from psychology and survey research about what citizens think about when they answer survey questions, it is possible to design surveys whose questions have clarity of purpose and universality of meaning. With such properties in mind, scholars can obtain increasingly valid measures of what citizens want and they can use these measures to develop more credible accounts of the role of preferences in political contexts.

Conclusion

Greater attention to institutions and cognition can help scholars improve what they claim and know about what citizens want. If greater attention to institutions and cognition has these effects, it can also improve the soundness of many normative arguments about democracy. Such improvements can be leveraged in the study of a range of important topics, including the extent and meaning of governmental accountability to citizens' desires.

Greater attention to institutions reveals that what feelings citizens should have about candidates or parties can depend on the institutional context in which they reside. The appeal of an extremist party, for example, may reflect citizens' own extremity or it may reflect a recognition that achieving desired policy outcomes requires legislators who are extreme in ways that give them the power to counter other legislators who are extreme in less desirable ways. To the extent that relevant institutional dynamics are understood, that knowledge can be used to build more appropriate empirical models (i.e., models that allow the effect of preferences to be conditioned in theoretically defensible ways on important properties of institutional contexts).

Lupia, Krupnikov, Levine, Piston, and Von Hagen-Jamar (2010), for example, use information about the range of different requirements for changes in the constitutions of each of the U.S. states to better explain the correspondence between citizen attitudes on gay marriage and the constitutional status of such marriages in each state. Using a model that incorporates state-specific institutional information, Lupia et al. show that in states where the support of a simple majority of voters is sufficient to amend their constitution, the state constitutional status of gay marriage is far more sensitive to evenly divided public opinion than is the case in states where substantial legislative supermajorities are required.

A consequence of this finding pertains to what types of legislators citizens should prefer. Consider citizens for whom the legal status of gay marriage is far and away their most important issue. I contend that their preferences over candidates for state-level office should depend not just on their feelings about the issue but also on the constitutional amending rules of their state. If they live in states where simple voting majorities can change the state constitutional status of gay marriage, the effect that any particular legislator can have on that issue is minimal. Hence, voters who care primarily about gay marriage gain little with respect to this issue by forming a strong preference over state-level candidates. In other states, such citizens should take more of an interest in how their representative can affect bargaining dynamics in the state legislature. Here, learning about whether candidates for office can tip the required legislative balance in their state can help citizens achieve their goals. Moreover, for advocates of a particular position on this issue who can select particular states as targets for their legislative ambitions, understanding the differences in state requirements can give them a better sense of the states in which their informational efforts can have the greatest effect on the likelihood of constitutional change.

Greater attention to cognition can have parallel effects. To see how, note that many analysts treat survey-based preference measures as context-independent traits that are measured effectively by the questions at hand. Greater attention to cognition can clarify when responses to preference-oriented survey questions reliably correspond to targeted respondent thoughts and feelings. Such attention can not only help analysts build more appropriate empirical models (i.e., models that base their inclusion of such variables on a coherent logic of how they relate to relevant thoughts and feelings), they can also guide survey researchers to ask questions in ways that make valid measurements of important citizen evaluations more likely.

Notes

I thank the volume's editors, Christopher Carman, and participants at the Inaugural Conference of the Centre for Elections and Representation Studies at University of Strathclyde in Glasgow, Scotland, for helpful comments on previous versions of this essay.

1. See, e.g., Gerber and Lupia (1995); Habermas (1996); Besley and Burgess (2001, 2002).

2. See, e.g., Riker (1982), and James Madison's argument in *Federalist* 10.

3. Riker (1965), p. 25.

4. Delli Carpini and Keeter (1996).

5. See, e.g., Page and Shapiro (1992).

6. See, e.g., Rawls (1971).

7. See, e.g., Bartels (2005); Lupia et al. (2007).

8. Kedar (2005); Sin and Lupia (2010).

9. See, e.g., Althaus (2003); Turgeon (2009).

10. Pasek and Krosnick (2010).

11. See, e.g., Bartels (1996).

12. In this essay, I focus on conceptualizing and measuring citizen preferences over small numbers of alternatives. I choose this focus for three reasons. First, in many of the most important democratic roles that citizens play (e.g., as voters or jurors), the number of options (i.e., candidates, potential verdicts) over which they are given the opportunity to express preferences is small (e.g., two or three candidates for an elective office). Second, survey research, a subject on which a substantial portion of this essay focuses, tends to measure a specific preference with respect to a small set of response options. For example, survey respondents are often asked about whether they support or oppose specific policy positions, but they are not allowed to amend the set of positions and express preferences over the larger set. They are rarely, if ever, asked to express more complicated preferences or to discuss trade-offs when issue-specific preferences come into conflict. Third, focusing on the conceptualization of preferences over a small number of options simplifies the conceptual parts of the narrative, though in most cases this simplification is without a loss of generality.

This focus means that this essay will not touch on debates about the extent to which citizens can express meaningful preferences over more complex sets of alternatives. On this topic, Bartels (2002b, p. 49) argues that "citizens have attitudes but not preferences." His rationale for the distinction is that an attitude is an evaluation of a single object, while preference is a ranked evaluation over sets of objects. Bartels argues that political objects are so complex that citizen preferences can be contaminated by a number of psychological biases and limitations related to complex and abstract reasoning. I agree with the idea that citizens have difficulty dealing with politically common types of complexity and abstraction. However, a careful review of logic and evidence about how citizens reason suggests that such difficulties need not be sufficient to render citizens' judgments meaningless. As Sniderman and Bullock (2004) argue, political institutions simplify citizen choices by significantly reducing the complexity of the set of alternatives over which they express preferences. While Bartels (2002b) expresses doubts about the validity of even simple preference statements, his main evidence comes from framing-induced preference reversals in psychology. As Druckman (2001) shows, when these experiments are replicated in political environments, framing effects disappear or are greatly diminished. One way to interpret the difference between these outcomes is that the studies that Bartels cites are institution-free, where Druckman's study introduces political content. Over the set of issues on which this essay focuses, the institutional simplifications described by Sniderman and Bullock and the limits of framing in such circumstances identified by Druckman support the idea that citizens can conjure ranked evaluations over the kinds of sets of alternatives the politics often presents.

13. For empirical studies that conceptualize and attempt to improve measurements of "correct voting," see Lupia and McCubbins (1998) and Lau and Redlawsk (2006).

14. For reviews and theoretical foundations, consider Laver and Schofield (1998) and Bergman, Strom, and Mueller (2008) on coalescence, and Bergman, Strom, and Mueller (2003) on delegation.

15. See, e.g., Lupia and Strom (2008) for a review of the role of time preferences in legislative bargaining.

16. See, e.g., Lupia and Strom (2008) for an overview of such effects.

17. Sin and Lupia (2010).

18. See, e.g., Gerber et. al. (2001).

19. Bergman, Mueller, and Strom (2000).

20. See, e.g., Sen (1970).

21. The next four paragraphs follow from a description of preference formation originally used in Druckman and Lupia (2000).

22. Lodge et al. (1990).

23. See, e.g., Fishbein and Ajzen (1975); Enelow and Hinich (1984).

24. See, e.g., Bruner (1957), p. 135.

25. See, e.g., Higgins and King (1981); Srull and Wyer (1989); Fazio (1995).

26. See, e.g., Tourangeau, Rips, and Rasinski (2000).

27. Weisberg, Krosnick, and Bowen (1996), pp. 87–88.

28. Holbrook et al. (2007), p. 341.

29. See, e.g., Malhotra, Krosnick, and Thomas (2007).

30. Gould (1996), p. 48.

31. Ibid., p. 280.

II

Purposive Mass Belief Systems concerning Foreign Policy

Benjamin I. Page and Tao Xie

IN THE DECADES SINCE PHILIP CONVERSE's pioneering work on mass "belief systems" (a term generally taken to include affective as well as cognitive elements), a number of scholars have argued that citizens' political attitudes are more tightly constrained or more closely linked together than Converse thought.[1] Several of these scholars have offered evidence of coherent patterns in which citizens' policy preferences tend to be linked to broader political ideologies or beliefs, in a more or less instrumental or purposive fashion.[2]

Elsewhere we have proposed a theory of "purposive belief systems," postulating an instrumental logic that we believe tends to form an important foundation for citizens' policy preferences. Empirically, we have found substantial evidence for the existence of such belief systems in the realm of foreign policy.[3] In this chapter, we illustrate and extend those findings, using recent data on the specific case of U.S.-China relations. We also explore the workings of policy preference heuristics that involve feelings toward foreign countries and investigate the ways in which such heuristics do or do not relate to purposive belief systems.[4]

The Theory of Purposive Belief Systems

Our theory of purposive belief systems is quite simple, perhaps embarrassingly so. It is based on the proposition that ordinary citizens are capable of—and tend to engage in—"rational," instrumental, purposive reasoning about politics. We assume that most individuals have a set of fairly stable and firmly held political values, interests, and beliefs, which they acquire (and in some cases modify) as a result of childhood upbringing, life experiences, and exposure to political events and political rhetoric. These values, interests, and beliefs are often translated into what we call "basic political attitudes" or "political predispositions," including positions on the familiar liberal-conservative ideological continuum, or adherence to a political party, or commitment to activism or isolationism in foreign policy.

According to the theory, individuals use these values and interests (and the basic attitudes that sum them up), together with perceptions of political realities and beliefs about how the political world works, to form assessments of political "threats" to their values and interests. They also formulate "goals" that they want government to pursue and attach priorities to those goals. (In principle, citizens' goals for government can be negative as well as positive: "stay out of that," or "just leave me alone," for example.)

Individuals then bring the whole complex of values, interests, beliefs, basic attitudes, perceived threats, and goals—together with specific perceptions relevant to particular government programs (or, in the foreign policy case, particular foreign countries)—to bear upon the formulation of policy preferences.

In a nutshell, the theory asserts that individuals' policy preferences tend to reflect—and tend to follow from, in a logical, instrumental fashion—a broad set of relevant political values, interests, attitudes, and beliefs. A schematic view of the theory is given in figure 2-1, in which causal impacts are assumed to flow from the more basic attitudes and beliefs at the top of the diagram down to the less firmly held policy preferences at the bottom.[5]

Nothing about this theory is limited to foreign as opposed to domestic policy. Indeed, we would argue strongly for applying it to the domestic realm. In practice, however, relevant data—particularly on perceived threats and favored goals, which are central to the theory—have been much more readily available with respect to foreign policy than domestic. Every four years since 1974 (and now every two years), the Chicago Council on Global Affairs (CCGA, formerly CCFR) has conducted surveys of the American public's views on foreign policy, producing a wealth of data on individuals' basic attitudes, perceived threats, favored goals, country-specific beliefs and attitudes, and a wide range of foreign policy preferences.[6]

The Case of U.S.-China Relations

We have used the 2008 "regular," or Global Views, or POS (short for public opinion survey) CCGA survey to illustrate and explore the workings of purposive belief systems with respect to U.S.-China relations, a topic that is well represented in that survey.[7] Here, we focus on what these data can tell us about the theory of purposive belief systems, rather than on the substance of the U.S.-China case itself. (Readers interested in the substance of Americans' views of China and U.S.-China relations may want to take a look at our recent book on the subject.[8])

We consider five dependent variables: (1) positive, neutral, or negative reactions to China's economy growing to be as large as the U.S. economy;

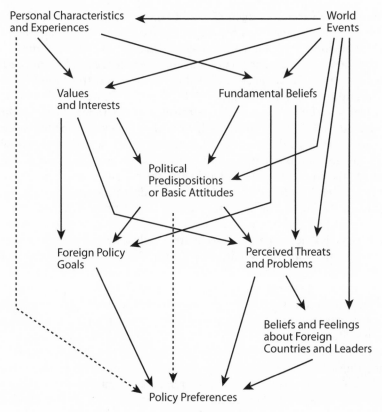

Figure 2-1
The theory of purposive belief systems.

(2) (in the context of a possible new agreement on climate change) support or opposition to providing U.S. aid to developing countries like India and China to help them limit the growth of emissions[9]; (3) support or opposition to allowing foreign government investors to invest in U.S. companies and banks; (4) support or opposition to using U.S. troops if China invaded Taiwan; and (5) support for undertaking friendly cooperation and engagement with China, as opposed to actively working to limit the growth of China's power. (Exact question wording is given in tables 2-1 through 2-5.)

For each dependent variable, we conducted a series of multiple regression analyses corresponding to the hierarchical model implied by the purposive belief system theory sketched in figure 2-1.[10] First (see column I of tables 2-1 through 2-5), we regressed policy preferences on thirteen demographic variables—such factors as the respondent's race, Hispanic ethnicity, religion, region of residence, gender, marital status, age, income level, education level, and employment status. We take these as measures of upbringing and life experience and consider them causally prior to the various attitudes and beliefs included in our later statistical models.

Second (see column II of tables 2-1 through 2-5), we included as independent variables—along with the thirteen demographic factors—three "basic attitudes": respondents' self-ratings on a seven-point liberal/conservative ideological scale; their locations on the standard seven-point party identification scale[11]; and their view on whether the United States should take an "active part" in world affairs or should "stay out" of world affairs. Liberalism/conservatism and party identification have long been known to be important influences on political attitudes and policy preferences, at least in the domestic realm. Ups and downs in collective responses to the "active part" question are widely taken as a prime indicator of the extent of internationalism or isolationism in the American public, and individuals' responses to this simple item have been found to have remarkably strong effects on a wide range of foreign policy preferences.[12]

Third (column III of each table), we added to all the preceding independent variables certain selected perceptions of the degree of "threat" to the vital interest of the United States from particular theoretically relevant potential threats (a "critical," "important but not critical," or "not important" threat), and judgments of how important to U.S. foreign policy should be certain theoretically relevant potential goals of U.S. policy ("very important," "somewhat important," "not important at all").[13] Note that our regressions of types I and II include an identical set of independent variables for each of our five dependent variables. For regression III, we added selected goals and/or threats (chosen to be theoretically relevant to a particular dependent variable), which vary by dependent variable.[14] For example, embrace of the goal of limiting climate change or global warming[15] would be expected to encourage support for aid to limit emissions; priority given to the goal of protecting the jobs of American workers should encourage negative reactions to China's economy growing as large as the U.S. economy; perceptions of a critical threat to the United States from the development of China as a world power ought to produce support for working to limit China's rise rather than cooperating with China.

Fourth and finally (see column IV of each table), we added to all the preceding independent variables a set of four general indices of support for different types of foreign policy goals: security goals not explicitly related to China, domestic welfare goals, humanitarian goals, and cooperation goals.[16] The purpose here is twofold: first, to consider a further set

Table 2-1. Determinants of Positive Reactions to China's Economy Growing as Large as the U.S. Economy

Independent variable	I	II	III	IV
Black	0.08*	0.08*	0.09*	0.07+
Hispanic	0.10**	0.12**	0.11*	0.10*
Evangelical	−0.07**	n.s.	n.s.	n.s.
Male	0.06**	0.07**	0.06*	0.06*
Married	0.08**	0.08**	0.09**	0.08**
Age	−0.08+	−0.09+	−0.10*	−0.08+
Income level	n.s.	n.s.	n.s.	n.s.
Education level	n.s.	n.s.	−0.08+	−0.08+
Employed	0.05+	n.s.	n.s.	n.s.
Conservatism		−0.16*	−0.17*	−0.15*
Republican Party loyalty		n.s.	n.s.	n.s.
Active part internationalism		n.s.	n.s.	n.s.
Threat of China's development as a world power			−0.20**	−0.21**
Goal of protecting jobs of American workers			−0.24**	−0.30**
Threat of economic competition from low-wage countries			n.s.	n.s.
Threat of China–Taiwan conflict			0.14**	0.12**
Domestic welfare goals				n.s.
Humanitarian foreign policy goals				0.17**
Security goals (non-China-specific)				n.s.
Cooperation goals				n.s.
R	0.255	0.272	0.380	0.398
Adjusted R-squared	0.047	0.050	0.116	0.125
Degrees of freedom	701	647	626	626

Source: 2008 CCGA U.S. general public survey.

Note: Entries are unstandardized OLS regression coefficients, with all variables rescaled to the 0–1 range. Thirteen demographic independent variables were included in all regressions; except as noted, only those with significant coefficients are shown. All attitudinal variables included in regressions are displayed.

Dependent variable: "If China's economy were to grow to be as large as the U.S. economy, do you think that would be mostly positive [1], mostly negative [0], or equally positive and negative [0.5]?" Goal and threat indices are described in the text and as follows.

$+p < 0.10$; $*p < 0.05$; $**p < 0.01$.

Table 2-2. Determinants of Favoring Aid to Developing Countries such as China and India to Help Them Limit the Growth of Emissions

Independent variable	I	II	III	IV
Black	n.s.	n.s.	n.s.	n.s.
Hispanic	0.11+	n.s.	n.s.	n.s.
Evangelical	–0.18**	–0.13**	–0.16**	–0.17**
Western	0.12*	n.s.	n.s	n.s.
Married	–0.14**	–0.14**	–0.11+	–0.12+
Age	n.s.	n.s.	n.s.	n.s.
Income level	n.s.	n.s.	n.s.	n.s.
Education level	n.s.	n.s.	n.s.	n.s.
Conservative ideology		–0.24*	–0.37*	–0.41*
Republican Party loyalty		–0.14+	n.s.	n.s.
Active part internationalism		0.13**	0.12*	n.s.
Goal of limiting climate change			0.16**	n.s.
Goal of combating world hunger			0.26**	n.s.
Humanitarian goals				0.40*
Security goals (non-China-specific)				n.s.
Domestic welfare goals				n.s.
R	0.276	0.357	0.458	0.480
Adjusted R-squared	0.059	0.105	0.163	0.176
Degrees of freedom	709	646	321	321

Source: 2008 CCGA U.S. general public survey.

Note: Entries are unstandardized OLS regression coefficients, with all variables rescaled to the 0–1 range. Thirteen demographic independent variables were included in all regressions; except as noted, only those with significant coefficients are shown. All attitudinal variables included in regressions are displayed.

Dependent variable: "In thinking about a new agreement on climate change, do you favor [1] or oppose [0] the U.S. providing technological and financial aid to countries like India and China to help them limit the growth of their emissions, if they agree to make efforts to reach this goal?"

$+p < 0.10$; $*p < 0.05$; $**p < 0.01$.

Table 2-3. Influences on Approval of Allowing Foreign Government Investors to Invest in U.S. Companies and Banks

Independent variable	I	II	III	IV
Black	−0.11*	n.s.	n.s.	n.s.
Northeastern	0.15**	0.14**	0.13*	0.12*
Western	0.09+	n.s.	n.s.	n.s.
Male	0.14**	0.13**	0.11**	0.12**
Age	−0.18**	−0.19*	−0.15*	−0.14*
Income level	0.23**	0.25**	0.23**	0.23**
Education level	n.s.	n.s.	n.s.	n.s.
Conservatism		n.s.	n.s.	n.s.
Republican Party loyalty		n.s.	n.s.	n.s.
Active part internationalism		n.s.	0.07+	0.07+
Threat of China's development as a world power			−0.13*	−0.13*
Goal of protecting jobs of American workers			−0.35**	−0.38**
Threat of economic competition from low-wage countries			n.s.	n.s.
Domestic welfare goals				n.s.
Cooperation goals				0.14+
Security goals (non-China-specific)				n.s.
Humanitarian goals				n.s.
R	0.349	0.353	0.418	0.426
Adjusted R-squared	0.105	0.103	0.150	0.151
Degrees of freedom	697	649	641	641

Source: 2008 CCGA U.S. general public survey.

Note: Entries are unstandardized OLS regression coefficients, with all variables rescaled to the 0–1 range. Thirteen demographic independent variables were included in all regressions; except as noted, only those with significant coefficients are shown. All attitudinal variables included in regressions are displayed.

Dependent variable: "Recently some foreign government-owned funds have made major investments in American companies and financial institutions. Some observers say that as their role is purely economic, we should welcome such investment. Others say that the risk of losing control of American companies and their technologies to foreign governments is too great. Are you in favor [1] or not in favor [0] of allowing foreign government investors to invest in U.S. companies and banks?"

+$p < 0.10$; *$p < 0.05$; **$p < 0.01$.

Table 2-4. What Affects Favoring U.S. Troop Use to Defend Taiwan against a Hypothetical Chinese Invasion

Independent variable	I	II	III	IV
Hispanic	0.13*	0.23**	0.23**	0.22**
Northeastern	0.10+	n.s.	0.10+	n.s.
Southern	0.15**	0.12*	0.12*	0.11*
Western	0.13*	n.s.	0.09+	0.10+
Male	0.19**	0.17**	0.16**	0.14**
Age	n.s.	−0.15*	−0.18*	−0.17*
Income level	n.s.	n.s.	n.s.	n.s.
Education level	n.s.	n.s.	n.s.	n.s.
Conservatism		0.20+	n.s.	n.s.
Republican Party loyalty		n.s.	n.s.	n.s.
Active part internationalism		0.22**	0.11**	0.10*
Threat of China's development as a world power			n.s.	n.s.
Threat of China–Taiwan conflict			0.18**	0.19**
Goal of protecting weaker nations against foreign aggression			0.34**	0.27*
Humanitarian goals				n.s.
Cooperation goals				−0.21*
Security goals (non-China-specific)				n.s.
Domestic welfare goals				n.s.
R	0.290	0.399	0.471	0.489
Adjusted R-squared	0.066	0.136	0.196	0.208
Degrees of freedom	658	603	586	586

Source: 2008 CCGA U.S. general public survey.

Note: Entries are unstandardized OLS regression coefficients, with all variables rescaled to the 0–1 range. Thirteen demographic variables were included in all regressions; except as noted, only those with significant coefficients are shown. All attitudinal variables included in regressions are displayed.

Dependent variable: "There has been some discussion about the circumstances that might justify using U.S. troops in other parts of the world. Please give your opinion about some situations. Would you favor [1] or oppose [0] the use of U.S. troops . . . if China invaded Taiwan?"

+$p < 0.10$; *$p < 0.05$; **$p < 0.01$.

Table 2-5. Influences on Favoring Cooperation and Engagement with China

Independent variable	I	II	III	IV
Catholic	0.09*	0.10*	n.s.	n.s.
Evangelical	−0.07+	n.s.	n.s.	n.s.
Western	0.10+	0.11+	n.s.	n.s.
Male	0.09*	0.08*	0.09*	0.09*
Married	0.12**	0.13**	0.13**	0.13**
Income level	n.s.	n.s.	n.s.	n.s.
Education level	0.31**	0.34**	0.27**	0.27**
Conservative		−0.27*	−0.28**	−0.25*
Republican		n.s.	n.s.	n.s.
Active part internationalism		0.09*	0.14**	0.14**
Threat of China's development as a world power			−0.37**	−0.38**
Threat of China–Taiwan conflict			n.s.	n.s.
Threat of low-wage economic competition			n.s.	n.s.
Goal of protecting the jobs of American workers			n.s.	n.s.
Security goals (non-China-specific)				n.s.
Humanitarian goals				n.s.
Cooperation goals				0.12+
Domestic welfare goals				n.s.
R	0.297	0.352	0.417	0.424
Adjusted R-squared	0.071	0.101	0.146	0.147
Degrees of freedom	685	637	621	621

Source: 2008 CCGA U.S. general public survey.

Entries are unstandardized OLS regression coefficients, with all variables rescaled to the 0–1 range. Thirteen demographic independent variables were included in all regressions; except as noted, only those with significant coefficients are shown in the table. All attitudinal variables that were included in the regressions are shown.

Dependent variable: "In dealing with the rise of China's power, do you think that the U.S. should undertake friendly cooperation and engagement with China [1] or actively work to limit the growth of China's power [0]?"

$+p < 0.10$; $*p < 0.05$; $**p < 0.01$.

of fairly basic attitudinal factors, roughly comparable to (though, in our view, causally subsequent to) our three "basic attitudes," and second, to make sure that in our selection of theoretically relevant goals and threats we did not omit an important factor that (perhaps for good though unexpected reasons) affects Americans' policy preferences.

Rather than marching through each of our five sets of regressions and discussing them one at a time, we will comment on general patterns that run through all five. Readers are invited to revisit these tables whenever and however often they want.

Effects of Demographic Factors on Policy Preferences

By glancing at column I of each regression, the reader can see that several demographic factors (four or five of the thirteen, on average) have a significant estimated impact on each of our five China-related policy preferences. Some of these effects are substantively interesting, though we will not discuss them here. And several of them (e.g., education in table 2-5) are fairly substantial in magnitude, with movement from the bottom to the top of a demographic measure accounting for movement of about one-fifth or even one-third along the 0-1 policy preference scales.

We take this as consistent with the idea, included in the purposive belief system theory (and of course in many other theories as well), that individuals' upbringing and life experience have effects—presumably working largely or wholly through intervening beliefs and attitudes—on their policy preferences. Our column I regressions can be taken as "reduced form" analyses, in which the demographic effects are real, but part or all of the effects may actually be indirect, working through attitudinal variables that are omitted from the column I equation—presumably including those that we add in later sets of regressions.

One surprise, however. Much of the estimated impact of demographic factors turns out to be "direct." If one looks at the coefficients for each demographic variable, moving to the right across columns of progressively larger and more inclusive regressions, it is apparent that most of the significant coefficients stay just about as large throughout this process. Neither basic political attitudes, nor specific theoretically relevant goals or threats, nor comprehensive orientations toward different types of foreign policy goals—at least as we have measured these factors[17]—can provide major mechanisms by which demographic effects occur. (One exception: The effects of being an Evangelical Christian apparently work partly through Evangelicals' generally conservative ideologies. When ideological self-ratings are included in regressions, the coefficients for being Evangelical tend to drop.) This is contrary to the impression given by our earlier research, an impression that now appears to be clearly incorrect.[18] Unless demographic characteristics somehow exert force at a distance (unmediated by any attitudes or beliefs), this suggests that important attitudinal factors are either very poorly measured or are omitted from the models we have specified.

Still, we must not lose sight of the major fact about demographic factors: they do *not* in general—either individually or all taken together—have a great deal of effect, either on these China-related preferences or on foreign policy attitudes more generally.[19] A glance at the upper rows in tables 2-1 through 2-5 reveals that the demographic coefficients are not very large, either in absolute terms (often clustering around 0.10) or relative to attitudinal coefficients for the same dependent variables—many of which are substantially larger. Moreover, a look across the row of adjusted R-squared coefficients near the bottom of each table makes clear that demographic factors alone (in column I) can account for only about one-third to one-half as much of the variance in responses as the full column IV models—including basic attitudes, specific threats and goals, and general goal orientations.

It would be a grievous error, then, to suppose that foreign policy attitudes can be sufficiently accounted for solely through demographic characteristics. It is important also to consider the sorts of beliefs, values, and attitudes postulated by the purposive belief system theory.

Basic Political Attitudes

As column II in each of the five regression tables indicates, our three "basic attitudes"—ideological liberalism/conservatism, party affiliation, and "active part" internationalism or isolationism—also have some significant effects on China-related policy preferences. Being conservative, for example, leads to somewhat more negative reactions to the prospect of China's economy growing as large as the U.S. economy, and to a substantial tendency to favor the U.S. "actively" working to limit the growth of China's power rather than engaging in friendly cooperation with China. Being a Republican leads to somewhat more opposition to aid to countries like China and India in order to limit their emissions, whereas being an active part internationalist tends to produce support for aid to limit emissions, support for using troops in a hypothetical Chinese invasion of Taiwan, and support for engagement with China rather than efforts to limit China.

Here we see more evidence in favor of the hierarchical aspect of the theory. The conservative opposition to emissions aid, for example, and the active part internationalist support for it, both appear to work mostly through more specific attitudes concerning limiting climate change and combating world hunger. (When these more specific opinions are added to regressions, they get substantial coefficients, and the coefficients for the basic attitudes drop.) Much the same is true of active part internationalists' support for troop use in the Taiwan invasion scenario.

This makes sense. The basic attitudes undoubtedly influence specific goals, values, and beliefs, which in turn often or usually have the main proximate impact on policy preferences.

But again, the effects of these basic attitudes are mostly not very large. Party identification, in particular, plays a far less important role in most foreign policy issues than in domestic policy. (Only when foreign policy issues have become clearly a subject of partisan debate, as in the case of climate change and the Kyoto Agreement, does party identification tend to have weak effects independent of ideology and other factors.) As comparison of the adjusted R-squared coefficients at the bottom of columns I and II indicates, the addition of the three basic attitudes to our regressions does increase explanatory power, but for the most part only by a small amount.[20]

Threats, Goals, and Purposive Belief Systems

It is in the column III regressions, when we add theoretically relevant perceptions of threats and high-priority goals, that we find a particularly strong improvement in explanatory power, particularly large coefficients, and substantial evidence for the purposive belief system theory.

Consider first the question of "explanatory power"—a sometimes-derided criterion that we believe is useful for judging the relevance of theories to the real world. When one moves from column II to column III in our tables—which involves adding only two or three attitudinal variables to the sixteen independent variables previously included—there is always a marked rise in adjusted R-squared values—usually a rise on the order of 50%, and in one case (reactions to growth of China's economy), a doubling of the adjusted R-squared coefficient. Key variables specified by the purposive belief system theory make a real difference.

Moreover, the effects of these variables make sense. Other things being equal, perceptions of threat from China's development as a world power—and embrace of the goal of protecting the jobs of American workers—lead to more negative assessments of China's economic growth, and more opposition to allowing foreign government investment in U.S. companies and banks. The goal of protecting weaker nations from foreign aggression, and perceived threats to vital U.S. interests from conflict between China and Taiwan, lead to support for U.S. troop use in the event of a Chinese invasion of Taiwan. Perceptions of threat from China's development as a world power lead rather strongly to favoring the U.S. working to limit the growth of China's power, rather than engaging in friendly cooperation with China.

To be sure, some of this seems obvious. Of course, commitment to the goal of limiting climate change leads to support for aid to limit emissions from China and India. (Both countries are emerging as major polluters.) And of course, seeing China's power as a threat to the United States leads to wanting to limit that power. Naturally, fears of job and wage losses lead to concern about economic growth or investments from China.

But that is precisely the point. The theory of purposive belief systems asserts that people tend to think sensibly about politics, instrumentally deriving their policy preferences from values they hold, threats they perceive, and goals they embrace. It may not be very exciting to find such sensible connections among attitudes, but they fit the theory. Note also that our findings directly contradict the "nonattitude" or "no constraint" perspective, which predicts no associations at all among these attitudinal elements. And our findings are not artifacts of short-term response-consistency effects; the relevant items are generally found widely separated from each other in the survey instrument.

General Goal Orientations

In our column IV regressions, we sought to do a sort of clean-up operation, checking whether we had omitted important explanatory factors, and also testing whether our highly rationalistic theoretical account—in which rather specific, logically relevant goals and threat perceptions affect policy preferences—might obscure a less sharply instrumental reality in which broader goal orientations or attitudinal tendencies (with which specific goals are often positively correlated) might be the real causal factors.

The short answer is no. In our column IV regressions, we included four indices of general goal orientations: embrace of domestic welfare goals, humanitarian foreign policy goals, security goals (not specific to China), and cooperation goals.[21] These cover all the major dimensions that emerged from factor analyses of CCGA goals. Yet seldom do they have much independent effect on policy preferences, once our specific, theoretically relevant goals and threats are taken into account. They add very little to explanatory power: the adjusted R-squared values at the bottom of column IV are only a bit bigger than those at the bottom of column III. Most of the individual coefficients are nonsignificant.

The main exception to this point is that a general embrace of human-itarian goals (combating world hunger, promoting democracy abroad, promoting and defending human rights, and protecting weaker nations from foreign aggression) does have some substantial effects: it leads to more positive reactions to China's economic growth and substantial sup-port for emission aid. This makes sense. Americans who care about peo-ple abroad and want to help them are more likely to take concrete stands that are consistent with their altruism. We had no single, specific goal capturing this stance that could be included in type III regressions. The other exception involves the negative effect of cooperation goals, which are explicitly multilateral, on the (implicitly unilateral) use of U.S. troops in the event of a Chinese invasion of Taiwan. Again, this seems consistent with the reasoning of the purposive belief system theory.

Thus, our findings support the purposive belief system theory much more strongly than they do a more psychologically oriented view that emphasizes "response tendencies" or broad attitudes. Strikingly, this is true even though the multiple-item measures of general goal orientations are presumably measured more accurately (and hence should more eas-ily produce significant coefficient estimates) than the single-item goal or threat indicators that get to the heart of the purposive belief system theory.

Feelings toward Countries as Heuristics

In the context of domestic political attitudes, Paul Sniderman and others have argued that feelings toward particular social groups can serve as heuristics in forming political attitudes and policy preferences. If a dis-tinct social group is seen as differentially benefiting from—or otherwise linked to—a given public policy, it could make sense for individuals to use their positive or negative feelings toward that group to form preferences about that policy. Positive or negative feelings toward African Americans, for example, apparently feed into judgments about civil rights policies.[22]

Here we inquire whether, in the realm of foreign policy, a similar logic might apply to preferences concerning policies that differentially affect particular countries. Do individuals' feelings toward a given country (to-ward China, for example) affect judgments about foreign aid for that country, or trade or diplomatic relations with it, or military policies con-cerning it?

We also inquire into the mechanisms by which such feeling heuristics may work. In particular, do feelings toward foreign countries consciously or unconsciously "sum up" a variety of beliefs and attitudes toward that country, such as beliefs that the country is a military ally (or enemy) of the United States, or that it engages in mutually beneficial (or harmful) economic relations with the United States, or that its political system respects (or represses) the human rights and democratic aspirations of its own people? If so, do Americans' feelings toward that country only indirectly affect policy preferences, working through more specific beliefs and attitudes? Or, indeed, are any apparent effects spurious, an artifact of positive correlations between feelings and the specific beliefs and attitudes that affect both feelings and policy preferences?

On the other hand, do feelings toward countries have independent effects on policy preferences, even when a variety of specific beliefs and attitudes are controlled for? Either way, how do feelings toward countries fit together with—or perhaps contradict—the logic of the purposive belief system theory?

Our own past research has indicated that feelings toward countries do in fact affect many sorts of foreign policy preferences—concerning matters from foreign aid, to diplomatic relations, to the use of U.S. troops—and that a substantial part of those effects is independent of other measured beliefs and attitudes. Americans' support for increasing economic aid to African countries, for example, is distinctly and independently affected by their feelings toward three very different countries on the African continent: South Africa, Nigeria, and Egypt. Feelings toward Israel affect judgments about using U.S. troops to defend Israel against a hypothetical invasion by "Arab forces." Feelings toward South Korea, Saudi Arabia, and Taiwan appear to play analogous roles in favoring or opposing defense of those countries. Individuals' support for trade with, diplomatic relations with, or economic sanctions against such countries as China, Cuba, Iran, or North Korea are also affected (independently of many other factors) by feelings toward those countries or their leaders.[23]

Our analysis of China-related policy preferences using the 2008 CCGA data confirms and extends these findings. We used "feeling thermometer" ratings of attitudes toward China—which run from 0 degrees ("very cold, unfavorable") through 50 degrees ("not particularly warm or cold") to 100 degrees ("very warm, favorable"), with respondents encouraged to pick any point in between—as imperfect but very helpful indicators of respondents' overall feelings toward China.[24]

In table 2-6, we present the ordinary least squares (OLS) coefficients for China feelings (recoded to the 0–1 range) in a series of regressions for each of our five policy preference–dependent variables. Each row (concerning a given dependent variable) begins with the coefficient from a simple bivariate regression of policy preferences on feelings toward China. The remaining coefficients, moving from left to right, are derived from regressions exactly the same as those in corresponding columns (I through IV) of tables 2-1 through 2-5, except for the addition in each case of the China feelings variable. The adjusted R-squared value for each regression is given in parentheses so that the magnitude of the China feelings coefficient can be put into the context of the explanatory power of all the variables included in that regression.

The first column of table 2-6 is definitely consistent with the idea that feelings toward foreign countries serve as heuristics in forming policy preferences. Feelings toward China are substantially related, at a high level of statistical significance, to most of the policy preferences (four of the five) that we consider.

The magnitude of the coefficient (0.52) for effects of China feelings on the most general policy item—whether to undertake "friendly cooperation and engagement" with China or work to limit the growth of China's power—is remarkably large, larger than one ordinarily encounters in the analysis of individual-level survey data. It indicates that movement from the bottom to the top of the thermometer scale produces movement of about half the distance between favoring active efforts to limit China and favoring friendly cooperation with China. Most of the other coefficients are also substantial, clustering around 0.30. Even the item concerning whether "foreign government investors" should be allowed to invest in U.S. banks and companies—which does not explicitly mention China, hence is not subject to any simpleminded process in which the term "China" itself triggers feelings regardless of their instrumental relevance or irrelevance to a given policy—shows a substantial relationship with feelings toward China (a prime candidate for undertaking such investments).

The sole exception to this pattern—the lack of any significant relationship between feelings toward China and support for or opposition to using U.S. troops in case China invaded Taiwan—is consistent with past findings that feelings toward the hypothetical victims of aggression, not feelings toward the hypothetical aggressors, affect Americans' policy reactions.[25] Presumably, the fact of attacking another country overrides any other feelings about the attacker.

Each of these possible uses of feelings as heuristics seems quite reasonable to us. But by what mechanisms do they work?

A glance from left to right across each row of coefficients in table 2-6 reveals that for the first three items (friendly cooperation with China, reactions to growth of China's economy, and foreign government investment in the United States), the "independent effects" hypothesis gets some support. The coefficients for China feelings do tend to drop a bit when certain other factors are considered—for example, the rather strong negative effects of embracing the goal of job protection, or perceiving a threat

Table 2-6. Effects of Feelings toward China on Policy Preferences

Dependent variable	Bivariate	I (Demographics only)	II (Demographics + basic attitudes)	III (Demographics + basic attitudes + threat/goals)	IV (Demographics + basic attitudes + threat/goals + goal indices)
Engage in friendly cooperation	0.52** (0.072)	0.59** (0.169)	0.57** (0.163)	0.46** (0.197)	0.45** (0.194)
Positive reaction to China economy as large as U.S. economy	0.33** (0.073)	0.27** (0.088)	0.22** (0.081)	0.16** (0.121)	0.17** (0.136)
Allow investments in U.S. companies by foreign governments	0.30** (0.024)	0.22** (0.102)	0.26** (0.097)	0.19* (0.140)	0.18* (0.139)
Favor aid to countries like India and China to limit emissions	0.27** (0.014)	0.27** (0.063)	n.s. (0.097)	n.s. (0.138)	n.s. (0.151)
Favor U.S. troop use if China invaded Taiwan	n.s. (0.000)	n.s. (0.058)	n.s. (0.118)	n.s. (0.197)	n.s. (0.200)

Source: 2008 CCGA U.S. general public survey.
Entries are unstandardized OLS coefficients for China feeling thermometer ratings (recoded, like all other variables, to the 0–1 range) in a given regression. The adjusted R-squared value for each regression is given in parentheses. Regression specifications in columns I–IV are exactly the same as in corresponding columns of tables 2-1 through 2-5, except for the addition of the China thermometer ratings.
+$p < 0.10$; *$p < 0.05$; **$p < 0.01$.

to U.S. interests from the development of China as a world power, on reactions to the growth of China's economy, or the big negative impact of the job protection goal on support for foreign government investment. (Compare columns II and III in table 2-6, and look back at tables 2-1 and 2-3.) Still, the first three rows of table 2-6 (we will indicate shortly why the fourth row is different) still show substantial, statistically significant coefficients for feelings toward China, even when some twenty other independent variables are taken into account.

The aid-to-limit-emissions item constitutes a special case because the question deals with technological and financial aid to "developing countries like China and *India* [emphasis added]," not just China, in order to help them limit the growth of their emissions. It turns out—for reasons that currently escape us but seem worth investigating—that feelings toward India are much more important than feelings toward China in affecting preferences on this matter. In fact, when feelings toward both countries are included at the same time in a series of regression analyses, the coefficients for China feelings become completely nonsignificant, while those for India are quite large and remain so through all the different types of regressions.[26]

To a substantial extent, then, whatever effects feelings toward China (or India) have on these policy preferences do *not* just work indirectly through—or spuriously result from—the impact of other factors we included in our analysis. Neither demographic variables (thirteen of them), nor our three partisan and ideological basic attitudes, nor specific China-relevant threats and goals, nor the four indices of general goal orientations—nor all of these factors taken together—can erase the estimated independent effects on policy preferences of feelings toward China.

This finding surprised us. We had been inclined toward the "summing up" rather than the "independent effects" hypothesis. We expected, in particular, that theoretically relevant foreign policy goals and perceived threats would turn out to account for most or all of the initial relationships between feelings and policy preferences, as the purposive belief system theory might be taken to predict. We resist any simple dichotomy between "rational" instrumental calculations and "emotional" reactions, whether in forming policy preferences or in human behavior generally, because we see cognitions and emotions as inextricably intertwined. (Human emotions presumably evolved largely for instrumental reasons related to survival and propagation.[27]) Still, the persistent independent effects of feelings, when so many logically relevant beliefs and attitudes are controlled for, seem somewhat troubling for the purely rationalistic and instrumental logic of the purposive belief system theory.

Of course, methodological considerations (similar to those discussed in connection with the persistent effects of demographic factors) might account for these findings and might leave our initial theoretical expectations intact. Perhaps the specific goals, perceived threats, and the like that we deal with are too poorly measured to do the job they should. Or (we think more plausibly) perhaps we have simply not had access to measures of certain important beliefs and attitudes that would change the picture if they could be included. These might include perceptions about China's role in the war on terror, reactions to the quality or price of imports from China, assessments of the state of human rights or democracy in China, and judgments about China's likely foreign policy actions as it gains power. One can imagine many other specific, China-related beliefs and attitudes that might fit into a full account of Americans' policy preferences concerning U.S.-China relations, and might affect (or be affected by) feelings toward China in such ways that all the apparent impact of China feelings on policy preferences would turn out to be spurious or indirect.

Further research seems indicated in order to work out the precise role in policy preferences of feelings toward foreign countries, and their place in (or contradiction to) the theory of purposive belief systems. Some of this research could be done with cross-sectional surveys that more fully spell out and measure relevant beliefs and attitudes. Some fundamental questions, however (including the extent to which country feelings are causes or are effects of other factors, and whether individuals consciously or unconsciously use feelings as running-tally summaries of various beliefs and attitudes), may be more effectively pursued through experimental research.

Conclusion

Generations of politicians, pundits, and foreign policy experts have denigrated public opinion on foreign policy as being ill-informed, unstructured, and capricious—hence as either irrelevant to policy making or as dangerous to the survival of the republic.[28] We believe that our findings that individuals tend to have purposive belief systems concerning foreign policy point in the opposite direction. They should be of interest not only for the patterns revealed in individual political behavior (ordinary Americans tend to bring logically relevant foreign policy goals, threat perceptions, and other factors to bear on the formation of policy preferences), but also for the implication they raise that policy makers should pay more respectful attention to the collective foreign policy preferences of the U.S. citizenry. Those preferences turn out to reflect more instrumental political reasoning, and to rest on more solid logical foundations, than is often supposed.

To be sure, we do not want to overstate the strength of our findings. Perusal of the adjusted R-squared values at the bottom of tables 2-1 through 2-5 indicates that even our full column IV models generally account for less than one-fifth of the variance in individuals' policy preferences. It is definitely not the case that every individual American has a tight, coherent, well-worked-out belief system related to each foreign policy issue. Far from it. We are dealing only with tendencies and with "on the average" patterns.

But these tendencies are rather solid. (Indeed, their strength may be understated here because of our particular method of analysis[29] as well as by the inherent limitations of available data that do not include every theoretically relevant independent variable.) The tendencies are strong enough, we believe, to say something interesting about individual political behavior. Perhaps even more important, we believe that the tendencies we have found are strong enough to help account for the "rational" characteristics that Page and Shapiro have attributed to collective public opinion.[30]

The empirical relationships among logically connected values, interests, beliefs and policy preferences are apparently strong enough so that if and when most Americans agree on centrally relevant values and beliefs, majorities of Americans will come to favor a set of policies that coherently and consistently reflects those values and beliefs. This helps clear up a mystery about how collective public opinion can look "rational" when individual opinions look so messy. The so-called miracle of aggregation, alone, will not do it; as a leading political scientist once pointed out, "a thousand times nothing is still nothing."[31] The aggregation of individual opinions can indeed dispose of off-setting random errors, but it will reveal something coherent at the collective level only if certain coherent tendencies are shared in the minds of individuals. We believe that we have uncovered such tendencies.

A final reflection: As we have noted, nothing about the logic of purposive belief systems is limited to foreign (as opposed to domestic) policy. If anything, foreign policy should be *less* amenable to logically structured, instrumentally oriented belief systems, since foreign affairs are complicated, fast-moving, and distant from the immediate lives of most Americans. One would expect, a fortiori, that if purposive belief systems are widely found in the foreign policy realm, they should be even stronger and more prevalent in the realm of domestic policy. We hope that future research will cast more light on this possibility.

Notes

1. Converse (1964, 1970).
2. See Feldman (1988); Hurwitz and Peffley (1987); Peffley and Hurwitz (1985); Herrmann, Tetlock, and Visser (1999).

3. Page with Bouton (2006).

4. The origins of Ben Page's thinking about purposive or "rational" political behavior go back to Raymond E. Wolfinger's Stanford University research seminar on Public Opinion and Voting Behavior, in which he and Harlan Robinson explored "rational voting" of the sort postulated by V. O. Key Jr. in his book *The Responsible Electorate* (1966).

5. We are aware that we cannot exclude the possibility of some effects proceeding upward in the diagram. To the extent that they do so, empirical coefficient estimates based on these hierarchical assumptions may be inflated by simultaneity bias. We believe, however, that any such effects are small. The hierarchical structure of these attitudes and beliefs (e.g., the relative stability of party identification, as compared with policy preferences) is fairly well established.

6. It is not entirely a coincidence that the CCGA surveys have produced relevant data. One of the present authors (Page) has participated in designing each of the CCGA surveys since 1974, with a theory of this sort in mind. See the reports of CCGA studies (now directed by Marshall M. Bouton) at the website www.thechicagocouncil.org.

7. The "regular" 2008 CCGA survey should be distinguished from the "Soft Power" U.S. survey, which was also conducted in 2008 by the CCGA as part of an interesting study that also involved parallel surveys in several Asian countries. See Whitney and Shambaugh (2009).

8. Page and Xie (2010).

9. In the following analyses, we report OLS regression coefficients, which—with dichotomous dependent variables like support for or opposition to emissions aid—assume a less plausible functional form, and can provide less accurate information, than logit or probit coefficients. But OLS coefficients are much more easily interpreted and compared both within and across regressions. Our explorations of logit models have revealed very few substantive differences.

10. Quantitatively inclined readers will note that our regression types I through IV correspond to a hierarchical causal model in which it is assumed that demographic factors affect subsequent attitudes but not vice versa, and the "basic attitudes" affect more specific goals and threats but not vice versa. We believe that any specification bias from violations of these assumptions is minimal. The coefficient for each independent variable in column IV can be interpreted as estimating the direct effect of that variable while controlling for all others in the regression; indirect effects can be calculated from earlier stages. All coefficients in stages prior to IV can be interpreted as "reduced form" coefficients that mix direct and indirect effects.

11. To facilitate interpretation of regression coefficients, all the independent variables that have more than two valid values were rescaled into 0–1 range.

12. Page with Bouton (2006), pp. 70–72.

13. In principle, it would be desirable to more explicitly allow for opposition to goals, rather than merely attaching low priority to them, since nearly all the potential goals are noncontroversial and very widely shared, with large majorities saying that all of them should be at least "somewhat important." Nevertheless, the "not important" responses are probably adequate to encompass the few cases of outright opposition as well as attachment of low priority.

14. An argument can be made for including all available measures of threats and goals—whether theoretically relevant or not—in all regressions, in order to

facilitate comparability across regressions and to ensure that no unforeseen influence is missed. But this is not feasible because of limited Ns and a high number
of often-collinear goal ($n = 14$) and threat ($n = 13$) items. Our step IV regressions,
described later, help ensure that no important unforeseen factors are missed.

15. The questions about climate change and global warming as foreign policy
goals were respectively asked of split samples. As such, it is impossible to include
both variables in regression analysis. In the end, we selected "climate change"
because it is a broader and less controversial term than "global warming." The
split-sample design was responsible for the sharp drop of N for columns III and
IV in table 2-2.

16. The goal indices are simple sums of responses (1 = should be a very important goal of U.S. foreign policy, 0.5 = a somewhat important goal, 0 = not an
important goal) to the following questions that loaded highly on a given factor
derived from varimax oblique rotation: (1) Security goals: "combating international terrorism"; "preventing the spread of nuclear weapons"; "maintaining su-
perior military power worldwide." (2) Domestic welfare goals: "protecting the
jobs of American workers"; "securing adequate supplies of energy"; "improving
America's standing in the world"; "controlling and reducing illegal immigration."
(3) Humanitarian goals: "protecting weaker nations against foreign aggression";
"helping to bring a democratic form of government to other nations"; "promoting and defending human rights in other countries"; "combating world hunger."
(4) Cooperation goals: "limiting climate change"; "strengthening the United Nations."

17. One reason for the persistence of significant demographic coefficients, despite their actually working through attitudes of the sort we specified, could be
that those attitudes are measured with substantial error. But unless the attitudinal
measures altogether lack validity (a possibility that is contradicted by abundant
evidence), measurement attenuation would account only for the persistence of
significant demographic coefficients, not for the persistence of estimated effects
of the same magnitude.

18. See Page with Bouton (2006). The balkanized 2002 CCGA data on which
those analyses were largely based provided very low Ns of respondents for type
III or type IV regressions, which rendered many demographic coefficients nonsignificant. Those coefficients were unfortunately displayed only as "n.s."(not significant) in tables, even when the best estimate was no smaller than in column I
or II—thus creating an impression of diminished effects.

19. See Page with Bouton (2006).

20. In the case of emissions aid (where the adjusted R-squared goes from
0.059 to 0.105), and a hypothetical invasion of Taiwan (from 0.066 to 0.136),
the impact of basic attitudes is more substantial.

21. For the sake of uniformity, the column IV regressions included all (except
for cooperation goals in table 2-2) goal indices, intact, along with any of their
specific components that were included separately, for comparability. This means
that column IV coefficients for general goal orientations control for certain specific goals, and vice versa.

22. Sniderman, Brody, and Tetlock (1991), especially chapters 4–6.

23. Page with Bouton (2006), pp. 123–127, 144–146, 182–184, 196; nn. 66–70.

24. The 100-point thermometer format may produce less reliable responses than a five- or seven-point feeling scale would, since respondents can easily use it in quite different ways: systematically choosing or avoiding the most extreme ("0" or "100" degree) responses, for example. Still, the substantial empirical relationships between thermometer ratings and many other variables indicate that they convey useful information. Sniderman et al. (1986) also used similar thermometer ratings in their analysis of the role that affect (i.e., feelings) plays in mass publics' policy reasoning.

25. For example, feelings toward South Korea but not toward North Korea appear to affect support or opposition to using U.S. troops to defend the South against a hypothetical invasion by the North (Page with Bouton 2006, pp. 123–124, and n. 66).

26. When thermometer ratings of both China and India were included in regressions for the aid-to-limit-emissions item, all coefficients for China feelings were nonsignificant at even the $p < 0.10$ level. The coefficients for feelings toward India (corresponding to each of the five columns of table 2-6) were 0.43*, 0.34*, 0.42*, 0.38*, and 0.37*.

27. See Marcus (2000).

28. For quotations from Madison, Hamilton, Lippmann, Kennan, Morgenthau, and others on the irrelevance or perniciousness of public opinion concerning foreign policy, see Page and Shapiro (1992), chapter 1; Page with Bouton (2006), chapter 1.

29. The proportion of variance that we can account is attenuated by our use of OLS estimates that assume linear rather than curvilinear probability functions for dichotomous dependent variables.

30. Page and Shapiro (1992).

31. Raymond E. Wolfinger, personal communication, c. 1967.

III

Cosmopolitanism

Simon Jackman and Lynn Vavreck

> I am a citizen of the world.
> —*Diogenes the Cynic, 412 B.C.*

ON APRIL 14, 2008, with Barack Obama only eight points behind her in the polls and the Pennsylvania Democratic primary only days away, Hillary Clinton downed a shot of whiskey and a beer at a campaign stop in Indiana. She was appealing to working class Americans, those "hardworking" Americans she claimed could not bring themselves to vote for the effete, well-educated Barack Obama.[1]

Clinton was capitalizing on revelations of remarks made by Obama at a closed-press fundraising event in liberal San Francisco. Obama said:

> You go into these small towns in Pennsylvania and, like a lot of small towns in the Midwest, the jobs have been gone now for 25 years and nothing's replaced them. And it's not surprising, then, they get bitter, they cling to guns or religion or antipathy to people who aren't like them or anti-immigrant sentiment or anti-trade sentiment as a way to explain their frustrations.[2]

Pennsylvania and the American Midwest versus the California coast—in America, geography and politics are related. But how? America is the third largest country in the world in terms of both square kilometers and population. Americans exhibit tremendous cultural diversity. Some of us hunt; some of us are vegetarian. Some of us believe that the Bible is the literal word of God; some of us are atheists. The social spaces we inhabit vary tremendously in extent and character. For some of us, social space is largely local, centered on social networks and institutions in one's neighborhood. For others, social spaces span the nation and the globe, encompassing people and cultures who are different from those in one's physical locale. These differences go a long way toward defining us socially, culturally, and spatially.

In this chapter, we explore the political implications of these differences. The distinction between a "local" or "global" orientation systematically affects political behavior both within and across parties. Borrowing a concept from 1950s sociology—but operationalizing it differently—we demonstrate that "cosmopolitanism" affects vote choice and is not well measured by typical demographic or attitudinal controls we routinely include in vote models. Further, we show that cosmopolitanism is not accounted for by mainstay geographic indicators such as the regional marker for South or non-South. Cosmopolitanism is a mix of attributes, local environment, and opportunity, and the means of taking advantage of those opportunities. But we measure it here through a series of behaviors (or self-reports of behaviors) that indicate the presence or absence of a cosmopolitan orientation.

What Is Cosmopolitanism?

Cosmopolitanism has its roots in ancient political thought. But contemporary, social-scientific treatments of cosmopolitanism begin with the seminal work of the sociologist Robert Merton. In operationalizing the concept, Merton[3] identified two types of community leaders, "cosmopolitans" and "locals." Cosmopolitans (or "cosmopolites" as they are sometimes called) are more attentive to the world than locals, who tend to be oriented toward the local community. Both groups have distinct bases of power, influence, and leadership. For instance, locals have interpersonal relationships, developed over time within their communities, which serve as the basis of their political power and leadership; cosmopolites have knowledge and skills acquired from (and valuable within) a broader social space, which in turn generate prestige, wealth, and, in turn, power.[4] This is an important point. Both groups are influential, but for different reasons, and the local-cosmopolitan distinction is not intended to be normative or pejorative.

For a brief period, several influential scholars investigated cosmopolitanism, albeit from varying theoretical perspectives and operationalizations. Katz and Lazarsfeld[5] operationalized the concept through news orientations; Gouldner[6] classified employees as cosmopolitans or locals depending on their loyalty to the company, commitment to developing their specialization, and whether their primary reference group was interior to the company or exterior to it; Abrahmson[7] used the construct to study geographic mobility; Filley and Grimes[8] used cosmopolitanism to study power.

In 1967, Kent Jennings showed that cosmopolitanism was markedly related to political behavior. Jennings[9] found that cosmopolitanism—as measured in a national sample of twelfth graders—was related to knowledge and discourse about larger political domains, interest in public affairs, evaluations of politics at multiple levels, and tolerance of political diversity. Compared to their parents, teenagers in the mid-1960s were more cosmopolitan. Jennings concluded that this was likely due to both generation and life-cycle effects. Jennings pointed out that political scientists have a tendency to forget that citizens interact with multiple systems of government, some local and some as broad as national. He argued that:

> There is a tendency in political studies to focus on one system at a time, as in community studies or in national participation studies. In so doing, some of the richness and complexity of how man relates to his political environment is sacrificed.

Ironically, it was Jennings's Michigan colleagues Campbell, Converse, Miller, and Stokes who started the American National Election Studies (ANES), utilizing national samples as a means of learning about political behavior. As the Michigan studies gained momentum, the study of local politics and local communities became rare. Cosmopolitanism faded from the research agenda both in political science and sociology.

Other disciplines, however, leveraged the concept in extremely important ways throughout the years. Most notably, cosmopolitanism has an extremely long lineage in political theory and philosophy, with an emphasis on many of the same facets of the concept that we attempt to operationalize here—e.g., a respect for "the other," a tolerance for things and people who are different, and the notion that morality is not rooted locally, but globally. Kwame Anthony Appiah[10] makes a compelling argument about morality and cosmopolitanism, and we adopt several of his ideas as we operationalize the concept. In addition, diplomatic and foreign policy specialists use the concept to explain and predict nationalism, ethnic conflict, tyranny, emancipation, and other important phenomena.[11]

Yet, for a concept that has been so widely used across disciplines, cosmopolitanism is underelaborated theoretically, to say nothing of our dearth of understanding as to its empirical content. There is a widely shared scholarly consensus that cosmopolitanism is largely driven by experience: how one relates to local community, the nature of work, how people treat their neighbors (especially if they are different). But another facet seems attitudinal: an openness to experience other cultures or customs and a belief that there is something to be gained from a connection to people and places beyond the local community. These dimensions return us to Merton's[12] original description of the concept: parochial versus ecumenical orientations and their behavioral manifestations.

We explore the local-cosmopolitan distinction in the pages to come, offering a new operationalization of the concept, based on self-reports of reasonably common behaviors: playing sports, traveling, and eating. For instance, we conjecture that those who report participating in locally organized, community-oriented sports, like softball, or who have not experienced foods different from their own nor traveled far from home are more likely to be one of Merton's "locals." At the other end of the dimension are people who report travel to places like South Africa or Asia, people who report eating ethnic foods, and people whose conception of community is much more broad. These people experience others who are different from them—and like Appiah,[13] we argue that this experience is critical.

We investigate the effect of cosmopolitanism on political behavior. The 2008 presidential election provides a unique opportunity for this investigation, because of Obama's inherent difference. Voters in this contest were faced with a choice between mainstay partisan regulars (Clinton and McCain) and a man about whom much was different—Barack Obama. We further believe that enthusiasm for or anxiety toward Obama among white voters is about more than Obama's race (although we have shown elsewhere[14] that attitudes about race certainly played a critical role in these contests). Specifically, we suspect that people with low levels of cosmopolitanism (Merton's "locals") should be less likely to vote for Obama, all else equal, since they have less appetite for things that are different from the environment with which they are locally familiar.

Appiah[15] writes of two strands in cosmopolitanism:

> One is the idea that we have obligations to others, obligations that stretch beyond those to whom we are related by the ties of kith and kind, or even the more formal ties of a shared citizenship. The other is that we take seriously the value not just of human life, but of particular human lives ... people are different, the cosmopolitan knows, and there is much to learn from our differences. There will be times when these two strands—universal concern and respect for legitimate difference—clash. There's a sense in which cosmopolitanism is the name not of the solution but of the challenge.

In the pages that follow, we argue that in 2008, voters in the U.S. presidential election and the Democratic primary were challenged by the limits of their cosmopolitanism—or perhaps we should say the strength of their "local" ties.

Operationalization and Data

We use data from a 2007–2008 panel study of registered voters. In 2008, we were the principal investigators (PIs) of the Cooperative Campaign Analysis Project (CCAP),[16] in which we investigated attitudes about the candidates, issues, race, and other political topics. CCAP was conducted in six waves between December of 2007 and November of 2008. The primary election waves, which were conducted in December (2007), January, and March, were followed by a post-primary survey in September. The September wave also doubled as the first general election wave, which was followed by another interview in October and a post-election followup in November. A total of 10,486 respondents were impaneled across each of these six waves, and we use these data in the analyses that follow.

CCAP was administered online by YouGov/Polimetrix, Inc., a survey research firm in Palo Alto, California. The project was a joint venture of 27 research teams around the world. For details on the structure of the cooperative projects see Vavreck and Rivers.[17] CCAP is designed to be representative of registered voters. Details on the construction of the sample and comparisons with other election studies can be found in Jackman and Vavreck.[18] For this paper, we use data from the "Common Content" portion of CCAP, containing 20,000 respondents.[19]

We operationalize cosmopolitanism with indicators fielded in the September 2008 wave of the study, after the party nominees are known and after each of the nominating conventions. The cosmopolitanism items ask respondents to report on their past behavior about a variety of topics, including travel, hobbies, and food, via seven binary response items. Respondents read the following stem:

> We are interested in the kinds of things people do for recreation. Tell us a little bit about yourself. In the last 10 years, have you . . .

The following list of seven items was then asked. Respondents could answer "Yes, I have done this" or "No, I have not done this" to these questions. Respondents were also free to skip any or all of these items:

1. Played softball on an organized team?
2. Gone hunting?
3. Been to Europe or Australia?
4. Traveled to Canada or Mexico?
5. Visited Asia, Africa, or South America?
6. Gone to an Indian restaurant?
7. Had Japanese food?

The items are designed to tap the dimensions of cosmopolitanism described by Merton, Appiah, and to some extent Jennings.[20] We were particularly sensitive to the need to write questions that would tap these dimensions that had nothing or very little to do with politics. We wanted the questions to seem politically benign so that the self-reports would be exogenous to political preferences and vote choice. This is why, for example, to tap into people's associations in their local community, we asked about playing softball on an organized team instead of whether they were members of the local Kiwanis Club. Similarly, in communities where hunting is popular, it is often done with family or friends from the local community. The travel items are designed to capture people's exposure to places and cultures different from their own. Finally, the food items are meant to gauge whether respondents do things (like eating foods) that reflect a cosmopolitan disposition or aspiration.

The focus on experience is important and drawn largely from the sociological work in the 1950s. More recently, Appiah[21] explains why experience and behavior are more powerful than attitudes when it comes to increasing levels of cosmopolitanism:

> I am a philosopher. I believe in Reason. But I have learned in a life of university teaching and research that even the cleverest people are not easily shifted by reason alone—and that can be true even in the most cerebral of realms. One of the great savants of the postwar era, John Von Nuemann, liked to say, mischievously, that "in mathematics you don't understand things, you just get used to them."[22]

Appiah goes on to argue that "getting used to things"—including people different from yourself—takes time and practice. The exercise he uses to demonstrate this process is conversation, but imagine substituting any kind of behavioral experience for conversation, and you get the basic idea behind Appiah's claim. Conversation, he says, is a metaphor for engagement with the experience and the ideas of others:

> Conversation, as I've said, is hardly guaranteed to lead to agreement about what to think and feel. Yet we go wrong if we think the point of conversation is to persuade, and imagine it proceeding as a debate. . . . Often enough, as Faust said, in the beginning is the deed: practices and not principles are what enable us to live together in peace. Conversation . . . doesn't have to lead to consensus about anything, especially not values; it's enough that it *helps people get used to one another* [emphasis added].[23]

"Getting used to one another." That is what happens as a by-product of daily life when people live or travel among others who are different. As much as possible, we try to capture this engagement, this experience, in our simple items. The travel and food items suppose differing underlying thresholds of cosmopolitanism in order to generate a positive, binary response. For example, we conjecture that it takes a higher level of cosmopolitanism to travel to South Africa than it does to travel to Canada from the United States. Similarly, even someone with a low level of cosmopolitanism might try Japanese food (or have the chance to go to a Japanese restaurant), but this same person might think twice before going to an Indian restaurant (curry is not as familiar to the American palate as teriyaki).

Finally, a word about why we chose to ask the questions retrospectively over a decade-long period. This represents an effort on our part to not have "one-off" cosmopolitan moments unduly contaminate our measure. We did not want to ask respondents whether they had "ever" eaten Indian or Japanese food: consider the respondent who tried sushi in a moment of youthful adventure, hated it (and perhaps many other "ethnic" foods, too), but would nonetheless self-report the behavior that we would score as evidence of cosmopolitanism. Likewise, we did not want to count "one-off" trips to international destinations—perhaps taken many years ago, and perhaps not undertaken voluntarily, for members of the armed forces—as evidence of cosmopolitanism. On the other hand, making the time window for self-evaluation too short would skew the measures toward finding cosmopolitanism confined to the wealthy (or—dare we say—the professoriate). In this way, we were attempting to operationalize cosmopolitanism as a more or less enduring element of a person's personality and lifestyle.

Constructing a Cosmopolitanism Scale

In our preliminary analyses of these data, we repeatedly find the incidence of reporting cosmopolitan activities to increase with income. Figure 3-1 shows the relationship between income and these incidence rates for the seven activities we consider here.

The overall incidence rates have a reassuring, superficial validity. For example, more registered voters have traveled to Canada or Mexico (about half) than have traveled to Europe or Australia (about a quarter). Similarly, in terms of ethnic foods, more of our registered voter sample report going to a Japanese restaurant than going to an Indian restaurant. Incidentally, these results are consistent with data from the U.S. Office of Travel and Tourism statistics on the locations to which Americans travel every year.

Just 1.1 percent of our respondents report engaging in all seven activities; 18.1 percent of respondents report engaging in none of the seven listed activities. The incidence of engaging in none of these activities is strongly associated with income: 38 percent of respondents in the lowest income categories report engaging in none of the listed activities; this rate falls more or less monotonically as income rises, to be around 6 percent among respondents earning more than $100,000 a year and about 2 percent when annual income rises above $150,000. For all activities—except

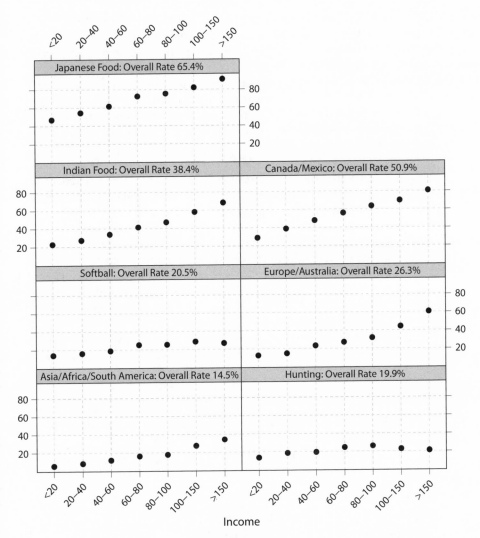

Figure 3-1
Incidence of self-reports of cosmopolitanism/localism indicators, by income.

for the softball and hunting items—we see a moderate to strong association with income in figure 3-1. It would seem that income supplies some of the resources necessary to engage in cosmopolitan behaviors.

Table 3-1 presents the tetrachoric correlation matrix[24] for the seven binary indicators (top seven rows of the table). The largest correlation is between the two food items (0.70), followed by some large correlations among the three travel items (0.67, 0.54, and 0.53). The softball and hunting items have a tetrachoric correlation of 0.40, and generally display small to moderate correlations with the other five items. The correlations between the three travel and two food items average about 0.5. Interestingly, none of the correlations are negative (this is also true if we naïvely compute a Pearson correlation matrix with these binary items), suggesting the possibility of a method factor or "response set" in the data. (We defer a consideration of these methodological issues for another time.)

The eigenstructure of the tetrachoric correlation matrix indicates that multiple dimensions structure the responses to our seven items. There are two eigenvalues greater than unity, and while the first eigenvalue is reasonably large relative to the second (3.37 versus 1.27), it is not so large for us to comfortably ignore the possibility of multidimensionality. We fit a series of exploratory factor analytic models to the tetrachoric correlation matrix: with seven indicators, we can fit up to three factors.[25] A one-factor model sees a pattern of reasonably strong loadings (0.69 to 0.76) among the travel and food items and modest loadings from the softball and hunting items (0.36 and 0.21); these estimated loadings are reported in the bottom row of table 3-1.[26]

In building a scale measure of cosmopolitanism, we draw on the results from the exploratory factor analysis. We conceive of and operationalize

Table 3-1. Tetrachoric Correlations among Binary Indicators of Cosmopolitanism, Eigenvalues, and Factor Loadings, September 2008 wave of CCAP.

	Softball	Hunting	E/A	C/M	A/A/SA	Indian	Japanese
Hunting	.40						
Europe/Australia	.18	.05					
Canada/Mexico	.32	.22	.55				
Asia/Africa/South America	.17	.12	.67	.53			
Indian food	.25	.11	.54	.49	.50		
Japanese food	.35	.22	.51	.49	.46	.70	
Eigenvalues	3.39	1.27	.70	.57	.46	.32	.29
Factor loadings	.36	.21	.76	.69	.72	.76	.75

Note: n = 14,942 complete cases; 15,272 partially observed cases. The lower triangle of the tetrachoric correlation matrix **R** appears in the top seven rows of the table, above the seven eigenvalues of **R**. The lower row reports maximum likelihood estimates of the loadings from a one-factor factor analysis of **R**.

Table 3-2. Item Parameter Estimates, Five Indicators of Cosmopolitanism, September 2008 Wave of CCAP

	Discrimination	StdDev	Difficulty	StdDev
Europe/Australia	0.93	0.03	0.81	0.02
Canada/Mexico	0.68	0.02	–0.21	0.01
Asia/Africa/ South America	0.92	0.03	1.49	0.03
Indian food	0.91	0.03	0.30	0.02
Japanese food	0.87	0.02	–0.74	0.02

Note: $n = 15,272$ partially observed cases. Cell entries are MCMC-generated estimates of the mean and standard deviation of the marginal posterior density of each item's discrimination and difficulty parameters.

cosmopolitanism as a unidimensional construct. The softball and hunting items—which we conjectured would measure "anti-cosmopolitanism" or "localism"—appear to load on a separate dimension, and, if anything, load weakly but positively when we impose unidimensionality on the seven items. So as to bolster the validity of our recovered dimension, we exclude these two anomalous items from the actual scaling. We fit the remaining five items using an item-response theory (IRT) model, identical to that used in the analysis of educational testing data and binary roll call data.[27] In this IRT model, we treat each subject's score on the latent cosmopolitanism dimension as a parameter to be estimated; we impose the identifying normalization that the scores on the latent dimension have mean zero and variance one across the respondents. Estimates of the item parameters are reported in table 3-2; the discrimination parameters are largely identical to one another, save for the slightly smaller Canada/Mexico travel item.

Correlates of Cosmopolitanism

Like many other enduring traits, we believe that cosmopolitanism is learned or experienced initially at an early age. In this view, children acquire tendencies toward cosmopolitanism along with other values that are normative from their social environment. Social pressure, as well as "the intrinsic strength of early learned attitudes" promotes the persistence of values like cosmopolitansim "through the vicissitudes of later life."[28] In this way, cosmopolitanism may be correlated with political attitudes of interest and other politically relevant variables.

We suspect that income and education are positively associated with cosmopolitanism; both increase resources and opportunities to experience different people and cultures. Religious affiliation and religiosity may also shape cosmopolitan orientations, as some doctrines are more parochial than others. The desire to experience new things may also be related to cosmopolitanism; we include traditional measures of personality to capture these tendencies. Finally, cosmopolitanism may be correlated with political attitudes such as attitudes about race, immigration, the war in Iraq, health care, and gun control.

We model the cosmopolitanism index using these predictors and a host of other controls (gender, age, ideology, marital status, partisanship). Finally, to account for the role that opportunity might play in increasing levels of cosmopolitanism, we also measure the urbanity of the respondent's residential locale, with the percentage of the households in the respondent's zip code that are deemed "urban."[29]

Summaries of the relationships between cosmopolitanism and these correlates appear in table 3-3. Each line of the table represents the results of a separate regression in which our cosmopolitanism measure is the dependent variable. Age, symbolic racism, and openness to experience enter their respective regressions as continuous variables and are modeled with thin-plate smoothing splines, while all other predictors enter their respective regressions as a series of mutually exhaustive and exclusive dummy variables (one for each unique level of the predictor).

Income and education are important drivers of cosmopolitanism, accounting for 27 percent and 22 percent of the variation in cosmopolitanism, respectively. We have already noted that the rates of reporting behaviors that are indicators of cosmopolitanism increase in income (figure 3-1); unsurprisingly, we find a monotonically increasing pattern between our scale measure of cosmopolitanism and income. Similarly, we find cosmopolitanism to generally increase with educational attainment, with over a standard deviation separating median levels of cosmopolitanism across the five categories of educational attainment we utilize (less than high school through to post-graduate degrees).

Other important predictors of cosmopolitanism include racial resentment, urbanity of the respondent's locale (zip code), and openness to experience. We operationalize the latter concept using a dimension of the personality battery commonly referred to as the "Big 5."[30] High scores on this particular dimension of the five-factor personality model are associated with intellectual curiosity, openness to emotion, interest in art, and a willingness to try new things. The trait is said to distinguish imaginative people from "down-to-earth," conventional people. Lower scores on this dimension are associated with conventional traditional interests. Low scores indicate a preference for the obvious over the complex and for the

Table 3-3. Correlates of Cosmopolitanism

Variable	r^2	F	df_1	df_2	p-value
Demographics					
Marital status	.01	21.8	6	15,265	<.01
Education	.22	843.3	5	15,266	<.01
Income	.27	569.0	4.6	13,885.4	<.01
Religion	.04	52.9	13	15,258	<.01
Race	.02	35.7	7	15,264	<.01
Gender	.02	297.5	1	15,270	<.01
Age	.07	41.8	2.5	15,265.5	<.01
Geography					
Percent urban (zip)	.11	103.3	7	14,620	<.01
State	.06	2.5	50	15,221	<.01
Battleground	.01	111.9	1	15,270	< .01
Attitudes					
Party ID	.02	35.8	9	15,262	<.01
Ideology	.08	25.6	5	15,100	<.01
Racial resentment (September)	.11	91.4	8.3	15,088.7	<.01
Openness to experience	.07	185.7	6	14,920	<.01
Issues					
Border fence	.07	177.9	6	14,372	<.01
Arrest immigrants	.04	228.9	3	15,268	<.01
Handgun ban	.02	48.6	6	14,372	<.01
Iraq withdraw	.02	53.8	5	15,266	<.01

Note: Each line represents a separate regression analysis. The relationship between cosmopolitanism and continuous predictors (income, age, percent urban in zip and racial resentment) are fit nonparametrically, via thin-plate smoothing splines.

familiar over the novel. In our model of cosmopolitanism, this relationship comes through plainly. There is a strong positive association between increasing levels of openness and cosmopolitanism.

We see a relationship between geography and cosmopolitanism, with state of residence accounting for 6 percent of the variation in cosmopolitanism, while urbanity of the respondent's zip code accounts for 11 percent of the variation. This is not unexpected. Living in a more urban area may bring more opportunity to engage in the cosmopolitan behaviors we ask about. The Census Bureau defines addresses as urban if they are located within an extended Metropolitan Statistical Area (MSA). Roughly

10 percent of our sample live in entirely rural areas (zip codes that are entirely nonurban) and slightly more than 30 percent live in zip codes that are entirely urban areas. The more fine-grained indicator of spatial setting—urbanity at the zip code level—accounts for almost twice as much variation in cosmopolitanism as state of residence.

We measure attitudes about race with the notion of symbolic racism,[31] operationalized with the racial resentment scale.[32] Instead of explicitly asking about overt racial prejudice, this scale (constructed from a four-item battery) taps prejudice cloaked as a legitimate disapproval and antipathy toward violations of traditional American norms of hard work, self-reliance, and equality of opportunity.[33] Increasing levels of resentment toward African Americans as expressed through symbolic racism are negatively related to cosmopolitanism, as we expected. The nonparametric fit of racial resentment to cosmopolitanism results in an r^2 of 0.11, making racial resentment one of the better predictors of cosmopolitanism we consider here. Figure 3-2 shows the relationship between the two variables, with a distinct drop in cosmopolitanism (vertical axis) occurring close to the middle of the racial resentment scale; respondents scoring high on racial resentment tend to be somewhat less cosmopolitan than respondents exhibiting low levels of racial resentment.

We also examine the association between cosmopolitanism and stances on issues relevant to the 2008 election. These issues include whether illegal immigrants should be arrested and deported, restrictions on handgun sales, and whether the United States should build a fence along the border with Mexico.[34] The immigration items correlate with cosmopolitanism as one might expect: those who want to take measures to keep illegal immigrants out of America are less likely to be cosmopolitan. Yet overall, none of these issues explain much variation in cosmopolitanism, and certainly do not rival education or income as predictors. These issues tap the facet of cosmopolitanism that Appiah[35] describes as ethical standards in a "world of strangers." Here, we find that having little tolerance for those "strangers" is positively associated with building border fence or deporting undocumented immigrants. In this way, we see that cosmopolitanism is not just related to any political issue, but specifically to those having to do with "others" or "strangers." On the other hand, ideological self-placement on a five-point scale ("very liberal" to "very conservative" plus a "not sure" outcome) accounts for more variation in cosmopolitanism (8 percent) than any particular issue; unsurprisingly, conservatives are less cosmopolitan than liberals, with those being "not sure" especially noncosmopolitan (a median score one standard deviation below the mean). Stances on issues such as when the United States should withdraw from Iraq and whether to ban handguns explain virtually none of the variation in cosmopolitanism.

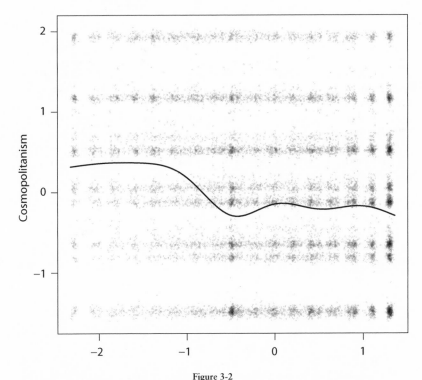

Figure 3-2

Cosmopolitanism, by racial resentment (measured contemporaneously in the September 2008 wave of CCAP). The solid line is a nonparametric fit (a thin-plate smoothing spline).

When we combine all of the preceding items in a multiple regression analysis—again with the continuous predictors entering nonparametrically—we explain about one-half of the variation in cosmopolitanism. The strongest correlates remain those described earlier: income, education, racial resentment, and the urbanity of zip code measure. We turn now to a brief elaboration of the geographic component of cosmopolitanism.

Cosmopolitanism and Geography

We further explore the geographic basis of cosmopolitanism in figure 3-3, plotting state-level average levels of cosmopolitanism. We limit the analysis of geography to states in which we have more than 75 respondents.[36] The most cosmopolitan states in the nation—at least as represented by the registered voter sample used by CCAP—are Virginia, Nevada, California,

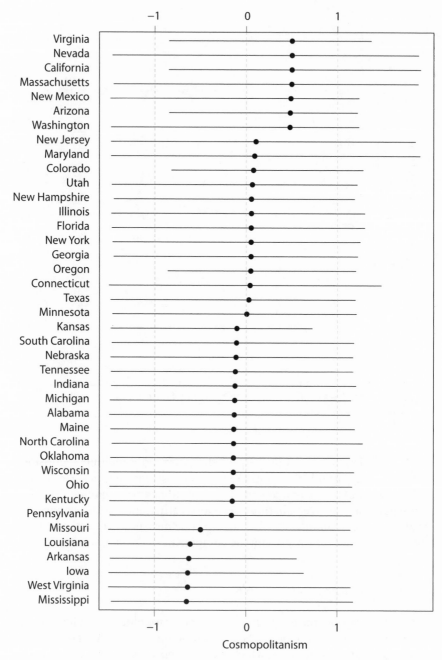

Figure 3-3
Cosmopolitanism, medians, and 10th and 90th percentiles, by state.

and Massachusetts, closely followed by Arizona, New Mexico, and Washington. The most locally oriented states are Arkansas, West Virginia, Iowa, and Missouri. While it looks like Southern states are populated with locals and non-Southern states with cosmopolites, consider that Georgia, Florida, and South Carolina are all in or above the middle of the list. This said, we note that the within-state variation in cosmopolitanism is very large relative to the between-state variation; recall that in table 3-3, we report that state of residence accounts for just 6 percent of the variation in cosmopolitanism.

We observe a slightly stronger relationship between urbanity of the zip code and cosmopolitanism. In table 3-3, we report that 11 percent of the variation in cosmopolitanism is due to this measure of urbanity, almost double the variation accounted for by state of residence. Moreover, the relationship is nonlinear, with average levels of cosmopolitanism increasing by about half a standard deviation (from −0.5 to 0) as urbanity of zip code increases from about 60 percent to 100 percent. Urban life would certainly provide more opportunities for cosmopolitan activities, at least as we have defined them here. Nonetheless, "opportunity" does not seem to be a sufficient condition for cosmopolitanism, with substantial within-unit variation in cosmopolitanism at either the state or zip code level.

We turn now to an investigation of whether our operationalization of cosmopolitansim predicts vote choice in the Democratic primary and the general election, and specifically whether cosmopolitansim has unique effects on vote choice that are not captured by typical predictors of these choices.

Cosmopolitanism in the Campaign for the Democratic Presidential Nomination

We consider the dichotomous choice between Clinton and Obama in the 2008 Democratic primary. We began this project believing that many Americans viewed Barack Obama as different—not just because of his race, but because of his connection to a broader world and his global sensibilities. We suspect that increasing levels of cosmopolitanism should be related to increasing probabilities of voting for Obama in both the Democratic primary and the general election. In order to assess this relationship, we use logistic regression of the binary vote choice (Obama versus Clinton), including measures of symbolic racism (our scaling of the racial resentment items), income, party identification, education, gender, age (entering the model nonparametrically), and urbanity in the respondent's zip code as determinants of the choice between Obama and Clinton.

We estimate the model at four points in time: December, January, March, and September,[37] restricting the analysis to white voters. What is driving Democratic vote choice between Obama and Clinton for these voters? As we and others have demonstrated,[38] racial resentment plays an important and robust role in the choice between Obama and Clinton. But gender and age matter, too.

We present a selection of the logistic regression estimates in table 3-4. The racial resentment effects and the gender offsets are not surprising. Unreported here, we also find that younger voters are more likely to vote for Obama than Clinton, all else equal. Clinton appears to fare better with the Democratic "base" than Obama, while Obama has more appeal to independents and Republican identifiers voting in the Democratic primaries.[39] The goodness-of-fit measures—the area under the receiver operating characteristic curve (ROC curve)—indicate that the models fit the data reasonably well.

Amid controls for various demographics, ideology, and even racial resentment, cosmopolitanism is a significant predictor of Obama vote in the Democratic primary, at least in the early going. The effects of cosmopolitanism wane over the course of the prolonged campaign for the Democratic nomination, and are not distinguishable from zero at conventional levels of statistical significance by September 2008. We compute the predicted effect of a two standard deviation change in cosmopolitanism on the probability of a report of an Obama vote (versus a vote for Clinton) in the Democratic primaries and caucuses, holding other predictors constant (see table 3-5). The change associated with a two standard deviation difference in cosmopolitanism is quite large in the early stages of the primary campaign, equivalent to a 10 percentage point swing in vote share among

Table 3-4. Cosmopolitanism and Obama-Clinton Primary Vote, 2007–2008, Logistic Regression Analysis, White Voters Only Who Prefer Either Obama (1) or Clinton (0)

	December		January		March		September	
	Est.	SE	Est.	SE	Est.	SE	Est.	SE
Cosmopolitanism	.30	.07	.22	.07	.09	.05	.05	.05
Racial resentment	−.59	.07	−.75	.07	−.75	.05	−.62	.05
Female	−.32	.12	−.52	.11	−.58	.08	−.41	.08
Area under ROC curve	.75		.76		.74		.71	
n	1,895		2,146		3,531		3,575	

Note: Models also include party identification, income, education, percent urban in respondent zip code, and a smoothing spline over respondent age.

Table 3-5. Changes in Probability of Obama Primary Vote (over Clinton) in Response to a Two Standard Deviation Change in Cosmopolitanism

| | Orientation | | |
	Local (−1 SD)	Cosmopolitan (+1 SD)	Change
December	.29	.43	.14
January	.44	.55	.11
March	.50	.55	.05
September	.44	.47	.02

Note: Predictions based on modeling reported in table 3-4. Continuous predictors held constant at their means; party identification set to Independent, education set to Some College, and gender set to Male.

otherwise reasonably typical looking primary voters. But by the March 2008 wave of CCAP, when the controversy over Obama's ties to Reverend Wright was raging, the effects of cosmopolitanism are dwarfed by racial resentment and gender.

That is, cosmopolitanism is related to initial preferences over Obama and Clinton as evidenced by its large effects in the early waves of the study, even as we control for income, education, racial resentment, and other things driving this choice. As the campaign wears on and information is revealed (and the dynamics of momentum begin to take shape), the effect of cosmopolitanism diminishes. Voters whose experiences take them beyond their local boundaries were more likely to vote for Obama than for Clinton in the Democratic contest. As primary voters evaluated whether it was reasonable to vote for a black man named Barack Hussein Obama, who had a Kenyan father and grew up all over the world, they drew upon their beliefs about that world—in Appiah's terms, cosmopolitan voters were "used to" someone like Obama already. Perhaps not directly, but people with cosmopolitan leanings were in "conversation" with strangers like Obama their whole lives, or at least a good portion of their lives, and that is what makes voting for him easier than it is for Democrats with more local orientations.

Support for Obama and Cosmopolitanism

We have claimed that cosmopolitanism has a distinctive role in shaping support for Obama. If this is correct, then we should see that cosmopolitanism is more strongly related to support for Obama than for other candidates. To examine this, we model support for candidates in the Democratic primary with a series of binary logistic models, repeating the specification used in the Obama-versus-Clinton analysis, earlier.

The goal of this analysis is to test whether cosmopolitanism is as important in the choices involving Obama but not in the other choices. For example, if cosmopolitanism really is primed in this election because of Obama's presence, it should matter (or matter more) when the choice is one with Obama in it compared to a choice without Obama in it. We expect cosmopolitanism to have an effect in the Obama-Clinton and Obama-Edwards evaluations, for example. If it really taps into the dimensions we think it does, cosmopolitanism should not matter much for choices between Clinton and Edwards, or between Clinton and the remainder of the field. Cosmopolitanism should matter for the choice between Obama and Clinton, Obama and Edwards, and Obama and the rest of the field. We present these results for the four primary election waves of the survey in table 3-6.

Table 3-6. Cosmopolitanism and Democratic Primary Matchups

	December		January		March		September	
	Est	SE	Est	SE	Est	SE	Est	SE
Obama versus Clinton								
Cosmopolitanism	.30	.07	.22	.07	.09	.05	.05	.05
Racial resentment	−.59	.07	−.75	.07	−.75	.05	−.62	.05
Obama versus Edwards								
Cosmopolitanism	.24	.08	.16	.07	−.01	.09	.08	.08
Racial resentment	−.16	.07	−.17	.07	−.30	.09	−.14	.08
Obama versus Other								
Cosmopolitanism	.20	.09	.11	.13	.13	.12	.03	.10
Racial resentment	−.08	.09	−.07	.13	−.32	.13	−.16	.10
Edwards versus Clinton								
Cosmopolitanism	.03	.07	.04	.07	.11	.09	−.00	.08
Racial resentment	−.47	.06	−.62	.07	−.50	.09	−.51	.08
Clinton versus Other								
Cosmopolitanism	−.08	.09	−.13	.14	−.01	.12	.01	.10
Racial resentment	.55	.09	.65	.14	.50	.13	.53	.10

Note: Cell entries are logit coefficients for white voters. Obama is always the "1" outcome if he is in the matchup. Edwards and Other are the "1" in their pairings with Clinton. Coefficients on other covariates are suppressed; see text for details of full specification.

In table 3-6, we present logit coefficients for the two covariates in which we are most interested: cosmopolitanism and racial resentment. Each column of the table represents a different wave of the survey, starting with the December 2007 baseline wave. The first three rows contain the choices in which Obama is a candidate. An examination of the coefficients on cosmopolitanism in the first three rows compared to the bottom two rows reveals the pattern we expect to find. Cosmopolitanism is a significant predictor for matchups including Obama, but for matchups without Obama, we cannot be sure that the effects of cosmopolitanism are different from zero. The effects in December and January, for example, translate into greater than 10 points in increased support for Obama as cosmopolitanism moves a standard deviation in each direction, regardless of whether the opposing candidate is Clinton or Edwards. But, in a matchup between Edwards and Clinton (row 4), the role of cosmopolitanism is nowhere near as clear and indeed, we cannot be sure it has any effect at all. In short, unless Obama is in the matchup, cosmopolitanism does not matter.

On the other hand, the fact that symbolic racism—operationalized here as racial resentment—continues to matter a great deal when Obama is not in the matchup is not at all surprising. The predictive power of racial resentment does not turn on the presence of a black candidate in the choice set, and this fact has been well known to students of American public opinion for some time.[40]

Preferences in the General Election

How does cosmopolitanism fare in the general election contest between Obama and his Republican opponent John McCain? In the presence of strong predictors like partisanship, ideology, withdrawal from Iraq, health insurance, and a host of other controls, does cosmopolitanism add any predictive or explanatory power to the model? The answer is yes—cosmopolitan still plays a vital role in choices about Obama, even in the general election contest.

We consider a reasonably simple model of general election vote choice between Obama and McCain in the baseline, December 2007, and post-election waves of CCAP (see table 3-7). In December of 2007, roughly 2,000 randomly selected respondents were asked to express a preference for either McCain or Obama—even though it was not expected that either one of them would be their party nominee.[41] We compare the structure of vote choice between these two candidates in December to the structure one year later in November of 2008. Predictors in the model include cosmopolitanism, racial resentment, retrospective assessments of

Table 3-7. Cosmopolitanism and Two-Party General Election Vote Choice, December 2007, and Post-Election Waves

	December 2007		November 2008	
	Est.	SE	Est.	SE
Intercept	−.82	.26	−1.32	.23
Cosmopolitanism	−.03	.08	.16	.05
Racial resentment	−.77	.09	−1.06	.06
Negative economic retrospections	.48	.16	.89	.20
Liberal	.47	.18	.99	.16
Conservative	−.44	.18	−.65	.12
Education > high school	.11	.16	.05	.11
Male	−.18	.14	.28	.09
Under 45	.30	.14	.36	.10
Democrat	.98	.19	1.77	.12
Republican	−.92	.22	−2.03	.12
Arrest/deport illegal immigrants	−.36	.15	−.58	.10
Leave Iraq now	.90	.16	1.04	.13
Government provide health insurance	.43	.15	1.10	.11
Ban handguns	.09	.16	.45	.10
Area under ROC curve	.92		.97	
n	2,295		9,932	

Note: Logit coefficients, white voters only. Dependent variable is vote report for Obama (1) versus McCain (0).

the economy, indicators of ideological self-position, educational attainment, age, party identification, and stances on a number of issues. Adding other controls (income, authoritarianism, etc.) does not substantively affect the results.

Party, ideology, and respondents' positions on issues all behave as we would expect. Increasing levels of symbolic racism are a strong predictor of vote against Obama even in the baseline, December 2007, wave of the survey. In December 2007, before people knew that Obama would be a focal candidate in the general election race, cosmopolitanism plays a small role in the choice between he and McCain. Over the course of the campaign—and indeed by late January after he emerges as the candidate most likely to defeat Clinton—cosmopolitanism starts to play an important role. Our estimate is that for an otherwise indifferent voter, a one standard deviation change in cosmopolitanism would have resulted in an 4 point change in the probability of voting for Obama in the general election, holding the other variables in the model constant.

Once again, we see that cosmopolitanism demonstrates two important features: (1) cosmopolitanism is a predictor of political choices even controlling for many other important and strong determinants of vote choice, and (2) cosmopolitanism is systematically related to vote for or against the most unusual presidential candidate America has recently seen.

Conclusion

We set out to test whether cultural, social, and experiential differences among Americans—indicators of cosmopolitanism—account for any of the variation in vote share in the 2008 Democratic primary and general election. Our conjecture was that Obama was thought of as different because of more than just his race. The way the candidates campaigned and where they were while they were campaigning, especially in the last weeks of the primary, led us to the notion of cosmopolitanism. If there were social and cultural differences separate from attitudes about Obama's race, could we uncover them through a set of questions aimed at illustrating Americans' local or cosmopolitan orientations toward the world?

Our preliminary exploration of cosmopolitanism has proven fruitful. We cannot claim to have measured the concept flawlessly. Rather, our aim has been to stake a claim for the concept, to show that cosmopolitanism has predictive power. Our analysis highlights that Obama had to first be identified as a viable candidate for cosmopolitanism to become important. Our investigation has also shown that cosmopolitanism is not the same as geography or the political and social attitudes we already measure. And even in the presence of the strong Obama vote predictor—symbolic racism—cosmopolitanism has a large and unique effect on vote choice.

The steady pattern of cosmopolitan's influence throughout the 2008 cycle suggests a new dimension in the study of race, ethnicity, and politics. Globalization is changing the political landscape, both in terms of the issues facing contemporary democracies and the candidates who run for office. In 2008, for the first time, a major American party made a man who was not white their presidential nominee. And the person who gave him the toughest challenge for the nomination was a woman. After President Obama's first State of the Union speech, the Republican reply was given by the governor of Louisiana, a young man of Indian descent, Piyush Amrit Jindal, who goes by "Bobby." The face of politics in America is changing, and to understand how voters are reacting to these changes, we may need to move beyond conceptions of prejudice that are literally black and white.

Appendix: Question Wordings

Racial Resentment

Please tell us how strongly you agree or disagree with the following statements:

> Generations of slavery and discrimination have created conditions that make it difficult for African Americans to work their way out of the lower class.
> Many other minority groups have overcome prejudice and worked their way up. African Americans should do the same without any special favors.
> Over the past few years, African Americans have gotten less than they deserve.
> It's really a matter of some people not trying hard enough; if African Americans would only try harder, they could be just as well off as whites.

Outcome categories: Agree strongly, agree somewhat, neither agree nor disagree, disagree somewhat, disagree strongly.

Immigration

Which comes closest to your view about illegal immigration?

> Illegal immigrants should be arrested and deported.
> Illegal immigrants now living in the United States should be allowed to become citizens if they pay a fine.
> I'm not sure; I haven't thought much about this.

Iraq

How long should the United States stay in Iraq?

> Should leave immediately.
> Should leave within one year.
> Should stay for at least another year but not indefinitely.

Should stay in Iraq as long as it takes to stabilize the country.
I'm not sure; I haven't thought much about this.

Border Fence

Tell us how much you agree with the following policy:

Building a 700-mile fence along U.S. border.

Outcome categories: Strongly agree, somewhat agree, somewhat disagree, strongly disagree, don't know.

Health Care

Which comes closest to your view about providing health care in the United States?

The government should provide everyone with health care and pay for it with tax dollars.

Companies should be required to provide health insurance for their employees, and the government should provide subsidies for those who are not working or retired.

Health insurance should be voluntary. Individuals should either buy insurance or obtain it through their employers as they do currently. The elderly and the very poor should be covered by Medicare and Medicaid as they are currently.

I'm not sure; I haven't thought much about this.

Personality—Ten-Item Personality Index (TIPI)

Here are a number of personality traits that may apply to you. Please rate the extent to which you agree that the pair of traits apply to you, even if one applies more strongly than the other:

Extraverted, enthusiastic.
Critical, quarrelsome.
Dependable, self-disciplined.
Anxious, easily upset.
Open to new experiences, complex.
Reserved, quiet.
Sympathetic, warm.

Disorganized, careless.
Calm, emotionally stable.
Conventional, uncreative.

Outcome categories: Disagree strongly, disagree moderately, disagree a little, neither agree nor disagree, agree a little, agree moderately, agree strongly.

Notes

We thank David Sears, Michael Tesler, and Brian Law for helpful discussions and comments on this work. We are grateful to David Barker and his colleagues at Pittsburgh, along with participants in the CCAP Lake Arrowhead Research Meeting for providing challenging questions and reactions that helped us strengthen and clarify the argument. We owe special thanks to Paul Sniderman for recognizing this work as interesting and inviting us to participate in this volume.

1. For example, this interview with *USA Today* from early May 2008.

2. Audio and a transcript of Obama's remarks were posted to Huffington Post and were quickly replayed and/or reported in the mainstream media.

3. Merton (1947).

4. Merton (1957).

5. Katz and Lazarsfeld (1955).

6. Gouldner (1957, 1958).

7. Abrahamson (1965).

8. Filley and Grimes (1968).

9. Jennings (1967).

10. Appiah (2006).

11. For example, Walzer (2006).

12. Merton (1957).

13. Appiah (2006).

14. Jackman and Vavreck (2010a).

15. Appiah (2006), p. xv.

16. Jackman and Vavreck (2009).

17. Vavreck and Rivers (2008).

18. Jackman and Vavreck (2010).

19. The Common Content portion of CCAP is the first 10 minutes of every respondent's survey. The total length of the survey is 20 minutes. After the common part of the survey, respondents are routed to any one of the many team studies, which make up the second half of the survey. For details on the mechanics of how this works and information about how panelists are recruited into the PollingPoint panel, see Vavreck and Rivers (2008).

20. Merton (1957); Appiah (2006); Jennings (1967).

21. Appiah (2006).

22. Ibid., p. 84

23. Ibid., p. 84.

24. The tetrachoric correlation between two binary variables y_j, j = 1, 2, is the correlation between their latent counterparts, y_j^*, where y_j = 1 $\Leftrightarrow$ y_j^* > 0 and y_j = 0 otherwise, and the y_j^* have a bivariate normal density with mean zero, unit variances and tetrachoric covariance/correlation r.

25. Each model is fit via the maximum likelihood factor analysis function factanal in R.

26. Going up to two factors sees the travel and food items separate, with the softball and hunting items loading modestly on the food factor (after a conventional varimax rotation of the estimated factor structure). The (nearly saturated) three-factor model results in quite distinct travel, food, and softball/hunting factors. Goodness of fit statistics suggest a modest improvement in going from a one- to a two-dimensional model, with the RMSE (root mean squared error) falling from 0.10 to 0.07; the nearly saturated three-factor model has RMSE of 0.01, consistent with overfitting the data.

27. Clinton, Jackman, and Rivers (2004).

28. Kinder and Sears (1981).

29. This proportion is generated with data from the 2000 U.S. Census by dividing the number of households in each zip code that are within an urban metropolitan statistical area by the total number of households in the zip code. The proportion ranges from zero to one, with a mean value of 0.78 and a standard deviation of 0.32.

30. The "Big 5" are five broad dimensions of personality developed by L. R. Goldberg in 1992 through lexical analysis. The traits are openness, conscientiousness, extraversion, agreeableness, and neuroticism (OCEAN). For a list of the questions used to generate the openness dimension used here, please see the appendix.

31. Kinder and Sears (1981).

32. Kinder and Sanders (1996).

33. See the question wordings in the appendix, or see our detailed analysis of how symbolic racism predicts the vote for Obama in the general and primary elections in Jackman and Vavreck (2010b). Here we construct a racial resentment score via factor analysis.

34. Exact question wordings appear in the appendix.

35. Appiah (2006).

36. This eliminates eleven states: Alaska, Delaware, the District of Columbia, Hawaii, Idaho, Montana, North Dakota, Rhode Island, South Dakota, Vermont, and Wyoming.

37. The December wave is a vote intention for everyone, and the September wave is a vote report for everyone. In the January wave, only people in Iowa, New Hampshire, Michigan, South Carolina, Nevada, and Florida had voted. By the March wave, nearly everyone had voted, but most notably, not people in Indiana, Kentucky, or Pennsylvania.

38. Tesler and Sears (2010); Jackman and Vavreck (2010a).

39. Jackman and Vavreck (2010a).

40. For example, Tesler and Sears (2010).

41. Respondents in our December 2007 wave were fielded three randomly chosen of twelve possible matchups between three Democratic contenders (Clinton, Edwards, and Obama) and four Republican contenders (Giuliani, Huckabee, McCain, and Romney), with one exception: the Clinton-Giuliani matchup seemed likely to eventuate in late 2007, and all of our December 2007 respondents were fielded this particular matchup.

IV

Running to the Right

EFFECTS OF CAMPAIGN STRATEGY ON MASS OPINION
AND BEHAVIOR

Diana Mutz and Susanna Dilliplane

IN THE ROUGH AND TUMBLE OF AMERICA'S two-party political contests, there are supposedly two main strategies for winning an election: candidates either woo the undecided middle or they fire up the base. As interpreted by political pundits and academic scholars alike, the former strategy is generally understood in terms of appealing to "swing voters," who are variously cast as undecided independents or moderates. The latter strategy entails stimulating enthusiasm and turnout among a party's generally loyal bloc of supporters.

Underlying this dichotomy of campaign strategy is an ongoing debate—both in political circles and in scholarly literature—about whether candidates' electoral fortunes benefit more when they run toward the center or as stronger ideologues. Must the fickle "median voter" be courted in order to build a winning coalition? Or is it best to ignore them and focus on galvanizing and motivating those already likely to support a party's candidate?

In this chapter, we focus on the occasion of Republican John McCain's selection of Sarah Palin as a vice-presidential running mate because this event signaled to many voters an abrupt change in McCain's ideological position. In other words, Palin served as an exogenous shock, with the potential to "send a message" to the public about McCain's ideological stance. Using panel data from the 2008 National Annenberg Election Study (NAES), we analyze: (1) the extent to which Palin's selection altered perceptions of McCain's ideology; (2) the extent to which the perceived ideological shift to the right benefited several election-related outcomes such as favorability toward McCain, vote preference, and turnout; and (3) the extent to which the net impact of the shift helped or harmed his candidacy. Because Palin's nomination conveniently occurred between two waves of a large panel study, we are able to study individual-level overtime changes in a large, representative sample of people interviewed both before and after the announcement.

To determine whether McCain's strategy of "running to the right" enhanced his support among Republicans and conservatives and/or backfired among other groups, we examine the effects of the candidate's perceived ideological shift on the preferences of voters across the ideological spectrum. To the extent that these effects are stronger among some groups than others, our analysis will reveal whether the strategy yielded a net advantage or disadvantage to the candidate. But rather than assuming, as in most spatial models, that all people receive and respond to the new information about ideological positioning to the same extent, we empirically examine the degree to which different groups perceived this ideological shift and the extent to which it subsequently produced changes in their candidate preferences.

The Context

It is worth remembering that throughout much of the 2008 primary season, McCain was said to be a long shot for the Republican nomination for president precisely because he was too liberal for many Republicans. Although he held conservative positions on many issues, he was known as a "maverick" for failing to toe the party line on others.[1] Nonetheless, by March 4, 2008, he had clinched a majority of the delegates for the Republican presidential nomination.

Perceptions of the ideology of presidential candidates tend to shift very slowly, if at all. A changed issue position here, perhaps another change there, and perceptions of candidate ideology could gradually shift. However, change of this kind seldom happens overnight with well-known politicians. In McCain's case, however, his selection of Alaska governor Sarah Palin as his vice-presidential nominee produced a sudden adjustment in people's perceptions of who he was ideologically.

Although Palin was relatively unknown outside of Alaska at the time, her reputation was clearly that of a social conservative.[2] She opposed same-sex marriage[3] and stem cell research[4] and supported allowing the discussion of creationism in public schools.[5] When it came to abortion, she called herself "as pro-life as any candidate can be,"[6] also supporting laws requiring parental consent for minors seeking an abortion.[7] Her conservative credentials included a lifetime membership in the National Rifle Association[8] and support for capital punishment.[9] In addition, as a self-described "Bible-believing Christian,"[10] Palin was portrayed by the McCain campaign as having "deep religious convictions."[11] In short, conservative credentials do not get much more convincing than hers. Moreover, this conservative image of Palin was quickly picked up by the press soon after her entry into the national spotlight.

To examine the impact of her selection on presidential candidate John McCain, we begin by reviewing what is known about the effects of playing to the base as opposed to shifting toward the median voter. We examine theoretical accounts of shifting ideological positions as well as empirical analyses of the strategies candidates actually choose and the effects produced by their ideological positioning.

Which Way to Run—Toward or Away from the Middle?

The two seemingly contradictory strategies for winning general elections are often framed in the language of "persuasion" versus "mobilization."[12] Candidates can either try to "persuade" swing voters by moving toward the political center (winning over independents or moderates) or "mobilize" the party base by taking more extreme positions (activating partisans).

A large theoretical and formal literature has accumulated about what candidates optimally should do—converge at the center or diverge to the extremes—usually using the Downsian spatial model as a starting point.[13] The median voter theorem posits that candidates should converge at the center (median voter) in order to maximize votes.

Despite the prominence of this model as a way to understand candidate and voter behavior, a number of qualifications of the basic convergence proposition have been advanced to explain instances of candidate polarization.[14] For example, concerns about abstention due to indifference (the candidates smack of Tweedle-dee and Tweedle-dum) and abstention due to alienation (neither candidate is ideologically close to the voter, such as when strong ideologues are turned off by centrist candidates) serve as a brake on candidates' tendency to converge at the center. Candidates may also be genuinely committed to issue positions that are ideologically more extreme than the median voter. Another potential factor producing divergence is the current nomination system, which may produce ideologically extreme candidates despite the more moderate hue of the general electorate.

The empirical scholarship evaluating what candidates actually do and whether their strategies help or hurt their chances of winning has suggested mixed results. Consistent with the median voter hypothesis, some research has provided empirical evidence of the link between ideological moderation and success in presidential elections.[15] Other evidence has confirmed that more ideologically extreme candidates tend to win the nomination, while more moderate candidates are more likely to win the general election.[16]

Moreover, it stands to reason that if the general public holds largely moderate rather than polarized attitudes, as some have argued,[17] then taking extreme ideological positions may not be the best candidate strategy for maximizing vote share. Providing another twist on these calculations, others have suggested that partisan biases affect voters' perceptions of candidates such that stronger party identifiers are more likely to perceive their party's candidate as closer to their own issue position, even when the opposing party's candidate is objectively closer.[18] This suggests that candidates have some leeway to ideologically maneuver their positions without necessarily alienating their base.

In contrast to this evidence in favor of the median voter strategy, other research points to the potential effectiveness of the reverse strategy—moving *away* from the political center. For example, the base mobilization strategy is a plausible means of achieving electoral success because most people have partisan preferences, even if they only "lean" toward one of the parties, and partisanship is a strong influence on voting behavior.[19] Such widespread partisan loyalties provide reason to question the notion that there is much of an actual "swing" vote to be won, and suggest that candidates would do better to galvanize their bases rather than chasing an illusory (or at least exaggerated) middle bloc of voters. Further, the more politically engaged segment of the public exhibits greater partisan polarization, and the voting public (those who actually turn out) is more partisan than the general population.[20] Strategically, it may be more advantageous for candidates to exploit the greater mobilizing potential of the party's base, given that those with stronger political views are more likely to make the trip to the polls than those with weaker or more ambivalent attitudes.

A popular case study of base mobilization is the 2004 reelection of George W. Bush. Post hoc media accounts widely attributed Bush's victory to strategic efforts to fire up the Republican Party's core voters, particularly around "moral values" issues. Empirical studies of voting behavior in this election, however, yielded inconclusive results. For example, some evidence was found for a significant impact of moral values on support for Bush, but it was most pronounced among Democrats and independents and thus fails to speak to Republican mobilization per se.[21] Others concluded that mobilization around moral values did not drive Bush's victory and that such issues exerted relatively little impact on vote choice (though the effect detected among Southern "Bible belt" voters suggests a pattern of reinforcement consistent with mobilization).[22]

Given the contradictory conclusions in the scholarly literature, it is perhaps unsurprising to find similar conflicting impulses in actual campaigns. For example, in listing the four things that the Republican Party needed to do coming out of its 2008 nominating convention, Steve Schmidt, senior adviser to McCain's campaign, said that two of them were "to appeal to the middle" and "to excite the base of the party."[23]

A similar tension may be located in McCain's "maverick" persona of bucking the party line and appealing to independents, which seems in line with a median voter approach, versus the nomination of Sarah Palin, who played well before crowds of the party faithful. In fact, it has been suggested that the selection of Palin was driven by contradictory aims: "to energize the social conservative coalition . . . [and] to reinforce his [McCain's] appeal to independent voters and perhaps appeal to some of the disenchanted Democrats who had supported Sen. Hillary Clinton."[24]

Regardless of what the McCain campaign was *trying* to do, a separate issue—and the one empirically examined here—is whether voters' *perceptions* of McCain's ideology changed, and whether those perceptions influenced his support in positive and/or negative ways. Did McCain's shift make him more ideologically distinct from his Democratic opponent, Barack Obama? Did this perceived shift to a more ideologically extreme position mobilize McCain's base? Did it also negatively affect his support among more moderate voters, or even galvanize greater opposition among liberals? To answer these questions, we now turn to an analysis of panel data.

A Panel Study of Change

The National Annenberg Election Study (NAES) Internet Panel began with a random probability sample of around 20,000 people in the fall of 2007. These same people were interviewed a total of five times during the course of the primary and general election periods, including a postelection wave. Knowledge Networks of Menlo Park, California, conducted the data collection, and respondents were interviewed either via an Internet connection on their personal computer or via WebTV. Retention rates between adjacent waves were quite high, averaging 82 percent.

In addition to interviewing the same people repeatedly over the course of the election, the design of the NAES was such that the date of interview within wave was randomly assigned so that any week's interviews could be considered a random subsample of the larger pool of interviews for a given wave. This design element of the study makes it possible to plot continuous over-time trends in aggregate populations as well as individual-level change between waves.

In this chapter, we focus primarily on the third and fourth waves of data collection, which occurred between April 2 and August 29, 2008, in the case of wave 3, and between August 29 and November 4, 2008, for wave 4. Waves 3 and 4 occurred cleanly on either side of the announcement of Palin's candidacy, thus offering us a clear pre-post picture of how the same group of 12,000 potential voters perceived McCain both before and after Palin was selected as his vice-presidential candidate.

The central independent variable in our analyses is individual-level over-time change in perceptions of McCain's ideology relative to each individual respondent's own ideological position; we call this variable Absolute Ideological Distance from McCain. To evaluate the net impact of these changes over time, we take into account both the proportion of people who perceived a shift in their proximity to McCain, and the impact of these shifts, whether in the direction of increasing or decreasing distance from the respondent.

Increasing ideological distance from a candidate may not necessarily have the same extent of impact as decreased distance, and this could have important implications for choice of campaign strategy. For this reason, we set up our analyses to make it possible to see these differences. In order to evaluate the relative magnitude of the impact among those whose distance from McCain increased ("increasers") compared to the impact among those whose distance decreased ("decreasers"), we created separate variables to capture the extent of increased ideological distance from McCain and the extent of decreased distance from McCain.[25] If the impact of these changes is symmetric, these two coefficients should look very similar in magnitude but of opposite signs; if change in one direction makes more of a difference than change in the other, this will be evident from the relative size of the coefficients as well.[26]

Our dependent variables include four separate outcomes related to the campaign. McCain Favorability is based on feeling thermometer ratings of McCain and is used to assess whether McCain's perceived ideological shift alienated those who increased in distance from him and/or enhanced liking among those who decreased in distance from him. McCain Issue Agreement is an additive index assessing the extent to which the respondent perceived him- or herself as agreeing with McCain on six different policy issues. Our hypothesis is that Palin's selection may have served as a cue to voters, prompting them to believe that they had greater issue agreement with McCain in the case of ideological decreasers, or lesser agreement in the case of ideological increasers. Our third dependent variable is a dichotomous indicator of McCain Vote Preference. Measures are available for each of these three dependent variables in waves 3 and 4, thus allowing us to assess the impact of a change in perceived ideological distance from McCain between waves 3 and 4 on *change* in respondents' favorability toward him, perceived issue agreement with him, and vote preference for him across the same two waves.

Our fourth dependent variable is Turnout. Here we are testing the expectation that a change in perceptions of McCain's ideological position had a mobilizing or demobilizing effect, changing the odds that voters turned out in 2008 relative to the 2004 presidential election. We use as a baseline a measure that was reported almost a year earlier indicating whether respondents voted in the 2004 presidential election, and combine that with the post-election (wave 5) report of whether they voted in 2008. Increased ideological distance is expected to decrease the odds of voting, while decreased ideological distance is expected to increase the odds of turning out.

To take full advantage of the panel design, we utilize fixed-effects regression models.[27] A key advantage that fixed effects regression offers over conventional regression with cross-sectional data is that it uses only within-person variation. Individuals serve as their own respective controls because each person is compared to him- or herself at an earlier point in time. By discarding all between-person variation, the models eliminate the "contaminated" variation that is likely to be confounded with unobserved characteristics of individuals. In other words, fixed effects regression controls for the constant effects of all preexisting stable variables (both measured or unmeasured) as if they had been included in the model.[28] In addition, by including a variable for time ("wave") that reflects change in the dependent variable between the two waves, the fixed effects models also account for the sum total effect of all other time-varying factors on change in the dependent variables over time.[29]

Because of their potential importance, we also included two over-time influences in our model that happened to be taking place at the same time, and whose effects were anticipated to be large. First, perceptions of collective economic conditions were obviously changing dramatically during the summer of 2008.[30] In addition, we took into account over-time change in perceptions of Obama's ideology, given that the ideological distance between respondents and McCain's opponent has direct implications for these outcomes. This variable is included in all models and is labeled Absolute Ideological Distance from Obama. Fortunately, both variables were also measured in waves 3 and 4.

Although our primary concern is whether increasers and decreasers respond in symmetric ways to McCain's ideological repositioning, we also wanted to see whether our hypotheses held among specific subgroups of the population based on ideology and party identification. Embedded in the expectations of the median voter and base mobilization strategies is the assumption that Republicans or conservatives would respond most favorably to McCain's shift to the right, while independents or moderates would respond more negatively. Democrats and liberals would also be expected to react more negatively to McCain's stronger conservatism, potentially producing a "backfire" effect of mobilizing the opposition. Thus, we would expect the strongest positive effect of decreased ideological distance among Republicans/conservatives, while a stronger negative effect of increased ideological distance is expected among independents/ moderates and Democrats/liberals.

In the next section, we answer the three main questions guiding our investigation. First, did perceptions of McCain's ideology change abruptly around the time of Palin's nomination? Second, did increased and decreased ideological distance affect people's favorability toward McCain, the extent to which they perceived issue agreement with him, their vote preference, and their likelihood of turning out to vote? Because people are being compared to themselves over time using a strictly within-subject design, we can be assured that these relationships represent the relationship between actual change in perceived ideological distance and change in each of these dependent variables, and that the variables are not spuriously related to one another. Finally, what was the net effect of McCain's strategy? We combine information about the prevalence of increasing or decreasing ideological distance with estimates of the effects of these shifts in order to render a summary judgment on the net impact of his ideological shift on the four election-relevant outcomes.

Did Perceptions of McCain's Ideology Change?

Immediately after Palin's selection, the previously stable perceptions of McCain's relatively moderate ideology shifted in a more conservative direction. Our evidence comes from questions asking respondents to locate the candidates on a standard seven-point left-right ideology scale. Figure 4-1 illustrates the change in perceptions of McCain's ideology that occurred following Palin's nomination on August 29, 2008. Marked by a vertical line in figure 4-1, this event was accompanied by an upward shift, indicating that McCain was being perceived as more conservative than before. Interestingly, this shift did not register to the same degree among various partisan subgroups. Republicans seem to have been particularly tuned in to the signal sent by Palin's nomination, perhaps because it was communicated during the Republican National Convention. Alternatively, Republicans may simply be more likely to pay attention to conservative messages. For whatever reason, this group perceived the greatest shift toward stronger conservatism in McCain's ideology (a within-subject paired samples t-test reveals a mean change of about 0.35 between waves 3 and 4). Although the trend among Republicans perceiving McCain as more conservative may have begun slightly before the date of Palin's nomination, this change in perception occurs across the board in the population at this juncture.

As figure 4-1 shows, Democrats and independents also abruptly changed their perceptions of McCain at this same point in time, though

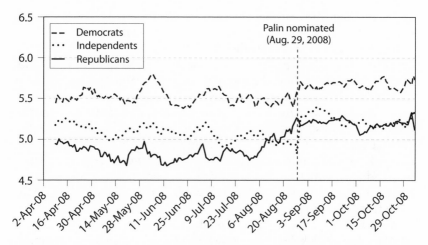

Figure 4-1

Perceptions of McCain's ideological placement over time, by respondent party. Note: The *y* axis is the perceived ideological placement of McCain (measured in waves 3 and 4), where 4 = moderate and 7 = extremely conservative. Respondent party identification was measured in wave 2. The figure shows ten-day moving averages; to separate averages during the period before Palin's nomination (wave 3) from averages during the period after her nomination (wave 4), the average of a given day and the prior nine days was taken for the wave 3 period, and the average of a given day and the subsequent nine days was taken for the wave 4 period. Source: 2008 National Annenberg Election Survey.

to a lesser extent. The mean change among these groups was about half the size of the shift in perceptions among Republicans (mean = 0.18).[31] For all three groups, these changes in perceptions of McCain's ideological position were statistically significant ($p < 0.001$).

McCain's choice of Palin as his vice-presidential candidate was widely interpreted as a deliberate strategic attempt to try to energize the conservative base. Notably, his positions on issues did not change radically, nor did he make any grand pronouncements at the convention that might have changed people's views of him. Many pundits thus interpreted Palin's selection as pandering to the right in order to win the election, rather than as an actual change in his ideology. Nonetheless, the public appears to have changed its views of where McCain stood, making it a potentially effective strategy for firing up the base. Although rolling samples cannot rule out all other possible causes, it appears that Palin's nomination served as an effective ideological cue, signaling by association that the candidate was more conservative than previously thought. This shift thus provides an opportunity to test the electoral consequences of this strategy, as the candidate moved from a position of ideological moderation to that of a stronger ideologue.

In table 4-1, we summarize the *absolute distance* between each respondent's ideological self-placement and his or her perception of McCain's ideological position both before and after the Palin announcement. If McCain's ideological repositioning were working as expected, one would see a significant *increase* in ideological distance on average between McCain and liberals/Democrats, and a significant *decrease* in ideological distance between McCain and conservatives/Republicans. The prediction for moderates and independents is less clear and would depend on where they had placed McCain to begin with, but overall, firing up the base is expected to leave those in the middle cold, increasing their absolute distance from McCain.

As shown in table 4-1, this predicted pattern held, regardless of whether the sample was broken down by ideology or by partisanship. On average, from pre- to post-announcement, liberals and Democrats perceived a significant increase in their absolute distance from McCain from pre- to post-Palin announcement, while conservatives and Republicans perceived a significant decrease in their absolute distance from McCain.

Table 4-1. Mean Absolute Distance between Respondent and McCain Ideological Placement, by Wave and by Respondent Ideology and Party

	Absolute Ideological Distance from McCain			
	Wave 3	Wave 4	Wave 3–4 change	N
By party:				
Democrats	2.84 (1.55)	2.99 (1.53)	0.15***	3,473
Independents (includes leaners)	1.83 (1.42)	1.85 (1.43)	0.02	3,038
Republicans	1.27 (1.17)	1.02 (1.01)	−.25***	3,572
By ideology:				
Liberals	3.45 (1.31)	3.62 (1.24)	0.17***	3,137
Moderates	1.42 (0.96)	1.54 (0.95)	0.12***	2,628
Conservatives	1.25 (1.18)	0.99 (1.02)	−0.26***	4,318

Note: Table reports mean absolute ideological distance between respondent and McCain, with standard deviations in parentheses. The significance of change in absolute distance between waves 3 and 4 is calculated using paired t-tests. Values for absolute ideological distance range from 0 (respondent and candidate are the same) to 6 (maximum distance). Includes respondents who were interviewed in waves 2, 3, and 4 and who gave a response for McCain's ideological placement in both waves. Respondent ideology and party identification were measured in wave 2.

*p < 0.05; **p < 0.01; ***p < 0.001.

Interestingly, moderates became more distant from McCain as well, but there was no significant change among political independents.

Of even greater interest is the relative size of the increases and decreases. McCain's perceived ideological shift registered at both ends of the ideological spectrum, but the increased ideological distance perceived by liberals and Democrats was about two-thirds the size of the decreased distance perceived by conservatives and Republicans. Meanwhile, the size of the increased distance among moderates was somewhat smaller than that among liberals (and nonexistent among independents). Although one might naturally expect these perceptions to mirror one another, they do not. The shift *toward* their own views that those on the right perceived in McCain was more sizable than the shift *away* perceived by those on the left and in the middle.

This asymmetry provides one clue to explain how such a strategy might work to produce a net benefit for the candidate. Even though he alienated some people by increasing his ideological distance from them, if voters on his own side of the political spectrum were more likely to pay attention to his friendly ideological repositioning, then the gains within his base may outweigh any losses among those in the middle or antagonistic mobilization of the left.

More generally, the evidence in table 4-1 makes it clear that when considering the value of the two competing electoral strategies, it would be a mistake to assume that all partisans receive the same message to the same extent. Intuitively, it makes sense that Republicans would pay more attention to the Republican candidate, and thus register this shift more profoundly than others. A particularly pronounced discrepancy may have emerged in this particular case because the announcement occurred during the Republican convention, which is more widely watched by sympathetic partisans.

Still, given that interviews with respondents were distributed over more than two months after the announcement, independents and Democrats had plenty of time to pick up on McCain's more conservative repositioning, but did not do so to the same extent. The implications of this differential point to the potential effectiveness of playing to the base; the damage inflicted by increasing ideological distance from the middle is muted by the fact that this group does not register the change to the same extent and thus is less likely to be adversely affected by it.

Interestingly, perceptions of Obama's ideological position also moved more toward the extreme end of the spectrum, though the magnitude of this shift toward greater liberal perceptions of Obama was far smaller than the shift toward greater conservatism perceived for McCain.[32] Thus, there is no evidence of ideological convergence on the part of the 2008 presidential candidates. At least on average, neither candidate was perceived as shifting closer toward the ideological middle over time; if anything, the median voter was abandoned during the course of the campaign.

Thus far, we have documented an abrupt shift in McCain's perceived ideology at the time Palin was selected, as illustrated in figure 4-1 and statistically confirmed in table 4-1. The next step is to examine the extent to which these shifting perceptions mattered to election-related outcomes—that is, whether voters' political preferences or propensity to vote changed as a result of McCain's perceived shift.

With What Effects on Political Attitudes and Behaviors?

Did McCain help or hurt himself by virtue of the signal he sent about his ideology? Did this shift in perceived ideological position deliver the intended benefit by mobilizing the party faithful or did it end up reducing the support of a larger group of moderates? We begin answering this question by analyzing the impact of changes in perceptions of McCain's ideological distance on changes in McCain Favorability, Issue Agreement, Vote Choice, and Turnout using fixed effects analysis.

In order to test the base mobilization hypothesis as well as look for potential backlash, table 4-2 reports the impact that changes in perceived ideological distance had on changes in each of the dependent variables, broken down by partisan group. The relationships represented by the coefficients reveal the amount and direction of change in the dependent variables produced by a one-unit, within-person change in the independent variables. For the McCain Favorability and McCain Issue Agreement linear models, the coefficients are interpreted as the impact of change in the independent variables on change in the dependent variable. For the McCain Vote Choice and Turnout logistic models, the coefficients are interpreted as the impact of change in the independent variables on change in the odds of a McCain vote choice or the odds of voting in 2008 relative to 2004.

Three findings immediately jump out from the patterns observed in table 4-2. First, the signs of the coefficients for the impact of changes in ideological distance are exactly as predicted for Favorability toward McCain, Issue Agreement, and Vote Choice. The coefficients are all negative for increased distance and positive for decreased distance, indicating that as the perceived distance between the respondent and McCain grew (shrank), respondents were more likely to change in negative (positive) directions with respect to these outcomes. In other words, the top row for each partisan group shows that the greater the increase in distance from McCain, the greater the negative change, while the second row shows that the greater the decrease in distance from McCain, the greater the positive change. Moreover, with only two exceptions (to which we'll return), these relationships are statistically significant.

The second important finding in table 4-2 is an exception to this general pattern. As shown in the last column, the odds of turning out in 2008 relative to 2004 were not significantly affected by shifts in perceived distance from McCain. Decreased ideological distance from McCain did not have a significant effect among Republicans (contrary to the notion of mobilizing the base beyond former levels of participation), while increased ideological distance failed to significantly affect turnout among independents (contrary to the idea that diverging from the middle alienates the median voter). Although most of the coefficients are in the expected directions, they do not reach statistical significance.

Nor did the same analysis substituting ideological groups for partisan groups produce significant effects on Turnout. Regardless of ideology or partisanship, changes in ideological distance from McCain did not affect respondents' odds of voting in 2008 relative to 2004. Given that the type of "mobilization" most hoped for by advocates of firing up the base is greater turnout, this finding should raise serious doubts. It is still possible that the increases in favorability and issue agreement are indicative of enhanced enthusiasm among those who came to perceive themselves as closer to McCain (and possibly greater fundraising capability, etc.). But in the end, turning out to vote is shown here to be the same habitual behavior as typically depicted and seems less likely to respond to short-term changes. The significant changes in vote preference could represent a direct electoral benefit for the candidate, but not through mobilization so much as persuasion or activation.

The third important finding in table 4-2 is evident in the patterns of asymmetry between the extent to which increases in perceived distance induce changes in the direction of anti-McCain outcomes, and the extent to which decreases in perceived distance induce changes toward pro-McCain outcomes. The impact of these changes in perceptions is strongly conditioned by party. Among Republicans, for example, a decrease in ideological distance from McCain has far stronger positive implications for his favorability ratings than the corresponding negative effect of increased distance. (The former coefficient is more than double the size of the latter.) Democrats, on the other hand, responded more strongly to increased distance from McCain than to decreased distance. This partisan pattern was visible for issue agreement and vote preference as well. In fact, the impact of increased distance from McCain on change in vote preference among Republicans was not significant, while decreased distance had no significant effect on the votes of Democrats. In short, when the shift in perceived ideological distance is in line with the preexisting party allegiance, it produces a stronger impact than when it is inconsistent.

Table 4-2. Effects of Increased and Decreased Ideological Distance from McCain on Voters' Political Attitudes and Behavior

REPUBLICANS

	McCain Favorability	McCain Issue Agreement	McCain Vote Choice	Turnout
	Coefficient (S.E.)	Coefficient (S.E.)	Coefficient (S.E.)	Coefficient (S.E.)
INCREASE in ideological distance from McCain (0–6)	−1.692 (0.571)**	−0.123 (0.050)*	−0.225 (.196)	−0.085 (0.216)
DECREASE in ideological distance from McCain (0–6)	4.543 (0.382)***	.207 (.033)***	0.485 (0.158)**	−0.240 (0.176)
Change in ideological distance from Obama	1.453 (0.389)***	0.193 (0.034)***	0.561 (0.151)***	0.228 (0.170)
Change in economic perceptions	0.465 (0.330)	0.096 (0.029)**	0.074 (0.142)	0.329 (0.178)
Wave	5.324 (0.388)***	.256 (0.034)***	0.214 (0.167)	0.215 (0.177)
Constant	59.768 (1.651)***	2.414 (0.143)***		
N	3,379	3,432	327	237

INDEPENDENTS

	McCain Favorability	McCain Issue Agreement	McCain Vote Choice	Turnout
	Coefficient (S.E.)	Coefficient (S.E.)	Coefficient (S.E.)	Coefficient (S.E.)
INCREASE in ideological distance from McCain (0–6)	−2.711 (0.572)***	−0.111 (0.037)**	−0.783 (.186)***	−0.140 (0.170)
DECREASE in ideological distance from McCain (0–6)	3.635 (0.582)***	0.129 (0.038)**	0.435 (0.157)**	0.271 (0.190)

	McCain Favorability Coefficient (S.E.)	McCain Issue Agreement Coefficient (S.E.)	McCain Vote Choice Coefficient (S.E.)	Turnout Coefficient (S.E.)
Change in ideological distance from Obama	0.810 (0.412)*	0.118 (0.027)***	0.524 (0.111)***	−0.258 (0.127)*
Change in economic perceptions	0.538 (0.526)	0.008 (0.034)	0.020 (0.139)	−0.119 (0.156)
Wave	1.467 (0.471)**	0.125 (.031)***	−0.074 (0.141)	0.116 (0.157)
Constant	46.174 (1.231)***	1.322 (0.080)***		
N	2,814	2,910	444	299
DEMOCRATS				
	McCain Favorability Coefficient (S.E.)	McCain Issue Agreement Coefficient (S.E.)	McCain Vote Choice Coefficient (S.E.)	Turnout Coefficient (S.E.)
INCREASE in ideological distance from McCain (0–6)	−2.670 (0.465)***	−0.125 (0.024)***	−0.514 (0.227)*	−0.102 (0.174)
DECREASE in ideological distance from McCain (0–6)	2.045 (0.570)***	0.085 (0.029)**	0.311 (0.223)	0.205 (0.228)
Change in ideological distance from Obama	−0.190 (0.347)	0.030 (0.018)	0.513 (0.145)***	−0.003 (0.159)
Change in economic perceptions	0.309 (0.551)	0.046 (0.028)	0.281 (0.199)	−0.034 (0.221)
Wave	−1.258 (0.404)**	0.085 (0.021)***	−0.654 (0.200)**	0.232 (0.167)
Constant	34.519 (0.878)***	0.603 (0.045)***		
N	3,295	3,384	239	261

Note: Unstandardized coefficients from fixed effects linear and logistic regression models reported, with standard errors in parentheses.
*$p < 0.05$; **$p < 0.01$; ***$p < 0.001$.

But what about independents? Here the pattern is far less predictable and varies by outcome. In general, a decrease in perceived ideological distance matters more to McCain's favorability ratings, but perceiving increased distance has the stronger impact on change in the odds of a McCain vote preference. Issue agreement is more or less a wash, with roughly equally sized coefficients in positive and negative directions.

Did Running to the Right Help or Harm McCain?

The bottom line when candidates make strategic choices about ideological positioning is whether the candidate will, on the whole, be helped or harmed. In order to assess the net effects of these perceived shifts in McCain's ideology, we need to take into account both the size of each of these subgroups (that is, increasers and decreasers), as well as the extent of impact from the changed perceptions for each group. To do this, we look first to figure 4-2, which shows the distribution of increasers and decreasers both overall and by subgroup. In the sample as a whole, the number of people who shifted closer to McCain between waves 3 and 4 (25.2 percent) was almost precisely the same proportion who became more distant from him during that same time (24.7 percent).

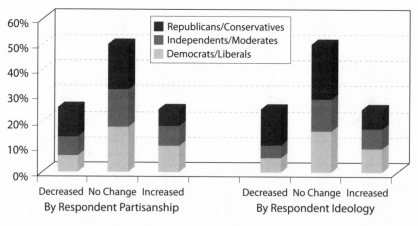

Figure 4-2

Proportions of all respondents perceiving an increase, a decrease, or no change in absolute ideological distance from McCain.

Note: Each set of three bars shows the proportion of total respondents (N = 10,083) who perceived an increase, a decrease, or no change in absolute ideological distance from McCain between waves 3 and 4, by respondent party and ideology.

Notably, not all of those who felt closer to McCain after his shift in ideology were Republicans, and not all of those who felt farther away were Democrats. In fact, when considered together, more Democrats and independents perceived themselves closer to McCain after his shift than Republicans. Likewise, when combined, more Republicans and independents perceived themselves as farther from McCain after his selection of Palin than did Democrats. It is obviously overly simplistic to assume that his shift to the right brought Republicans closer and Democrats farther away. Based on this evidence alone, one might infer from the even numbers of increasers and decreasers that the effects of this strategy were a wash; the net impact would be small because just as many people were alienated as elated.

But as suggested by the results in table 4-3, increasing ideological distance and decreasing ideological distance cannot be assumed to have the same impact. Table 4-3 illustrates the pooled analysis including all potential voters in order to summarize the net impact of shifts in ideological distance for each of the outcomes under study. As shown in the fourth column, consistent with previous analyses, turnout remains unaffected even with the larger pooled sample. However, as shown in the other three columns of table 4-3, where the coefficients for changes in ideological distance are significant, the effects are not always symmetric. In particular, McCain experiences far more of a boost in Favorability from a given decrease in ideological distance than he takes a hit from the same amount of increase in ideological distance. Taken alone, this suggests that his move may indeed have been an effective strategy for electoral success. Likewise, the coefficients for Issue Agreement suggest that decreasing the ideological distance from some potential voters produces more of a benefit than the parallel cost of increasing distance from others.

However, neither of these outcomes is as close to what candidates care about as Vote Choice. And here, although the difference between the positive and negative coefficients is modest relative to the size of the standard errors, it suggests a stronger negative than positive impact, or at best, a wash. In other words, what the candidate loses by virtue of increased ideological distance from some voters outweighs what is gained by moving closer to others.

If these groups of increasers and decreasers were of different sizes, to calculate a net impact it would be necessary to weight the impact of decreasing distance by the number of decreasers and the impact of increasing by the number of increasers. However, given that the groups are of equal size, as shown in figure 4-2, this is not necessary, and the coefficients should reflect the relative net positive and negative effects.

Taken together, what these patterns suggest is that the Republican Party's base responded more strongly and positively to decreased ideological

Table 4-3. Net Effects of Increased and Decreased Ideological Distance on the McCain Campaign

	McCain Favorability	McCain Issue Agreement	McCain Vote Choice	Turnout
	Coefficient (S.E.)	Coefficient (S.E.)	Coefficient (S.E.)	Coefficient (S.E.)
INCREASE in ideological distance from McCain (0–6)	−2.843 (0.307)***	−0.132 (0.021)***	−0.575 (0.114)***	−0.129 (0.104)
DECREASE in ideological distance from McCain (0–6)	4.242 (0.285)***	0.171 (0.019)***	0.466 (0.097)***	0.040 (0.108)
Change in absolute ideological distance from Obama	0.817 (0.222)***	0.110 (0.015)***	0.531 (0.074)***	−0.076 (0.083)
Change in perceptions of economic conditions (better)	0.189 (0.258)	0.054 (0.018)**	0.060 (0.087)	0.029 (0.100)
Wave	1.836 (0.245)***	0.159 (0.017)***	−0.118 (0.093)	0.188 (0.095)
Constant	48.440 (0.692)***	1.573 (0.047)***		
N	9,488	9,726	1,010	797

Note: Unstandardized coefficients from fixed effects linear and logistic regression models reported, with standard errors in parentheses.
*$p < 0.05$; **$p < 0.01$; ***$p < 0.001$.

distance, while those in the middle and on the left punished McCain in terms of vote choice but otherwise responded ambivalently to increases and decreases in distance. This is roughly as the base mobilization strategy predicts, though the effect is not one of enhanced turnout rates per se, nor of a net increase in the odds of voting for McCain. Overall, Republicans and conservatives may have felt more positive about their candidate as a result of his choice, but there is little evidence that his electoral prospects were enhanced by this strategy.

Implications

Given that roughly as many people perceived McCain as ideologically farther away from them as perceived him as ideologically closer to them after he selected Palin, one might simply call it even in terms of the effectiveness of this strategy, citing no net gain overall. However, our more nuanced analysis of change over time in perceptions of ideology and its effects on favorability, issue agreement, vote choice, and turnout tells a more complex story. First, when a cue suggesting ideological change such as Palin's selection is released into the election environment, not everyone is equally likely to receive it. Those attempting to model and empirically assess the impact of ideological convergence and divergence thus need to take this imperfect information environment into account. Democrats generally perceived McCain as more conservative to begin with, but on average they perceived *less* of a shift in McCain's ideology from before to after Palin's selection (as did independents). The cue still reached them to some extent, to be sure, but the magnitude of perceived change was far greater for Republicans.

Interestingly, Republicans not only "got the message" about the ideological shift more loudly and clearly than others, they also responded more strongly to it in terms of their *attitudes* toward McCain. They viewed him in a more favorable light as a result, and perceived themselves as having greater issue agreement with him as well. One might assume that the increased enthusiasm for McCain could translate to greater turnout or to more votes, but this was not the case. We find no evidence that McCain gained more votes than he lost from this strategy, either from increased odds of turnout or increased odds of voting for him. Although voter preferences suggested significant effects in both positive and negative directions, they essentially canceled out one another in the aggregate, or even slightly depressed the likelihood of a vote choice for McCain. For turnout, there is no evidence of changes in behavior relative to the previous presidential election as a result of McCain's shift. Voters still voted and nonvoters did not, and among the small portion of the sample that did, in fact, change from one category to another, the shift in their perceptions of McCain's ideology had no significant relationship with this change.

Of course, this analysis cannot rule out the possibility that those who became closer to McCain became more enthusiastic about his candidacy and perhaps engaged in other kinds of activities to support the candidate, which they would not otherwise have engaged in. We can only assess the outcomes measured repeatedly in the panel study, and thus this is one limitation to our conclusions. However, the panel characteristics of these data and the repeated measurement of all dependent measures produce a much stronger causal case than has heretofore been possible. The only rival interpretation of these data that fixed effects analysis cannot rule out is reverse causation. In this particular case, this possibility seems highly unlikely, however. If for some unrelated reason, Republicans came to feel more favorably toward McCain, and this, in turn, caused them to perceive him as more conservative than they did previously, then one might make a plausible case for reverse causation. But this seems unlikely. Moreover, by using a wave 2 baseline measure of the respondent's own ideology as the basis for ideological distance, we have ruled out the possibility that the effects we uncovered are due to people moving their own ideologies toward or away from McCain to match their feelings toward him.

These findings also underline the ongoing importance of party, both in registering the candidate's change in ideology and in how people respond to it once it has been registered. Our analyses demonstrate evidence of resistance to responding negatively to increased ideological distance among those of the same party as McCain, and resistance to positive reassessments as a result of decreased ideological distance among those of the opposing party.

In short, playing to the base can indeed make the party faithful happier, but that does not change the fact that they are the party faithful. In terms of the actual outcomes of elections, this strategy seems unlikely to help a candidate achieve electoral success. Throughout the course of the 2008 election, neither Republican John McCain nor Democrat Barack Obama shifted significantly toward the ideological middle to pursue a median voter strategy. As a result, we cannot say whether and what benefits might have accrued as a result of this alternative strategy. But it appears relatively certain that McCain shifted perceptions of his ideology significantly to the right at the time of Sarah Palin's selection as a vice-presidential nominee. While some were undoubtedly thrilled with this move on his part and rated him more favorably as a result, it did not increase the probability of his election in any of the direct ways we have examined.

Notes

1. See, for example, Continetti (2008); Robb (2008).
2. See *Anchorage Daily News* (2008).
3. See Ontheissues.org (2008). (Source: 2008 vice-presidential debate against Senator Joe Biden.)
4. See *ABC News* (2008).
5. Kizzia (2006).
6. Demer (2008).
7. See *New York Times* (2008).
8. See *ABC News* (2008).
9. Goldenberg (2008).
10. Newton-Small (2008).
11. Kaye (2008).
12. See Holbrook and McClurg (2005) (though cf. Hillygus and Shields 2008). In the mobilization-versus-persuasion literature, key studies of partisan mobilization confirm that campaigns do have mobilizing effects (e.g., McGhee and Sides forthcoming; Hillygus 2005; Holbrook and McClurg 2005). However, these studies focused on campaign activity—e.g., get-out-the-vote efforts, ads, campaign spending—rather than ideological placement of the candidates.
13. Downs (1957); Adams and Merrill (2003); Groseclose (2001); Plane and Gershtenson (2004). See Green and Shapiro (1994) for a review.
14. See Fiorina (1999b) for a review.
15. For example, Bartels and Zaller (2001); Zaller (1998).
16. Kenny and Lotfinia (2005).
17. See Fiorina et al. (2006); Ansolabehere et al. (2006); though cf. Abramowitz and Saunders (2008).
18. Van Houweling and Sniderman (2005).
19. Keith et al. (1992); Bartels (2000).
20. Abramowitz and Saunders (2008); Fiorina (1999b); Prior (2007).
21. Knuckey (2007).
22. Burden (2004); Hillygus and Shields (2005).
23. Jamieson (2009), p. 29.
24. Caswell (2009), p. 392.
25. To create these variables, we first calculated the absolute distance between the respondent's ideology (measured in wave 2) and the respondent's perception of McCain's ideology in wave 3 and wave 4, producing a measure of absolute ideological distance for each wave ranging from 0 to 6. We then created two separate indicators of absolute ideological distance for each wave, one for those whose distance increased over time ("increasers") and one for those whose distance decreased ("decreasers"). For example, for the wave 3 indicator for ideological distance among "increasers," respondents whose distance increased over time retained the same values (0–6) as the original wave 3 distance measure, while those who did not change or who decreased in distance were coded 0. And for the wave 3 indicator for ideological distance among "decreasers," respondents whose

distance decreased over time retained the same values as the original wave 3 distance measure (though with the opposite sign so that higher values indicated less distance), while all other respondents were coded 0. This process was repeated for the wave 4 measures, yielding a total of four indicators of absolute ideological distance (two per wave). In the case of the indicators capturing distance among "decreasers," the values of absolute ideological distance were reversed in sign in order to produce an easily interpretable pattern of results. If the hypotheses are correct, the coefficient for change in distance among increasers should be negative (bad for McCain), and the coefficient for change in distance among decreasers should be positive (good for McCain).

26. In addition, to ensure that we captured changes in ideological distance due to movement in perceived candidate ideological placement rather than respondents' own ideological placement, we used the wave 2 measure of respondent ideological placement as the basis for these distance assessments.

27. We ran linear and logistic fixed effects models using Stata's "xtreg" and "xtlogit" commands, respectively. Using this approach, the measures of the predictor and outcome variables from each wave are simultaneously entered into the model to produce estimates of the impact of within-person, over-time change in each predictor on change in the dependent variable. For example, to capture the distinct effects of increased and decreased distance from McCain, the two absolute ideological distance indicators (for increasers and decreasers) for each wave were entered simultaneously into the model to evaluate the impact of *change* in absolute ideological distance (either increase or decrease) on change in the dependent variables.

28. See Allison (2009). The fixed effects models control for the constant effects of all stable characteristics (ruling out the sources of spuriousness usually plaguing cross-sectional models); however, they cannot take into account all potential interactions between these characteristics.

29. Sample sizes vary across analyses for several reasons. Over 12,000 people were interviewed in waves 2, 3, and 4; this sample was used in the linear fixed effects regression models used to predict change in McCain favorability and issue agreement. However, just over 10,000 placed McCain and themselves on the ideological scales. This number drops to about 9,500 when modeled along with perceptions of Obama's ideological placement and sociotropic perceptions of economic conditions. In the binary logit fixed effects models used to predict change in the odds of McCain vote choice and turnout, respondents who did not change on each dependent variable over time automatically drop out of the analysis, thus greatly reducing the sample size. In addition, the sample size for the turnout model was reduced because this model employed the wave 5 post-election measure of turnout; about 10 percent of respondents interviewed in waves 2, 3, and 4 were not interviewed in wave 5.

30. The absolute distance between the respondent's ideology and the respondent's perception of Obama's ideology was calculated for wave 3 and wave 4. Higher values correspond to greater distance from Obama, so in the regression models, we expect that change toward greater distance from Obama will be associated with greater support for McCain (i.e., a positive coefficient). For per-

ceptions of collective economic conditions, we used an item asking respondents whether they thought the economy had gotten better, worse, or stayed the same (1 = gotten a lot worse, 5 = gotten a lot better).

31. In this analysis, leaners are included as independents. Although those who indicate "leaning" toward one of the parties tend to behave like partisans rather than "pure" independents (see Keith et al. 1992), they represent the bulk of the bloc of voters typically referred to as the "middle" or the "swing vote." In contrast, those who insist that they have no preference for either major party make up less than 3 percent of the sample.

32. For example, the mean shift in perceptions of Obama's ideology between waves 3 and 4, by partisan group, was as follows: Republicans = 0.18; independents = 0.09; Democrats = 0.05 ($p < 0.01$ in each case, based on paired t-tests). All of these perceived shifts were toward the liberal end of the spectrum.

V

Pathways to Conservative Identification

THE POLITICS OF IDEOLOGICAL CONTRADICTION IN THE UNITED STATES

Christopher Ellis and James A. Stimson

WHAT DO AMERICANS WANT FROM THEIR GOVERNMENT? Do they prefer a government that intervenes in economic life to regulate the market and to confer benefits? Or would they prefer that government stay out? Do they want government to enforce traditional moral and religious codes, or would they prefer a government that took no position on these controversies? These are among the most basic questions about American public opinion—matters, it would seem, of simple description. Are Americans, in general, "liberal" or "conservative"? Anything so basic should long ago have found an answer. And indeed the question has been answered, many times over. The problem is that the answers conflict.

The reason for ongoing controversy over what might seem a simple fact is a long-standing paradox in American public opinion: the American public is, on average, *operationally* liberal and at the same time *symbolically* conservative.[1] When asked about specific government programs and specific social goals, the American public generally wants the government to do more, spend more, and redistribute more. But at the same time, citizens are considerably more likely to identify as conservatives than liberals. The public, in other words, generally wants more government-based solutions to social problems, but overwhelmingly identifies with the ideological label that rejects those solutions. At the individual level, this implies that a great many Americans hold conflicted beliefs, thinking of themselves as "conservative" while supporting predominantly liberal public policies.

This paradox presents an important puzzle for scholars of public opinion. While we know that citizens vary widely in their ability to interpret and use ideological terms and that many people will choose ideological self-identifications for random, idiosyncratic reasons, this disconnect between operational and symbolic ideology suggests that many citizens identify as "conservatives" for reasons that are *systematically* different from those which reflect preferences on the underlying dimensions of ideological and issue conflict.[2]

This "paradox" is our take-off point. We will discuss the reasons for and implications of it, working to understand why so many citizens who hold predominantly liberal policy preferences identify as ideological conservatives. We argue that because of its nonpolitical connotations and the way in which it is used by political elites, the ideological label "conservative" is both more popular and more multidimensional than the label "liberal."

We suggest three general "pathways" through which individual can approach the decision to identify as ideological conservatives. Although some citizens identify as conservatives as part of a sophisticated political worldview, many others choose to do so for systematically different reasons, reasons grounded in citizens' nonpolitical (particular, religious) orientations or the ways in which ideological labels and issue positions are framed in elite political discourse. Different groups of self-identified conservatives approach the meaning of the term "conservative" itself in fundamentally different ways, identifying with diverse connotations of the term, many of which have little to do with their own operational preferences on salient matters of public policy. This stands in contrast to the broadly singular way in which self-identified "liberals" approach their self-identification. Taken together, an understanding of the different ways in which self-identified conservatives come to their ideological identification can explain both the reasons for the operational-symbolic paradox in public opinion and shed light on its political implications.

The Longitudinal Evidence

We begin by more formally defining the disconnect between operational and symbolic ideology that sets the stage for this essay. In the aggregate, Americans are always operationally liberal on average. They prefer a government that does and spends more to solve social problems. And they are always symbolically conservative on average: they consistently prefer the conservative label to the liberal one.[3] To illustrate this, we display commonly used measures of both "operational" and "symbolic" beliefs on the same graph (figure 5-1).

For a basic measure of operational views, we choose Public Policy Mood.[4] Mood essentially measures—through answers to over 1,600 survey questions regarding specific issues and social programs—public opinion on issues related to the size and scope of the federal government for the period 1970 to 2004. The measurement scheme for Mood (and for symbolic ideology to come) is such that items are scaled as the percentage of liberal responses divided by the percent that are liberal plus the percent

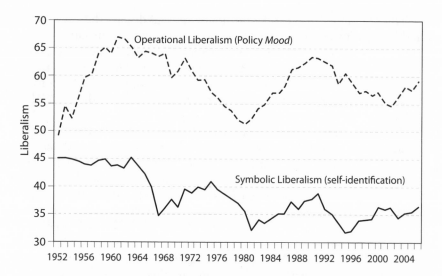

Figure 5-1

Operational and symbolic liberalism in the American electorate. Sources: Public Policy Mood (Stimson 2004); Ideological Self-Identification (Ellis and Stimson 2008).

that are conservative. Values above the neutral point of 50 thus indicate a predominance of liberal over conservative responses.

The graphs show a clear preference for operational liberalism in every survey year: the dominance of liberal over conservative is the normal state of Mood. It varies within a relatively small range, never quite touching the neutral point even at its most extreme conservative moments. This is obviously not true for every single issue, all the time. But whether one employs this summary measure or looks more closely at preferences for the hundreds of different policies and programs of which the measure is composed, the basic fact is that Americans in the norm hold liberal preferences for public policy.

The measure of symbolic ideology in figure 5-1 is composed of items, now thousands of them, that ask respondents some form of the "How do you think of yourself?" questions that allow liberal, moderate, or conservative self-designations. The pattern of ideological self-identification is also strikingly consistent: a preference for "conservative" over "liberal." Of those Americans who give a self-designation, there are almost two conservatives for every liberal. There is a consistent 20- to 25-point gap between "operational" and "symbolic" preferences in the aggregate, a sizable gap. (In comparison, the within-series variance for both self-identification and Mood are only 12 to 15 percentage points over this time span.)

The question now is simple: Why? What, at the level of the individual citizen, lies beneath these aggregate tendencies that explains the evident conflict between them? A potential explanation will have to explain both why Americans tend to like government solutions and why they tend to identify with a government-rejecting ideological label. It will also have to go beyond simple aggregates to a deeper understanding of the relationship between different types of issues (including issues that lie outside the long-standing "scope of government" divide) and self-identification among diverse groups of citizens.

The Cross-Sectional Evidence

Cross-sectional analysis allows for a nuanced understanding of the relationship between certain issue types and ideological self-identification, and is thus useful in explaining the roots of this operational-symbolic paradox. Although in the aggregate and over time, most of explicable variance in macro-level public opinion falls on one dimension, individual-level public opinion at any given time is usually multidimensional.[5] Scholars have generally recognized two central organizing dimensions in contemporary American politics: a (loosely labeled) "economic" or "scope-of-government" dimension, containing preferences on taxation, redistribution, government spending, and other major issues of the role of the federal government in solving social problems, and a smaller, more focused "cultural" dimension, dealing primarily with issues related to enforcement of traditional moral and religious norms.[6] The former of these dimensions reflects the long-standing party divide over the proper size and scope of the federal government, tapping preferences on the same general concept of policy sentiment as Mood.[7] The "cultural" dimension is comparably newer, having emerged as a dividing line in American politics as a result of the actions of strategic elites and activists over the past few decades.[8]

We begin by isolating these two dimensions in the modern American electorate with a simple exploratory principal components analysis using a battery of policy preference questions asked of respondents in the 2000 American National Election Study (ANES).[9] This very basic analysis is designed to devise quick, substantively reasonable measures of mass preferences on each of these dimensions. The analysis, shown in table 5-1, returns two clearly interpretable factors with eigenvalues greater than 1.0, with most questions relating to spending on social welfare programs residing on one dimension, and questions relating to culture and traditional morality residing on the other. Consistent with much previous research, we find that despite the fact that these dimensions have essentially

Table 5-1. Exploratory Factor Analysis of Policy Preferences in the American Electorate, 2000

	Dimension 1: "Scope of Government"	Dimension 2: "Cultural"
Spending on welfare	0.69	0.06
Spending on foreign aid	0.31	0.08
Spending on food stamps	0.67	0.06
Spending on reducing illegal immigration	0.14	0.22
Spending on the poor	0.51	−0.00
Spending on Social Security	0.18	−0.06
Spending on the environment	0.19	0.16
Spending on education	0.17	0.13
Spending on child care	0.25	0.16
Spending on improving the conditions of blacks	0.49	0.05
Spending on AIDS research	0.19	0.18
Adoption of children by homosexuals	0.12	**0.61**
Abortion	0.03	**0.49**
Gays in the military	−0.00	**0.50**
Spending to improve roads	−0.03	−0.08
Spending on reducing crime	−0.00	−0.12

Note: Table entries are principal-axis factor loadings (varimax rotation). **Bold** entries indicate that an issue was retained for use in forming additive scales for the designated factor. Factor scores correlate with the additive scales at 0.82 (dimension 1) and 0.97 (dimension 2).

been collapsed into one at the elite level, they remain only loosely correlated with one another (0.23) at the mass level.[10]

This simple analysis shows the presence of two dominant organizing dimensions in modern public opinion, a "scope-of-government" dimension and a "cultural" dimension. We classify individuals as either operational "liberals" or "conservatives" on each of these using an additive scale of preferences for each dimension. Those who give more conservative than liberal responses are classified as operational conservatives on that dimension, and those who give more liberal than conservative responses are classified as operational liberals.

Table 5-2 shows the distribution of preferences on both issue domains. Results for the scope-of-government set confirms what we have long known: on this dominant dimension of conflict, operational liberalism

Table 5-2. Operational Preferences for Scope of Government and Cultural
Dimensions, 2000

Scope of government issues	
Conservative	25%
Moderate	9%
Liberal	66%
Cultural issues	
Conservative	39%
Moderate	9%
Liberal	52%

Source: American National Election Studies, 2000.

dominates. For the "cultural" domain, it is a closer call, with the numbers
of liberals and conservatives roughly equal.[11]

How does the introduction of the second dimension affect the relationships between operational and symbolic ideology? To explore this
question, we examine the distribution of operational preferences *within*
the groups of ideological identifiers. In the top half of table 5-3, we observe operational preferences for citizens who identify as ideological "liberals." This table shows a high level of consistency between *identifying*
as a liberal and holding views which are, in fact, liberal. A considerable
majority (66 percent) of self-identified liberals are liberal on *both* issue
dimensions. To call oneself a liberal is, more or less, to be one.

Table 5-3. Operational Preferences among Self-Identified "Liberals" and
"Conservatives"

Self-identified liberals	
Liberal on both dimensions	66%
Liberal on scope-of-government issues only	22%
Liberal on cultural issues only	7%
Liberal on neither dimension	4%
Self-identified conservatives	
Conservative on both dimensions	21%
Conservative on scope-of-government issues only	16%
Conservative on cultural issues only	29%
Conservative on neither dimension	34%

For self-identified conservatives, the story is different. In the second half of table 5-3, we present a parallel breakdown of issue preferences. Only about one in five self-identified conservatives holds "consistently" conservative issue positions: right of center positions on both dimensions. Put another way, *almost 80 percent of professed conservatives are not conservative on at least one of these dimensions.* A larger group (30 percent) of conservatives are operationally conservative *only* on the narrow set of issues related to culture and traditional morality, not the broader scope-of-government dimension. The "scope-of-government conservatives," conservative on scope-of-government issues alone, are not very numerous (15 percent). But the largest group (34 percent) of self-identified conservatives reject operationally conservative beliefs on both the scope-of-government and the cultural issue domains. This stands in contrast to the less than 4 percent of self-identified liberals who hold no liberal issue views.

These numbers are clearly rough estimates: the number of citizens that fall into each of these categories will vary from year to year, and will vary as a function of the particular mix of policy questions asked in any given survey. But the larger pattern in the figures, easily generalizable to other years and other survey contexts, is clear. Liberals are a pretty homogeneous lot. Conservatives, in contrast, are heterogeneous, a coalition of people with differing political worldviews, many of which are not at all conservative. This analysis suggests that there are three large-sized groups of ideological conservatives with diverse sets of policy preferences, to which we attach labels. "Constrained conservatives" are those who combine conservative identification with consistently conservative policy views. "Cultural conservatives" are conservative on the three traditional morality issues but little else. And truly "conflicted conservatives" combine conservative identification with left-of-center views on both the scope-of-government *and* cultural dimensions.

Who Are the Constrained, Cultural, and Conflicted Conservatives?

Our data shows us that we have three groups of conservatives of roughly equal size, each with a different combination of policy preferences to complement their conservative self-identification. Here, we ask the basic question, are these groups of conservatives fundamentally different from one another? For an answer, we examine demographic, social, and political characteristics of the three groups of conservatives. For comparison, we also examine the same characteristics for constrained liberals, the only group of self-identified liberals large enough for meaningful analysis.

Table 5-4 presents the data. A comparison of the characteristics of the three groups of conservatives reveals that the groups of self-identified conservatives are indeed substantively different from one another, and their characteristics are generally supportive of the "three pathways" idea. Constrained conservatives are, as would be expected, disproportionately educated, interested in politics, and politically knowledgeable. They are overwhelmingly attached to the party and political candidate of their ideological "side" and are likely to hold a personal worldview (e.g., a distaste for government, a preference for individualism over egalitarianism) that is consistent with more abstract understandings of conservatism.

The other types of conservatives look quite different from both the "constrained conservatives" and from each other. The difference between constrained and cultural conservatives is especially interesting. Both groups are highly religious, and more likely than the others to believe in the inerrancy of the Bible—a standard indicator of doctrinal conservatism.[12] This is to be expected from the two groups that hold conservative positions on issues of traditional morality. But constrained conservatives are far more educated, have higher incomes, and are more interested in politics than our cultural conservatives. Cultural conservatives, in contrast, are less skeptical of the federal government and more receptive to the abstract notion of economic "equality." Constrained and cultural conservatives are similar with respect to religious characteristics (and beliefs on the dimension of issues directly connected to religious orthodoxy), but cultural conservatives exhibit no other evidence of looking (demographically) or thinking (operationally) like constrained conservatives.[13]

Of course, religiously conservative people of all kinds are obviously more likely to hold conservative positions on issues of traditional morality, so it is not surprising that our constrained and cultural conservatives look similar on indicators of religious traditionalism but different on other matters. But in addition to that, there is some evidence that cultural conservatives do not necessarily understand the politics of cultural issues. Purely "cultural" conservatives, for example, are far less likely than constrained conservatives—and not much more likely than would be expected by random guessing—to be able to correctly place George W. Bush to the right of Al Gore on the issue of abortion.

Cultural conservatives, in other words, are largely unable to connect a religiously conservative position—even one to which they presumably attach great importance—to its political meaning. It is thus difficult to suggest that cultural conservatives are "issue publics" in the sense that they are conservative on the only issues they truly care about politically, and thus align their political ideology to be consistent with these preferences. Rather, it appears that the *political* implications of these opinions are simply not visible.

Table 5-4. Selected Social, Demographic, and Political Attributes of Different "Types" of Conservatives

	Consistent conservatives	Cultural conservatives	Conflicted conservatives	Consistent liberals
Education/sophistication				
% college degree or more	30%	23%	31%	43%
% high school degree or less	30%	54%	35%	22%
Mean score: 8-point political knowledge scale	4.58	3.12	3.72	4.22
% "very interested" in 2000 presidential campaign	44%	27%	25%	34%
Demographics				
Female	40%	57%	62%	61%
Nonwhite	9%	31%	18%	22%
South	40%	45%	31%	29%
Religion				
% who believe that the bible is "the literal word of god, to be taken word for word"	51%	63%	28%	10%
% who attend church almost every week or every week	60%	57%	31%	20%
Political attributes				
Bush % of vote, 2000	91%	65%	51%	9%
% Republican	81%	49%	48%	11%
% placing Republicans to the ideological right of Democrats	77%	55%	55%	72%
% placing Bush to the right of Gore on services/spending	72%	45%	46%	56%
% placing Bush to right of Gore on abortion	72%	44%	46%	64%
% saying abortion issue is very or extremely important	65%	69%	51%	59%

Table 5-4. (*continued*)

	Consistent conservatives	Cultural conservatives	Conflicted conservatives	Consistent liberals
Symbolic attitudes				
% who feel that government has gotten bigger because social problems have (as opposed to government meddling in things people should do for themselves)	24%	59%	54%	77%
% agreeing with statement "we'd have fewer problems if we treated people equally"	40%	58%	58%	65%

Note: Exact estimates of significance vary, but as a rough guide, any between-group difference of roughly 10% or more can be considered statistically significant ($p < 0.05$, two-tailed).

Truly "conflicted" conservatives look little like constrained conservatives or cultural conservatives. They are less committed to religious principles and practice. They are not as secular as are consistent liberals but look more like liberals with respect to religion than either of the other groups of conservatives. They are educated at roughly the same rates as consistent conservatives, but score at or slightly below average in terms of political knowledge and interest. Demographically and socially, and with respect to many broad attitudes on the role of government and fundamental political values, they look much like consistent liberals, whose policy preferences they share. In terms of electoral behavior and partisan identification, they split almost evenly between Democrats and Republicans.

The result of this exercise is to show that the differences between types of conservatives are meaningful. The groups differ markedly with respect to knowledge, education, income, religious commitment, and other symbolic attitudes. Constrained conservatives are disproportionately educated, sophisticated, religiously orthodox, and skeptical of government intervention. Cultural conservatives are religiously orthodox, but are more likely to be poorly educated, low-income, uninterested in politics, and more supportive of governmental efforts to solve social problems. Conflicted conservatives look in many ways more like consistent liberals than either other group of conservatives. But they are less politically knowledgeable.

The general lesson of this exercise is that the differences between types of conservatives are meaningful. The groups differ markedly with respect to knowledge, demographics, religious commitment, and other attitudes. Constrained conservatives appear to be people able to understand and use ideological terms. Cultural conservatives look like religious citizens who do not understand the political implications of ideological terms. And conflicted conservatives hold operational and social attitudes similar to those of operational liberals.

Explaining Conservative Dominance: Three Pathways to Conservative Self-Identification

It is, of course, not new to suggest that Americans are poorly equipped to use broad ideological concepts to structure their thinking on particular matters of public policy. From the early, seminal literature on ideological constraint, researchers have soundly dispelled the normatively appealing notion of widespread ideological thinking in the American electorate.[14] Citizens often cannot discern the "liberal" or "conservative" positions on issues and often misunderstand how these labels apply to political parties and candidates. Even among those who understand the meaning of ideological terms, the ability to use these terms to structure policy preferences is weak and inconsistent.[15]

None of this implies, of course, that people do not *hold* ideological identifications. People may still identify as ideologically "liberal" or "conservative," and this ideology may even exert an independent impact on political choices, but it is not necessarily grounded in an understanding of the specific issue positions that the ideological label implies.[16] Given that many people hold ideological identifications without a clear understanding of how they apply to either specific policy domains or the whole of elite-structured political conflict, we might reasonably expect that large segments of the public citizens will form and report ideological self-identifications that are more or less random, essentially unconnected with other political beliefs. They may be formed arbitrarily, from citizen-specific misunderstandings of what "liberal" and "conservative" actually mean politically, or from symbolic attachments to one ideological term or the other for no generalizible reason. But in the aggregate, these responses are *not* random: the ideological label "conservative" dominates despite demonstrated preferences for operational liberalism. Many of the people who call themselves "conservative," in other words, do not do so because of preferences on the underlying dimension of political conflict. But neither do they do so arbitrarily. Rather, we argue that they do so because they approach the meaning of the ideological term *itself* from substantively different places.

More specifically, we suggest that there is potential for generalizibility in understanding why citizens identify as "conservatives" for reasons that go beyond policy preferences. We propose *three* general ways that people can approach the ideological label "conservative." These three different pathways produce three distinct groups of conservatives, united by the ideological label but far different in terms of demographics, policy preferences, and political and social worldviews. In what follows, we outline and provide some preliminary evidence for the existence and pervasiveness of these three "pathways," using this analysis to make some general sense of the reasons behind the operational-symbolic disconnect and the dominance of conservative self-identification, in American politics.

Pathway 1: Ideological Constraint

We begin with the obvious group, and the obvious explanation: that some people identify as conservatives (or liberals) because they are conservatives (or liberals). Scholars have long recognized that some people can use abstract ideology to organize a consistent, belief system.[17] For some, ideology represents an effective way to link together a system of beliefs on specific policy issues, integrate unfamiliar issue content into their existing belief systems, and understand how their own policy attitudes correspond to those of political elites.[18] These citizens understand the meaning of ideological terms and use them to structure their own political attitudes. The mechanism of self-identification here is simple cognition. We call such people "constrained conservatives" (and "constrained liberals") reflecting the Converse usage.

Such citizens were falsely seen as typical before the advent of serious scholarship on mass opinion. But we now know this is not the case: possession of a high level of ideological sophistication and the capacity for ideological thinking are conditioned to a large degree by factors such as education, political knowledge, and interest in politics.[19] Although "constrained" liberals and conservatives will obviously differ politically, socially, and demographically, constrained ideologues on both the liberal and conservative side will be disproportionately educated and knowledgeable, possessing the understanding of politics necessary to hold a constrained issue belief system. Their level of political engagement will reflect the fact that they know both the meaning of abstract ideological terms and how the terms relate to concrete political issues. We thus expect that those who claim an ideology that matches their actual views to be mostly citizens with the education, sophistication, and beliefs necessary to conceptualize politics in ideological terms and incorporate ideology into a larger political belief system. In this sense, and despite their other differences, constrained conservatives should look much like constrained liberals.

To gain leverage on this idea, we estimate a logit model (table 5-5) that predicts whether citizens hold consistent operational and ideological preferences. We estimate three models: the first, examining the likelihood of being a "consistent" ideologue in the population at large, and the second two asking the same question for citizens whose ideological identifications are either liberal or conservative. This basic analysis is supportive of the descriptive evidence in table 5-4: among both symbolic liberals and conservatives, as well as in the public as a whole, indicators of education and political engagement predict whether someone holds operational and ideological beliefs in line with one another. Consistent conservatives, much like consistent liberals, understand elite ideological discourse and structure their own attitudes accordingly. Although there are obviously many other important differences between them, consistent conservatives are much like consistent liberals in the sense that they are disproportionately likely to bring explicitly political meanings to ideological terms.

This is to be expected. The first "pathway" to conservatism—constrained conservatives as politically sophisticated ideological conservatives—is consistent with what we have long known about the role of knowledge and sophistication in political belief systems. But this "constrained" group is a minority—albeit a highly influential one—of all self-identified conservatives. We need more to systematically explain the identifications of the rest. Unlike the left-right symmetry of the constrained ideologues, however, our additional two pathways lead only to conservative identifications—and go to the heart of the operational-symbolic gap in American politics.

Pathway 2: From Theology to Politics

As we have seen, the "conservative" label appears to have a disproportionate draw among citizens who hold conservative "cultural" preferences but operationally liberal views on scope-of-government concerns. In principle, this could be attributable to the disproportionate salience of cultural and religious issues to politics in general, and to these types of citizens in particular. This argument, however, meets resistance on two counts. First, recent research suggests that both at the level of the aggregate public and at the level of important political subgroups, the "scope-of-government," rather than cultural, dimension remains the dominant dividing line in American politics.[20] Second, as we have seen earlier, a disproportionate number of citizens with these kinds of culturally conservative but economically liberal views are unlikely to understand the politics of cultural issues—at a minimum, which party stands for what. While undoubtedly true for some citizens, the possibility that the draw of the

Table 5-5. Effects on the Likelihood of Holding "Consistent" Operational-Ideological Preferences

	Among all citizens	Among those with symbolically conservative preferences	Among those with symbolically liberal preferences
Education (highest degree earned)	0.07 (0.05)	0.20* (0.07)	0.17* (0.07)
Political knowledge (8-point scale of factual questions)	0.13* (0.04)	0.10* (0.05)	0.23* (0.07)
Political interest (3-point scale)	0.22* (0.10)	0.52* (0.12)	−0.00 (0.18)
Partisanship	−0.10* (0.03)	0.31* (0.06)	−0.05 (0.09)
Strength of partisanship	−0.05 (0.07)	−0.09 (0.11)	−0.16* (0.15)
Nonwhite	−0.60* (0.18)	−0.74* (0.32)	−0.53 (0.28)
Female	−0.02 (0.14)	−0.54* (0.20)	−0.77* (0.25)
South	−0.15 (0.14)	−0.03 (0.20)	−0.35 (0.26)
Northeast	−0.15 (0.18)	−0.68* (0.29)	0.20 (0.32)
Strength of scope-of-government preferences	0.19* (0.03)	0.11* (0.04)	0.16* (0.05)
Strength of cultural preferences	0.64* (0.06)	0.38* (0.09)	0.95* (0.11)
Constant	−2.83* (0.31)	−3.05* (0.46)	−3.18* (0.64)
N	1,276	794	482
Pseudo-R^2	0.15	0.24	0.24
Log-likelihood	−725.07	−358.64	−233.70

Note: Entries are logit coefficients (standard errors in parentheses).
*$p < 0.05$.

"conservative" label for culturally conservative citizens is driven purely
by the political salience of these issues seems quite unlikely. Instead, we
argue that it is aspects of the religious experience itself, far removed from
the substance of day-to-day politics, that drives this "conservative" symbolic identification.

The term "conservative," of course, has meaning in contexts other than
politics. One particular place that it has a relatively clear meaning—and
potential implications for political conservatism—is in the context of religion. Religion is central to the lives of many Americans. And in a world
where politics is central for few, it is quite likely that religion is perceived
as more important than politics for the vast majority of church-going
Americans. Thus if there is transfer of concepts between the domains of
religion and politics, for most the dominant domain would be religion.
Concepts originating in religion would find their way into politics, with
transfer in the other direction much less likely.

The term "conservative" has a rich connotation in religious practice
and religious doctrine. Usually applied to Protestant Christians, there is a
large parallel movement also inside Roman Catholicism. Those who style
themselves "conservative" in religious terms tend to believe in the verac-
ity of traditional religious teachings—of the biblical account of creation,
of Heaven and Hell as literal places, and the like.[21] Against the backdrop
of modernism—the increased tolerance for nontraditional sexual practices, sex outside of marriage and homosexuality, for example—doctrinally conservative Christians hew to the original view, that sex is permitted
only in the context of (heterosexual) marriage blessed by the Church.
They strongly oppose abortion, birth control, and homosexuality. Perhaps the most important aspect of this conception of religious conservatism is the idea of biblical literacy—that the text of the Bible is literally
true, and should be interpreted as such.

We posit that Christian conservatives are quite aware of their conservative self-identification, at least when it comes to religion. Regular
church-goers are exposed to a level of theological education that vastly
exceeds anything that happens in politics. Many Americans combine an
interest in politics that occurs only at two- or even four-year intervals
with going to church—and often Sunday School as well—*every* Sunday.
Thus, where confusion about the meanings of ideological labels is normal
in politics, most conservative Christians should know quite firmly that
they are conservatives in the religious sense: it is, at least for many, a vital
component of self-identity.[22]

So long as religion and politics remain separable domains, this usage
of the same language has no consequences. But we postulate that millions of Americans who know that they are religious conservatives are
simultaneously confused by what "conservative" means in politics. When

asked to choose a political ideology, they draw upon the only connotation of "conservatism" with which they have a deep understanding—religious conservatism. They thus translate their religious self-identification directly to their political self-identification, adopting at least the name of the political ideology associated with small government, low taxes, and freedom from economic regulation. Since moral traditionalism is associated with some aspects of modern political conservatism, that is not entirely wrong. But since the "moral" side of conservatism is but a slice of the whole of modern policy conflict, it is mainly wrong. Thus, people who may call for more regulation of business and support fundamental equality in the economic sphere end up identifying themselves as "conservative."[23] Further, and just as importantly, because politics is so peripheral for so many, even many citizens who hold doctrinally "conservative" positions on issues such as abortion and sexual morality may be largely *unaware* that these positions also happen to be politically conservative—for them, the attitudes are religious, not political ones.

We thus expect that a number of self-identified conservatives are actually religious conservatives who translate the doctrinal conservatism with which they identify into political conservatism regardless of their political opinions and, in many cases, without an understanding that their culturally conservative positions on issues that tie directly to religious orthodoxy are, in fact, politically conservative. This is not simply identifying as politically conservative because of one's positions on cultural issues: it is the direct (mis-)application of the label one attaches to his or her religious identity to political self-identification, without an understanding of its political consequences.

Given that this religious conservatism does manifest itself in some politically conservative preferences, the idea that religious conservatism is being translated directly to political identification is a subtle point, and one for which it is difficult to amass direct evidence. To provide at least indirect leverage on this idea, we examine whether positions on this narrow cultural dimension of preference are, in fact, more closely related to ideological self-identification than are positions on other issues, and whether our "cultural" conservatives are more likely to hold the religious beliefs that would lead to a conservative identification than citizens with similar issue positions, but who choose to identify as "moderate" or "liberal" politically.

We first explore the relationship between the two dimensions of policy preferences and ideological self-identification. Doctrinal beliefs have clear implications for political beliefs only on the "cultural" dimension, not for most issues on the dominant "scope-of-government" dimension. We know that, in general, the majority of elite and mass policy conflict is structured around broader scope-of-government concerns.[24] If the

Table 5-6. Predicting Ideological and Partisan Identification in the Electorate

	Ideological self-identification base category: liberal		Partisanship base category: Democrat	
	Pr (Conservative)	Pr (Moderate)	Pr (Republican)	Pr (Independent)
Scope-of-government preferences (standardized)	−0.47* (0.08)	−0.37* (0.10)	−0.67* (0.08)	−0.35* (0.10)
Cultural preferences (standardized)	−0.69* (0.08)	−0.30* (0.10)	−0.37* (0.07)	−0.16 (0.10)
Nonwhite	0.13 (0.18)	0.19 (0.21)	−1.23* (0.19)	−0.79* (0.22)
Female	0.10 (0.15)	0.02 (0.18)	−0.02 (0.14)	−0.25 (0.18)
Age	0.007 (0.004)	0.006 (0.005)	−0.019* (0.004)	−0.021* (0.005)
Education (highest degree obtained)	−0.07 (0.05)	−0.22* (0.06)	0.20* (0.05)	0.11 (0.06)
Political knowledge	0.05 (0.04)	−0.09 (0.05)	−0.00 (0.04)	−0.34* (0.05)
Partisanship (3-point scale)	0.98* (0.04)	0.14* (0.05)		
Ideological identification (3-point scale)			−1.03* (0.09)	0.27* (0.10)
Constant	−0.53 (0.32)	−0.16 (0.41)	−0.27* (0.32)	0.65 (0.37)
Log-likelihood	−1,268.78		−1,186.43	
N	1,550		1,550	
Pseudo-R^2	0.18		0.22	
(Cultural preferences—scope-of-government preferences)	0.22	0.07	−0.30	−0.19

Table 5-6. (*continued*)

	Ideological self-identification base category: liberal		Partisanship base category: Democrat	
	Pr (Conservative)	Pr (Moderate)	Pr (Republican)	Pr (Independent)
χ^2 test that coefficients for cultural and scope-of-government preferences are different from one another	30.68 ($p < 0.06$)	00.08 n.s.	60.78 ($p < 0.01$)	10.51 n.s.

Note: Entries are multinomial logit coefficients (standard errors in parentheses).
*$p < 0.05$.

political connotations of "liberal" and "conservative" are all that matter to ideological self-identification, then this first dimension should be more closely associated with ideology. But if *religious* conservatism is being translated to *political* conservatism, we should see that the issues connected to the religious liberal-conservative divide should have a disproportionate association with self-identification, as many would be translating their religiously driven beliefs directly to political ideology.

To examine this idea, in table 5-6 we estimate a multinomial logistic regression predicting ideological self-identification in the electorate ("conservative" [–1], "moderate" [0], "liberal" [+1]) as a function of standardized additive measures of policy preferences on each of these two issue dimensions and some standard covariates of self-identification. Results are shown in the first two columns of table 5-6. On average, preferences on cultural issues are modestly but significantly more powerful in differentiating self-identified liberals and conservatives than are scope-of-government issues. Figure 5-2 graphs the estimated impact of preferences on these two dimensions on self-identification, displaying the probability that an ideological identifier is "conservative" given his or her policy preferences on each dimension. The effect of holding strongly "conservative" or "liberal" preferences relative to the population on this dimension is greater than the effect of holding similarly extreme preferences on the scope-of-government dimension.

The fact that the narrow dimension of issues with a direct relationship to doctrinal orthodoxy have a greater association with ideological

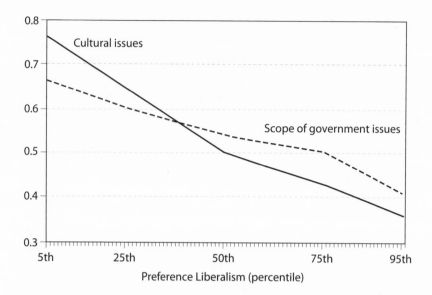

Figure 5-2
Probabilities of identifying as "liberal" and "conservative" as a function of policy
preferences. Note: Figure entries are predicted probabilities generated from multinomial logit estimates reported in table 5-4. The lines represent the effects of
the variables of interest, while all other variables are held constant at their mean
(or modal) values.

self-identification than scope-of-government preferences is supportive of
the idea that explicitly *political* liberalism and conservatism is not the
only liberalism and conservatism that people associate with ideological
terms. Of course, the issues on the cultural dimension are also symbolically "easy" issues for which citizens are more likely to understand the
political implications.[25] It could simply be the case, then, that the cultural
dimension is more closely related to ideology because it is simply easier
for all types of citizens to both understand and base decisions upon.

It is thus important to note that while cultural issues are disproportionately important in predicting *ideological* identification, they are far
less effective in predicting *party* identification. Replicating the models
with a trichotomous measure of partisanship (Republican, independent,
Democrat) instead of ideology as the dependent variable yields results
nearly opposite to those of the ideological self-identification model. Scope-
of-government issues are far more relevant than are cultural issues in
distinguishing Democrats from Republicans (see columns 3 and 4 of
table 5-6). Cultural issues matter disproportionately to ideology, but not
to partisanship. The exceptionally strong relationship of cultural preferences to conservative identification thus suggests that the "ideology"

that citizens associate with these issues has, at least for some citizens, an extrapolitical meaning.

The pathways idea also suggests that the large group of "cultural conservatives" often misdefine "doctrinal conservative" to also mean "political conservative," and identify politically accordingly. We thus must understand whether the "cultural conservatives" are largely identifying as conservative because of their politics, or their adherence to conservative religious doctrine.

One way to find support for this idea is to examine the self-identifications of a broader group of "cross-pressured" citizens: those who are conservative on issues of traditional morality but hold liberal preferences on scope-of-government issues. Our cultural conservatives fall into this group, but so do many others who consider themselves nonideological "moderates" and a smaller group that identifies as "liberal." While religious orthodoxy is obviously highly correlated with conservative opinions on cultural issues, people can come to politically conservative positions on cultural issues for reasons other than religious orthodoxy.[26]

But if the idea that religious conservatism is being transferred to conservative identification is correct, then among people with this combination of preferences—liberal on scope-of-government issues, conservative on cultural issues—it is the *doctrinally* conservative—those who have an overarching understanding of religious conservatism from which their cultural preferences are derived—that should identify as *politically* conservative. Conversely, for those whose "conservative" positions on the cultural dimension are not being shaped by a conception of religious commitment, but by other factors, there is no reason to think that they should be disproportionately conservative in self-identification. For these people, cultural issues are simply political issues, much like any others, on which they happen to take conservative positions. Among these citizens with these operational cross-pressures, doctrinal conservatism should have a clear and strong link to the probability of identifying as politically conservative.

We estimate multinomial logit models of ideological self-identification for people with liberal New Deal preferences but conservative cultural issue preferences. The sample here includes those classified as "cultural conservatives" earlier, as well as those with the same combination of preferences who are ideological "liberals" or "moderates." If the pathways theory is correct, then we should see a direct relationship between biblical literalism and ideological conservatism among this group.

Results are reported in table 5-7. Column one includes standard demographic and social predictors, as well as a measure of biblical orthodoxy: a three-point scale asking respondents about the degree to which they believe the Bible to be literally true. This orthodoxy measure has

Table 5-7. Predicting Ideological Conservatism among "Culturally
Conservative," "Scope-of-Government Liberal" Citizens

Partisanship	0.32*
	(0.07)
Nonwhite	−0.21
	(0.28)
South	0.09
	(0.28)
Northeast	0.11
	(0.37)
Female	0.15
	(0.27)
Education	0.01
	(0.09)
Political knowledge	0.16
	(0.08)
Political interest	0.13
	(0.18)
Religious orthodoxy	0.64*
	(0.23)
Log-likelihood	−194.45
Pseudo-R^2	0.09
N	316

Note: Entries are logit coefficients (standard errors in parentheses).
*$p < 0.05$.

powerful statistical and substantive effects on conservative identification.
Among those who hold conservative positions on cultural issues, it is the
religiously conservative who are most likely to be *politically* conservative.
It appears, in other words, that those whose conservative preferences on
cultural issues are more likely a reflection of their own doctrinally conservative beliefs do translate their religious beliefs into conservative identification. Those whose conservative cultural beliefs are driven by factors
other than orthodoxy are more likely to identify as political "moderates"
or "liberals." [27]

In sum, we have evidence that, at least for some segments of the population, political ideology is related to the extrapolitical meaning of "conservative" grounded in religious orthodoxy. Issues directly related to religious orthodoxy are more strongly related to political ideology than
are scope-of-government issues, even though the scope-of-government

dimension encompasses most of what we think of as elite policy debate (and is by far the more important dimension in explaining mass partisanship). And among citizens who hold conservative positions on "cultural" issues, biblical orthodoxy has a direct relationship to self-identification.

This is, of course, a general point: We cannot claim that ideological identification of all "cultural conservatives" comes directly from religious orthodoxy. But at least for many citizens, the meanings of political liberalism and conservatism—and the decision to identify as politically "conservative"—are contaminated by the use of the terms in the religious context. These conservatives may actually *be* conservative on some political issues, but the "conservatism" that is used to structure these beliefs is principally of a religious, not a political, nature. For many, there is no contradiction between one's ideological self-identification and holding liberal issue preferences on the dimension that structures most policy conflict, because that self-identification is not explicitly political.

Pathway 3: Responsiveness to Elite Political Discourse

While misapplication of religious labels and symbols provide some leverage on understanding why a disproportionate number of "cultural" conservatives identify as politically conservative, no such explanation exists for the third—and perhaps largest—group of self-identified conservatives: those with no conservative issue views. The "conservatism" that these citizens espouse, we argue, is a result of something entirely different: the reception and acceptance of the dominant messages of political elites.

On many questions of politics, there exist dominant frames, shared conceptions of politics and policy that define issues in the context of standard and widely believed stories. Such stories embed issues and controversies in a framework that emphasizes some aspects of the issue and downplays others. The dominant frames become answers to the questions of politics. The benefit of the frame to the citizen is context: issues embedded in frames become more meaningful. The cost is objectivity; the stories tend to point to answers that are far from neutral.

Dominant frames originate in the culture and find expression in the rhetoric of elites, reaching the general public through the mass media. We like to think that in an ideal polity, everyone would be exposed to a balance of frames, a competition of ideas. But in reality, some messages dominate others. We thus expect to see the public reflect such dominance in its own beliefs. What do the messages from American elites tell us about how symbolic ideology and specific social programs are framed for American citizens? What they tell us is that for both "symbolic" and "operational" messages, there exist dominant frames that shape how at least certain segments of the public view their own relationship to the political world.

On the symbolic side, the public is consistently exposed to frames that revere conservative symbols and slur liberal ones. The term "conservative" is held in far greater esteem than the term "liberal."[28] Elite conservatives, as a result, talk a great deal about the principles of a "conservative" approach to politics and the way in which this general value will affect one's approach to political problems, doing little to explain the concrete implications of this conservatism for policy. Conservatives boast about their conservatism, treating it as a badge of honor.[29] Liberals, in contrast, attack conservative politicians, but usually not their conservatism. Because liberals know the public affection for "conservative," they will call their opponents fools or extremists, and go after their stands on specific issues. But they will not say "my opponent is a conservative" as a means of disparagement. Conservatives play up the positive implications of a "conservative" approach to politics, but "liberals" do not do the same.[30]

When it comes to operational messages, the story is reversed. People prefer government action to meet specific social needs because they like the benefits that government action confers, especially for programs (to improve education, clean the environment, and the like) that benefit all groups of citizens. Liberal politicians thus usually frame their political appeals in terms of *specifics*, since government action at the operational level (that is, to meet a specific social need), generally leads to popular support.[31] Further, these policies are often framed in terms of the worth of the specific social goals (e.g., education, environmental protection, income security) themselves, not the more complex budgeting and policy trade-off issues that may underlie them.[32] These polices may, in fact, be "liberal," but the use of the label liberal, with its connotations of intrusiveness, recklessness, and more recently, elitism, is avoided. Conversely, conservatives may attack popular social programs at the margins, saying that they are inefficient, poorly administered, or the like, but rarely directly attack the worth of the specific social programs themselves.[33]

This divide in elite framing of general and specific political appeals is especially important when considering what we know about how citizens form operational and symbolic opinions. Ideology is principally a symbolic, evaluative orientation, developed from affective reactions to broad, *general* concepts.[34] Influences on issue attitudes vary considerably by domain, but—at least for the large segment of the population that does not structure preferences ideologically—are principally formed from reactions to the worth of *specific* social goals or programs.[35] For those without the ability to engage in abstract ideological thinking, self-identification and policy preferences are formed in response to substantively different political stimuli. Ideology and issue preferences, in other words, are a formed as a reaction to evaluations that differ in scope and generality, with ideological identifications formed largely as a function of general feelings about politics, with operational preferences formed largely as a function of reactions to specific social goals and problems.

The dominant frames in American politics, the ways in which liberal and conservative elites describe and defend their own actions, thus conflict, but do so in ways that may not be apparent to large segments of the general public. When it comes to ideological symbols, "conservatism" dominates, as people hear about the value of "conservative" approaches to politics, with far less mention of the specifics of what this approach may entail. But when it comes to specific social programs, spending and government action to solve specific social problems is lauded—again, with comparably little discussion of the costs and trade-offs inherent in solving such problems. It is, of course, the case that the real policy implications of these "conservative" and "liberal" messages conflict with one another. But since they deal with different things—liberal specifics, conservative symbols—and since neither is given much opposition in mainstream political discourse, the context necessary for citizens who are only vaguely involved in politics to reconcile their competing implications and choose between them is not apparent. As a result, people may internalize *both* types of messages, espousing beliefs of ideological and symbolic conservatism, while holding predominantly liberal operational beliefs on both relevant dimensions of conflict. A citizen who does not carefully sort through the conflict will end up with inconsistent views. The story here is thus straightforward: some citizens will be identify as ideologically conservative while simultaneously holding liberal issue positions as a reflection of the conflicting political messages to which they are exposed.

Converse and Zaller provide some insight on who these citizens will be, as the reception and acceptance of these elite messages is crucial in determining who is likely to hold conflicted preferences.[36] They will not be sophisticates, interested and informed enough to sort through and resolve conflicting messages. But they will also not be those completely disengaged from politics, those not paying enough attention to pick up the dominant frames sent by political elites. Those in the "middle"—who receive competing cues but lack the contextual knowledge to sort through their competing implications—are more likely to accept *both* dominant messages, holding attitudes that are both operationally liberal and ideologically conservative.

Although citizens learn about politics in a number of ways, most who obtain political information do so through the mainstream press. Paying regular attention to the news media is often thought of as one of the hallmarks of an informed and engaged citizen. But if one of the functions of the mass media is to transmit the competing messages of political elites, exposure to news may exacerbate the potential for operational-symbolic conflict. Those who pay more attention to the news will be more exposed to the conflicting dominant frames—they will receive a greater number of both symbolic appeals from conservatives and operational appeals from liberals. It is individuals who receive these messages and do not understand their conflicting implications who are good candidates to hold "conflicted" operational-symbolic preferences.

To explore this conflicting frames idea, we estimate logit models predicting "conflicted conservative" preferences as a function of contextual and demographic factors. The dependent variable is a simple "1" for individuals who are operationally liberal on both issue dimensions and identify as a conservative (a "conflicted conservative") and "0" for otherwise. We expect that the likelihood of holding conflicted conservative preferences will be a function of education, knowledge, and interest (as those with higher levels of all of these should be less likely to hold operational-symbolic conflict) and of news media exposure. It is impossible in the survey setting to tell how many political messages a person has received. But we do have a measure of the amount of exposure that citizens have to new content from television, radio, and print sources. This can measure, albeit imperfectly, the number of political cues to which one has been exposed.

We expect that political knowledge will mediate the relationship between media exposure and micro-level conflict. Conflicted conservatives, rather than being people entirely "tuned out" of politics, should be those who are most likely to receive "conflicting" dominant elite cues without the contextual information necessary to reconcile conflicting implications. Those with especially low levels of knowledge—even if they receive a great deal of mainstream news—will not pay attention to or process the political messages of elites. If they are reading or watching news, they are doing so for reasons other than politics. Conversely, those with high levels of knowledge will receive messages but will also understand that the operational messages of elite liberals and the symbolic messages of elite conservatives actually do conflict and will process them accordingly. It is those with modest amounts of knowledge—those who receive and process political messages but are not necessarily able to understand or resolve their conflicting implications—who are likely to internalize the messages of both operational liberalism and symbolic conservatism.

We address the issue in table 5-8. The first, baseline, model (column 1) tests the direct impact of each of the concepts of interest on the likelihood of holding conflicted preferences. As expected, higher levels of education and interest decrease the likelihood of operational-ideological conflict, as does holding of relatively moderate (weak) issue beliefs. We would

Table 5-8. Predicting "Conflicted Conservative" Preferences in the Electorate

	(1)	(2)
Political knowledge	−0.04 (0.04)	
News exposure	0.20* (0.09)	
Highest 1/3 of knowledge (dummy)		−0.27 (0.46)
Middle 1/3 of knowledge (dummy)		−0.66* (0.33)
High knowledge * news exposure		0.08 (0.18)
Medium knowledge * news exposure		0.40* (0.12)
Low knowledge * news exposure		−0.00 (0.15)
Strength of scope-of-government preferences	−0.10* (0.03)	0.09* (0.03)
Strength of cultural preferences	−0.26* (0.07)	0.26* (0.07)
Partisanship	0.08* (0.04)	0.08* (0.04)
Political interest	−0.29* (0.12)	−0.29* (0.12)
Education	0.06 (0.05)	−0.05 (0.05)
Log-likelihood	−617.94	−615.52
Pseudo-R^2	0.04	0.04
N	1,276	1,276

Note: Entries are logit coefficients (standard errors in parentheses).
*$p < 0.05$.

expect those whose issue preferences are only marginally liberal to be more likely to identify as ideological conservatives than those who are extremely liberal, and that is the case.[37]

The second model (column 2) analyzes the effects of exposure to the news media across three levels of political sophistication (operationalized by dividing the population into the top, middle, and lower "thirds" of knowledge based on responses to an eight-point battery of factual questions). The results show that exposure to conflicting elite cues increases the likelihood of "conflicted conservatism" only among those in this "middle" tier of sophistication: only among these people is the effect of political news media significantly different from zero. The news media transmit conflicting cues to the public in a way that may increase the likelihood of operational-symbolic conflict among those unable to reconcile the conflicting implications of the cues.[38]

There are undoubtedly individual-level, idiosyncratic differences among self-identified conservatives that are ignored with this predictive analysis. But as a general explanation, it seems that these citizens hold "conflicted" beliefs in large part because they have internalized and accepted the messages of both conservative and liberal political elites. They identify as conservative because they like the ideological label as it is used in elite discourse but are unaware of how it relates to the larger political context. "Conflicted conservatives," in other words, are conservative in name only: they like (and are persuaded by) symbolic conservative messages but show no evidence of operational conservatism.

Conclusions and Implications

This chapter, part of a larger project examining ideological politics in the United States, works to provide a broad foundation from which to understand the operational-ideological "paradox" in American public opinion. We have shown that there are three different "pathways" through which people can approach the ideological term "conservative," pathways rooted in three different *meanings* of the term itself. For some, self-identified "conservatism" is part of a constrained system of issue beliefs. For some, doctrinal conservatism is translated to political conservatism with little understanding of the broader political meanings of the term. For still others, ideological conservatism represents an affinity for the symbol of conservatism, a function of the esteem in which the label is held in elite discourse. These diverse pathways to conservatism stand in contrast to the relatively homogenous reasons that people choose to identify as ideological "liberals."

Conover and Feldman argued that in the minds of the general public, "liberal" and "conservative" are not opposites, but are instead separate concepts, evaluated in light of feelings toward separate groups.[39] This work takes that argument a step further, arguing that the term "conservative" is itself multifaceted, as different groups of people bring substantively different ideas to the meaning of "conservatism" and identify as conservative for systematically different reasons. Most research examining the role of symbolic ideology to mass choices frames the issue as one of a continuum of influence, conditional on a citizen's level of political sophistication—either a citizen has the sophistication and political awareness to understand and conceptualize political ideology (in which case, ideology will be a meaningful guide to political choice), or he or she lacks this sophistication and awareness (in which case, ideology will not be particularly meaningful). This project suggests a different view: that ideological self-identification may be important for all types of conservatives, but may matter in systematically different ways for different types of people—especially different types of symbolic "conservatives."

We have long known that ideology is a source more of stability in electoral outcomes than of change. Consistent ideologues, those who match a liberal or conservative identification to a consistent set of policy views, constitute the partisan and ideological bases of the two major parties. Because they loyally support their own side, they produce almost no longitudinal variation in electoral outcomes. Purely nonideological moderates, on the other hand, do not respond to ideological appeals and thus are most susceptible to persuasion by popular or eloquent candidates or the "nature of the times." But the two other groups of conservatives, those who either take consistently liberal positions or hold conservative positions only on issues where doctrinal conservatism is relevant, may be especially important to understanding the dynamics of mass electoral behavior.

For the citizens that we have labeled "cultural conservatives," the idea that doctrinal conservatism can be translated directly into political conservatism is not simply a curious artifact of the survey context, but can have real political implications. Candidates can occasionally gain electoral advantage by mobilizing religiously conservative voters around some manufactured "social issue" of the time (gay marriage, for example). But individual "social issues" generally have little staying power in American politics, and the number of religiously orthodox voters who will care a great deal about any given issue is likely quite small. Most religiously conservative citizens, for example, are likely to oppose gay marriage. But finding a large number of religiously conservative voters who care enough about gay marriage (or any other particular issue) to have the issue drive their vote choice is another matter.

But if politicians can connect religiously conservative positions on these individual issues to a broader message of ideological "conservatism," then it is possible to mobilize a large group of religiously conservative voters not around transient political issues of limited import to most, but rather under the guise of protecting a "conservative" value system that voters both identify with and care deeply about. More closely tying the symbols of *political* conservatism to the value system implied by *religious* orthodoxy may be an effective way to generate long-term change in the behavior of religious conservatives.

Truly "conflicted" conservatives, with the capacity to be persuaded both by liberal issue positions and conservative symbols, represent an interesting and politically important "swing" group. When specific issues and policy proposals dominate political discourse, liberal candidates will generally earn the support of conflicted conservatives. When symbols and ideological rhetoric dominate, conservative candidates can expect to win. Because of this, the conflicted conservatives become the dynamic element in electoral politics, producing much of the cyclical change that is such a hallmark of the American polity.

Notes

1. For the first major treatment of this topic, see Free (1967).
2. Knight (1985); Jacoby (1991).
3. This also holds true, to a very similar extent, to new labels that Democratic politicians have tried to use in place of the label "liberal"—e.g., "progressive."
4. Stimson (1999).
5. There is no logical disconnect here. At any given time, there can be one or two especially relevant "social," "racial," or other issues that do not clearly load on a single dimension. But these issues tend to be either transient (and thus not important to the long-term dynamics of public opinion) or gradually "usurped" into the standard scope of unidimensional conflict.
6. Ansolabehere, Rodden, and Snyder (2006); Gelman et al. (2008); Miller and Schofeld (2003).
7. Ellis, Ura, and Ashley-Robinson (2006); Enns and Kellstedt (2008).
8. Adams (1997).
9. We choose to employ the 2000 study because of the breadth and depth of its issue-related questions, although parallel analyses using the issue-related content data from more recent (or more distant) National Election Studies (NES) produce very similar results. The reliance on only spending questions to measure "scope-of-government" preferences was chosen because past work (e.g., Ellis, Ura, and Ashley-Robinson 2006; Stimson 2002) has shown that measures comprised solely of spending items provide good longitudinal proxies for the Mood measure shown in figure 5-1, and thus can be considered reasonably valid measures of the concept of "operational ideology" on scope-of-government matters.
10. See Layman and Carsey (2002).
11. Note that this stands in contrast to much popular commentary, which tends to assume conservative dominance on these types of issues.
12. Kellstedt and Smidt (1991).
13. Perhaps the most striking difference between consistent and moral conservatives is that of race. A plurality of blacks are self-identified political conservatives, even though only 11 percent are operationally conservative on the "New

Deal" dimension of conflict and only 8 percent are Republicans. By far the largest group of ideologically conservative blacks are those who hold conservative preferences only on "moral" issues. This does still more to imply that some factors that are associated with citizens' liberal-conservative ideology are *not* directly associated with either issue preferences or partisanship.

14. Converse (1964); Jacoby (1986).

15. Jacoby, (1995).

16. Holm and Robinson (1978); Jacoby (1991).

17. Campbell et al. (1960).

18. Sharp and Lodge (1985).

19. Stimson (1975); Knight (1985).

20 Ansolabehere, Rodden, and Sndyer (2006); Ellis (2010).

21. Wald (2003).

22. Leege and Kellstedt (1993).

23. This is especially important given the homogeneity of preferences on scope-of-government issues among various types of "doctrinally conservative" churches. Some doctrinally conservative churches send very (politically) conservative messages to parishioners on issues of social welfare and redistribution of wealth, others pay little attention to them, and still others (notably some African American and Catholic churches) hold liberal preferences on these issues (see, e.g., Cavendish 2000). Doctrinally liberal churches, in contrast, are generally politically liberal across the board (see, e.g., Green 2003). So the cross-contamination of ideological terms is far less likely to be an issue here: these citizens are by and large politically liberal on all relevant dimensions.

24. Stonecash (2001); Erikson, MacKuen, and Stimson (2002); McCarty, Poole, and Rosenthal (2006).

25. Carmines and Stimson (1980).

26. Loftus (2001).

27. It is also important to note that it is not other aspects of religious commitment, but religious conservatism explicitly that relates to political conservatism. If we estimate a similar model adding in other indicators of religious beliefs and behavior (church attendance, relationship with God, moral traditionalism, and frequency of prayer), only biblical literalism stands out as a significant predictor of conservative identification. This provides some supportive evidence that it is doctrinal conservatism itself that relates directly to ideological self-identification.

28. Jennings (1992); Schiffer (2000).

29. In addition, as in religion, the use of the labels "conservative" and "liberal" also have connotations in fields other than politics—and, as with politics, the "conservative" label is typically held in higher esteem than the "liberal" one. In large part, that is because "conservatism" is associated with temperance, prudence, restraint, and respect for traditional social standards—all attributes highly prized in the American electorate. In finance, for example (and especially) in the modern context, "conservative" approaches to investments are lauded, and society tends to respect citizens who are "conservative" in their budgeting and approach to personal finance. These uses of the labels, despite their nonpolitical origins, also have implications for why the "conservative" label is so much more popular than the liberal one. For an extended discussion of this point, see Stimson (2004).

30. The idea that the "conservative" label carries more popular connotations in the electorate is often discussed, but rarely tested. Many studies have alluded to, and/or provided indirect tests of, the idea that the label "conservative" is now typically held in higher regard than the label "liberal" (see, e.g., Schiffer 2000; McGowan 2007; Rotunda 1989). And there is certainly evidence of popular commentators (and political candidates) recognizing the advantages of "conservative," and disadvantages of "liberal," labeling (e.g., Reardon 2005; Lakoff 2004). But few studies have tested the claim directly and empirically. It would be helpful to know, for example, whether media frames and usage of the "liberal" and "conservative" labels reflect disproportionately positive or negative connotations, for example, to be able to put these claims to better empirical scrutiny. Without such tests, our claims to follow rest on the assumption that the electorate views the conservative label more positively than the liberal one, though we cannot provide direct evidence for this assumption here.

31. Sears and Citrin (1982).

32. But it is not simply the case that people support a stronger government role in a variety of social realms simply because they forget that these programs are not free. Analysis of earlier General Social Survey data, for example, shows that support for many major government programs dip a bit, but still gain clear majority support, when citizens are reminded that a tax increase might be required to pay for them.

33. Jacoby (2000); Stimson (2004).

34. Conover and Feldman (1980).

35. Jacoby (2000).

36. Converse (1964); Zaller (1992).

37. Including "strength of preference" variables also serves as an implicit control for the fact that both measures of issue preferences are based on non-random samples of political issues, and that the categorization of respondents as operational "liberals" or "conservatives" was based on knife-edge coding decisions (e.g., a respondent who gave seven conservative responses and six liberal responses was classified as conservative, while a respondent who gave six conservative responses and seven liberal was considered a liberal). The inclusion of this control guards against the notion that measurement and classification error drives the results.

38. It is possible that the frame of reference of this model is incorrect: perhaps it makes more sense to predict "conflicted conservatives" from a population as a whole, but rather we should be focusing on who, *among operational liberals*, chooses to identify as conservative or (conversely) who, *among self-identified conservatives*, is consistently operationally liberal. It is worth noting that in models estimated with either of these restricted samples, the effects of the variables of theoretical interest are similar to those in the "full population" model.

39. Conover and Feldman (1980).

Part II

POLARIZATION AND THE PARTY SYSTEM

VI

Partisan Differences in Job Approval Ratings of George W. Bush and U.S. Senators in the States

AN EXPLORATION

Gary C. Jacobson

AFTER SEVERAL DECADES OF NEARLY CONTINUAL EXPANSION, the partisan divide in Washington reached its widest extent in a century during the George W. Bush administration. By every systematic measure, members of Congress grew increasingly polarized along ideological and party lines between the 1970s and the 109th Congress (2005–2006), when, according to Poole and Rosenthal's DW-NOMINATE scale, the gap was wider than at any time since before World War I.[1] Conflicts between Congress and the White House also became more heatedly partisan, most conspicuously in the Republican Congress's failed attempt to impeach and remove President Bill Clinton during his second term. The sources of this polarizing trend in national politics are diverse and still in some dispute among scholars, but its reality is not.[2]

Ordinary Americans, though remaining considerably less divided by party and ideology than politicians, activists, or pundits, have not been mere bystanders in this process. They, too, have increasingly sorted themselves into the partisan camp that best suits their policy preferences and ideological leanings.[3] Partisan differences in political opinions have widened, most notably in attitudes toward presidents, with G. W. Bush provoking the most polarized responses of any president since polling on presidential job approval began more than 70 years ago.[4] Party-line voting in the congressional and presidential elections of 2004, 2006, and 2008 reached its highest levels since the 1950s. Individual ticket splitting declined, as did the proportion of states and districts delivering split electoral verdicts—majorities for a president of one party, for a representative or senator of the other. With specific regard to Senate elections—senators in the 109th Congress (2005–2006) are the principal focus of this chapter—27 of 34 contests in 2004 were won by the party whose presidential candidate won the state's electoral votes, tying 1964 and 2008 for the highest level of such congruence in the past half century. With the 2004 winners added to the continuing Senate membership, fully 75 percent of senators in the 109th Congress represented states won by their party's presidential candidate in the most recent presidential election, the highest proportion in at least 50 years.[5]

Despite these trends, more than a few senators still manage to win and hold seats against the partisan grain. In 2004, for example, the voters in Indiana, where Republicans outnumber Democrats, elected Democrat Evan Bayh to the Senate with 62 percent of the vote while giving G.W. Bush 60 percent. North Dakota, a predominantly Republican state taken by Bush in 2000 and 2004 with more than 60 percent of the vote, is represented in the Senate by a brace of Democrats.[6] After 2006, 26 of the 100 senators represented states where their party has fewer identifiers than its rival.[7] How do these senators do it? More generally, how is it that, while operating in a highly partisan and sharply polarized national arena, most senators have been able to avoid becoming polarizing figures themselves, not only but especially in contexts where offending the other party's adherents would threaten their careers? What does determine the degree to which senators inspire divergent ratings from partisans in their states? And how were partisan assessments of senators related to partisan assessments of President Bush?

In this chapter, I address these and related questions by examining a unique set of state-level public opinion surveys. From May 2005 until November 2006, SurveyUSA, a polling firm whose main clients for its political surveys are local news media, conducted monthly statewide polls in all 50 states. Their automated telephone surveys asked samples of approximately 600 respondents in each state whether they approved of the performance of G. W. Bush, the state's governor, and both of its senators, as well as questions about each respondent's party identification, ideology, religious service attendance, and demographic characteristics (age, education, sex, race, and in some states, region). In some months, they also asked respondents' positions on policy issues. The aggregate results, including breakdowns of the approval questions by all of the respondents' other characteristics, are posted on the Internet shortly after the surveys are taken.[8] These data, if reliable, obviously have great potential value for addressing a variety of interesting questions about state-level political attachments and opinions. I thus examined the survey results carefully for internal and external consistency as well as intuitive plausibility and they passed all of the tests very satisfactorily.[9] For the analyses reported here, I use the data produced by the thirteen monthly surveys taken from May 2005 through May 2006.

The chapter proceeds as follows. First, I compare the state-level determinants of the job approval ratings of the president and the senators and find that they have almost nothing in common. I then compare the sources of partisan differences in states' ratings of the president and senators and again find that they have almost nothing in common. Next, I explore in greater detail the sources of variation in the degree of polarization inspired by senators' ratings, finding that these differ somewhat between Republican and Democratic senators but remain to an important degree under a senator's control. I then show how senators have adapted their roll-call behavior to the political leanings of their states. My conclusion is that senators have both the motive and means to mitigate partisan divisions when they choose, although they do not always do so and they cannot completely avoid the fallout from participation in the intensely partisan national arena.

Determinants of Approval Ratings of the President and Senators

As a prelude to considering the sources of state-level partisan differences in job approval ratings of G. W. Bush and the state's senators, it is instructive to compare the determinants of their overall statewide ratings during the period under review. Figure 6-1, which displays the kernel density distributions of responses to the job approval question from all 650 statewide surveys taken over the thirteen months from May 2005 through May 2006, shows that, for the most part, senators were rated more favorably than the president during this period. Bush's average approval

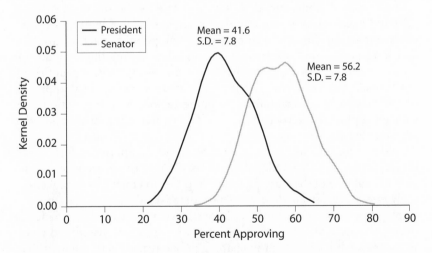

Figure 6-1

Distribution of approval ratings of senators and G. W. Bush, by state. Source: Thirteen monthly statewide polls taken between May 2005 and May 2006 by SurveyUSA and reported at http://www.surveyusa.com/50StateTracking.html.

rating of 41.6 percent is very close to his average in major national polls taken over the same months.[10] This was a time when Bush's approval ratings were sagging to their lowest levels to that date; had the surveys been taken in 2002 or 2003, his ratings would of course have been much higher. Senators' average ratings were about 15 points higher than Bush's, with Democratic senators (58.1 percent approving) rated a bit higher than Republicans (54.9 percent approving).[11] Perhaps more surprising, and certainly noteworthy, the ratings of Bush and the state's senators were nearly orthogonal; the correlation between ratings of Bush and Republican senators was only 0.15; ratings of Bush and Democratic senators were also positively if weakly related ($r = 0.13$), not negatively, as might be expected.

These results suggest that state-level evaluations of the president and senators were shaped by divergent sets of political forces, a conclusion amply confirmed by the regression results reported in table 6-1.[12] Variations in reactions to Bush mirrored his electoral performance in 2004 very closely and were almost completely explained by partisan makeup of the state and its balance between conservatives and liberals. Bush's standing in 2005–2006 is predicted with great precision by his 2004 vote, albeit at a substantial discount (of about 22 percent) because he had become noticeably less popular after May 2005 than he had been at the time of his reelection. The partisan and ideological makeup of the state predicts Bush's approval ratings almost as accurately.[13] Bush's approval ratings rise with the proportion of Republican identifiers in a state, fall with the proportion of Democratic identifiers, and rise as the state's ideological balance becomes more conservative.[14] These results highlight the decisive effect of partisanship and ideology in shaping popular reactions to Bush that have been found in national surveys taken during this period.[15] Of these factors, partisanship was clearly the most important, accounting by itself for 83 percent of the variance in state-level presidential approval. No other variables I examined, including region, state population, and state unemployment level had any additional discernable effect on Bush's approval level.

In sharp contrast to evaluations of the president, approval of U.S. senators is almost entirely unrelated to the distribution of partisans or the ideological balance in the state (the third and fourth equations in table 6-1). Only one of the six coefficients achieves statistical significance, and two display the wrong sign. Both equations leave almost all the variance in senators' approval ratings unexplained. Clearly, partisanship and ideology were far less important in shaping public reactions to senators than to G. W. Bush. What did affect constituents' reaction to senators? We can begin answering this question by observing the rank ordering of senators according to their average approval ratings in the thirteen monthly polls

Table 6-1. Partisanship, Ideology, and Job Performance Approval of the President and Senators in the States

	President Bush		Republican senators		Democratic senators	
	Coefficient	S.E.	Coefficient	S.E.	Coefficient	S.E.
2004 presidential vote	0.80***	0.03				
Percent Republican			0.41***	0.08	-0.20	0.26	-0.06	0.26
Percent Democrat			-0.32***	0.06	-0.40*	0.18	-0.32	0.20
Ideological balance[a]			0.34***	0.05	0.21	0.20	0.08	0.17
Constant	-1.40	1.70	32.34***	3.23	69.92***	10.33	70.40***	10.27
Adjusted R^2	0.93		0.91		0.05		0.00	
Root MSE	1.87		2.16		6.99		7.10	
Number of cases	50		50		55		45	

Note: Except for the 2004 presidential vote, the variables are the average statewide percentages from thirteen monthly SurveyUSA surveys taken from May 2005 through May 2006.

[a] Percent conservative minus percent liberal.

Table 6-2. State-Level Approval of U.S. Senators

Senator	Party/state	Approval	Senator	Party/state	Approval
Snowe	R-ME	73.8	Salazar	D-CO	55.5
Collins	R-ME	72.8	Dole	R-NC	55.2
Obama	D-IL	69.8	Gregg	R-NH	55.0
Conrad	D-ND	69.2	Lincoln	D-AR	54.8
Leahy	D-VT	68.9	Feingold	D-WI	54.3
Inouye	D-HI	68.9	Harkin	D-IO	54.2
Johnson	D-SD	68.7	Bond	R-MO	54.1
Dorgan	D-ND	68.4	Murray	D-WA	53.8
McCain	R-AZ	67.8	Kerry	D-MA	53.8
Reed	D-RI	67.2	Feinstein	D-CA	53.8
Rockefeller	D-WV	65.8	Alexander	R-TN	53.7
Ben Nelson	D-NE	65.8	Spector	R-PA	53.4
Jeffords	I-VT	64.8	McConnell	R-KY	53.1
Grassley	R-IO	64.7	Levin	D-MI	52.9
Stevens	R-AK	64.5	Allen	R-VA	52.7
Lott	R-MS	63.9	Roberts	R-KN	52.6
Domenici	R-NM	63.5	Coleman	R-MN	52.4
Carper	D-DE	63.3	Chafee	R-RI	52.4
Byrd	D-WV	63.3	Brownback	R-KA	52.3
Lieberman	D-CT	63.2	Landrieu	D-LA	52.2
Clinton	D-NY	62.5	Frist	R-TN	51.7
Bayh	D-IN	62.5	Ensign	R-NV	51.3
Biden	D-DE	61.8	Cantwell	D-WA	51.1
Lugar	R-IN	61.1	Smith	R-OR	51.0
Cochran	R-MS	60.8	Murkowski	R-AK	51.0
Crapo	R-ID	60.7	Boxer	D-CA	51.0
Vitter	R-LA	60.2	Isakson	R-GA	50.2
Schumer	D-NY	60.1	Sarbanes	D-MD	49.8
Hatch	R-UT	60.1	Durbin	D-IL	49.5
Baucus	D-MT	60.1	Talent	R-MO	49.0
Mikulski	D-MD	59.9	Sununu	R-NH	49.0
Thomas	R-WY	59.8	DeMint	R-SC	48.9
Bingaman	R-NM	59.5	Voinovich	R-OH	48.7
Shelby	R-AL	59.4	Chambliss	D-GA	48.7

Table 6-2. (*continued*)

Senator	Party/state	Approval	Senator	Party/state	Approval
Kennedy	D-MA	59.4	Bill Nelson	D-FL	48.7
Hutchison	R-TX	59.2	Stabenow	D-MI	48.0
Craig	R-ID	59.1	Corzine	D-NJ	47.8
Enzi	R-WY	58.9	Coburn	R-OK	47.5
Warner	R-VA	58.7	Inhofe	R-OK	47.0
Akaka	D-HI	58.7	Allard	R-CO	46.7
Wyden	D-OR	58.6	Kyl	R-AZ	46.5
Hagel	R-NE	58.5	Burns	R-MT	46.4
Dodd	D-CT	58.1	DeWine	R-OH	45.5
Kohl	D-WI	57.5	Dayton	D-MN	45.4
Graham	R-SC	57.5	Bunning	R-KY	45.3
Session	R-AL	57.1	Burr	R-NC	45.2
Pryor	D-AR	57.1	Martinez	R-FL	44.1
Thune	R-SD	56.7	Cornyn	R-TX	43.4
Bennett	R-UT	56.2	Lautenberg	D-NJ	43.2
Reid	D-NV	55.6	Santorum	R-PA	43.1

(table 6-2). Maine's Olympia Snowe and Susan Collins top the list, while Rick Santorum edges out Frank Lautenberg and John Cornyn for last place. A visual scan of the list suggests that, consistent with previous research,[16] moderates and senators from less populous states receive higher marks than ideologues and senators from more populous states. The rankings of Snowe and Collins raise the possibility that women might be better regarded as well.

These and other hypothetical determinants of senators' approval ratings are tested by the regression equations in table 6-3. Under controls, the state's partisan balance is still irrelevant, but the state's ideological balance now makes a significant difference; a senator with the most favorable ideological balance is estimated to be rated about 8 points higher than a senator with the least favorable balance. Senators who are more extreme (measured here by the natural log of the senators absolute DW-NOMINATE score for the 109th Congress[17]) or more loyal to their party (average for the two sessions of 109th Congress[18]) win significantly lower approval ratings than their more moderate or less partisan colleagues. The coefficients indicate that, other things being equal, the most

Table 6-3. Approval of Senators' Performance

	Coefficient	S.E.	Coefficient	S.E.
Senator's partisans (%)	0.07	0.11	0.04	0.11
Other party's partisans (%)	0.07	0.11	0.02	0.11
State ideological balance[a]	0.23*	0.09	0.25**	0.09
Ideological extremity[b]	−4.80***	1.34		
Party unity score[c]			−0.26**	0.07
State population[d]	−3.29***	0.64	−3.16***	0.65
Senator is Republican	−12.24***	3.70	−12.43***	3.76
Senator is a woman	2.19	1.79	2.75	1.76
Partisan leader	−0.36	2.19	0.01	2.20
Terms served	0.97**	0.36	0.16***	0.35
Constant	54.96***	5.85	3.75***	8.87
Adjusted R^2	0.42		0.42	
Number of cases	100		100	

[a] Percent conservative minus percent liberal for Republicans; percent liberal minus percent conservative for Democrats.
[b] Log of absolute DW-NOMINATE score.
[c] CQ party unity score.
[d] Log of the number of House seats in the state.
* $p < 0.05$; ** $p < 0.01$; *** $p < 0.001$.

moderate senator would be rated 15 points higher than the most extreme senator; the least partisan would be rated 15 points higher than the most partisan.[19] Senators tend to receive higher ratings the less populous the state; according to the estimated coefficient, a senator from a state with only one House seat would be rated about 13 points higher than a senator from California. Republicans are rated about 12 points lower than Democrats.[20] Women receive slightly higher ratings than men, but the pertinent coefficients are not significant. Partisan leaders, here defined as the Senate majority and minority leaders and whips plus Trent Lott (former majority leader), John Kerry, Ted Kennedy, and Hillary Clinton, are neither helped nor hurt by that status. Senators were rated about 1 point higher for each term served, although it is not clear whether this means that longer service increases public regard, that higher public regard is a condition of longer service, or both.

These equations leave a good deal of variance in job approval unexplained. I examined several other potential explanatory variables, including a crude measure of senators' success in delivering local benefits (the state's ratio of federal transfers to federal taxes paid), state per capita income, state unemployment rates, and the senator's location in the six-year electoral cycle, none of which had any discernable systematic effect on senators' job approval ratings.

Party Polarization in Ratings of the President and Senators

The overall ratings of G. W. Bush and U.S. senators bear little relationship to one another and are shaped by different sets of state-level factors. Not surprisingly, then, the degree of partisan polarization they inspired is also shaped by different sets of variables. The unusually wide partisan divisions provoked by Bush are explicable in good part by his leadership style, policy goals, decisions (especially on Iraq), and political strategies. His administration's relationship with the Democratic opposition epitomized polarized national politics, and his example shows that presidents do much to shape how they are perceived by their own and the other party's identifiers and therefore how far they polarize the public. Bush's immediate predecessor, Bill Clinton, also inspired wide partisan differences in performance ratings, as (so far) does his successor, Barack Obama, again reflecting their choice of political objectives and actions as well as the intensely partisan political environment prevailing during their presidencies.[21]

Although the Senate as a whole has clearly contributed to the trend toward intensified partisan conflict, its individual members enjoy the leeway, and often the incentive, to limit their participation in it. Presidents serve national constituencies; senators need worry only about pleasing their state's electorate—unless, of course, they aspire to the White House themselves. As with presidents, senators' decisions and actions should help determine how partisans in their states assess their performance. The more they are identified with the ideological and partisan clashes that have divided the parties in Washington, the more polarized their constituents are likely to be in evaluating their job performance. Hard-line ideologues ought to provoke more divergent reactions than moderate centrists. Senators who lead or stand loyally with their parties on the fundamental issues that divide Democrats and Republicans ought to be more polarizing than party mavericks or those who keep low national profiles and busy themselves delivering local benefits. And because they can cultivate personal connections with a larger share of their electorates, politicians serving relatively small, homogenous populations should find it easier to reach across party lines than should those serving large, heterogeneous populations.[22]

Senators cannot, of course, affect state populations, and they cannot do much if anything to affect the general level of partisan dissensus among their constituents. But they can decide how conservative or liberal a voting record to compile and how consistently to support their party's and the president's legislative proposals. Thus, they can, if they choose, adapt their behavior to the local political context, and senators representing states where their party is in the minority will naturally have the strongest incentive to compile more centrist, less partisan voting records.

In light of these options and incentives, it is not surprising to find that senators provoked far smaller divisions between partisan identifiers than did the president during the period under review. Figure 6-2 displays the distribution of party differences in approval ratings for senators and Bush in the 650 surveys. The mean partisan difference across states in evaluations of Bush, 64 points, is not far below the national average during these months (70 points)[23]—that is, Bush was, on average, nearly as polarizing a figure within each state as he was nationally. The average gap for senators is much smaller, 29 points, and displays much greater variance; a few senators even received higher approval ratings from the opposing party's identifiers than from their own. In only 17 of 1,300 possible comparisons were respondents more divided by party in their evaluations of a senator than of the president; in no state was the average partisan gap across the thirteen monthly surveys wider for any senator than for Bush. [24]

Figures 6-3 and 6-4 offer more detailed comparisons of the distribution of partisan approval ratings across the three offices using a common scale. Figure 6-3 documents the widely separated statewide evaluations

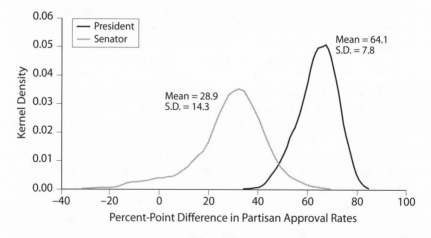

Figure 6-2
Party differences in approval ratings of senators and G. W. Bush in the states.
Source: Thirteen monthly statewide polls taken between May 2005 and May 2006 by SurveyUSA and reported at http://www.surveyusa.com/50StateTracking.html.

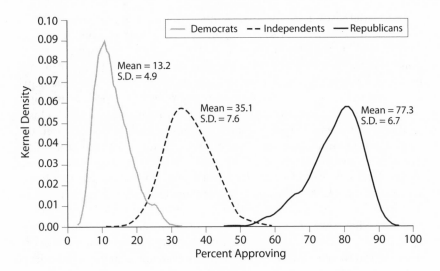

Figure 6-3
Distribution of president's approval in states, by party. Source: Thirteen monthly statewide polls taken between May 2005 and May 2006 by SurveyUSA and reported at http://www.surveyusa.com/50StateTracking.html.

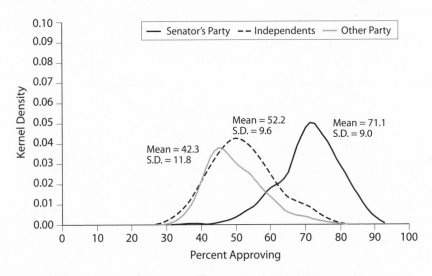

Figure 6-4
Distribution of senators' approval ratings, by party. Source: Thirteen monthly statewide polls taken between May 2005 and May 2006 by SurveyUSA and reported at http://www.surveyusa.com/50StateTracking.html.

of Bush offered by Republicans, Democrats, and independents. There is no overlap between partisan categories; Bush's worst showing among Republicans in any state in any month (47 percent approving) was 15 points higher than his best showing among Democrats (32 percent approving). There is also little overlap between evaluations of independents and partisans of either stripe. As in national polls of the period, approval of Bush's performance among independents was on average much closer to that of Democrats than to that of Republicans.[25] In comparison, the partisan distributions of senators' approval rates are considerably less distinctive and much flatter (figure 6-4). State-level approval reached as low as 33 percent among a senator's own partisans and as high as 84 percent among the other party's partisans. The data indicate that senators were less polarizing figures than the president because they typically got somewhat lower ratings from their own partisans and, more importantly, much higher ratings from the other party's adherents. As with approval ratings, the simple correlation between the extent of state-level polarization provoked by the president and the state's senators is modest ($r = 0.17$).

The sources as well as degree of polarization differ between the two offices. Of the variety of models I explored estimating the level of state-level polarization on Bush's performance, the equation reported in table 6-4 appears to offer the most parsimonious explanation. Partisans in states with a larger proportion of independents and a relative preponderance of conservatives over liberals tended to be more divided by party over Bush's performance.[26] The Northeast was less polarized (mainly because of comparatively lower enthusiasm for Bush among Republicans in the

Table 6-4. Partisan Polarization on President Bush's Performance

	Coefficient	S.E.
Independents (%)	0.38***	0.10
Ideological balance[a]	0.18*	0.09
Northeast	−4.38*	1.76
Midwest	4.26*	1.65
Constant	48.82***	4.36
Adjusted R^2	0.42	
Number of cases	50	

Note: The dependent variable is the difference in presidential approval ratings of Democrats and Republicans in the state.

[a] Percent of conservatives minus percent of liberals.

*$p < 0.05$; **$p < 0.01$; ***$p < 0.001$.

region), and the Midwest was more polarized (mainly because of the unusually low ratings Bush received from Democrats in the region).[27] Overall, though, these equations suggest that most of the action is in the constant term—that is, a wide partisan divide was characteristic of all the states.

The same set of variables explains exactly *none* of the variance in degree to which senators receive divergent evaluations from partisans in their states. What does determine the extent of polarization provoked by senators? Table 6-5, which lists all 100 senators in rank order of the difference in average approval ratings between their own and the other party's identifiers, provides some impressionistic evidence regarding several of the explanatory hypotheses sketched out earlier. Senators identifiable as fervent ideologues or as partisan national leaders tended to provoke the most polarized responses. Ted Kennedy and John Kerry topped the list, with Hillary Clinton not far behind. John Thune, who had defeated minority leader Tom Daschle in the most hotly contested Senate contest of 2004—together, Thune and Daschle spent more than $34 million courting South Dakota's 502,000 registered voters—also generated widely divergent partisan responses. So did James Jeffords, whose defection in 2001 cost Republicans control of the Senate for 18 months. Barbara Boxer (sixth) and Russ Feingold (eighth) had the most liberal voting records among Democrats in the 109th Congress. Majority leader Bill Frist, his predecessor, Trent Lott, and Democratic minority leader Harry Reid were also among the top twenty polarizers. At the other end of the list are five senators who won higher evaluations from the opposition party than their own. Three were moderate northeastern Republicans often at odds with their party (Collins, Snowe, and Lincoln Chaffee); the other two, Democrat (later, independent) Joseph Lieberman and Republican Chuck Hagel, defied their party's orthodoxy on Bush's Iraq War, Lieberman as an enthusiastic supporter, Hagel as vocal critic.

Table 6-6 presents a more systematic analysis of the sources of partisan differences in evaluations of senators' job performance. The most consequential variable is clearly the senator's pattern of roll-call votes, measured either as ideological extremity or party unity; the more ideologically extreme or more partisan the voting record, the wider the partisan division on job approval. Setting the other variables at their means, the coefficient estimates the partisan gap to vary from –1 point for the most moderate senator to 42 points for the most extreme senator. Similarly, the gap would vary from –6 points for the least partisan to 36 points for the most partisan senator. Other things equal, prominent partisan leaders provoked substantially more polarized responses, as did—unexpectedly, given the positions of Collins and Snowe on the list in table 6-3—women senators. The gap is also positively related to partisan polarization in

Table 6-5. Partisan Differences in Approval of Senators

Senator	Party/state	Partisan difference	Senator's party	Other party
Kennedy	D-MA	56.8	82.4	25.5
Kerry	D-MA	56.8	77.5	20.7
Thune	R-SD	51.5	81.8	30.3
Clinton	D-NY	49.8	83.7	33.9
Coleman	R-MN	46.7	79.6	32.9
Boxer	D-CA	45.2	72.4	27.2
Murray	D-WA	45.2	76.4	31.2
Feingold	D-WI	43.7	74.1	30.4
Jeffords	I-VT	43.2	80.7	37.5
Leahy	D-VT	43.2	85.8	42.6
Talent	R-MO	42.9	73.2	30.2
Burns	R-MT	41.9	68.3	26.4
Hatch	R-UT	41.8	77.1	35.3
Reid	D-NV	41.2	76.5	35.3
Frist	R-TN	40.8	74.1	33.3
Mikulski	D-MD	39.8	76.2	36.4
Allen	R-VA	39.5	74.4	34.8
Lott	R-MS	39.0	83.8	44.8
Harkin	D-IO	38.9	73.4	34.5
Salazar	D-CO	38.9	77.2	38.3
Lincoln	D-AR	38.2	72.4	34.2
Chambliss	D-GA	37.8	68.5	30.7
Byrd	D-WV	37.7	80.3	42.6
Bond	R-MO	37.5	76.2	38.7
Sununu	R-NH	37.1	69.5	32.4
Feinstein	D-CA	36.8	71.8	35.0
Landrieu	D-LA	36.6	70.2	33.5
Dorgan	D-ND	36.4	87.7	51.3
Craig	R-ID	36.1	74.9	38.8
Cantwell	D-WA	36.1	70.1	34.0
Dole	R-NC	35.5	75.6	40.2
Obama	D-IL	34.9	86.3	51.4
Bennett	R-UT	34.6	70.2	35.6
Brownback	R-KA	34.6	69.8	35.2

Table 6-5. (*continued*)

Senator	Party/state	Partisan difference	Senator's party	Other party
Murkowski	R-AK	33.8	67.7	33.9
Biden	D-DE	33.7	76.9	43.2
Gregg	R-NH	33.2	73.8	40.5
Conrad	D-ND	32.5	86.3	53.8
Isakson	R-GA	32.5	67.0	34.5
Cochran	R-MS	32.3	77.9	45.6
Corzine	D-NJ	32.1	63.9	31.8
Santorum	R-PA	32.0	62.2	30.2
Rockefeller	D-WV	31.7	81.1	49.4
Roberts	R-KN	31.6	69.1	37.5
Inhofe	R-OK	31.5	65.3	33.8
Allard	R-CO	31.5	64.9	33.5
Dayton	D-MN	31.5	60.7	29.2
Martinez	R-FL	31.4	61.9	30.5
McConnell	R-KY	31.3	70.5	39.2
Shelby	R-AL	30.9	76.2	45.2
DeMint	R-SC	30.8	65.5	34.6
Hutchison	R-TX	30.8	76.7	45.8
Crapo	R-ID	30.8	74.5	43.8
Coburn	R-OK	30.3	64.6	34.3
Stevens	R-AK	30.0	80.0	50.0
Session	R-AL	29.8	73.3	43.5
Thomas	R-WY	29.7	73.9	44.2
Kyl	R-AZ	29.4	63.5	34.1
Ensign	R-NV	29.4	69.7	40.3
Enzi	R-WY	29.1	72.6	43.5
Bunning	R-KY	28.5	60.8	32.4
Cornyn	R-TX	28.4	59.2	30.8
Grassley	R-IO	28.1	80.8	52.7
Vitter	R-LA	27.4	77.2	49.8
Pryor	D-AR	27.4	69.8	42.5
Reed	D-RI	27.4	77.4	50.0
Durbin	D-IL	26.8	61.1	34.3
Levin	D-MI	26.6	66.0	39.4

Table 6-5. (*continued*)

Senator	Party/state	Partisan difference	Senator's party	Other party
Kohl	D-WI	26.2	71.1	44.8
Burr	R-NC	25.6	60.5	34.8
Johnson	D-SD	24.9	83.2	58.2
Smith	R-OR	24.8	68.2	43.4
Akaka	D-HI	24.5	72.2	47.8
Alexander	R-TN	24.0	66.6	42.6
Dodd	D-CT	23.8	69.1	45.3
Baucus	D-MT	23.5	75.2	51.7
Wyden	D-OR	23.5	72.4	48.9
Stabenow	D-MI	23.1	58.6	35.5
Bayh	D-IN	22.3	75.5	53.2
Schumer	D-NY	21.9	71.4	49.5
Graham	R-SC	21.4	69.3	47.9
Sarbanes	D-MD	21.4	59.5	38.2
DeWine	R-OH	21.0	58.5	37.5
Lautenberg	D-NJ	21.0	53.7	32.7
Domenici	R-NM	20.2	78.3	58.2
Inouye	D-HI	19.2	80.2	61.0
Warner	R-VA	18.1	69.4	51.3
Lugar	R-IN	15.5	69.8	54.3
Bingaman	R-NM	14.8	68.2	53.4
Voinovich	R-OH	12.5	57.3	44.8
Carper	D-DE	8.8	67.9	59.2
Ben Nelson	D-NE	6.8	72.0	65.2
Bill Nelson	D-FL	4.7	52.8	48.1
McCain	R-AZ	2.6	70.9	68.3
Spector	R-PA	1.9	56.1	54.2
Collins	R-ME	−0.8	72.5	73.3
Lieberman	D-CT	−2.1	63.7	65.8
Snowe	R-ME	−6.6	69.8	76.5
Hagel	R-NE	−7.8	57.3	65.1
Chafee	R-RI	−17.4	42.3	59.7

Note: Data are averages of thirteen monthly polls taken between May 2005 and May 2006 by SurveyUSA; available at http://www.surveyusa.com/50StateTracking.html.

Table 6-6. Partisan Polarization of Senators' Approval Ratings

	Coefficient	S.E.	Coefficient	S.E.
Ideological extremity[a]	13.89***	1.94		
Party unity score[b]			0.73***	0.10
State population[c]	−1.44	1.07	−1.56	1.07
Senator is Republican	−1.02	2.11	−2.03	2.09
Senator is a woman	8.78**	3.10	6.87*	3.05
Partisan leader	13.45***	3.84	11.62**	3.88
Terms served	0.76	0.63	0.15	0.62
Bush polarization[d]	0.64**	0.20	0.58**	0.20
Constant	0.89	13.48	−71.13***	15.19
Adjusted R²	0.44		0.43	
Number of cases	100		100	

Note: The dependent variable is the difference in senatorial approval ratings of Democrats and Republicans in the state.

[a] Log of absolute DW-NOMINATE score.

[b] CQ party unity score.

[c] Log of the number of House seats in the state.

[d] Absolute difference between Republicans' and Democrats' approval of the president in the state (average).

*$p < 0.05$; **$p < 0.01$; ***$p < 0.001$.

evaluations of Bush, suggesting some systematic underlying variation across state electorates in the intensity of partisan divisions. Contrary to expectation, however, state population, though related to overall approval, is not related significantly to partisan polarization.

Why Don't Senators Vote More Moderately?

If ideological extremity and party loyalty cost senators support, why don't they vote more moderately and less loyally? One reason is that ideological extremity and party loyalty do not cost support among the voters who are likely to matter to them. The equations in table 6-7 separate respondents by party identification to show more precisely how a senator's extremity and party loyalty affect partisan performance evaluations. Ideological extremism has a large negative effect on approval ratings offered by people who identify with the party opposite the senator's; the coefficients indicate that approval is about 35 percentage points lower for the most compared to the least extreme Democratic senator and about 27 points lower for the most compared to the least extreme Republican

Table 6-7. Ideological Extremism and Approval of Senators' Performance

Republican senators	Republicans		Democrats		Independents	
	Coefficient	S.E.	Coefficient	S.E.	Coefficient	S.E.
Ideological extremity[a]	3.11[†]	1.84	−8.65***	2.57	−3.92*	1.89
State population[b]	−1.58[†]	0.92	−0.72	1.32	−1.63	0.93
Terms served	1.79**	0.62	2.28*	0.91	1.92**	0.65
Partisan leader	6.38[†]	3.63	−2.67	5.23	2.76	3.76
Woman senator	8.84*	3.20	8.24[†]	4.65	9.49**	3.26
Bush approval (%)	0.66*	0.25	0.35	0.35	0.21	0.24
Constant	17.85	21.37	23.75***	7.14	35.06***	10.10
Adjusted R^2	0.39		0.41		0.41	
Number of cases	55		55		55	
Democratic senators						
Ideological extremity[a]	−12.44***	2.86	1.99	3.24	−2.36	2.70
State population[b]	−1.58	1.25	−4.14**	1.31	−4.59***	1.09
Terms served	−0.17	0.61	0.67	0.67	0.05	0.53
Partisan leader	−11.25**	3.66	6.05	3.80	−0.23	3.14
Woman senator	−9.50**	2.98	4.82	3.14	−1.44	2.61
Bush approval (%)	−0.47[†]	0.23	0.21	0.32	−0.36	0.22
Constant	72.99***	18.15	75.61	5.53	73.22***	7.67
Adjusted R^2	0.57		0.22		0.41	
Number of cases	45		45		45	

Note: The dependent variable, percent approving of the senator's performance, is from the average of thirteen monthly polls taken between May 2005 and May 2006 by SurveyUSA; available at http://www.surveyusa.com/50StateTracking.html.

[a] Log of absolute DW-NOMINATE score.

[b] Log of the number of House seats in the state.

[†] $p < 0.10$; *$p < 0.05$; **$p < 0.01$; ***$p < 0.001$.

senator among such respondents. In contrast, ideological extremism has no significant effect at all on how partisans rate senators of their own party. More extreme senators get lower marks from independents, although the effect is statistically significant only for Republicans. In sum, ideologues in office may alienate rival partisans, but they do not appear to displease their own partisans in the least and do not put off independents to the extent that it might raise serious political problems.

Note also that Republican respondents' ratings of senators are related to their ratings of Bush; the larger the proportion who approve of Bush, the larger the proportion who approve of Republican senators and the smaller the proportion who approve of Democratic senators. There is no significant aggregate relationship, however, between Democratic or independent respondents' ratings of the president and senators of either party. A similar pattern of results appears when the senator's party unity score replaces ideological extremity in the equation (results not shown). Party loyalty has its largest effect on the approval ratings of partisans of the opposite party, with approval among Democratic respondents estimated to be 32 points lower for the most compared to the least partisan Republican senator, and approval among Republican respondents 27 points lower for the most compared to the least partisan Democratic senator. Again, party loyalty hurts Republican senators among independents (a 16-point decline from least to most loyal), but it does not affect ratings of Democratic senators by either Democrats or independents.

A third measure of roll-call behavior, presidential support, reiterates these patterns but with a notable twist: presidential support affects evaluations of Republican senators more powerfully than it does evaluations of Democratic senators. The evidence is in table 6-8. Senate Republicans apparently partook of Bush's status as a highly polarizing figure to the extent that they did his bidding on the floor. Democrats rated them lower the more they lined up with the president, as did, to a lesser but still notable extent, independents. Republican senators' approval ratings among Republican identifiers are positively related to their level of support for the president's policies even when approval of the president is also included in the equation. Republican respondents also regarded Democratic senators more favorably the greater their support for the president's agenda, but ratings offered by Democrats and independents were, in the aggregate, unaffected one way or the other. Observe that coefficients in tables 6-7 and 6-8 indicate that approval of Republican but not Democratic senators increases with years of service among respondents in all partisan categories.

Overall, these results suggest that the variables affecting partisan responses differ for Republican and Democratic senators and thus so must the sources of partisan polarization. Analyses replicating the equations

Table 6-8. Presidential Support and Approval of Senators' Performance

Republican senators	Republicans		Democrats		Independents	
	Coefficient	S.E.	Coefficient	S.E.	Coefficient	S.E.
Presidential support[a]	0.38†	0.19	−1.07***	0.23	−0.53**	0.19
State population[b]	−2.16*	0.98	0.78	1.28	−0.78	0.98
Terms served	1.40*	0.57	3.37***	0.76	2.40***	0.57
Partisan leader	6.22†	3.60	−2.05	4.81	2.77	3.64
Woman senator	7.85*	3.00	9.31*	4.03	9.98**	3.02
Bush approval (%)	0.62*	0.25	0.25	0.30	0.28	0.23
Constant	−13.32	17.21	122.82***	18.52	80.59***	13.71
Adjusted R²	0.40		0.50		0.44	
Number of cases	55		55		55	
Democratic senators						
Presidential support[a]	0.60***	0.16	−0.17	0.17	0.12	0.15
State population[b]	−2.55*	1.25	−4.11**	1.25	−4.76***	1.05
Terms served	−0.30	0.63	0.60	0.66	0.03	0.53
Partisan leader	−11.05**	3.83	5.87	3.78	−0.11	3.16
Woman senator	−9.57**	3.12	4.99	3.13	−1.47	2.62
Bush approval (%)	−0.59*	0.26	0.29	0.33	−0.38	0.24
Constant	67.64***	19.03	80.62***	8.52	70.92***	8.32
Adjusted R²	0.53		0.23		0.40	
Number of cases	45		45		45	

Note: The dependent variable, percent approving of the senator's performance, is from the average of thirteen monthly polls taken between May 2005 and May 2006 by SurveyUSA; available at http://www.surveyusa.com/50StateTracking.html.
[a] CQ presidential support score averaged for 2005 and 2006.
[b] Log of the number of House seats in the state.
†$p < 0.10$; *$p < 0.05$; **$p < 0.01$; ***$p < 0.001$.

in table 6-6 but with senators separated by party confirm this conclusion (tables 6-9a and 6-9b). The extent of polarization provoked by ideological extremity, party unity, and presidential support tends to be greater for Republican than for Democratic senators, as is the effect of partisan differences on approval of President Bush. Perhaps because Republicans exercised majority control at the time and shared a highly divisive president's party label, partisan evaluations of Republican senators were more acutely sensitive to the degree of partisanship and presidential support displayed in their roll-call voting. It is also evident from these equations that only the Democratic women were significantly more polarizing then men and that Democrat partisan leaders were more polarizing than their Republican counterparts.

In general, Republicans paid a political price for polarizing their constituencies; there is a modest but statistically significant negative relationship ($r = -0.35$) between degree of polarization and a Republican senator's overall approval rating, and regression estimates suggest that the most polarizing Republican senator would be rated about 13 points lower than the least polarizing. Among Democratic senators, in contrast,

Table 6-9a. Partisan Polarization of Republican Senators' Approval Ratings

	Coefficient	S.E.	Coefficient	S.E.	Coefficient	S.E.
Ideological extremity[a]	12.91***	2.52				
Party unity score[b]			0.84***	0.13		
Presidential support score[c]					1.55***	0.25
State population[d]	–1.15	1.51	–1.24	1.35	–3.40*	1.45
Senator is a woman	1.20	5.37	–0.56	4.60	–1.16	4.77
Partisan leader	1.38	6.17	6.43	5.60	9.11	5.76
Terms served	–0.20	1.03	–1.07	0.88	–1.89*	0.90
Bush polarization[e]	0.98**	0.32	0.77**	0.29	0.71*	0.30
Constant	–21.72	21.38	–91.98***	20.95	–144.79***	26.81
Adjusted R^2	0.44		0.55		0.52	
Number of cases	55		55		55	

Table 6-9b. Partisan Polarization of Democratic Senators' Approval Ratings

	Coefficient	S.E.	Coefficient	S.E.	Coefficient	S.E.
Ideological extremity[a]	11.72**	3.66				
Party unity score[b]			0.41*	.16		
Presidential support score[c]					−0.55**	0.19
State population[d]	−2.57	1.62	−2.06	1.68	−1.71	1.58
Senator is a woman	14.36***	3.71	13.64**	4.02	14.42***	3.96
Partisan leader	16.47***	4.69	16.15**	4.92	16.05**	4.81
Terms served	1.20	0.80	1.26	0.84	1.35	0.81
Bush polarization[e]	0.40	0.24	0.44[†]	0.25	0.44[†]	0.25
Constant	12.50	17.47	−37.85[†]	20.59	22.25	19.76
Adjusted R^2	0.47		0.42		0.45	
Number of cases	45		45		45	

Note: The dependent variable is the difference in senatorial approval ratings of Democrats and Republicans in the state.
[a] Log of absolute DW-NOMINATE score.
[b] CQ party unity score, average of 2005 and 2006.
[c] CQ presidential support score, average of 2005 and 2006.
[d] Log of the number of House seats in the state.
[e] Republican minus Democratic approval of the president in the state (average).
[†] $p < 0.10$; *$p < 0.05$; **$p < 0.01$; ***$p < 0.001$.

polarization is unrelated to overall approval rating ($r = -0.05$). Moreover, as noted in the discussion of table 6-3, Republican senators generally tended to receive lower approval ratings. This difference may simply expose one cost of majority control, which Republicans enjoyed in 2006: the exigencies of party discipline and pressures to remain loyal to a controversial president may have compelled Republicans to take divisive or unpopular positions, while Democrats—at least those without aspirations to national party leadership—were freer to back the president selectively as it suited their personal preferences or political needs.

Adapting to Constituencies

The results presented so far suggest that ideological extremism and party loyalty should be a problem only for senators representing states tilting away from their party, which leaves senators the option of avoiding political problems by adapting their roll-call behavior to local political sentiments. The wisdom of doing is apparent from the literature, as is, by various measures, the practice.[28] Despite historically high levels of partisanship and ideological polarization on the Hill, the senators in the 109th Congress continued to display considerable strategic adaptation to local political leanings. Initial evidence is provided by the regression equations in table 6-10, which examine the effects of state partisanship on ideological extremism and party support among senators.

The distribution of partisans clearly affects a senator's ideological extremism and level of party support, but it is the relative proportion of Republican identifiers that evidently matters for senators of both parties; the proportion of Democratic identifiers has no significant effect and, for Republican senators, displays the wrong sign. These party differences arise because an unusually large proportion of respondents in the very liberal states of the Northeast (especially Massachusetts, Rhode Island, Vermont, and Connecticut) identify themselves as independents rather than as Democrats.[29] Thus, the decisive component of state partisanship seems to be the proportion of Republicans relative to that of non-Republicans. The greater the proportion of Republican identifiers in the state, the more conservative and loyal to party a Republican senator was likely to be; the smaller the proportion of Republicans represented, the more liberal and partisan the Democratic senator. The coefficients estimate Republicans' DW-NOMINATE scores to vary from 0.115 to 0.793, and Democrats' scores to vary from −0.712 to −0.199, between the least and most Republican states they represent.[30] Similarly, Republicans' party unity scores are estimated to vary from 67 percent to 100 percent, and Democrats' party unity scores, from 100 percent to 71 percent, as the proportion of Republicans in a state ranges from its lowest to highest values.

Presidential support scores offer additional evidence that senators adapted their voting patterns to local sentiments (table 6-11). Controlling for party (which of course makes a huge difference), the higher Bush's approval rating in a state, the higher a senator's presidential support score; for every additional percentage point approval, support for the president's agenda is estimated to rise 0.6 percentage points. When senators and respondents are separated by party, the results suggest that senators were more responsive to their own than to the other party's partisans and that Democratic senators were affected more strongly by their constituents' views of Bush than were Republican senators. This latter result probably reflects differences in the pressure to support or oppose the president between the two party coalitions noted earlier; Republican senators, under greater compulsion to stick with their party's leader, tended to offer high levels of support across the board, while Democrats were freer to support or oppose the president selectively as circumstances dictated.[31]

Table 6-10. State Partisanship and Senators' Voting Patterns

| | Republican senators | | | | Democratic senators | | | |
| | DW-NOMINATE | | Party support | | DW-NOMINATE | | Party support | |
	Coefficient	S.E.	Coefficient	S.E.	Coefficient	S.E.	Coefficient	S.E.
Republicans (%)	0.058***	0.012	1.05***	0.20	−0.042***	0.009	−1.10***	0.20
Democrats (%)	0.023†	0.012	0.28	0.20	0.013	0.010	0.29	0.22
Constant	−3.84***	0.677	41.64***	11.4	−0.207***	0.479	110.37***	10.4
Adjusted R2	0.28		0.31		0.34		0.42	
Number of cases	55		55		45		45	

Note: The dependent variables are the log of absolute DW-NOMINATE score and average CQ party support score for the two sessions of the 109th Congress (2005–2006).

†$p < 0.10$; ***$p < 0.001$.

Table 6-11. State Presidential Approval and Presidential Support among
Senators

	All senators		Republican senators		Democratic senators	
	Coefficient	S.E.	Coefficient	S.E.	Coefficient	S.E.
Statewide approval (%)	0.61***	0.09				
Senator is Republican	37.60***	1.32				
Democrats' approval (%)			0.20	0.18	0.83**	0.25
Republicans' approval (%)			0.67***	0.18	0.55**	0.20
Constant	23.04	3.64	32.84*	13.42	−5.81*	15.14
Adjusted R²	0.93		0.27		0.31	
Number of cases	100		55		45	

Note: The dependent variable is average CQ presidential support score for 2005 and 2006.
$*p < 0.05; **p < 0.01; ***p < 0.001$.

Discussion

By the evidence presented here, polarized politics may be a prominent
feature of national politics, but the extent to which the public responds
to politicians in partisan terms depends on how closely they are identified
with their own side in the partisan battles waged in the capitol. When it
comes to provoking widely divergent partisan reactions, George W. Bush,
as the alpha Republican, was in a class by himself. Partisanship and ideology almost completely determine the state-level distribution of popular
responses to the president, just as they determined his vote in the ex-
traordinarily partisan election of 2004.[32] Yet these variables have little
to do with senators' job approval ratings. Even though senators usually
receive higher ratings from their own than from the other party's partisans, the effect of variation in the distribution of partisans across states
is swamped by the much larger interstate variations in approval within
partisan categories (evident in figure 6-4).

Senators inspire polarized responses from their constituents mainly
to the degree that they vote like ideologues or party loyalists and take a
leading role in the partisan skirmishes on the Hill. Senators who compile
more moderate voting records and avoid high national profiles as partisan

leaders enjoy greater cross-party support; those displaying the opposite characteristics tend to be the leading polarizers. The most prominent national figures among Democratic senators—Kerry, Kennedy, and Clinton, once and future presidential candidates all—were only a little less polarizing than Bush. National prominence and presidential ambitions are not inevitably divisive, however; John McCain had approval ratings nearly as high among Arizona's Democrats (68 percent) as among its Republicans (71 percent). He was, not coincidentally, 49th in presidential and party support and 37th in roll-call conservatism among the 55 Republican senators in the 109th Congress. Barack Obama, who announced his presidential candidacy only at the end of the period surveyed, also enjoyed bipartisan support; he was approved by an average of 51 percent of Republicans as well as 86 percent of Democrats in his state during this period despite a voting record to the left of the Democratic average.

Moderation among senators represents strategic adaptation as well as, presumably, personal preferences. Senators' roll-call ideologies, party unity scores, and presidential support scores all reflect the ideological and partisan makeup of their states (as well as, of course, their party affiliation). Senators representing states where the opposing party predominates are of necessity inclined to moderation and consequently tend to be less polarizing figures than senators enjoying a better partisan and ideological fit with their constituencies. Indeed, senators holding seats against their state's partisan grain could not survive politically without the kind of cross-party appeal that reduces polarization.[33] Not every senator puts prudence ahead of principle, but those who don't pay a political price: lower approval ratings and greater electoral risk. Pennsylvania's Rick Santorum, a dedicated social conservative representing a moderate, Democratic-leaning state, is a case in point. He was the lowest rated senator during the period analyzed (43 percent approving) and lost in 2006, winning only 41 percent of the vote.

Santorum is, however, only the most extreme exemplar of a more general implication of the results presented here: most senators would be more popular with their constituents if they were more moderate and less partisan. Put another way, they would receive higher approval ratings if they moved closer to the state's median voter. That most senators do not do so is open to several explanations. First, most are popular enough to retain their seats already; more than three-quarters enjoy the approval of a majority of their constituents (recall figure 6-1). Second, they have to worry about primary as well as general elections and so must pay attention to their own partisans, whose views may diverge significantly from the median constituent's. This is, of course, the canonical if not unchallenged explanation for the absence of Downsian convergence on the position of the median voter,[34] and the 2006 election provided some

concrete examples in the form of Lieberman, defeated in the Connecticut Democratic primary by liberal insurgent Ted Lamont for supporting
Bush's Iraq war too enthusiastically, and Chaffee, by far the most liberal
Republican, who won renomination by only 54–46 against a conservative primary challenger.[35] Third, and probably most important, most
senators prefer to support their party and its positions because they are
themselves partisans and ideologues (through self-selection and social-
ization into political careers[36]) and so act as such unless moderation is a
condition of political survival.

Santorum's fate raises the question of how accurately approval ratings
predicted election results in 2006 for senators seeking reelection. The answer is quite accurately indeed, especially among Republicans (table 6-12).
For example, the equation predicts the lowest rated Republican in 2005
(Santorum at 50 percent) to win 40.9 percent of the vote; his actual vote
was 41.3 percent. It predicts the highest rated Republican (Snowe at 78
percent) to win 79.7 percent; her actual vote was 78.2 percent. A full analysis of the electoral consequences of senators' approval ratings required
a separate study.[37] Its most salient finding is that the lower a Republican
senator's 2005 approval ratings (average from May through December),
the stronger the opposition he or she attracted, and the stronger the opposition, the more the approval rating declined over the election year, and
the worse that Republican did on election day. Among Democrats, the
strongly pro-Democratic political climate yielded relatively weak opponents and comfortable reelection margins, although their 2005 approval
ratings also had a significant effect on just how comfortable they were
(table 6-12). Among the six losing Republicans, only Santorum was conspicuously out of ideological sync with his state.[38] Most of them were,

Table 6-12. Approval in 2005 and Election Results in 2006

	Republican senators		Democratic senators	
	Coefficient	S.E.	Coefficient	S.E.
Approval, May–December 2005	1.39***	0.13	0.71***	0.17
Constant	−28.37**	7.90	19.32	10.95
Adjusted R^2	0.91		0.56	
Number of cases	13		13	

Note: The dependent variable is senator's share of the major-party vote in 2006; omitted are Luger (IN), who ran unopposed, and Lieberman (CT), who lost his primary and ran as an Independent against both a Democrat and a Republican.
**$p < 0.01$; ***$p < 0.001$.

however, relatively unpopular well before the election year and faced an unfavorable state partisan balance, which proved to be a major burden in a year when Democratic voters were eager to express their unhappiness with the Bush administration. The most notable example was Chaffee, who lost his reelection bid in Rhode Island, where Democrats outnumber Republicans two to one, despite having by far the most liberal voting record of any Republican senator and higher approval ratings from Democrats than from Republicans in his state (table 6-5).

Electorates became more polarized during the campaign in their reactions to the twenty-nine senators who ran for reelection in 2006; nineteen provoked wider partisan differences in the November 2006 SurveyUSA polls than they had in the May 2005–June 2006 polls, with an average increase in the partisan gap of about 5 percentage points. Most of this increase came from a decline in approval among opposite-party identifiers and was largest in the most competitive races.[39] For senators not on the ballot in 2006, the average partisan gap remained virtually unchanged.

Perhaps the most surprising finding here is that women senators, at least the nine Democrats, tended to be significantly more polarizing than the men. This pattern holds at the level of individual states as well as across the entire set of senators; in the eight states with Senate delegations split by gender, the woman was the more polarizing figure in seven. (Debbie Stabenow of Michigan was, by a small margin, the exception.) The average partisan approval gap is 10 points wider for the female than for the male senators in these states. The equations in table 6-7 suggest that this phenomenon was driven largely by Republican identifiers, who gave Republican women significantly higher ratings and Democratic women significantly lower ratings than their male counterparts. Democratic identifiers, in contrast, rated women higher than men regardless of party, although the estimated coefficient achieves statistical significance only when both parties' senators are analyzed together (results not shown). I have no satisfactory explanation for these patterns, but they might reflect stereotypes. Democrats may perceive women as more inclined to share their concerns regarding health, education, the environment, welfare, and so forth, regardless of party. The same image may lead Republican identifiers to regard and disdain Democratic women as bleeding heart liberals, while the Republican label offsets the stereotype as it applies to the Republican women.

Finally, it is worth considering whether George W. Bush was a uniquely polarizing figure or whether evaluations of any contemporary president would divide state electorates along party lines more widely than would evaluations of the typical senator. There is no question that Bush was the most polarizing president since approval data have been gathered, but the average partisan differences in evaluations of Clinton (55 percentage points in the 209 surveys taken by Gallup during his administration) and Ronald Reagan (53 points in 134 Gallup surveys) were also much wider than the 2005–2006 average for senators, as were partisan differences in approval of Bush's father by the final year of his administration (54 points). One has to go back to Jimmy Carter (26 points in 90 surveys) and Gerald Ford (31 points in 35 surveys) to find presidents with average partisan approval gaps similar to those of the typical senator in the 109th Congress. But back then, assessments of senators were almost certainly much less partisan than they have since become, for the American polity as a whole was much less polarized along party lines that it had become by the this century.

The tendency for people to assess presidents in more distinctly partisan terms than senators probably arises from differences in both the offices and their electoral constituencies. It is not simply that executives are inherently more polarizing than legislators; in the SurveyUSA data, evaluations of governors are actually slightly less polarized by party than evaluation of senators.[40] But the president is a national executive with a national constituency who attains office through a thoroughly partisan electoral process. Although in times of national crisis, leaders and ordinary Americans of all political persuasions have rallied to the president (the partisan gap in approval of Bush averaged only 18 points in the months after the terrorist attacks of September 11, 2001), under more normal circumstances, partisanship dominates the entire process of policy making in Washington and thus also public reactions to its leading participants. It is not hard to imagine a contemporary president less polarizing than George W. Bush, but it is hard to imagine one who could govern in a truly bipartisan fashion without alienating his own political base.

Serving narrower statewide rather than national constituencies, senators can (and as we have seen, often do) tailor their actions to fit local political conditions. Although constrained by party, they enjoy substantial leeway in responding to constituents' interests and opinions as they deem prudent. They also enjoy ample opportunities for advertising, position-taking, and credit claiming (notably for "pork"), as well as a variety of procedures for avoiding the traceable actions that might offend constituents.[41] All of them maintain local offices that deliver a variety of constituency services on a nonpartisan basis. It is thus not surprising that many senators are able to attract bipartisan support; more than half of the 100 senators examined here were approved by at least 40 percent of opposition partisans, and 23 were approved by majorities of them. Not coincidentally, election results mirror senators' advantages over presidents in this regard. In the American National Election Studies (ANES) conducted from 1992 through 2004, an average of 28.5 percent of partisans reported defecting to incumbent senators, only 9.3 percent to their opponents.

The comparable figures for the three presidents seeking reelection during this period are 12.7 percent and 8.2 percent, respectively.

Notes

1. For a full set of citations to this extensive literature, see Jacobson (2011).

2. See, for example, Sinclair (2006); Fiorina, Abrams, and Pope (2006); Bond and Fleisher (2000); Jacobson (2007); McCarty, Poole, and Rosenthal (2006); Stonecash, Brewer, and Mariani (2003).

3. Jacobson (2011); Abramowitz (2010); Levendusky, (2010); Bafumi and Shapiro, (2009).

4. Jacobson (2011).

5. After 2008, it was 77 percent; Jacobson (2005), pp. 206–210.

6. Similar cases appeared in 2008—for example, Susan Collins won 61 percent of the vote while Barack Obama was winning 59 percent in Maine.

7. Based on the SurveyUSA data I describe later.

8. The data can be accessed at http://www.surveyusa.com/50StateTracking .html.

9. Jacobson (2006b), appendix.

10. In 129 media-sponsored surveys taken over the same period, Bush's average approval rating was 40.4 percent; the population-weighted national average from SurveyUSA's polls is slightly smaller than the unweighted average of the state data.

11. In the 1,300 possible direct comparisons, the senator was rated higher than Bush in 91.8 percent of the cases, Bush higher in 6.8 percent, with the rest tied. Nearly every Democratic senator enjoyed higher approval ratings than Bush in his or her state (98.8 percent), as did most Republican senators (86.2 percent).

12. For this and subsequent analyses, I use the averages from the thirteen monthly surveys, producing 50 or 100 rather than 450 or 900 observations; this avoids artificially inflating the precision of the estimated coefficients and the problem of correlated errors across repeated observations for the same state. The standard deviation of the thirteen monthly ratings of senators averaged 2.63 percentage points across the fifty states. (The standard deviation of this mean standard deviation was 0.77 point.) There was no discernible overall trend in senators' approval rates over this period. For Bush, the standard deviation of the thirteen monthly ratings averaged 3.58 points across states. (The standard deviation of this average was 0.67 point.) The higher state-level variance of Bush's ratings is an artifact of the downward trend in his approval levels, which fell from about 45 to about 36 percent approving over the thirteen months examined here.

13. These variables also, as would be expected from the first equation, predict his 2004 vote with great precision; for that equation (not shown), the adjusted R^2 is 0.93 and the root mean square error is 2.23.

14. I did not enter percent conservative and percent liberal separately because they are so highly collinear ($r = -0.94$).

15. Jacobson (2011).

16. Binder, Maltzman, and Sigelman (1998); Hibbing and Alford (1990); Oppenheimer (1996).

17. Available courtesy of Keith T. Poole at http://voteview.com/dwnl.htm; I choose the log transformation on the basis of fit.

18. From *CQ Weekly*, January 9, 2006, p. 99, and January 1, 2007, p. 42.

19. These two variables are correlated at .90 and thus need to be entered separately to avoid multicollinearity.

20. The party difference is largely a product of controlling for ideological balance. On average, conservatives outnumber liberals by 19 percentage points. If this variable is normalized around its mean value, the coefficient on Republican falls to –3.35, near its value when the ideological balance variable is omitted entirely.

21. Jacobson (2011), p. 6.

22. Hibbing and Alford (1990); Oppenheimer (1996).

23. Based on 59 *CBS News/New York Times* and Gallup polls take between May 2005 and May 2006.

24. The 17 cases involved four senators: John Kerry (5), Ted Kennedy (5), Hilary Clinton (6), and Barbara Boxer (1), a list pointing to one obvious source of variation in partisan differences in assessments of senators; I will have more to say about this shortly.

25. Jacobson (2011), p. 267.

26. In states where the local ethos produces a large proportion of self-declared independents, the remaining party identifiers are probably on average more determinedly partisan than elsewhere.

27. Jacobson (2006b).

28. Erikson (1990); Whitby and Bledsoe (1986); Binder, Maltzman, and Sigelman (1998); Wright and Berkman (1986); Canes-Wrone, Brady, and Cogan (2002); Wright (1989); Wood and Andersson (1998); Shapiro et al. (1990); and Bishin (2000).

29. The percentage of Republicans and conservatives is highly correlated across the states ($r = 0.78$), but there is virtually no relationship between the percentage of Democrats and liberals ($r = 0.04$); rather, positive relationship is between the percentages of independents and liberals ($r = 0.61$).

30. With the proportion of Democrats set at the mean; recall that the DW-NOMINATE takes values from 1 (most conservative) to –1 (most liberal).

31. Cohen et al. (2000) also find that out-party senators are more sensitive to state-level approval, but they do not detect the more general effect of presidential approval documented here.

32. Jacobson (2005), pp. 209–210.

33. The average partisan gap in approval of the 27 senators representing states where their party has fewer partisans than the other party is 23 points; for the other 73, it is 30 points, a significant difference ($p = 0.013$). The entire difference is accounted for by the higher approval ratings offered by the rival party's partisans (an average of 47 percent for the former group, 40 percent for the latter).

34. Aranson and Ordeshook (1972); Aldrich (1983); and Ansolabehere, Snyder, and Stewart (2001).

35. Lieberman eventually won reelection as an independent by winning support from Republican voters. Chaffee received the lowest approval rating from his own partisans of any senator (42.3 percent); remarkably, Rhode Island Republicans gave Democrat Jack Reed higher ratings (50.0 percent) than they did Chaffee, even though Reed was far more liberal and more consistently opposed to Bush's agenda.

36. Fiorina, Abrams, and Pope (2006).

37. Brown and Jacobson (2008).

38. The other losers were Allen (VA), Burns (MT), Chaffee (RI), DeWine (OH), and Talent (MO).

39. For details, see Brown and Jacobson (2008).

40. Jacobson (2006b).

41. Mayhew (1974a); Arnold (1990).

VII

Political Participation, Polarization, and Public Opinion

ACTIVISM AND THE MERGING OF PARTISAN AND IDEOLOGICAL POLARIZATION

John H. Aldrich and Melanie Freeze

THE STUDY OF THE POLITICS of the post–World War II era has benefited greatly from what is now a considerable period of systematic data gathering. What Stimson and his colleagues have called "macro-politics"[1] is only possible because of the fifty years or more of such systematic and consistent measurement. One of the consequences of this cumulative database has been the identification and study of a number of dynamic aspects important to American politics, such as those studied in the Stimson et al. program. For example, it has enabled the study of issue evolution and the effect of civil rights and social issues such as abortion on party coalitions,[2] the variation in partisanship as a function of changes in the economy,[3] and so on.

Here, we propose one new variable for consideration, an apparent increase in the use of the liberal-conservative dimension in American politics by elites, activists, and, most surprisingly, the general public. We thus consider how dynamics in public opinion combine with changes in participation and in the degree of elite (specifically, congressional) polarization in this regard. We take the importance of changes in the participation and polarization factors to be evident. Certainly, variation in political participation, especially turnout, has garnered a great deal of attention for decades. The existence, cause, and effects of elite polarization originally went less fully noticed, but it has recently become one of the most widely studied dynamics by scholars and is regularly discussed by the public. We therefore begin by discussing the systematic changes in polarization and participation. Since the importance of a liberal-conservative dimension and left-right thinking in the public may be of less obvious importance for understanding American politics, given its peripheral position in the study of public opinion since Campbell et al. and Converse,[4] we develop a set of claims regarding its existence and relevance and then consider how it might fit into the polarization-participation-public opinion dynamics. We draw on data from American National Election Studies

(ANES) surveys, surveys of donors to political campaigns, and surveys of delegates to national conventions to support our arguments.

Outline of Some Systemic Changes

Elite polarization, we claim, had among its many results one effect of particular importance for our account. The increased homogeneity of public pronouncements and of the actual behavior of political elites—candidates, officeholders, activists—imbued the party label with more meaning. In the language favored by game theoretic accounts,[5] the party has a "reputation" that provides substantive content to its label and "separates" it (in equilibrium) from its opponent's reputation. While in principle, a party reputation could be about many things, in practice, as in this particular case, the reputation is about what the party stands for—and acts on—in terms of policy. Further, it is not just that the two parties differ consistently on one or two issues, but they do so over a whole range of issues. The sufficiently large clustering of partisan differences on this set of issues has come to define at the same time what we mean by what Democrats and what Republicans stand for and differ on, and also what we mean by what liberals and what conservatives stand for and differ on. That is, party and ideology have become bundled and interwoven.

As a result, the party affiliation of the candidate or officeholder increasingly conveyed policy content to the public. Indeed, at the extreme, even longtime members of Congress (MCs) who had developed a close, personal following in their constituency were affected by their party's reputation. Or, at least, it is alleged that MCs such as Senator Lincoln Chafee (Republican, Rhode Island) and Representative Christopher Shays (Republican, Connecticut) were weakened in the electorate because, even though the constituents favored their personal policy stances and actions, by voting for them, the public knew that they were also voting to strengthen a Republican Party whose stances and actions the constituents did not favor. And the conservative white southern Democrat was vulnerable on the other side. As Senator Jesse Helms (Republican, North Carolina) liked to say in his campaigns, his opponent was just another "liberal, Massachusetts Kennedy Democrat."

The development of a policy-based party reputation at the elite level, in turn, had two results at the mass level. First, partisanship, which had at least marginally weakened in the late 1960s and into the 1970s, stopped such a "decline," quite possibly because it began to become increasingly clear what the party with whom one identified actually stood for.[6] As we will see shortly, party identification became increasingly entwined with left-right ideology in the public. Second, not only did the public begin to see bigger differences between the two parties, but they, too, began to act on it. Turnout, that is, which either slumped in the same period as party identification or at least was stagnant,[7] began to rise. Currently, the United States no longer competes with Switzerland for the status of lowest rate of participation among advanced democracies, but it has moved up to challenge other advanced democracies such as Canada and Britain.

The argument, to this point, takes the political elite as the driving force of these dynamics. But, of course, if by "political elites" we mean officeholders such as members of Congress, then it is not particularly obvious why they would be leading such a set of changes if all they want is to be Mayhew's "seekers of reelection."[8] The question is why polarization?

Rohde and Aldrich give one answer.[9] The effect of civil rights legislation was to fundamentally alter the South and make it possible for Republicans to contest there, and once contesting, to take over the conservative wing of southern electorates and congressional delegations. The inclusion of African Americans (and many poorer whites) in the southern electorate greatly expanded its left wing, so that southern Democratic officeholders would have reelection constituencies that were now at least moderate in national terms. That is, from a very diverse coalition, the Democratic Party at the national level lost most of its conservative wing and picked up at least moderate seats in their place. Furthermore, the Republican Party lost its liberal "Rockefeller Republican" wing, quite possibly in reaction to the party's "southern strategy," and thus lost its hold on New England, California, and so on. Of course, there was more than "just" race, but also the coming of social issues and so forth that reinforce this basic story. By picking up conservative seats and losing liberal ones, the Republican Party, too, became more homogenous.

What is unexplained in this account is why Republican and Democrat officeholders with the exact same constituency are at times ideologically different. The evidence is quite clear that the gap between senators from the same state but different parties is just as large as the gap between those who are from different states.[10] There are, of course, a number of answers. One possibility is that candidates and officeholders are not Mayhew's single-minded seekers of reelection, but have policy preferences of their own (and act on them, as in Fenno's "seekers of good public policy"[11]). If so, homogenous parties might well be attracting potential candidates who personally agree with the party's stance. Republicans can no longer attract many Rockefeller Republicans, nor can Democrats attract those as (racially) conservative as was Senator Richard Russell (Democrat, Georgia).

Alternatively, there might be centrifugal pressures in addition to the centripetal ones that dominate such majoritarian accounts of elite politics as Krehbiel's.[12] Primary elections (or their caucus/convention counterparts) make it important that candidates for nomination be at least marginally pleasing, if not much more so, to partisans in the nominating constituency, and these are less likely to be the moderates found in larger proportions in general elections. (Note that this requires voters to employ some sort of liberal or conservative ideas; see the following discussion.)

A second, and not independent, source of external centrifugal pressures is from activists. Indeed, not only primary voters but activists of all kinds with resources at their command exert considerable centrifugal pressure on candidates and officeholders, we believe. Their ability to contribute scarce—and necessary—resources is valuable in the primary campaign, of course, but not only there. It is also at least as valuable in the general election and usually more so as the resource demands are usually far higher for general than primary campaigning. Indeed, activists' contributions of resources may be valuable even before the nominations, in amassing a war chest to ward off potential challengers. More recently, MCs have even found such resources valuable within office, as, at the extreme, the Republican House leadership, when it was in the majority, selected committee chairs based in part on what they had contributed to the House Party and its other candidates.

The theory on activists and their typically more extreme views on policy dimensions is well developed.[13] Partisan activists are, according to this model, toward the extreme on the major dimension of party cleavage, in equilibrium. Indeed, they may define what the dimension of partisan cleavages is. Of course, "party activists" is a generalized term that includes not only those directly working within the party, but a term that applies to those who contribute to its candidates, and applies even to interest groups and political action committees (PACs) that have become formally or informally affiliated with a party.[14] In any event, the seeking of resources requires working with activists who typically are more extreme than voters or even officeholders—and as we will see, increasingly so over this period.

The result is, we believe, a strong step toward a more complete explanation of the dynamics in recent decades among polarization, participation, and public opinion (particularly partisanship and its relationship to ideology). Let us briefly consider those dynamics and how they may relate this set of forces we have identified.

Dynamics and Their Linkages

Consider first polarization. There is no question in the discipline about its increase at the elite level, such as among MCs. The linkage between any apparent enhanced relevance of liberal-conservativeness in the public with increased ideological divergence between the parties is straightforward. Indeed, it may be a part of what we *mean* by "increased polarization." While it is unclear just how much of an increase there is in partisan polarization of the public,[15] there is no doubt about increased polarization among politically active groups, the two parties, and their respective candidates and their officeholders. What we show is that there is such a connection, and it appears that the public follows the parties in this regard, or perhaps more accurately, the relevance of liberal-conservative considerations to the citizen depends on it being a politically potent tool for understanding the choices with which they are faced.

Consider next political participation. Turnout slumped over the 1960s and 1970s. Wolfinger and Rosenstone studied the differences between individuals and among electoral rules in their landmark study.[16] Their work was often used to address Brody's famous "puzzle" of declining electoral participation. The decline in turnout was a puzzle because it happened in spite of many things that should have led to increased turnout in the United States in this period.[17] Rosenstone and Hansen added a key new element to the account when they found that declines in turnout were due to decreased mobilization efforts by the parties.[18] The parties at this time tended to spend their resources more on broadcast advertising (aka the "air wars") at the expense of securing activists to conduct direct contacting to mobilize (aka the "ground wars"). As they were writing, however, turnout in the United States began to increase and is now approaching levels of other advanced democracies.[19] A part of this increase is attributed to the actions taken by political parties—that is, to their use of activists and resources that party activists command to generate more and more effective mobilization. Martinez has studied this increase and found that "[a] little more than half of the recent increase in turnout can be attributed to the continuing growth of educational opportunities in the United States," while

> Most of the rest of the recent surge in turnout reflects the uptick in contacting by groups and especially by parties, as well as a greater ability on the part of the public to discern differences between the two major parties. These findings underscore the robustness of Rosenstone and Hansen's explanation that mobilization was the key to understanding patterns of electoral participation, as contacting was a significant correlate of participation both as turnout declined and as it rebounded. While differences in individuals' abilities, opportunities, and incentives explain much of the cross-sectional variation in turnout, changes in the level of campaigns' direct interactions with potential voters drives much of the aggregate variation in turnout over time.[20]

This relationship between having forces to mobilize the vote in a context in which the voter sees greater differences between the two parties, differences often rooted in left-right divisions, is the first major component in our explanation of the relationship among these various systemic changes.

In this inquiry, we examine these questions through use of the seven-point left-right continuum to shed light on these various changes and how they may—or may not—be related. In particular, we examine self-placement of a variety of political actors on this scale as a means of assessing the relationship between ideology, participation, and polarization. The idea of the public thinking and acting along liberal-conservative lines runs contrary to the thrust of the literature on public opinion and voting behavior, so we next develop the theory underlying that notion.

Theory: Left and Right in Mass Publics

Converse famously argued that the American public was unable to use a simple liberal-conservative conception of politics to make sense of politics.[21] In this, he did not really disagree with Lane when Lane found that careful in-depth analysis revealed that even ordinary voters held reasonably complex understandings about politics.[22] Lane, however, was discovering relationships among policies, parties, and candidates in the thinking of the particular individuals he interviewed. Converse was looking at a different question—how can mass and elite communicate effectively with each other? His assumption was that if voters and actual or prospective political leaders shared at least a common metric for discussion—and one obvious candidate for such a metric was the left-right dimension—then there would not only be a way for candidates to ask the public to vote for them (the Downsian ideology-as-informational-short-cut idea),[23] but voters could also hold them accountable for failure to do so. If individuals, however, held their own unique lens through which they viewed politics, then no matter how sophisticated their thinking, collective choice and collective accountability would simply be impossible.

In this, Converse echoed Key, who found that a one- (or perhaps no-) party South failed to have such a mechanism during the Jim Crow, solid, lily-white Democratic Party days.[24] In Key's case, the fault lay with the political party and its candidates and officeholders who intentionally sought to avoid accountability. As Key put it elsewhere:

> Even the most discriminating popular judgment can reflect only ambiguity, uncertainty, or even foolishness if those are the qualities of the input into the echo chamber. . . . Fed a steady diet of buncombe, the people may come to expect and to respond with highest predictability to buncombe. And those leaders most skilled in the propagation of buncombe may gain lasting advantage in the recurring struggles for popular favor.[25]

Obviously, outside the South there was a competitive two-party system, and so Converse's findings had to have a different source. Most scholars have concluded that fault lay in the electorate—it was simply not sufficiently politically sophisticated to employ even a simple left-right scale in considering parties, candidates, and policies—and there was lots of evidence for such a position.[26] Reinforcing this position was that mass publics in other nations (perhaps especially France)[27] were rather more inclined to see politics in these terms and to apply them to their perceptions and evaluations of parties. Of course, this being the era of the end of ideology,[28] a time when the Democratic Party was internally divided North from South, when both parties were nominating moderate candidates, and when conservative Republicans were still chastising their party for "me-too-ism" in such as the nominations of Thomas Dewey and Dwight Eisenhower, it was at least possible that the relatively more similar alternatives at the elite level were insufficiently distinct in the public to be completely free of buncombe. And, of course, there might not be a unique source of "fault" in this failure; it could come from any and all sources involved or perhaps even be the wrong question. Indeed, Converse's answer was, at least in part, the latter: It was not a question of whether left-right could serve as that metric or nothing could, but whether it was an ideological scale or a partisan one.

The idea that political parties could stand as that metric for communication—for making claims on voter preferences and for holding political elites accountable—requires that the party label have sufficient content for precisely that kind of communication. It could be, of course, that the content is one or more identities for the partisan. And, there is good reason to think that race, ethnicity, religion, class, and so on are bundled within a party label. This was especially true of the New Deal coalition, which could easily be defined as a collection of groups. With the exception of race, those classic definitions of the New Deal coalition have, however, consistently declined over the postwar period.[29] Of course, some new social divisions have arisen, particularly the new definition of religion and especially the religious right. Note, however, that it is referred to as the religious *right* and is meant to convey "right" in the sense of "conservative right," an explicitly ideological label with a clearly understandable set of policy positions.

Alternatively, a party label could convey competence, an ability to run government, an avoidance in particular of Hooverism and acceptance of the optimism that Franklin Roosevelt brought to the notion that he could secure freedom from fear, etc., that happy days are here again, with an effective running of government. But the failures of Johnson, Nixon, Ford, and Carter; the success of Reagan, but not his successor, and of some of Clinton and of Gingrich's opposing leaderships in the 1990s, but also their failures; and the clear failure of the younger Bush suggest that competence and effectiveness at running government, as a label of positive retrospective revaluations, in the sense of Key's rational god of vengeance and reward,[30] is not a very partisan cue and thus is not the basis by which party label could serve as meaningful guide. That pretty much leaves content, especially policy content, and thus the potential for partisanship to be defined in increasingly left-right terms.

Evidence: First Indications

We first examine three pieces of evidence in support of our argument. These are drawn from reasonably standard (and often already analyzed) data. In the next section, we add new data to support our claims about activists. The first evidence supports the claim that the two parties at the elite level have clearly polarized. Figure 7-1 reports the distance between the centers of the two parties in the U.S. House and Senate on the first dimension of the Poole-Rosenthal scaling procedure in one dimension. We can see there the relatively low levels of the polarization measure in both the U.S. House and Senate in the 1970s, which extend back through the 1950s as well. Then, the measures of elite polarization begin to change,

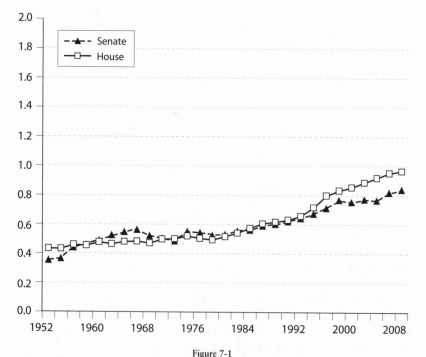

Figure 7-1

Polarization in House and Senate, 1952–2008. Source: Calculated using legislator and senator DW-NOMINATE estimates available from Poole and Rosenthal's Voteview database.

and the net revealed voting behavior (what DW-NOMINATE actually measures) of Democrats and Republicans in Congress diverge systematically and substantially.

The second piece of evidence examined suggests that the elite polarization is apparently perceived by the electorate. In figure 7-2, we show the percentage (of the total asked) who report seeing large differences between the two parties and, when available, the percentage of the electorate who describe the Republican Party as more conservative than the Democratic Party. As is seen in the figure, about half the sample throughout the 1950s, 1960s, and 1970s reports seeing large differences between the major parties. This proportion of people seeing large differences between parties begins to increase systematically around 1980, with the election of Reagan, a Republican Senate, and a closely divided House.

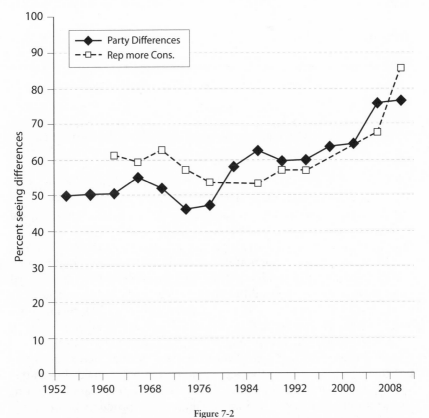

Figure 7-2
Perception of party differences, 1952–2008. Source: ANES surveys, various years, compiled by the authors.

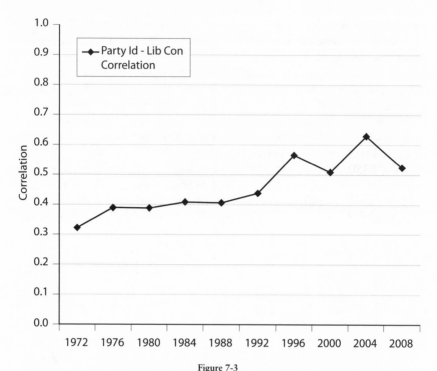

Figure 7-3
Correlation between party identification and liberal-conservative position,
1972–2008. Source: ANES surveys, various years, compiled by the authors.

It began to increase, that is, just as the polarization figures began to increase, as in figure 7-1. While in 1952 only one in two people saw much
of a difference between the two parties, by 2004 and 2008 this increased
to three in four. That is, the public was far more likely to perceive significant differences between the two parties in recent years than earlier. The
percentage of people saying that Republicans are more conservative than
Democrats at the national level also appears to follow the same upward
trend as perception of party differences. Between 1960 and 1992, at most
62 percent saw Republicans as more conservative. In 2004, this number
rose to 67 percent, and by 2008 it increased to over 80 percent, revealing
a major shift in public perceptions of political party polarization.

So political elites began to diverge by party in their actual behavior,
and this was observed, in the aggregate, by the public. Did this matter
to the public? Only later did the consequences of polarization begin to
appear in the public's own thinking. Figure 7-3 reproduces and extends
a similar figure in Abramowitz and Saunders to show that there was an
increasing coincidence between party and ideology.[31] Reported are the

correlations between the respondents' seven-point partisan identification and their self-placement on the seven-point liberal-conservative dimension. The latter was asked for the first time in 1972, so our series starts there. The correlation begins at typical levels, falling in the 0.3 range from 1972–1980. It increases slightly to the lower 0.4s in 1984 and 1988 and then begins to increase in earnest, rising to a robust level of nearly 0.6 in 2004 and 0.5 in 2008.

This set of observations suggests a relationship between what political elites do and how the public reacts. There is, however, a great deal of action between the survey response of a typical citizen and the floor voting of a member of the U.S. House. We are in the fortunate position of being able to fill in some of those intervening steps, some with extensions of already studied data, some with data heretofore unreported.

The Ideological Stances of Partisan Voters, Activists, and Officeholders

The central idea we present here is that there is a relationship between political activity and polarization between the two parties. Mayhew taught us long ago that much can be understood about what members of Congress (MCs) do in Washington by imagining that they were conditioning their actions on the implications for their reelection.[32] He argued that the MCs focused on three categories of acts—advertising, credit claiming, and position taking. And they did them in that order of priority. Not only was position taking third among the three major actions, it was *taking* a position, not *working* on the passage of legislation to *enact* that position. There is nothing obvious in Mayhew's account that would explain why the MCs began to polarize in their position taking—and voting—over time. How then might we account for these changes? Earlier, we argued that one important step in the argument was the centrifugal pressures of activists.

Political Activists and Ideology

Even within the set of activities in which people engage in support of partisan electoral campaigns, there is a large array of activities and of the kinds of people likely to engage in particular activities. What we offer here is measurement of a wider array of such individuals than usual, and we do so in the context of putting them in a common measurement of key variables. That way, we can see how those who engage in relatively low levels of activity compare with those who contribute at much higher levels, and thus have something close to a continuum of activists, from mass public to highest elite.

In particular, we have common measures of the following four sets of individuals. First, of course, we have the public, as represented by the various ANES election surveys. From them, we can also extract estimates of those who participate in sufficiently common ways to show up on national surveys. These are the activists that we identify in the same way as in Aldrich—that is, those who said that they had displayed a bumper sticker or worn a button, contributed money to a party or candidate, or attended a rally or meeting (see this chapter's appendix for details on this and all other measures).[33] We add to that two more sets of activists. One is the set of people who made "large" (at least $100 to $200) contributions to presidential candidates in 1972, 1988, 2000, or 2004. We were fortunate to be able to use the four random national surveys of campaign donors. For two of those years (1988 and 2000), we were also able to use surveys of the delegates to the two party's national conventions, but we are also able to measure national convention delegates at other points in time. All of these surveys have a measure of ideology similar or identical to the ANES seven-point liberal-conservative scale, making it possible to place these four types of activists on (nearly) the same scale. Of course, a fifth sort of activist, successful candidates for the House, are relevant to this story and are measurable on the DW-NOMINATE scale, as shown in figure 7-1. We can at least get some sense of dynamic, even if we cannot actually put them on the same scale as our other activists.

Results

Details of specific responses can be found in the appendix. The major result to focus on here is found in figure 7-4. We calculated the mean response of Democrats and Republicans: (1) in the full sample (called "partisans" in the figure, because that is the variable we use to distinguish Democrats and Republicans [excluding independents]); (2) in those partisans who reported that they had engaged in at least one campaign activity in the ANES; (3) in the samples of those who contributed at least $100–$200 to a Democrat or Republican candidate for president; and (4) in the samples of those who were delegates to the national party conventions. Our central measure is the difference between the average Democrat and average Republican liberal-conservative positions in each election year in each category of activism.

First, we find that there are regular and systematic differences between Republicans and Democrats, on each measure, at each point in time. Second, there is a general ordering, such that the smaller the percentage of the public engaged in an activity, the more extreme are the activists.[34]

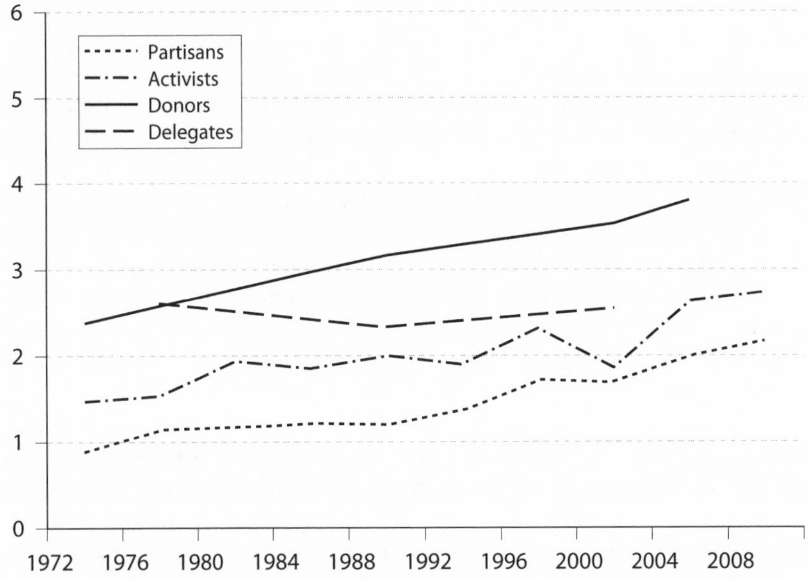

Figure 7-4
Liberal-conservative differences by party among different activists. Source: Compiled by the authors from various sources.

That is, partisans in the public are overall the least polarized from 1972 through 2004. The most general sort of activists, those measurable via the ANES, are considerably more polarized than the partisans in most years, but considerably less so than large donors or delegates, and this is true in 1972 and through 2004, although the ANES activists are approaching the level of polarization of the national convention delegates by 2004 (the last year for which we have either delegates or donors to compare). Third, excepting the delegates, there is a regular and substantial increase in polarization over time.[35] Finally, the differences and their increases are generally substantial. There is a maximum of a 6-point difference. Thus, for the general population, a difference of a full point in 1972 is reasonably large. That it essentially doubled by 2004 is quite impressive. That the approximately 20 percent of the general population who engaged in some sort of campaign activity were 1.5 and 3 points apart in 1972 and 2004, respectively, indicates very substantial differences. And that donors started at a quite large difference but by 2004 were nearly 4 points apart on self-identified liberal-conservatism is very impressive, indeed.

Thus, we conclude that in 1972, there was clear distinction, on average, between the typical Democrat and Republican in the population. This is at a level not really unlike that of the MCs in Congress, in which the two parties are distinguishable, but clearly overlapping. Each level of intensity of activity up the scale results in increased distinctiveness between the two parties' activists. Except for our delegate population, there was considerable increase in polarization in 1988, 2000, and especially 2004 or 2008 when the data is available. The level of polarization was very large by the end of the time period, and it is hard to imagine it much more distinctive, given that this is a set of survey responses. It again seems not at all unlike what has happened in Congress. And, the donor population polarized almost linearly and more steeply than the others, with general activists next and the partisan in the public least so.

Conclusion

It would be helpful if we could have a more dense set of measurements, but we are fortunate to be able to have even four measures of campaign donors. We would like to be able to assess the ordering of these changes, for we have implied a sequencing. But even with measures available in every election year since 1972, we would still be well short of having sufficient data to sort out any empirical estimation of causal ordering.

Our data, however, provide strong support for our basic argument. The general public appears to follow changes at a more elite level. They began to see differences between the parties only after we saw increased divergence in the roll-call behavior of MCs. That, of course, is not a particularly controversial causal claim. The public could hardly see increased differentiation between the two parties until there was some. Of more interest but well beyond what the data support, the intertwining of party identification and liberal-conservative placement in the public seems to be a consequence of elite bundling, and there is certainly theory to support that claim. However, the claim is not self-evident. Indeed, if elected officials respond to the public, how do we explain their polarization in the first place?

We argued that there were two forces at work. One was compositional and the other the influence of polarized activists. As to the first, the inclusion of the fuller electorate into southern politics induced one sort of polarization, as the total number of liberals and conservatives might not have changed in Congress, but it needed nothing beyond a simple sorting, whereby southern conservatives increasingly became Republicans rather than Democrats, and moderate to liberal northern MCs were increasingly Democrats rather than Republicans.

But that story is insufficient to account for the full process. There are still such anomalies as the dramatic differences between Democrats and Republicans elected from the same constituency, such as same-state senators. Here, then, we added the account of activists, and demonstrated that the higher the level of activity, the more divergent are Democrats from Republicans at every time point, and that such polarization has increased dramatically over the last few decades.

We have, of course, only correlations. Activists seem likely to exert centrifugal forces on elected officials to the extent that the resources they command are of value to those officials. But, of course, the relationship is dynamic. In the spatial theory of party activists,[36] activists are the sources of centrifugal pressures even were the extremely unlikely case of a centripetal, median-voter equilibrium to exist. But activists are engaged to become so by their views of where the party already stands. In the model, that was made fully endogenous and self-referential, in that activists cued off the spatial location of the existing distribution of activists. In reality, activists' decisions are all but certain to be based at least in part, perhaps in very large part, on what the incumbent officeholders of the two parties are doing in office.

If all parts of this account are interrelated and reinforcing, and given that polarization is increasing, is there any way in which this apparent equilibrium of two highly polarized parties will ever end? The answer seems most likely to be found in conditions that would divide currently unified parties. The most likely source is the arrival of new issues, ones that are cross-cutting. In this regard, perhaps the most interesting question is whether the parties' abilities to absorb new and divisive issues in the fashion outlined in the issue evolution account is a permanent feature.[37] If the two parties can absorb new issues into their line of cleavage quickly enough, then their position as duopolists in polarized, divergent, equilibrium is, to that extent, safe. After all, as the data in Aldrich, Rohde, and Tofias demonstrate,[38] the conditions for party government have been in place for most of the post–Civil War period. The only anomaly was the 1950s–1970s, and it was in place in large part because of the peculiar combination of southern democracy eliminating a substantial portion of their polity and the odd rules of the so-called "textbook Congress" that gave those particular MCs hold over many positions of power in Congress through seniority rights.[39] Democratizing both the southern electorate and the House removed this period of unique historical oddity. If that is the case, the textbook Congress period is the historical anomaly, and the increasing polarization we consider in this chapter is simple the return to the standard two-party, polarized equilibrium, the return to what members of Congress might call "regular order."

Finally, note that the theory we have been testing is based on the idea that polarization is an elite phenomenon (including candidates, officeholders, and activists, especially those providing greater resources), with people responding. The evidence is not decisive about the direction of causality, although it points toward one in which people respond to elite polarization by bringing their ideology and partisanship into closer harmony. The signaling, such as it is, however, appears to go from elite to the public, rather than the reverse. There is a modicum of accountability in this—votes reinforce the signal from elites, putting those inconsistent at electoral risk (as, for example, Lincoln Chafee), but it is a particular kind of accountability. Missing is the more direct accountability of elites responding to the public's political preferences (over policy and whatever else is measured by the seven-point ideology scale).

Appendix: Data Description

The data used to create figure 7-4 were drawn from three main studies that span multiple years: the 1972, 1988, and 2000 Convention Delegate Studies (CDS); the 1972, 1988, 2000, and 2004 Presidential Donor Studies (PDS); and the 1972–2004 American National Election Studies (ANES) Cumulative Data File and 2008 Time Series. Using these data, the American electorate was divided into four participation types: convention delegates, campaign donors, activists, and the major party identifiers in the mass electorate (partisans). The following section provides a brief description of the data sources, the data cleaning and coding choices we made to increase comparability of surveys, and the wording of the ideology variable examined across the multiple surveys and years.

While the individuals conducting the Convention Delegate Study surveys changed over the years,[40] all were modeled after a similar design in which delegates to the Republican and Democratic national party conventions were surveyed before or soon after the respective party conventions. A postconvention personal interview was conducted of a delegate sample in 1972, but our results rely only on responses from the preconvention mail questionnaire to ensure comparability with the later delegate surveys that were conducted solely as mail surveys. The 1972 CDS has a response rate of 58 percent, with a total of 2,587 delegates (1,722 Democrats and 864 Republicans) who returned the 1972 mail questionnaire. The 1988 Convention Delegate Survey was conducted in the early months of 1989 in the form of a mail questionnaire. Because delegates to pre-1988 conventions were also surveyed for the 1988 CDS in addition to 1988 convention delegates, we removed all non-1988 delegates from this year's survey before we conducted our analyses. The 1988 CDS response rate was 40 percent, with a total of 4,516 surveys returned (2,814 Democrats and 1,702 Republicans). The 2000 CDS[41] was conducted from the fall of 2001 through late spring 2002. Of the 4,284 Democrats and 2,049 Republicans surveyed, 38 percent (1,547) of Democrats and 40 percent

(780) of Republicans responded. Because the entire universe of national convention delegates was sampled for all of the CDS surveys, no weights were created or used for the convention delegate data.

Like the Convention Delegate Studies, a number of people collaborated to create the relatively comparable Presidential Donor Study surveys.[42] Individuals who contributed more than $100 (there was no upper contribution limit) to presidential campaign committees between April 7, 1972, and December 31, 1972, were sampled (with an oversample of Wallace donors) for the 1972 Presidential Donor Study mail survey following the 1972 election. The overall response rate of the 1972 PDS mail survey was 48.3 percent. The resulting data set has a total of 1,797 unweighted observations. Weights for the 1972 PDS correct for the oversample of Wallace donors and other unequal sampling probabilities.

In 1988, contribution limits restricted the sample of donors for the 1988 PDS to individuals who had contributed between $200 and $1,000 to presidential candidates before July 1988. The 1988 PDS has a response rate of approximately 37 percent, with the final data set containing 1,248 unweighted total observations. In the population list, donors were stratified by the eleven candidates and then randomly sampled to ensure that there would be enough data to allow candidate-level analysis. Furthermore, those donors to candidates who had fewer contributors were oversampled. To analyze contributors overall, this chapter relies on weights created by the 1988 survey's authors that are constructed to correct for (1) artificially high probabilities of being sampled for individuals who gave to multiple candidates and (2) oversampling of candidates with fewer contributors. The final probability weights were constructed using survey items asking about giving to multiple candidates and estimates of total donor distributions for all candidates.

The 2000 and 2004 Presidential Donor Study surveys closely follow the methodology used in the 1988 survey, as they both also draw on a random sample of donors stratified by candidate from public Federal Election Commission (FEC) donor lists. Paper questionnaires were sent by mail during 2001 and 2005 to a nationally representative sample of individuals who contributed between $200 and $1,000 to presidential candidates during the 2000 campaign and between $200 and $2,000 during the 2004 presidential election season. The 2000 and 2004 studies also sampled modest donors (less than $200). These modest donors were excluded from our analysis to enable greater comparability across the different years of the donor surveys. Weights similar to those constructed in 1988 were created and used for the 2000 and 2004 Presidential Donor Study data. Bush and Kerry donors were oversampled in 2004; therefore, the weights constructed for the 2004 PDS correct for these as well as the other unequal sampling probabilities. The final response rate for 2000

Presidential Donor Survey is about 50 percent, which is relatively high compared to past donor surveys. The final response rate for the entire 2004 survey is approximately 44 percent.

The Survey Research Center (SRC) of the University of Michigan has conducted the American National Election Studies (ANES) using pre- and post-election face-to-face interviews based on national samples in every presidential election since 1948.[43] To enable comparison of the mass electorate with the donor and delegate populations sampled through the CDS and PDS surveys, we conducted analysis on the ANES Cumulative Data File using years 1972 through 2004. Because 2008 has yet to be included in the cumulative file, we conducted a parallel analysis on the 2008 ANES time series study. While the basic design and content of the ANES is largely comparable across years, some experimentation in the design introduced a degree of variation in the studies. For example, in 2000, some respondents were selected by a traditional area probability sampling and interviewed face-to-face. Other respondents were sampled by a Random Digit Dialing (RDD) method and interviewed over the phone. Because of the small number of responses, we combined responses from the phone and face-to-face modes. Weights were used for our analysis when they were made available in the data set (for years 1976, 1992–2008).

Then, using a series of participation variables available in the ANES, a subgroup of the ANES respondents were classified as activists according to the method outlined in John Aldrich's *Why Parties*.[44] An individual was identified as an activist if he or she participated in any of the following activities: attending a political meeting; working for a party or candidate; wearing a button, putting a sticker on a car, or putting up a sign; or giving money to a political party or individual candidate.[45]

One of the consequences of compiling multiple surveys over many years is the lack of comparable questions available for examination. Of the hundreds of questions asked over the entire set of surveys, only six questions were asked consistently enough to enable some cross-survey and cross-time comparison. These include a question asking about the respondent's self-reported ideology on a seven-point scale ranging from "very liberal" to "very conservative." While most surveys relied on the standard seven-point ideology scale ranging from extremely liberal to extremely conservative (1 = Extremely Liberal, 2 = Liberal, 3 = Slightly Liberal, 4 = Moderate Middle of the Road, 5 = Slightly Conservative, 6 = Conservative, 7 = Extremely Conservative), a different set of response options was provided in the 1972 CDS (Radical, Very Liberal, Somewhat Liberal, Moderate, Somewhat Conservative, Very Conservative, Reactionary), so these responses are excluded from the analysis.

Finally, because of the systematic difference between respondents of different partisan identifications, our analysis examines the differences

Table 7-1. Population Percentages for Different Participation Pools

| | Partisans | | Activist | Donors | Delegates |
	Republicans	Democrats			
1972	44,000	26,000	19,000	—	—
1988	37,000	29,000	15,000	—	—
2000	42,000	24,000	14,000	0.004	0.003
2004	34,000	30,000	26,000	0.005	0.003
2008	34,000	26,000	27,000	0.006	0.003

Source: The statistics for partisans and activists were calculated using weighted ANES data. The percentage of the adult population (over 18 years) who donated over 200 dollars to a presidential candidate is as reported by the Center for Responsive Politics, at www.opensecrets.org. Convention delegate population percentages were calculated using historical presidential convention information from www.greenpapers.com.

between responses of Republicans and Democrats. Respondents are coded as Democratic if the respondent self-identified as Democrat on a three-point scale in the ANES or as Strong Democrat or Not Very Strong Democrat on the Donor Surveys, or were classified as a delegate for the Democratic Party Convention for the Convention Delegate Surveys (and vice versa for Republicans).

In table 7-1 (referenced in note 34), we present the sizes of the various groups for the years analyzed in the chapter relative to the total adult population in the United States.

Question Wording

Because our data draws on a range of surveys often created for distinct purposes, we have included in this section the exact question wording of the liberal-conservative ideology variable used in our chapter's analysis. While there is some variation in the wording of the question across the different surveys, the differences are relatively trivial and should not unduly influence any of this chapter's results.

1972 ANES IDEOLOGY

We hear a lot of talk these days about liberals and conservatives. I'm going to show you a seven-point scale on which the political views that people might hold are arranged from extremely liberal to extremely conservative. Where would you place yourself on this scale, or haven't you thought much about this? Extremely Liberal, Liberal, Slightly Liberal,

Moderate—Middle of the Road, Slightly Conservative, Conservative, Extremely Conservative.

1988, 2000, AND 2004 ANES IDEOLOGY

We hear a lot of talk these days about liberals and conservatives. Here is a seven-point scale on which the political views that people might hold are arranged from extremely liberal to extremely conservative. Where would you place yourself on this scale, or haven't you thought much about this? Extremely Liberal, Liberal, Slightly Liberal, Moderate—Middle of the Road, Slightly Conservative, Conservative, Extremely Conservative.

1988 CDS IDEOLOGY

We hear a lot of talk these days about liberals and conservatives. Here is a seven-point scale on which the political views that people might hold are arranged from extremely liberal to extremely conservative. Where would you place yourself on this scale, or haven't you thought much about this? (1: Extremely Liberal) (2) (3) (4) (5) (6) (7: Extremely Conservative).

2000 CDS IDEOLOGY

We hear a lot of talk these days about liberals and conservatives. Here is a seven-point scale on which the political views that people might hold are arranged from extremely liberal to extremely conservative. First, where would you place yourself on this scale? (1: Extremely Liberal), (2), (3), (4: Moderate), (5), (6), (7: Extremely Conservative).

1972 PDS Ideology

We hear a lot of talk these days about liberals and conservatives. Where would you place yourself on this scale? (Please circle the number of your choice) (1: Extremely Liberal) (2) (3) (4) (5) (6) (7: Extremely Conservative).

1988, 2000, and 2004 PDS Ideology

Here is a seven-point scale on which the political views that people might hold are arranged from extremely liberal to extremely conservative. Where would you place yourself . . . on this scale? Extremely Liberal, Liberal, Slightly Liberal, Moderate Middle of the Road, Slightly Conservative, Conservative, Extremely Conservative.

Notes

Data analysis reported here was supported in part by a grant from the National Science Foundation (NSF SES 0350936), for which we are grateful. This chapter also draws on data from the 2000 and 2004 Presidential Donor Studies, which were supported in part by the National Science Foundation through award numbers 0213643 and 0350936. We would like to thank Lynda Powell for providing us with the 1972 and 1988 Presidential Donor Studies. We alone are responsible for the research and its interpretations reported here.

1. See, especially, Erikson, MacKuen, and Stimson (2002).
2. Carmines and Stimson (1989); Adams (1997).
3. Or not, as argued in Green, Palmquist, and Schickler (2002).
4. Campbell et al. (1960); Converse (1964).
5. For example, Snyder and Ting (2002); Grynaviski (2010).
6. For data on partisanship since 1959, see Abramson, Aldrich, and Rohde (2009).
7. As shown by the data in McDonald and Popkin (2001).
8. Mayhew (1974a).
9. Rohde (1991); Aldrich (1995); Aldrich and Rohde (2000).
10. For example, Grofman, Griffin, and Glazer (1990).
11. Fenno (1973, 1978).
12. Krehbiel (1991, 1993).
13. Aldrich (1983); Aldrich and McGinnis (1989).
14. Cohen et al. (2008).
15. For an argument that there has not been much, if any partisan polarization in the public, see Fiorina, Abrams, and Pope (2006).
16. Wolfinger and Rosenstone (1980).
17. Brody (1978).
18. Rosenstone and Hansen (1993).
19. By that, we mean levels no longer as low as Switzerland's but more similar to Britain and Canada, among others.
20. Martinez (2009).
21. Converse (1964).
22. Lane (1962).
23. Downs (1957).
24. Key (1984 [1949]).
25. Key (1966). Key may have drawn the idea from his coverage of Senator Robert Rice Reynolds (Democrat, North Carolina, 1933–1945), whom he discussed in (1949) and whose nickname was "Buncombe Bob." See, for example, Pleanants (2000).
26. Converse's own article, of course, as well as Campbell et al., among many others. Converse (1964); Campbell et al. (1960).
27. Converse and Dupeaux (1962).
28. Bell (2000 [1960]).
29. See the Abramson et al. series, such as (2009), where this is laid out empirically.

30. Key (1966).

31. Abramowitz and Saunders (2005).

32. Mayhew (1974b).

33. Aldrich (1995).

34. Percentages of the adult population involved in the different levels of these four sets (partisans, activists, donors, and delegates) can be found in this chapter's appendix, in table 7-1.

35. It is at least possible that the 1972 Democratic Convention, with the fight over the Vietnam War and related issues between supporters of George McGovern and those of Hubert Humphrey and the other candidates, combined with this being the first time under (and with the fight over) the McGovern-Fraser Commission recommendations. It is also possible that the 1972 delegate survey is different due to somewhat different wording (see appendix).

36. Aldrich (1983); Aldrich and McGinnis (1989).

37. Carmines and Stimson (1980).

38. Aldrich, Rohde, and Tofias (2007).

39. Shepsle (1989).

40. The Convention Delegate Study of 1972: Women in Politics was conducted by Warren E. Miller, Elizabeth Douvan, William Crotty, and Jeane Kirkpatrick. The Convention Delegate Study, 1980, was conducted by Warren E. Miller, Kent M. Jennings, and Barbara G. Farah. The Convention Delegate Study, 2000, was conducted by Richard Herrera, Thomas Carsey, and John Green.

41. More details regarding the 2000 CDS can be found in Carsey, Green, and Herrera (2003).

42. The 1972 Presidential Donor Study was conducted by Clifford Brown, Roman Hedges, and Lynda Powell. The 1988 Presidential Donor Study was modeled after the 1972 study by Clifford Brown, Lynda Powell, and Clyde Wilcox. The principal investigators of the 2000 Presidential Donor Study were John Green, Mark Rozell, Alexandra Cooper, Michael Munger, and Clyde Wilcox. Finally, Michael Munger, John Aldrich, and Alexandra Cooper conducted the 2004 Presidential Election Study.

43. See http://www.electionstudies.org/ for more details on ANES design and content.

44. Aldrich (1996), p. 186.

45. In 1972, respondents were asked only whether they gave money to a political party. (They were not asked whether they contributed to an individual candidate.)

VIII

Political Parties in the Capital Economy of Modern Campaigns

Jonathan Krasno

A STANDARD STORY ABOUT American politics is that the last half century has seen a marked rise in "candidate-centered" campaigns. Like any broad narrative, this one is designed to fit some of the notable facts about recent American politics—the increased cost of campaigns (a by-product of candidates' efforts to present themselves as individuals to the public), the high reelection rate of incumbents (who attempt to convert their time in office into personal followings), and the advent of television advertising as the vital component of any campaign. If candidates are now the central feature of campaigns, parties apparently used to be. Thus, Wattenberg famously juxtaposed the "rise of candidate-centered politics" against the decline of parties and Herrnson described the earlier period as the "golden age of parties."[1]

Comparing the relative importance of candidates and parties is inherently difficult because of the trouble pinning down a single meaning of "party."[2] Political scientists divide American parties into three separate and distinct parts—in government, in the electorate (party identification), and as organizations—making it hard to determine what "the party" is and whether it is strong or weak. Nonetheless, there has been a fair amount of consensus that, at very least, the *national* party organizations were weak in the decades preceding the rise of candidate-centered campaigns and remained weak for much of the time after. The 1950 study group of the American Political Science Association (APSA) made creating (as opposed to restoring) vibrant national organizations essential for "responsible" parties its key mission. Just over a decade later, Cotter and Hennesey titled their book about the national committees *Politics without Power*.[3] So while there was debate into the 1970s and onward about the health of state and local party organizations, the national parties were largely consigned to life support.

Thus, it is perhaps somewhat miraculous that those organizations—the parties' national committees and their congressional campaign committees—have emerged in recent decades as financial powerhouses. How powerful? In the 2008 elections, the six national committees combined to raise over $1.2 billion.[4] For scholars long used to rooting for parties, this financial renaissance is good news for the political system since parties are associated with, among other things, greater electoral competition, higher voter turnout, and enhanced citizen connection to the political system.[5] It is also the latest sign of American parties' historic ability to adapt to and remain relevant through a variety of circumstances.[6] In this case, scholars argue that parties managed to adapt to candidate-centered campaigns by remaking themselves as major providers of campaign services to candidates.[7] Today's parties, especially the well-organized and well-heeled national organizations, are able to supply the latest campaign services to help candidates from voter lists and all manners of consulting, to providing polling, direct mail, phone banks, and even TV ads. National parties have clearly become major players in federal campaigns (and in some state and local contests).

In a series of essays prepared for federal courts, Frank Sorauf and I have argued that there is far less to parties' apparent health and their involvement in campaigns than meets the eye. In particular, we questioned whether parties' health can be measured accurately with dollars raised and spent, and we argued that the positive consequences of richer parties have been meager to nonexistent. Theory holds that formidable and active parties should lead to a variety of useful side effects such as increased electoral competition and voter turnout, improvements that did not appear to occur in American politics as national parties assumed more prominent roles in the 1980s and 1990s. In the current essay, I take those claims a step further by arguing that this lack of improvement is not coincidental—parties that depend on financial muscle are fundamentally different from traditional party organizations and unlikely to deliver the same benefits.

How is that possible? My explanation revolves around two central and related claims. First, I take issue with the conventional wisdom about the rise of candidate-centered campaigns sometime following 1950. In fact, there is ample anecdotal evidence that at least for the highest profile offices, American campaigns have always centered on candidates. The emphasis on candidate-centered campaigns obscures a much more fundamental transformation, especially for parties, from a campaign economy based mainly on labor to one based mainly on capital. Second, I posit that parties' and candidates' goals, though overlapping, are distinct and separate. This has always been true, but the parties' transition from mobilizing election workers and volunteers to providing money or paid services exposes a fundamental conflict between the interests of parties and of candidates. This conflict has had immediate and serious ramifications for how parties allocate their resources, present themselves to the electorate, and mobilize voters, ultimately calling into question many of scholars' assumptions about parties. I proceed in the next two sections to take up these claims before concluding with a broader discussion of parties' role in the modern campaign economy and the lessons for political scientists.

The Myth of Party-Centered Campaigns

Campaigns centered on the personality, experience, virtues, and even policy positions of the candidates are so familiar that the alternative of emphasizing parties instead seems difficult to imagine. There is good reason for incredulity, especially in the context of today's politics. Decades of survey research show that political parties are unpopular, even as a large majority of Americans continue to choose sides, whether explicitly or implicitly.[8] Candidates may not necessarily be all that popular either, but it is certainly easier to make the case that a person is honest, intelligent, and looking out for the voters' interests than it is to make the same case for a political party about which much of public already believes the opposite. Many candidates have already invested heavily in promoting themselves in order to win a primary. Furthermore, party-based appeals are not likely to attract many swing voters for whom partisanship is a less relevant concern, while doing little to persuade or mobilize voters from a candidate's own party who are already likely to support her. Thus, candidates generally have little incentive to do much to emphasize their party and plenty to emphasize themselves, an expectation supported by studies of campaign advertising.[9]

We have no survey data with which to assess the popularity of political parties prior to 1950, but there is plenty of anecdotal evidence to suggest that parties were not exactly beloved institutions. The Progressives made reining in parties a main goal, and were rewarded with millions of votes and some significant policy victories. Much of the nineteenth century and early twentieth century was marked by the rise and fall of sizable third parties, a sign of a fair amount of dissatisfaction with existing parties.[10] And, of course, George Washington devoted his farewell address to warning Americans about the evils of political parties, a sentiment that many of the other founders shared. In short, Americans have shown a distinct animosity toward political parties throughout their history.[11]

Of course, a lack of appreciation for parties does not mean that they cannot be effective rallying points during a campaign. Again, our ability to observe campaigns conducted before 1950 is limited, but what is known supports the contention that candidates were central to a campaign's message.[12] Glassman coded several thousand campaign buttons from 1896 to 1972 and found that images of candidates were plentiful while references to parties were rare throughout this period.[13] Even early TV commercials overwhelmingly focused on the candidates, an

easy choice for the Republicans given the popularity of General Eisenhower.[14] It is possible that other mediums featured more party-centered
messages, but there is no particular reason to believe that they did. In
fact, American parties have always gone to great lengths to recruit attractive candidates, such as the string of war heroes elected president
in the nineteenth century, and to create compelling stories and slogans
about their candidates' virtues and humble upbringings.[15] Even at the
local level, political machines engaged in ticket balancing and recruited
respected citizens to stand in for party bosses who were not considered
particularly electable.[16] It seems obvious that it has almost always been
easier to sell individuals—whether soldiers, athletes, businessmen, or log-
cabin dwellers—than it is to sell parties, even if most voters continue to
make partisan choices. Such efforts were not limited to presidential politics, although candidates near the top of the ticket always received more
attention than candidates at the bottom.

In short, American elections—at least for the offices to which people
pay the most attention—have always been candidate-centered. What has
changed for parties is not their dedication to helping their candidates get
elected, but the type of aid they provide. "Traditional" parties, the type
of state and local, often patronage-based, organizations that dominated
party politics through most of the nineteenth and twentieth centuries,
mainly supplied labor to campaigns; they measured their strength by
their ability to mobilize campaign workers and turn out voters, practic-
ing what Frantzich calls a "labor-intensive" form of politics.[17] Today's
party organizations, on the other hand, supply money or services they
purchase. To be sure, money mattered in the old system, too, but the
amounts were much smaller and much of it was used for organization
and payoffs.[18] Modern campaigns, however, have less use for labor than
for capital since television and polling and phone calls all cost large sums
of money.[19] As the emphasis on recruiting and mobilizing campaign
workers has waned in favor of raising money to purchase services, the
traditional party organizations have largely passed from the scene, their
demise hastened in some cases by the efforts of reformers eager to bust
political machines. In their place, service parties have come to the fore
because of their ability to raise and spend money. That transformation
from a labor to a capital economy has had profound consequences for
parties and for the candidates they support.

The Interests of Parties versus the Interests of Candidates

Scholars who have written of traditional party organizations have occasionally gone to pains to define their specific organizational structures
as a way to distinguish between more and less effective parties, and espe-

cially between parties engaged in winning elections and those interested in other goals.[20] Here, however, I follow Schattschneider and Downs, among others, by simply specifying that parties' overriding goal is and has always been to win elections.[21] This is equally true of traditional parties and service parties. It is true that parties, and especially partisans, have ideologies and remain fairly constrained in their ability to remake themselves to win an election. Still, winning remains the primary goal of party leaders and even of the rank and file who, for instance, are motivated by electability in selecting presidential nominees.[22] Minor parties may be content to compete or make a symbolic statement through their presence. The two major parties want to win. Not only is victory its own reward, winning elections is the main way to publicize the party's work and burnish its image. Winning now also helps the victor claim a greater share of resources, laying the groundwork for future victories.

Despite the shared goal of winning, candidates' and parties' interests diverge in two important ways. First, parties seek to maximize their victories—to win more legislative seats and executive offices, to control federal, state, and local governments. Some offices and some governmental bodies have more value than do others, and particular seats—like Tom Daschle's or Tom DeLay's—may carry special symbolic value, but, generally speaking, successful parties simply win more elections. Congressional campaign committees, at least in theory, seek to increase their parties' share of seats in the legislative chamber.[23] Candidates naturally care overwhelmingly about a single election—their own—but parties must prevail in many contests to succeed.

Second, parties also seek future victories. That is not to say that parties do not heavily discount future events in favor of the present; parties routinely go into debt during election cycles, although not to the point of selling their headquarters, and they exhort their followers with messages about the overriding significance of the coming election. Painful as a single loss may be, parties must survive to fight another day. Indeed, one of the important characteristics that distinguishes the Democratic and Republican parties from minor parties has been their ability to survive through defeats. History is littered with examples of third parties that experienced short-term success (often with the help of a single charismatic candidate) and then disappeared. Thus, winning later, while never as good as winning now, is essential for the parties' health and well-being. In both of these ways, parties differ from individual candidates whose goals are necessarily immediate and selfish.

That sets up a conflict of interest that modern parties with their emphasis on capital over labor have a difficult time resolving. The key problem is that money is fungible while labor is not. Money raised in Manhattan or Los Angeles can flow to races anywhere in the country and be used to purchase every service that is sold. Furthermore, as a result of a series of campaign finance rulings, there are practically no limits on the amount of money that parties can spend on behalf of the candidates they help (along with no minimum amount for the candidates whom they deem poor investments).[24] Labor or organization, however, is essentially local, tied to the area where the campaign workers live. One indication of the difference between labor and capital is that the campaign service industry offers for sale little of the grassroots campaigning that parties once provided. Networks of volunteers and paid campaign workers are expensive to create, and, more importantly, are not portable like other services.[25] While a phone bank can be used for candidates all around the country, grassroots networks can be sold only to local candidates. This combination of factors—candidates' (and consultants') demand for expensive services coupled with ability to move money and spend it in unlimited amounts versus the difficulty of creating an organization and its lack of portability—leaves a situation where the interests of candidates and parties clash. I focus here on three distinct areas where candidates' interests are served at the expense of parties': resource allocation, advertising, and voter mobilization.

Resource Allocation

Each year, would-be congressional candidates troop to Washington in search of financial and organizational help for their campaigns. The campaign committees are their main stop: the blessing of the Democratic Congressional Campaign Committee (DCCC) and National Republican Congressional Committee (NRCC) not only means substantial support from the committee, but also a much-improved opportunity to raise money elsewhere.[26] Parties try to decide whom to help by determining where their help is likeliest to do the most good. That is, they try to play in the closest contests where their support might make the difference between victory and defeat for their candidate.[27] It is an approach that makes intrinsic political sense. Why waste their money on lost causes or certain winners?

One reason is that parties exist or hope to exist in every corner of the country—if not today, then in the future. Indeed, every election brings the plaintive calls of Democrats and Republicans in various locales pleading for the national committees to campaign more actively in their areas to raise their spirits and boost the rest of the ticket. According to press reports, for example, California Republicans succeeded in convincing the Republican National Committee (RNC) and Bush campaign to divert resources from Florida and other close states in the final days of the 2000 campaign to avoid appearing to concede the state to the Democrats. It is a mistake that leading Democrats feared that Democratic National Committee (DNC) chairman Howard Dean was repeating with his "Fifty-State Strategy."[28] Dean argued that the practice of targeting a handful of close races or close states is contrary to the notion of a national party. That is surely right as a matter of philosophy and may very well help the Democrats win elections at some point, though Dean claimed some credit for Democratic victories in the 2006 and 2008 elections.

Were Dean's critics correct that parties are smartest to concentrate on the closest races? The U.S. House of Representatives is a useful case to consider. Two things stand out about the parties' allocation strategy in House elections. First is that the number of races they have recently targeted is small, shockingly small. In 2004 and 2006, the two parties (led mainly by the DCCC and NRCC) spent more than half of their money in just 11 races and 15 races, respectively, compared to 83 and 73 in 1992 and 1994.[29] This was the culmination of a decade-long trend of focusing more money in fewer races. In 1992, party committees gave at least some support to 91 percent of candidates; by 2006, they supported just 60 percent. More important, average support for the 5 percent of candidates on whom parties spent the most skyrocketed from $63,000 to $1.72 million. Almost all of parties' spending in 2004 and 2006 races came as independent expenditures,[30] meaning that the party officials who made the decisions to allocate this money were prohibited by law from having contact with the candidates, their representatives, or even other party officials. In other words, as closely as is possible this represents a decision by parties themselves and not outsiders seeking to influence them.

Second, the best predictor of the amount of money that each party spends on a given House race is spending by the opposite party. That is true for both hard-money expenditures from 1994 to 2006 and soft-money expenditures from 1998 to 2000.[31] More important, it holds up when controlling for measures of preelection vulnerability (including the closeness of the previous election, the presidential results, open seats, and candidate quality), the structure of the media market (in the case of issue ads), and even election results themselves, the ultimate measure of a competitive contest. This is not difficult to understand given the sheer size of parties' expenditures in a handful of races where both sides seem to get locked into a spending battle. Either the parties were impelled by the same unobserved strategic information to spend so heavily in these races versus other *equally* close contests, or they were determined not to let their counterparts get too much of an upper hand. Either way, the end result is huge inequalities in the amount of money that the parties invest in specific campaigns. Most races get little or no attention; a few attract substantial funds; and a select few get lavish support, although that support may vary from lavish to obscene.

Obviously, the parties were acting in what they perceived as their strategic interest by focusing more money in fewer contests. Their judgment that there were only a handful of close contests in most recent election cycle echoes assessments by independent observers like *Congressional Quarterly* and Charlie Cook, yet it also has the flavor—assuming that parties are consequential actors—of a self-fulfilling prophesy. Indeed, it is true that the number of close House elections from 1992 to 1996, when parties were forced because of campaign finance laws to spread the wealth, was much higher than in the 1998 to 2006 cycles, when these rules were relaxed: 81 and 85 races were decided by 10 points or less in 1992 and 1994, versus 22 and 60 in 2004 and 2006. That is not proof, of course, that parties create electoral competition as opposed to following in its path.[32] Whether parties are smart or stupid to focus so intensely on such a small number of races, their decision to do so in the last four or five election cycles constitutes an odd abandonment of most of their candidates and their fundamental mission of electoral competition. If parties do not compete, what do they do? If parties do not contest elections, how can they win control of government?[33]

Advertising

The hallmark of modern campaigns, and their single most expensive component, is television advertising. TV ads are thought to be an especially powerful persuasive tool because of the ability to deliver the candidate's message to a television audience of swing voters.[34] Those swing voters might be wobbly partisans or pure independents. Either way, advertisers seem to believe that they are unlikely to respond to overtly partisan appeals since they are not strongly attached to either party. The most obvious way to attract them is by selling the attributes of one candidate or disparaging the other candidate without mentioning parties at all.[35] That is a very familiar style of campaigning, the essence of candidate-centered politics.

Since 1998, parties have joined candidates as major advertisers in congressional campaigns, first by using soft money on issue ads and then, following 2002, by using hard money for independent expenditures. Media tracking data from 1998 and 2000 show just how big advertisers parties have become: in these two years, parties sponsored spots that aired more than 315,000 times in the nation's top 75 media markets at a minimum cost of at least $75 million.[36] Parties may produce these spots, but they certainly do not star in them: less than 10 percent of these ads aired mentioned either party in their text or visuals (aside from the barely legible disclaimers), while virtually all of them (99 percent) identified a particular candidate by name. They were also almost all strongly negative in their tone. Undergraduate coders ranked almost half of the spots aired by parties as pure attack ads versus about a quarter of candidate spots.

It is apparent that parties do candidates' bidding with their advertising. Candidates are featured, but the parties rarely figure in the message relayed. One particularly memorable spot run by the Republican Party of Wisconsin even praised its Senate candidate in 1998 for "standing up to his own party." This approach fits candidates' need to attract swing voters. The attack advertising represents a division of labor where parties do some of the dirty work of dismantling the opposition, while leaving the candidates with the happier and less controversial task of spreading the good word about themselves.[37]

The question, however, is whether parties hurt themselves in the process of helping their candidates or whether no conflict exists. I think, at very least, that the parties have ignored an opportunity to help themselves by doing nothing or next to nothing to promote themselves. No one knows whether parties can attract new partisans through advertising, but it is striking that neither party has even tried despite the vast sums of money available to them. Even generic, electoral advertising like 1982's "Vote Republican for a Change" or 1994's "Contract with America" has been abandoned in favor of candidate-specific advertising that makes no reference to party. This is a version of Coleman's observation that it is difficult to understand what resurgent party organizations do if they do not make partisans.[38] We know that they do not because the American National Election Studies (ANES) time series shows no more than an uptick in the strength of party identification or number of identifiers in the last decade as parties have spent *billions* of dollars.[39] The mere fact, as well, that parties readily engage in the sort of attacking behavior that candidates try to avoid to protect their own image lends further suspicion that parties' advertising in elections has the potential to hurt them even as it aids individual candidates.

Organization and Voter Mobilization

The defining characteristic of traditional parties was their ability to marshal labor, albeit with varying levels of success, to staff campaigns and get-out-the-vote drives. They managed this feat on what seems by today's standards shoestring budgets, with few paid employees outside of elected officials. In contrast, modern party organizations, including the federal committees as well as many state parties (who receive aid from the national committees), are awash with funds, employees, office space, etc. How do these resources affect parties' organizational capacity, especially their efforts to mobilize voters? The answer is not very much.

My evidence about organizational capacity comes from in-depth case studies of the Colorado and Missouri Republican parties conducted in conjunction with a pair of court cases.[40] Both parties were thoroughly well-to-do, largely on the strength of funds provided by national Republican committees. Despite the millions of dollars of support received, neither party managed to do very much by themselves. The Colorado Republicans, for example, tried and failed to organize a mailing to its own members (a very small subset of the registered Republicans in the state) or establish a phone bank for volunteers. They ended up paying vendors for these services. The Missouri Republican Party exhibited the same behavior, using its financial resources to pay outside vendors for these services.[41] The money that these state parties received appeared to flow through them unimpeded by any demands of the party itself. Rather, the federal committees used the state parties in a soft-money accounting game in which they sought the least restrictive regulatory environment for their campaign funds.[42] The state organizations showed many of the signs that analysts associate with strong parties—including professional staff, budget, and headquarters—without demonstrating much ability to engage in other electoral activities beyond receiving and writing checks.[43]

Even if parties no longer perform electoral tasks themselves, they may still act by hiring others. Of all the tasks attributed to parties, probably the most important is voter mobilization. Nearly every account of political parties makes special reference to their traditional role of getting out the vote. Aldrich describes mobilization as the overriding reason why Jacksonian operatives led by Van Buren created party organizations in the mass electorate in the first place during the 1820s.[44] Congress and the courts paid special attention to the parties' potential as mobilizers in McCain-Feingold, especially in light of the potential devastating impact of the ban on soft money.[45] Perhaps parties now pay to get out the vote.

La Raja offers some relevant evidence by examining parties' expenditures on Federal Election Commission (FEC) reports for activities like canvassing or phone banking in the weeks immediately preceding the election that can plausibly be characterized as mobilization.[46] He finds parties' mobilization expenditures increased monotonically from $10 million in 1992 to $314 million in 2004. The latter figure, of course, is the eye-popping one. Carman, Farrell, and Krasno obtain similar results for 2000 ($84 million), but a much smaller amount for 2004 ($183 million).[47] Even if La Raja's estimates are correct, several cautions apply. First, spending for mobilization constitutes 28% of parties' expenditures in 2004, and less than 15% in earlier years—not an insignificant sum, but also a sign that parties' greater priorities lay elsewhere. Second, the huge increase from 2000 to 2004 is largely attributable to Bipartisan Campaign Reform Act of 2002, which made it more difficult for parties to spend their money on television ads.[48] Regulation appears to have made the parties more "party-like."

But sheer spending tells little about the ultimate success of parties' mobilization programs.[49] Green and Gerber provide one important gauge for measuring their effectiveness with a series of experiments showing that canvassing has a far bigger impact on voting than other mobilization techniques.[50] Unfortunately, parties spent less than 5 percent of their mobilization dollars for canvassing in both 2000 and 2004.[51] Rather, this category of expenditures is dominated by phone banks and direct mail, two methods of contact that Green and Gerber find markedly less effective than canvassing. The question, of course, is why so little money was spent for canvassing and why so much was spent for phone calls and mail. The answer is evident from closer examination of these outlays: parties wrote huge checks to outside vendors for phone banks and direct mail, but they were forced to take care of canvassing in-house because of the inability to purchase these services. Thus, organizational capacity is relevant to parties' ability to mobilize voters. Parties that cannot organize a phone bank for volunteers seem ill-equipped to organize volunteer or paid canvassers. As Gerber and Green speculate: "the long term decay of civic and political organizations may have reached such a point that our society no longer has the infrastructure to conduct face-to-face canvassing on a large scale."[52]

The Future of Political Parties

The conversion of the campaign economy from one based largely on labor to one based almost entirely on capital has had a profound effect on parties. While parties once measured their strength by their ability to supply campaign workers and mobilize their supporters, today's parties think primarily in terms of dollars. That is not to say, of course, that money did not matter at all in the past or that modern campaigns have no use for volunteers or organization. And, it is certainly not to say that parties were ever routinely well organized; for every Jersey City or Chicago once run by party machines, there were other cities and states where party organizations were inefficient or sporadic. Nonetheless, it is generally true that parties' main asset was once their ability to muster campaign workers and now is their ability to raise money.

Labor and money have fundamentally different consequences for the relationship between candidates and parties. While individual candidates naturally seek all of the resources they can get their hands on for their own campaign, parties would like to see as many of their candidates win as possible, all while hopefully ensuring their chances to win in future

elections. When parties primarily offered labor to candidates, these disparate goals posed relatively little problem. Campaign workers could be de-
ployed, where parties were sufficiently organized, on the behalf of many
candidates on the ticket without costing any single candidate much. That
is, parties could mobilize the vote for an array of federal, state, and local
candidates all at the same time. Since political organizations take time
and effort to assemble, parties prospered by building up and sustaining
their ability to muster labor both in the present and the future. None of
this is true where money is concerned. Not only can money from all over
the country be concentrated in a single election, much of what money
purchases cannot be shared with other candidates. TV ads, for example,
cover the merits or demerits of a single candidate, not teams of candidates. Like ads, most of the services that money buys have a very limited
half-life. When the election is over, the consultants and ad agencies and
phone banks all pack up, only to reappear somewhere else in the next
election cycle. Little, if anything, is left over to help the state and local
parties contest later elections. Even the contributor lists likely belong to
the federal committees. In short, money is fungible and organization is
not. The result is that when individual candidates make selfish demands
on parties to benefit their campaign and no others, in the capital campaign economy parties can respond with aid that helps one candidate
and no others.

If parties and candidates do conflict, it is clear whose interests end up
being served in the current system: individual candidates, but only certain
ones. Parties allocate their resources to benefit a small subset of candidates. Parties make short-term investments and ignore their own organizational needs to help these candidates, even at the cost of hindering their
own ability to get out the vote. It is clear that the immediate needs of a
handful of candidates take precedence over the broader electoral goals of
the party and the immediate electoral needs of the vast majority of candidates running on its ticket. This sort of pattern might make sense for a
party and its other candidates if the object of the party's investment is at
the top of the ballot and could provide coattails to everyone below. It is
difficult, however, to make that argument about House candidates or to
claim that many races have particular symbolic significance to a party.[53]

This tension should not be mischaracterized as a conflict between parties' organizational needs and candidates' electoral ones. I have argued,
instead, that the stakes on both sides are primarily electoral. No matter
what else activists or scholars may find in them, the fundamental purpose
of party organizations is to help its candidates win. Thus, any tension
between them is reducible to a clash among candidates actively seeking
their aid right now or intending to seek it in the future. I have no direct
evidence about why parties lean so decisively toward satisfying the im-

mediate needs of a handful of favored candidates rather than trying to provide some level of meaningful assistance to many candidates both now and in future elections except to note the obvious: these decisions must reflect some sort of deliberate, strategic judgment. What informs that judgment is unclear. It is apparent from the gnashing of Democratic teeth over Dean's Fifty-State Strategy that parties discount future elections very heavily, thus explaining the lack of investment in organization or a more party-centric approach to advertising. That still leaves the matter of how parties allocate resources in *current* elections. Does their narrow focus on a sliver of candidates to the near exclusion of all others reflect a response to unobserved measures of competitiveness like polls? To each other? To the clamoring of consultants or funders or journalists? To something else? No matter its source, there is good reason to question the tactical wisdom of this pattern of allocation and to wonder about parties that deny help to so many candidates running under its banner.[54] What is clear is that all these sorts of questions about what parties do and do not do—their extreme emphasis on current elections over future ones and their coldhearted culling of today's candidates—are the result of a system where parties' resources are centralized and fungible, money not manpower. Parties' accommodation to the new campaign economy that values capital over labor has fundamental implications for what parties do and for whom they do it.

Beyond any specific empirical or theoretical claims, this account serves as a reminder that political parties vary. Variation qualifies as a theme of the vast literature on parties, so it comes as no surprise. Still for scholars inclined to thinking of parties as a single category of phenomena, particularly those who have celebrated their resurgence in recent decades, the message that today's parties act very differently from yesterday's offers a note of caution. Not everything with the name "Democratic" or "Republican" on its letterhead is the equivalent (in almost any respect) of every other party committee. While it is fair to marvel again at parties' ability to adapt to new regulatory regimes (e.g., Epstein 1986; Aldrich 1995), those adaptations do not come without costs to what parties are or what they do. Parties emerged vastly richer in dollars out of what first appeared as a hostile era of campaign finance reform, but possibly poorer in other ways. Simply assuming that their money at minimum compensates for their loss of other resources misses the bigger picture of how the capital economy has affected parties' behavior.

This set of empirical findings could be taken as confirmation of Aldrich's view that parties are endogenous institutions that exist to serve politicians who "use or abuse" them as they like.[55] There is certainly more than a grain of truth in that view, although it leaves unsettled how certain groups of politicians manage to get control of parties and what they try to do with their control. More important, it sets aside any normative concerns about parties' actions, a perspective contrary to much of the literature on parties. Scholars have come to appreciate party organizations not merely for existing, but for what they contribute to the political system. If it turns out that their contributions are surprisingly minimal, then surely we should make much less of them. Unfortunately, we have seen that economic transformation of political campaigns has fundamentally affected parties' incentives or, at least, their judgments; it is no longer inevitable that parties will contest many elections, mobilize many voters, or present images of themselves to the public. Scholars will continue to study party organizations that eschew these tasks and others, but they have little reason to value them as reflexively as they did past incarnations of parties. The alternative is not to think of parties as less than essential institutions, but to distinguish between different types or forms of parties for their intrinsic usefulness (e.g., national committees compared to locally based traditional organizations) and even to consider reforms that would enhance their positive role in American politics. The reformist tradition in political science, especially as represented by the "responsible parties" movement endorsed by the 1950 APSA Committee on Political Parties, has been justifiably critiqued as naïve.[56] That may be so, but parties remain too important to political scientists' theories of democracy to sign them over fully to ambitious politicians.

Notes

I am grateful to Frank Sorauf for sharpening my thinking about parties and contributing many of the better ideas here, to the Pew Charitable Trusts for their support of much of the research cited, and to Ray Wolfinger for teaching me to be productively skeptical.
   1. Wattenberg (1992); Herrnson (1994).
   2. Schlesinger (1994).
   3. Cotter and Hennesey (1964).
   4. http://fec.gov/press/press2009/05282009Party/20090528Party.shtml. The six national committees are the Democratic National Committee (DNC), Democratic Senatorial Campaign Committee (DSCC), Democratic Congressional Campaign Committee (DCCC), Republican National Committee (RNC), National Republican Senatorial Committee (NRSC), and National Republican Congressional Committee (NRCC). This figure does not include an additional quarter of a billion dollars spent by state and local parties in federal elections, often with the help of the national committees.
   5. La Raja (2003); Milkis (2003).
   6. For example, see Epstein (1986). One development that helped national parties was federal campaign finance law, an ironic twist of fate given the par-

ties' persistent and ongoing complaints that the law handicaps them. The 1974 Amendments to the Federal Election Campaign Act (FECA) created higher limits on contributions to parties than to candidate or PACs and allowed parties multiple routes to aid candidates, advantages that parties later expanded on through legislative, administrative, and legal means.

7. Frantzich (1984, 1989); Herrnson (1988); Aldrich (1995); Shea (1995); Menefee-Libey (1999). Recently, some scholars have begun to identify another form of parties, the "expanded party" made up of loose networks of major donors and campaign consultants (see Bernstein and Dominguez 2003; Cohen et al. 2008). For my purposes, expanded parties share the salient features of service parties, so I deal explicitly only with the latter here.

8. Keith et al. (1992).

9. Krasno and Seltz (2000); Krasno and Goldstein (2002).

10. Rosenstone, Behr, and Lazarus (1996).

11. Silbey (1994).

12. Tulis (1988) ascribes the rise of candidate-centered politics to the campaigns of Theodore Roosevelt (1904 and 1912) and Woodrow Wilson (1912 and 1916), further indication that putting the candidate front and center far precedes the advent of television.

13. Glassman (2002).

14. See www.livingroomcandidate.org for a remarkable archive of presidential TV ads dating from the first spots broadcast in 1952. The vast majority of these commercials, including the earliest ones, feature very personal appeals and make no reference to political parties.

15. Beard's (1928, pp. 1–2) account of political parties begins by quoting a contemporary observer who noted, "If the Republicans can find the proper candidate, any kind of slogan will do; and if the Democrats can find the proper slogan almost any kind of candidate will do."

16. Rakove (1975).

17. Frantzich (1989), p. 208. Riordan (1963, pp. 8–9) provides a typically colorful example from the rise of George Washington Plunkitt.

18. Key (1949).

19. Accompanying this, of course, is the rise of the professional campaign industry capable of consuming every dollar that candidates, parties, and groups raise for its expanding list of services. For a list, see http://www.politicsmagazine .com/resources/the-political-directories. The service industry is frequently interpreted as a product of candidates' desire to craft candidate-centered campaigns, but I think the more straightforward explanation is that it is a response to the rising amounts of money raised and spent.

20. See, for example, Eldersveld (1964); Key (1949).

21. Schattschneider (1942); Downs (1957).

22. Bartels (1988).

23. Kolodny (1998). Not all numbers are equally valuable. Winning a majority of legislative seats is any party's overriding concern, a factor that likely alters strategies, as the majority is at greater or lesser distance.

24. The lack of limits on parties is not a result of intentional design by policy-makers, but due to the intervention of judges. There have been two distinct eras of unlimited party involvement. The first occurred between 1996 and 2002, when parties began to use soft money to fund so-called issue ads attacking or promoting candidates (Moramarco 1999). The second began in 2004, after Congress banned soft money and party issue ads, when parties began taking advantage of an earlier decision in *Colorado I* to begin airing independent expenditures (Krasno and Dowling 2008).

25. Green and Gerber (2004).

26. Sidlow (2003).

27. Jacobson (1985–1986).

28. Bai (2006).

29. Krasno and Dowling (2008), p. 35.

30. Krasno and Dowling (2008); Krasno (2005).

31. See note 30.

32. Krasno and Dowling (2008) simulate the impact of alternative allocation strategies to show that parties could have increased the number of competitive contests without appreciably affecting their number of expected victories.

33. See Karp (1993) for a contrarian view of parties' competitive impulses.

34. Jamieson (1996).

35. See note 14.

36. Krasno and Goldstein (2002).

37. Magleby (2002).

38. Coleman (1996).

39. For instance, 30 percent of NES respondents described themselves as strong partisans and 10 percent described themselves as pure independents in 1996, as the parties embarked on their binge of spending, versus 32 percent and 11 percent in 2008. It is true that the percentage of respondents who are strong partisans has increased from a low of 23 percent in 1978, and the percentage of respondents who are pure independents has decreased from a high of 18 percent in 1974. Most of the change, however, came during the 1980s, well before the parties became major advertisers. See www.electionstudies.org/nesguide/toptable/tab2a_3.htm.

40. Sorauf and I worked as expert witnesses for the Federal Election Commission in 1997 for *Colorado Republican II* and for the State of Missouri in 2000 for *Missouri Republican Party v. Lamb*, two cases where the plaintiffs were state Republican parties suing on the grounds that different regulations illegally restricted their operations and harmed them. As a result of the litigation, we had the opportunity to review confidential documents from both parties, including internal communications and financial reports, as well as sworn depositions from party officials. We cited many of the relevant portions of our testimony in these cases in our later testimony in *McConnell v. FEC* (2003) which later appeared as Krasno and Sorauf (2003).

41. One of the more remarkable findings from our study of the Missouri Republican Party is that, at the time lacking any limits on the size of the donations it could accept, 80 percent of its receipts came from just 36 contributors (excluding

the national parties) from a total list of just 1,000 donors (Krasno and Sorauf 2003). Aside from the concerns about corruption that this raises, we argued that this indicates a lazy and unhealthy state party. It is hard to imagine that Missouri's Republicans could find so few contributors in a politically competitive state with more than 5 million residents, but the party had no incentive to try.

42. Corrado et al. (1997).

43. Gibson et al. (1983).

44. Aldrich (1995).

45. Ansolabehere and Snyder (2000b).

46. La Raja (2008); La Raja and Jarvis-Shean (2001).

47. Carman, Farrell, and Krasno (2008). The FEC required parties to include a short description of each expenditure. This results in thousands of entries, many of which describe the same activity, like "canvass" and "door-to-door," leading to obvious problems with replication (Krasno and Sorauf 2003, p. 151).

48. Krasno and Sorauf (2003). Parties managed to work around these impediments (mainly related to independent expenditures) as Election Day neared in 2004, a trend that carried over to the 2006 and 2008 elections. Under the circumstances, it remains to be seen whether the surge in mobilization spending in 2004 was a unique event or the beginning of a trend.

49. Turnout was significantly higher in 2000 than in 2004, but it is difficult to attribute this entirely to parties, since there was simultaneously heightened interest in the election and a great deal of activity by nonparty groups, especially on the Democratic side.

50. Green and Gerber (2004).

51. Carman, Farrell, and Krasno (2008).

52. Gerber and Green (2000), p. 662. This concern may have been alleviated somewhat by the substantial and successful efforts to mobilize voters in 2004. It remains to be seen, however, whether this was a one-time set of circumstances or the beginning of a longer trend in which the parties will become major players.

53. Two exceptions, of course, are when the opposing candidate is particularly noxious to partisans, as Senator Tom Daschle (Democrat, South Dakota) was to Republicans in 2004 or the Clinton impeachment managers were to Democrats in 1998, or when a single seat might shift control of a legislative body. In the latter case, I would argue that parties have a better chance of picking up the needed seat by putting more seats in play (Krasno and Green 2005).

54. Krasno and Green (2005).

55. Aldrich (1995), p. 21.

56. Ranney (1954).

IX

Candidates and Parties in Congressional Elections

REVISITING CANDIDATE-CENTERED CONCLUSIONS IN A PARTISAN ERA

Eric McGhee and Kathryn Pearson

SINCE THE 1950s, the reelection of nearly all House incumbents has been a constant in American political life. On average, incumbents were re-elected 93.3 percent of the time between 1952 and 2000 and 95.2 percent of the time between 2002 and 2008.[1] Significant and sustained interest in the incumbency advantage among political scientists has been a constant as well, as scholars have employed a variety of methods to analyze the sources and consequences of the incumbency advantage throughout this time period. Even as incumbency reelection rates remain essentially unchanged, changing political conditions warrant a reexamination of the roots of the incumbency advantage. In this chapter, we reassess the candidate-centered model of congressional elections during an era of heightened polarization.

The high incumbent reelection rates that began in the 1950s have been linked to the concomitant rise in candidate-centered campaigns. With the decline of strong party operations, members of Congress (MCs) responded strategically by drawing upon the resources and opportunities that come with membership in the House to build their own, personal reelection constituencies.[2] In a candidate-centered political world, incumbents are far better positioned than challengers because they can help their constituents, generate publicity, raise money, and scare off quality challengers.[3]

Mann and Wolfinger offered what remains one of the most complete expositions of this candidate-centered model.[4] Using new questions about incumbent members of Congress from the 1978 National Election Study (NES), Mann and Wolfinger showed that voters could generally recognize and evaluate the candidates running in their own district, particularly the incumbent, even when they were unable to recall candidates' names from memory. Further, they showed that these candidate evaluations mattered at least as much as—if not sometimes more than—political party affiliation when it came to vote choice. Voters were increasingly crossing party lines, and crossover support disproportionately benefited incumbents.

As much as this scholarship has contributed to our understanding of candidate-centered congressional elections, it emerged during a low point for parties in American public life. In recent years, parties have rebounded in significant ways. Since 1978, voters have "sorted" themselves more effectively into parties; the number of independent identifiers has decreased; the national party organizations are more involved in campaigns and campaign finance; and the parties play a more important role on Capitol Hill. How well does the candidate-centered model survive in this new era of party discipline?

In the analysis that follows, we test a party-centered and candidate-centered model of vote choice with more recent data. As might be expected, certain aspects of the candidate-centered model require revision. Partisanship has become more important to voters' evaluations and candidate choices. We focus on voters who identify with the same party as the candidate challenging their incumbent member of Congress, whom we refer to as "challenger partisans." (Likewise, we use the term "incumbent partisan" to refer to voters who identify with the incumbent's party.) Challenger partisans showed the strongest tendency to vote across party lines in 1978, but they are also the ones who have returned to the partisan fold in greatest numbers in recent years.[5] However, many important early conclusions about congressional incumbents withstand changing political currents. Although parties are more central to the average voter's calculus, images of the incumbents as representatives of the parties, rather than images of the parties themselves, are behind this change. Challenger partisans have grown more dissatisfied with their incumbents *as individuals*, and have turned to the challenger as a meaningful way to express this dissatisfaction.

Party-Centered and Candidate-Centered Models of Congressional Elections

Political parties are more central to American political life than they have been in nearly a century. In the electorate, there is evidence that individuals are increasingly likely to identify as partisans rather than pure independents, and that partisans are increasingly likely to support their party's candidate in the voting booth.[6]

In Congress, party loyalty in roll-call voting has reached record levels as the two parties have become more internally homogeneous and ideologically distinct. Members of Congress have ceded more power to their leaders than at any time since the downfall of Speaker Joseph Cannon in 1910.[7] Moreover, parties have become substantially more involved in congressional elections. Since the early 1980s, national party organizations have raised record amounts of money and have helped their respective candidates in competitive races with increasing frequency, particularly since 1995.[8] Congressional parties provide generous resources to their most vulnerable incumbents and their most promising challengers, and safe members of Congress are increasingly helpful in financing the races of colleagues in the same party.[9] These changes are profound and well-documented enough to make an anachronism of assertions that American parties are weak. Instead, in a striking reversal since calls for responsible party government in the 1950s, many congressional observers worry that excessive partisanship is responsible for a host of problems in Congress.[10]

What does the increased significance of party and partisan polarization mean for congressional elections? During the 1970s, there was considerable ideological overlap among party coalitions in the electorate and in Congress, and the national parties were only beginning to play a financial role in elections. House elections appeared to be very much in harmony with this broader notion of weak parties. Vote choice in House elections was strongly personal. The great majority of voters cast ballots for the candidate they preferred. In cases where partisan identification and candidate preference conflicted, voters more often than not prioritized candidate preference. Parties were not irrelevant to the vote, to be sure, but their role was notably weak and growing weaker.[11] This personal vote tilted heavily toward incumbents, who retained support from the vast majority of their own partisans, while challengers lost a majority of theirs. All of these findings came at a time when incumbent margins of victory were on the rise.[12]

The source of incumbents' appeal was as much weak challengers as strong incumbents. Incumbents were better liked than their opponents and also far better known. The few challengers who managed to become well known tended to win back voters of their own party—the challenger partisans who would have otherwise supported the incumbent. In fact, Mann and Wolfinger found that favorable impressions of incumbents were grounded in almost no ideological or issue content whatsoever.[13] Without a credible challenger, there was nobody to call attention to the details of an incumbent's record. More recently, Burden and Kimball have shown that voters cast their ballots for presidential and congressional candidates of opposite parties due mainly to a lack of competition in congressional elections (and sometimes popular presidential candidates of the other party), not from a desire to pursue a middle ground between the two parties.[14]

It is easy to imagine that today's party polarization might undermine this highly personalized portrait of House elections by discouraging partisan defection toward increasingly partisan incumbents. There is some evidence for a decrease in partisan defection, at the level of both individual voters and congressional districts.[15] And the more often incumbents vote with their party in Washington (as measured using Americans for Democratic Action scores), the lower their vote share is at home.[16]

Yet there is also reason to think that polarization by itself would have little impact. After all, incumbents are still far better positioned than their challengers to attract publicity, pursue particularistic benefits for their constituency, and provide nonpartisan constituent service. In fact, since the 1970s, incumbents have raised even more money and faced still weaker opponents.[17] Can challenger partisans become significantly more loyal to their party if they do not even know the identity of their party's candidate?

We seek to determine whether renewed partisan loyalty in voting is a response to parties or candidates, and if it is the latter, are challengers attracting votes or are incumbents repelling them? As the parties have polarized, they have developed clearer and more divergent images than they have had at any time since before World War II. Voters could be excused for mechanically attributing these partisan images to individual candidates in their local House race. But these party images emerge largely from the behavior of individual politicians serving in public office. Polarized voter behavior might simply be a reaction to individual candidates who have voted more frequently along party lines than in the past, rather than to the broader party images.

The first model of change is "party-centered," and it is well documented in the literature. Voters are more likely than in the past to give partisan reasons for their candidate evaluations, and the divergence of parties on Capitol Hill is strongly correlated with changing voter perceptions of the parties as a whole.[18] On the other hand, Fiorina et al. have argued strenuously for the second model, which we call "candidate-centered."[19] Just as Mann and Wolfinger argued in 1980, Fiorina et al. assert that voters can respond only to the candidates that they are offered. If voters are becoming more polarized, it is because they must choose between candidates who are themselves polarized along party lines. Given a choice, voters should still support attractive candidates who distinguish themselves from their parties.

Analyzing NES data from 1978 to 2008, we test these models in an era of increased partisan polarization. We explore the causes behind the changes we identify in voters' evaluations of candidates, asking whether they are party-centered or candidate-centered. At issue is whether candidates are trapped by larger party images that are essentially beyond their control, or whether their own partisan decisions on the House floor hinder their ability to win over wavering partisans from the other side. If candidates continue to be relevant to the process, the basic outlines of

House elections described in earlier research would still hold in today's era of strong parties.

The Importance of Party, Revisited

In the late 1970s, party identification was losing some of its centrality to vote choice.[20] Defectors—those who identify with one party and vote for the House candidate of the other—were becoming much more common. The proportion of defectors increased from just 9 percent in 1956 to 22 percent in 1978.

This trend of increasing partisan defection has now reversed itself, as shown in figure 9-1. In fact, 1980 was the high-water mark: since then, party-line voting in House elections has increased, and the percentage of voters self-identifying as pure independents has declined. In 1978, 10 percent of the electorate considered themselves pure independents, 68 percent of the electorate voted for their party's candidate, and 22 percent defected. There have never been so many pure independents since, and party loyalty among voters has fallen below 76 percent only once since 1990. Indeed, after 1980, party loyalty increased to levels that had not been seen since the 1960s.

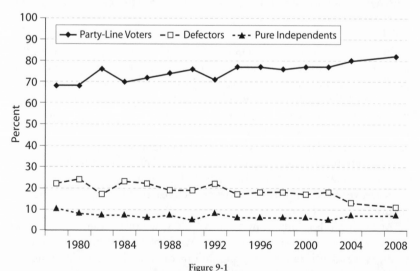

Figure 9-1

The composition of the vote in House elections, 1978–2008. Note: Data come from the National Election Studies Cumulative File, 1978–2008. No independent values are plotted for 2006 because no National Election Study was conducted that year.

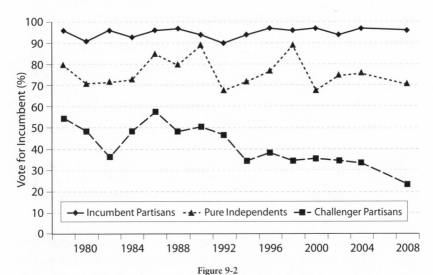

Figure 9-2

Incumbent support by partisan identification, 1978–2008. Note: Data come from the National Election Studies Cumulative File, 1978–2008. No independent values are plotted for 2006 because no National Election Study was conducted that year.

We should not imagine, however, that party loyalty increased equally among all groups of voters. After all, the growth in defection rates before 1980 did not occur in a "politically neutral manner": defection rates among incumbent partisans hardly changed at all, while defection rates among challenger partisans rose steeply.[21] We expect, then, that a return to party loyalty has also been concentrated among challenger partisans, since they were the ones who started defecting in the first place.

Defection rates from 1978 to 2008 confirm that incumbents consistently attract the overwhelming majority of their own partisans. As shown in figure 9-2, incumbents in 1978 drew 95 percent of voters from their own party, whereas challengers won only 46 percent of theirs. Since then, incumbent support from incumbent partisans has never dipped below 89 percent, and has climbed as high as 96 percent in several recent cycles. Incumbents continue to earn support from the great majority of pure independents, as well: three in four usually vote for the incumbent, and this number has never fallen below two-thirds. More to the point, independents are as likely to vote for the incumbent in recent years as they were two decades ago.

However, our analysis shows an important decline in support for incumbents among challenger partisans. Incumbents have not received the support of a majority of these voters since 1986, and the support rate dropped sharply from 54 percent in 1978 to 23 percent in 2008. There is a particularly striking 13-point drop between 1992 and 1994, after which support for the incumbent among challenger partisans never again exceeds 40 percent. Thus, while incumbent reelection rates are just as high as ever, incumbents increasingly face levels of challenger partisan loyalty not seen in decades.[22]

The high rates of challenger party defection in the late 1970s were primarily the product of an imbalance between weak challengers and strong incumbents: incumbents were far better known and better evaluated than their opponents, and these advantages allowed them to draw voters across party lines. It was a highly personal, candidate-centered phenomenon. What, then, are we to make of growing party loyalty in the electorate? Should this personal, candidate-based model now be revised?

The answer to that question depends a great deal on *why* challenger partisans have grown more loyal. The party-centered model suggests that challenger partisans have become more committed to their party in the abstract, without reference to individual candidates. As such, these partisans find the incumbent's personal appeals fundamentally less tempting. According to this model, we should see an increase in the percentage of challenger partisans who strongly identify with their party, because strong identification would suggest greater a priori commitment to the party. We should also see a decrease in the importance of candidate-centered factors such as candidate recognition and evaluation in predicting vote choice, since a stronger commitment to the party should overrule personal considerations. In contrast, the candidate-centered model suggests that loyalty is driven by candidate behavior, not by polarized voters. Candidate recognition and evaluation remain central to this perspective: defection is down among challenger partisans because challengers are better known or better liked relative to their incumbent opponents.

To adjudicate between these models, we first estimate a probit model of defection among challenger partisans, where the dependent variable is coded 1 if the respondent voted for the incumbent and 0 otherwise. In the first model, the election year is the only independent variable. The coefficient on this variable should be negative, reflecting the declining defection rate among these voters. We then add a variety of independent variables to the model and observe which most explains the time trend by bringing its coefficient closest to zero. The goal is to identify which factors have brought challenger partisans back into the fold.

We test four different possibilities. The first two variables test the party-centered model. We create a party preference variable, coded with relative feeling thermometer ratings. Respondents who give a higher thermometer rating to the incumbent's party are coded 1, those who give the challenger's party the higher rating are coded –1, and if both parties receive the same rating, the code is 0. A respondent who declines to rate a party for any reason is assumed to be perfectly neutral about the parties for the sake of coding this preference variable. If challenger partisans have grown loyal because they increasingly prefer their own party, then this variable should account for a significant portion of the trend over time. We then add strength of partisan identification to tap a similar idea: voters who have come to prefer their own party should be more likely to identify strongly with it, and so to avoid voting for the opposing party's candidate. Since the analysis is limited to challenger partisans, strength of partisanship is a dummy variable coded 1 for those who strongly identify with their party.

The second two variables test the continuing relevance of the candidate-centered model. Because feelings about the candidates might have changed without any change in feelings about the parties, we add candidate preference, coded with relative candidate feeling thermometers in the same manner as the party preference variable described earlier.[23] Finally, although the literature is filled with descriptions of the declining competitive position of the average challenger,[24] challenger partisans might still be motivated to learn more about their own party's candidate. Thus, we include a dummy variable indicating those respondents who can both recognize and rate the challenger, suggesting an awareness of that candidate that might lead to decreased support for the incumbent.

The results of these probit regressions are presented in table 9-1, and they support the continuing relevance of the candidate-centered model. The time trend, shown in model 1, is negative as expected (–0.60), indicating that challenger partisans have grown less likely to defect from their party in recent years. But of the four variables included to explain this decline, only candidate preference, added in model 4, has an effect: it significantly shrinks the magnitude of the time trend, cutting the coefficient from –0.55 to –0.28. Models 2 and 3 add the measures of party-centered behavior, but neither of these variables has much effect on the time trend, which drops from –0.60 to only –0.55 across these different specifications. Finally, the effect of recognizing and rating the challenger, added in model 5, is small, and generally leaves both the time trend and the effects of the other variables unchanged.[25]

These results suggest that growing loyalty among challenger partisans is a response to candidates more than parties. Figure 9-3 unpacks this result by looking at feeling thermometers of challengers and incumbents separately. The results suggest that feelings about incumbents are driving

Table 9-1. Explaining Vote Choice, 1978–2008

	(1)	(2)	(3)	(4)	(5)
Election year (1978 = 0, 2008 = 1)	−0.60*** (0.07)	−0.57*** (0.07)	−0.55*** (0.07)	−0.28** (0.08)	−0.25** (0.08)
Party preference	—	0.66*** (0.05)	0.54*** (0.05)	0.42*** (0.05)	0.43*** (0.05)
Strong partisan	—	—	−0.51*** (0.05)	−0.49*** (0.06)	−0.50*** (0.06)
Candidate preference	—	—	—	1.08*** (0.03)	1.06*** (0.03)
Recognize and rate challenger	—	—	—	—	−0.19** (0.06)
Constant	0.12*	0.60***	0.68***	0.26***	0.37**
−2*log likelihood	4566.97	4338.37	4228.32	2914.16	2902.91
χ^2	68.72***	255.94***	361.25***	1204.39***	1208.44***
Pseudo R^2	0.01	0.06	0.09	0.37	0.37
N	3384	3384	3384	3384	3384

Note: Data come from the National Election Studies Cumulative File, 1978–2008. 2002 is excluded from all models, since party feeling thermometers were not asked that year, and 2006 is excluded because no National Election Study was conducted.

$*p < 0.05; **p < 0.01; ***p < 0.001.$

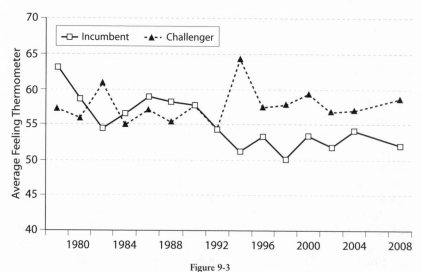

Figure 9-3

Candidate ratings over time (challenger partisans only). Note: Data come from the National Election Studies Cumulative File, 1978–2008. No independent values are plotted for 2006 because no National Election Study was conducted that year.

most of the party loyalty trend because they are the only ones that have changed over time. Though ratings rise and fall somewhat, challenger partisans give their party's candidate the same thermometer rating in 2008 as in 1978. In contrast, their average rating of the incumbent has fallen from 63 in 1978 to 52 in 2008. Challenger partisans are not drawn to their party's candidate so much as repelled by their incumbent.

Evaluating Polarized Incumbents

If favorable opinions of the incumbent are declining, what explains this change? Though candidate evaluations are clearly important to vote choice, partisan considerations might still enter a voter's calculus further back in the "funnel of causality" by shaping opinions of the incumbent, which in turn inform vote choice.[26] In particular, as congressional parties have become more polarized along ideological lines, challenger partisans might observe the incumbent's party drifting away from their own ideological position and simply assume that this movement applies to their own incumbent as well. In this way, the incumbent would be tarred with the behavior of the party, making general party polarization and increased party loyalty among members of Congress the most significant factors behind growing loyalty by voters.

The question, then, is whether party or incumbent ideology has a greater effect on incumbent evaluations. To explore this question, we first calculated the absolute distance between the respondent's ideological self-placement, compressed onto a scale from −1 to 1, and the incumbent's first-dimension DW-NOMINATE score, which falls within the same range.[27] We then calculated a similar distance measure using the average DW-NOMINATE score for every member of the incumbent's party in the House of Representatives. The first measure captures ideological distance from the incumbent, while the second captures distance from the incumbent's party. Because this approach uses actual voting behavior in Congress rather than the respondent's best guess of that behavior, it avoids the projection effects that can otherwise complicate measures of ideological distance.[28]

We then regressed challenger partisans' feeling thermometer ratings of the incumbent on these ideological distance measures, using a process similar to the one employed in table 9-1. Specifically, the first model includes only a time trend to capture the declining opinion of incumbents over time, the second and third models include each of the measures of ideological distance by themselves, and the last model includes both measures of distance simultaneously.[29] The goal, as before, is to account for as much of the time trend as possible. The results are presented in table 9-2.

Both candidate-specific and partisan considerations appear to be driving the change in incumbent evaluations over time. Each measure of ideological distance explains about as much of the time trend, reducing its size from −10.29 to either −6.61 or −6.95. This suggests that something common to both ideological distance measures is driving the broader trends—most likely the fact that parties and individual incumbents have both become more ideologically polarized over time. However, if both measures are included in the model together, ideological distance from the incumbent has by far the larger coefficient (−11.60 versus −4.39). Thus, feeling thermometer scores are still in part based on personal evaluations of each incumbent individually. Incumbents who distinguish themselves from their partisan colleagues can still influence their evaluations among challenger partisans through the roll-call votes they cast.[30]

Discussion

Our examination of House elections since 1978 reveals an important consistency between voter behavior in the era of weak parties and voter behavior in today's partisan era: the central role of the candidates. Partisanship in the electorate has increased, party organizations have increased their support for candidates in competitive races, and parties in government have become more ideologically distinct and powerful. Yet

Table 9-2. Explaining Incumbent Thermometer Scores, 1978–2008

	(1)	(2)	(3)	(4)
Election year	−10.29***	−6.61***	−6.95***	−6.44***
(1978 = 0, 2008 = 1)	(1.34)	(1.35)	(1.35)	(1.35)
Ideological distance	—	−15.10***	—	−11.60***
from incumbent		(1.21)		(2.27)
Ideological distance	—	—	−14.27***	−4.39#
from incumbent's party			(1.27)	(2.35)
Constant	59.91***	66.67***	66.87***	67.25***
Root MSE	23.76	23.17	23.27	23.16
Adjusted R^2	0.02	0.07	0.06	0.07
N	3231	3231	3231	3231

Note: Data come from the National Election Studies Cumulative File, 1978–2008. 2006 is excluded from all models because no National Election Study was conducted that year.
#$p < 0.1$; ***$p < 0.001$.

despite these changes, a candidate-centered model of congressional elections remains appropriate. Evaluations of individual candidates continue to drive many, if not most, voting decisions. Increasingly negative views about one's own incumbent, as opposed to negative feelings about the parties as a whole, are the most important factor explaining a return to higher levels of party loyalty among challenger partisans today. Moreover, incumbent behavior in office has a meaningful effect on these evaluations: the greater the ideological distance between an incumbent and a constituent, the lower the feeling thermometer rating, at least among constituents of the challenger's party. In short, challenger partisans have recommitted themselves to their parties, but for largely candidate-centered reasons that leave open the prospect of greater cross-party voting in the future.

This is not to say that the parties as a whole are unimportant. They help voters construct their feelings about incumbents in the first place. In addition, the parties play a larger role in campaign finance today than in the past, helping voters become aware of the candidates that they are meant to evaluate. Moreover, there is more to vote choice than just the candidates. In fact, the most notable break in our time series falls between 1992 and 1994, when support for the incumbent among challenger partisans dropped permanently and to a degree that is not easily explained from a candidate-centered perspective.[31] Finally, evidence from other studies suggests that voters have "sorted" more appropriately on the basis of ideology into the two parties: partisan identification is a stronger predictor of vote choice today than in the past, which means that a voter who identifies with a particular party is more likely to actually agree with that party on most issues.[32] The broader political landscape clearly matters.

Nonetheless, it is important to avoid assuming that "big-picture" changes such as partisan sorting, growing party campaign coffers, and polarized party images will lead to a deeper commitment to the parties under all circumstances. Feelings about the candidates continue to sway voters even as a variety of forces also work to line up voters more consistently on one side of the aisle.

We also identify an important point of departure from the candidate-centered model, at least as it came to be understood in the period before polarization. While much past research has found that political substance plays a small role in opinions of incumbents, we find that role to be somewhat larger: large enough, at any rate, for incumbent behavior in office to contribute to the trend toward greater party loyalty in vote choice. Incumbents have not lost support because they face strong challengers with the resources to publicize their potentially controversial positions. Instead, the polarized behavior of individual incumbents trickles down to enough voters that they are able to make evaluations on that basis.

Incumbents' partisan behavior in Washington has an important effect on how voters in their districts evaluate them.

This is perhaps the most important implication of our analysis. It is easy to believe that the trends that drive party loyalty in the electorate are beyond the control of individual candidates, yet we find that incumbents can and do help shape their own fates. Members of Congress have been increasingly likely to toe the party line, reflected in rising party unity in roll-call voting in the past two decades.[33] The partisan behavior of some members of Congress in recent years has made it harder for them to attract the cross-party voters that will help keep them in office.[34] In most districts, defecting voters are not essential for victory, and it is certainly possible that an increase in uncompetitive districts has compensated for the loss of challenger partisan support.[35] We believe, however, that there is no substitute for "running scared" to keep an incumbent secure over the long run, especially when many if not most of the wayward challenger partisans could be won back with a little dose of independence from the party.[36] Given that voters in many districts seem to want more moderate candidates than they are getting, it is remarkable that incumbents are not fighting harder to provide that moderation for them in Washington.

Notes

1. See Davidson et al. (2009), p. 64.
2. See Fenno (1978); Mayhew (1974b).
3. See Box-Steffensmeier (1996); Cox and Katz (1996); Jacobson (2004); Mayhew (1974b).
4. See Mann and Wolfinger (1980).
5. Ibid.
6. See Bartels (2000); Brady, d'Onofrio, and Fiorina (2000).
7. See McCarty, Poole, and Rosenthal (2006); Rohde (1991).
8. See Green and Herrnson (2002); Herrnson (2000).
9. See Kolodny (1998); Cann (2008).
10. For an example of a call for responsible party government, see Ranney (1954). For an example of concern about the effect of partisanship on Congress, see Mann and Ornstein (2006).
11. See Mann and Wolfinger (1980).
12. See Erikson (1972); Ferejohn (1977); Fiorina (1977); Mayhew (1974b).
13. See Mann and Wolfinger (1980).
14. See Burden and Kimball (2002).
15. See Bartels (2000); Brady, d'Onofrio, and Fiorina (2000).
16. See Canes-Wrone, Brady, and Cogan (2002).
17. See Abramowitz, Alexander, and Gunning (2006); Ansolabehere and Snyder (2000a); Campbell (2003); Jacobson (2004).

18. See Jacobson (2004); Hetherington (2001).

19. See Fiorina, Pope, and Abrams (2005).

20. See Mann and Wolfinger (1980).

21. See Mann and Wolfinger (1980, p. 620). Throughout this study, independents who lean toward either party are classified as partisans.

22. Incumbents are also more likely to represent districts that favor their party, so they have fewer challenger partisans that they need to convert. See Abramowitz, Alexander, and Gunning (2006).

23. We chose this categorical approach instead of subtracting one thermometer score from the other because it allowed us to include the large number of challenger partisans (about 50 percent) who decline to rate the challenger, without assuming too much about the specificity of their opinion. That is, we assume only that such respondents prefer the incumbent to the challenger (whom they do not rate), but not *how strongly* they hold that preference.

24. See Abramowitz et al. 2006; Ansolabehere and Snyder 2000; Campbell 2003.

25. The results are the same if the variables are added to the model in a different order.

26. See Campbell et al. (1960) for details on the "funnel of causality" concept.

27. See Poole and Rosenthal (1997).

28. See Brady and Sniderman (1985). This process does assume that the DW-NOMINATE score captures the same ideological dimension as the respondent's self-placement, but any error in this measurement should apply equally to ideological distance from the incumbent and from the parties.

29. We add each variable separately because the results are different when we do. In contrast, the results in table 9-1 are identical regardless of the order in which the variables are added.

30. One advantage of using actual voting records is that the measures of ideological distance differ only in terms of the measure of roll-call voting: a largely exogenous referent. The respondent's ideology is the same in both cases. Thus, there is little concern that one variable might be causing the other in a voter's internal decision-making process, and such questions of endogeneity become moot.

31. A dummy variable for the years since 1994 exerts a modest effect in our fully specified vote choice model (i.e., model 5 in table 9-1), suggesting something broader and more fundamental at work than we have otherwise identified.

32. See Abramowitz and Saunders (1998); Fiorina, Pope, and Abrams (2005).

33. See McCarty, Poole, and Rosenthal (2006); Layman et al. (2010).

34. See Canes-Wrone, Brady, and Cogan (2002).

35. See Oppenheimer (2005); Stonecash, Brewer, and Mariani (2003).

36. See Jacobson (1987).

X

The Myth of the Independent Voter Revisited

David B. Magleby, Candice J. Nelson, and Mark C. Westlye

FOR HALF A CENTURY, party identification has been seen as a fundamental, long-term influence on Americans' political attitudes and behavior, and as the single most important predictor of the vote.[1] In 2008, more respondents classified themselves as independents than as Democrats or Republicans; they comprised 39 percent of the American electorate, with Democrats at 34 percent and Republicans at 26 percent.[2] In eight of the last ten elections, independents have constituted a plurality of the electorate or been tied for that status.[3]

The increase in the number of citizens identifying as independent began in the 1960s, as figure 10-1 shows. By the 1970s and 1980s, this rise had been noted—sometimes with alarm—by political scientists, members of the media, and politicians alike. At the same time, the number of strong partisans was diminishing. The decline in strength of partisanship and the growth in independents were considered to have profound potential consequences for American politics and for democracy itself. Independents were seen as unconstrained by partisanship in responding to election-year appeals; they were "adrift without an anchor in a political world full of strong eddies and currents."[4] Their votes were "up for grabs."[5] With more and more voters becoming independents, there could be wider and wider swings between the parties.[6] Other anticipated consequences included weaker presidential mandates,[7] greater opportunities for third parties,[8] party realignment,[9] and an increasingly fragmented Congress.[10] Perhaps the most alarming potential development was that the rise in independents might bring an end to the current party system.[11] Such a "dealignment" not only portended "the deterioration and disarray of *both* parties,"[12] but "political instability and ineffective performance on a scale without recent precedent"[13] or—simply put—"a loss of democracy."[14]

The prevalence of these concerns prompted us and three colleagues, including Ray Wolfinger, to look closely at independents in the electorate from 1952 (the first year in which the American National Election Study [ANES] asked respondents for their party identification) through 1988, in *The Myth of the Independent Voter*.[15]

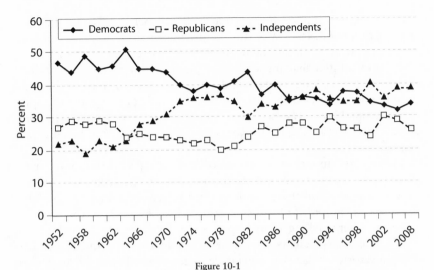

Figure 10-1

Republicans, Democrats, and independents in the United States, 1952–2008. Source: Sapiro, Virginia, Steven J. Rosenstone, and the National Election Studies. 2008. *American National Election Studies Cumulative Data File, 1948–2004* [computer file]. Ann Arbor: University of Michigan, Center for Political Studies [producer] and Inter-University Consortium for Political and Social Research [distributor]; the ANES 2008 Time Series Study [data set]; and Stanford University and the University of Michigan [producers].

NES first asks respondents whether they generally identify as Democrats, Republicans, or independents, and then asks those answering "independent" whether they lean toward one of the parties or not. Those identifying with a party are asked whether they do so strongly or weakly.[16] We looked at how each of the seven types of identifier responded on various attitudinal and behavioral measures relating to politics, political parties, and candidates and found that leaning independents ("leaners") were just as partisan in their attitudes and behavior as declared partisans, or more so. Differences between Independent Democrats and Independent Republicans were in most instances substantial. And Pure Independents consistently differed from partisan independents in their backgrounds, political perceptions, and behavior.

The speculation that independents might conceivably detach from the parties could realistically be applied only to Pure Independents, and their increases over time had been rather modest: they rose from 6 percent of the electorate in 1952 to 13 percent in 1972, and leveled off at 11 percent in 1988. Moreover, the proportion of Pure Independents who actually vote in elections comprised, on average, about 8 percent. *Myth* concluded that party identification was still the driving force of political behavior for most voters, including the majority of self-described independents. It also demonstrated that most of these findings about independents had been true for as long as data had been collected—a pattern that had been overlooked in much of the original analysis of party identification in the seminal book *The American Voter*.[17] Properly measured and interpreted, "independent" citizens were not nearly as influential as many had claimed.

In the years since the publication of *Myth*, the proportion of independents in the electorate has not diminished, nor has the proportion of their subcomponents: two-thirds of them remain leaners. Table 10-1 presents the seven categories of identifier produced by the two-part ANES survey question. After reaching 13 to 15 percent of the electorate throughout the 1970s, Pure Independents have since hovered between 8 and 12 percent. The trajectory for partisan independents has been similar. In the 1950s, both groups of leaners were in the single digits; Independent Republicans have, since the mid-1980s, constituted 11 to 13 percent of the electorate, and Independent Democrats have moved from an average of 12 percent in the 1970s and 1980s to 15 to 17 percent in more recent years.

The persistently large proportion of independents in the population has continued to prompt some pundits and politicians—and more than a few scholars—to believe that over one-third of the electorate have no party allegiance and are therefore up for grabs in a given election. Concern has continued to be expressed about possible dealignment and the consequent health and stability of the American political system. But these assumptions about independents, and the concerns that followed, are simply unfounded. The real differences between partisan and Pure Independents that we found in *Myth* have continued through the 2008 election. In this chapter, we will revisit the findings and conclusions reached in *Myth*, and address, where needed, some of the claims and concerns that still circulate regarding the large bloc of independents.

In previewing the 2008 presidential election campaign, a report by the *Washington Post*, the Henry J. Kaiser Foundation, and Harvard University called attention to "a broad segment of the electorate—about three in ten voters call themselves independents—. . . [which] is poised to play the role of political power broker in 2008."[18] Candidate McCain claimed a special affinity with "independents,"[19] while candidate Obama claimed to be "post-partisan" in his orientation.[20]

As candidates and political operatives searched out the independent vote, a number of scholars presented justification for the hunt. Kenneth Janda et al., for example, defined two-fifths of the electorate as independents, meaning persons with "no party attachment."[21] Martin Watten-

Table 10-1. Party Identification, 1952–2008

	Strong Democrats	Weak Democrats	Independent Democrats	Pure Independents	Independent Republicans	Weak Republicans	Strong Republicans	Apolitical
1952	22	25	10	6	7	14	14	3
1956	21	23	6	9	8	14	15	4
1958	27	22	7	7	5	17	11	4
1960	20	25	6	10	7	14	16	3
1962	23	23	7	8	6	16	12	4
1964	27	25	9	8	6	14	11	1
1966	18	28	9	12	7	15	11	1
1968	20	25	10	11	9	15	10	1
1970	20	24	10	13	8	15	10	1
1972	15	26	11	13	11	13	10	1
1974	18	21	13	15	9	14	8	3
1976	15	25	12	15	10	14	9	1
1978	15	24	14	14	10	13	8	3
1980	18	23	11	13	10	14	9	2
1982	20	24	11	11	8	14	10	2

1984	17	20	11	11	12	15	12	2
1986	18	22	10	12	11	15	11	2
1988	18	18	12	11	13	14	14	2
1990	17	19	12	11	13	17	11	2
1992	18	18	14	12	12	14	11	1
1994	15	19	13	11	12	15	15	1
1996	18	19	14	9	12	15	12	1
1998	19	18	14	11	11	16	10	2
2000	19	15	15	12	13	12	12	1
2002	17	17	15	8	13	16	14	1
2004	17	16	17	10	12	12	16	0
2006	No ANES survey conducted							
2008	19	15	17	11	11	13	13	1

Source: Sapiro, Virginia, Steven J. Rosenstone, and the National Election Studies. 2004. *American National Election Studies Cumulative Data File, 1948–2004* [computer file]. Ann Arbor, MI: University of Michigan, Center for Political Studies [producer]; Ann Arbor, MI: Inter-University Consortium for Political and Social Research [distributor]. The American National Election Studies (ANES; www.electionstudies.org). 2008. *The ANES 2008 Time Series Study* [data set]. Stanford University and the University of Michigan [producers].

Note: Cross-section samples only, except in 2000; pre-election surveys in presidential election years. The ANES was not conducted in 2006.

berg, a dedicated scholar of partisan decline, stated in 1998 that "for over four decades the American public has been drifting away from the two major political parties."[22] At the same time, Harold Clarke and Marianne Stewart claimed that "the most salient characteristic of partisanship since it was first measured in national election surveys in the 1950s has been its long-term erosion in what has become a protracted era of dealignment in the United States and other democracies."[23] And Marjorie R. Hershey, while acknowledging the distinction between leaners and Pure Independents, nevertheless seized on the size of the three independent subgroups combined (one-third of the electorate) to conclude that "because so many Americans consider themselves independent of party, it is also an electorate capable of producing mercurial election results."[24] Other scholars have continued to link the "bloc" of independents to the possibility of successful independent candidacies or of flourishing third parties.[25]

But if there is no such bloc, these foregoing conclusions are tenuous at best.

Basic Characteristics of Independents Unchanged

In *Myth*, we presented data showing that leaners tended to be more educated, more interested in politics, and more politically aware than many partisan identifiers. They also were not neutral in their opinions about the political parties. In contrast, Pure Independents were typically the least educated group in the electorate, were among the most politically unaware and disinterested in campaigns or elections, and were inclined not to express an affinity toward the parties or the party system. Morever, these patterns had already been consistently evident for decades.

Examination of data from elections occurring since the publication of *Myth* reveals that leaners remain just as well-educated as partisans, and sometimes more so than weak partisans. Pure Independents remain, as in the past, the least educated of the seven groups, and markedly so. In 2008, 54 percent of Pure Independents had no more than a high school education and only 13 percent reported having a college degree. In contrast, 60 percent of leaners had at least a high school diploma, and fully a quarter reported holding a college degree.

As had been the case previously, strong partisans since the 1990s have been consistently the most interested in politics and the current presidential campaign. Between 1992 and 2008, four-fifths (on average) of Strong Republicans and Strong Democrats reported following politics most or some of the time. In this more recent period, leaners still resemble weak partisans, although in some years their level of interest surpasses that of the weak partisans (2000 and 2004 for interest in general and 1992,

2000, and 2004 for interest in the presidential campaign). Although Pure Independents' interest has fluctuated depending on the election year, they remain the least interested in politics and campaigns.[26] In 2008, the percentage-point difference in interest level between the Pure Independents and leaners reached double digits.

The value of separating the leaners from Pure Independents may be illustrated by reviewing a conclusion recently reached by the authors of *The American Voter Revisited*. Examining the idea presented in *The American Voter* that party identification is a long-term cue for how to view politics, Lewis-Beck et al. posited that "the stronger a person's partisan attachment, the greater the person's involvement in politics."[27] They produced a table showing that in 2004, 57 percent of strong partisans, 28 percent of weak partisans, and 40 percent of independents (who in their table constituted 40 percent of all identifiers) were "very much interested" in the political campaign. Ignoring the nonlinearity of these findings, Lewis-Beck et al. concluded that independents are "less interested and involved in politics than are partisans."[28] This conclusion is correct despite the contradictory data in their table—so long as independents are considered to be those without partisan leanings. In fact, 35 percent of Independent Democrats and 42 percent of Independent Republicans reported being very much interested in the 2004 campaign compared to only 25 percent of the Pure Independents. When independents are aggregated, this distinction is lost. Indeed, partisan independents have frequently been more interested in presidential campaigns than have weak partisans.

Another political characteristic discussed in *Myth* was the extent to which Americans are knowledgeable about politics. On the measure "knowing which party has a majority in the House of Representatives," in *Myth* we found leaners to be nearly as knowledgeable as strong partisans, and consistently more knowledgeable than weak partisans. Pure Independents were notably the least knowledgeable, having provided the correct answer at an average rate—53 percent—that was little higher than would be yielded by guessing. Since 1992, the average proportion of Pure Independents who know which party controls the House has dropped to 43 percent. In that same period, Independent Democrats were on average 11 percentage points more knowledgeable than Pure Independents, and Independent Republicans 20 points more knowledgeable.

In examining independents' views of the two political parties, we noted in *Myth* that one of the reasons some political scientists gave for considering leaners as "true independents" was their apparent lack of psychological ties to party. Not surprisingly, we found that almost all strong party identifiers gave their parties very favorable ratings and were decidedly cool toward the other party. Pure Independents were neither favorable nor unfavorable toward either party—they were neutral and often inclined to have no opinion on the question. Leaners resembled weak partisans in giving strong positive ratings to the party toward which they leaned, but being unwilling to rate the other party negatively.

For an update on this question, we looked at identifiers' evaluations of the parties on the ANES 100-degree thermometer scales for all presidential and off-years since 1978. Strong partisans' ratings of their own party are remarkably high, and have remained constant over the period—hovering around 80 degrees. Their ratings of the other party have become even cooler than in prior years, dropping from the 40-degree mark in the 1980s to below 30 degrees by 2008. Thus, the distance between strong partisans' ratings of the two parties has grown over time. Figure 10-2 shows this difference for each type of identifier by subtracting the rating of the Republican Party from the rating of the Democratic Party and averaging these scores for two periods, 1978–1988 and 1990–2008. To continue with the example, the disparity between Strong Democrats' ratings of the two parties went from 44 points in the earlier period to 46 points in the more recent period. Indeed, looking at particular elections, the difference went from 40 points in 1978 to 58 points in 2008. Pure Independents, at the other extreme, rated both parties around the thermometer's 50-degree midpoint in 1978 and in 2008 and in all years between.

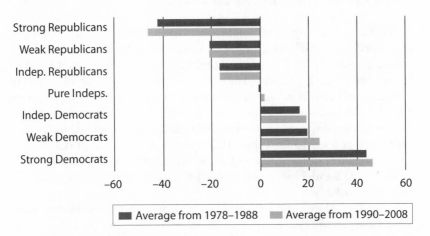

Figure 10-2
Party identification and attitudes toward the Democratic Party, 1978–2008. Note: The numbers provided represent the mean thermometer score for each group. This measure is achieved by subtracting the respondent's score for the Republican Party from his or her score for the Democratic Party. Source: The American National Election Studies (www.electionstudies.org). 2010. *Time Series Cumulative Data File* [data set]; Stanford University and the University of Michigan [producers and distributors].

Leaners and weak partisans have not changed much over time, either; they continue to view the parties in non-neutral terms. Independent Democrats rate their own party favorably, on average about 6 points less positively than do Weak Democrats. Independent Republicans rate their party about 5 points less positively than do Weak Republicans. Both groups of leaners rate the other party just a bit cooler than neutral. In terms of trends over time, Independent Democrats' feelings about the two parties have diverged in recent years. Democratic leaners' score differential increased in the two most recent presidential elections from the mid-high teens in the 1990s to the low 20s in 2004 and 2008. There is no corresponding change among Independent Republicans. Leaners remain partisans, and Pure Independents remain neutral in their view of the parties.

Overall, then, differences between leaners and Pure Independents over the last two decades have remained substantial. Leaners are better educated and more interested in and knowledgeable about politics, and in these respects they differ little from identifiers with the party toward which they lean. Leaners continue to resemble weak partisans in their evaluations of the major parties. In contrast, Pure Independents are a separate group, resembling none of the other six.

Voting Behavior of Independents Unchanged

Perhaps the most important implication for the political system of a rise in independents is whether and how Americans vote, in presidential and other elections. In *Myth*, we found that leaners were just as likely to turn out to vote as weak partisan identifiers, though somewhat less likely than strong identifiers. In contrast, the roughly 10 percent of the electorate who did not lean toward either party were the least likely to vote. Again, this significant difference between leaners and Pure Independents had existed since at least 1952. Table 10-2 presents ANES turnout data for all seven categories of identifier, giving the average for presidential elections between 1952 and 1988 and then for 1992 to 2008 (the period since the publication of *Myth*).

Table 10-2 shows the familiar pattern: leaners are considerably more likely to vote in presidential elections than are Pure Independents.[29] The proclivity to turn out has decreased slightly among all three types of independent identifier, while the turnout level for strong and weak identifiers has remained fairly constant.[30] As a result, in the last two presidential elections, leaners' propensity to vote dropped below that of their respective weak partisans. The drop in turnout is more striking among Pure Independents, starting in 1996. Where turnout among Pure Independents had averaged over 60 percent, that proportion dropped to 48 percent in

Table 10-2. Party Identification and Turnout in Presidential Elections, 1952–2008

	Percentage Who Voted						
	Average 1952–1988	1992	1996	2000	2004	2008	Average 1992–2008
Strong Democrats	83	86	88	85	90	89	87
Weak Democrats	71	76	67	69	74	77	72
Independent Democrats	72	74	66	65	68	68	68
Pure Independents	63	62	48	54	50	52	53
Independent Republicans	78	73	72	73	72	76	73
Weak Republicans	80	78	77	74	83	87	80
Strong Republicans	90	88	94	92	94	95	93

Source: The American National Election Studies (www.electionstudies.org). 2010. *Time Series Cumulative Data File* [data set]. Stanford University and the University of Michigan [producers and distributors].

Note: Self-reported turnout.

the Clinton-Dole election (1992) and has not topped 55 percent since. Pure Independents comprised only 7 percent of the electorate in 2008, which is below their average for the 1952–2008 period.

In our view, one of *Myth*'s most compelling findings was partisan independents' "impressive tendency to vote for the candidate of the party they feel closer to; indeed in presidential elections *they are generally more loyal to their party than weak partisans.*"[31] That pattern holds today. Table 10-3 shows the average vote for presidential elections between 1952 and 1988 and for each election since. In 1992, Independent Democrats' loyalty rate dropped to a still-impressive 67 percent (most of the defectors voting for Perot). Since then, Independent Democrats have become increasingly loyal in each of the last four presidential elections such that in 2008 fully 90 percent of them—the highest rate since ANES polling began—voted Democratic. Independent Republicans have also remained loyal, although Perot in 1992 and Clinton in 1996 were able to draw more than 20 percent of them away from the Republican standard-bearer.

Table 10-3. Party Identification and Vote for Democratic Presidential Candidates, 1952–2008

		Percentage Who Voted for the Democratic Presidential Candidate						Vote for Perot, 1992	Vote for Perot, 1996	Vote for Nader, 2000
	Average 1952–1988	1992	1996	2000	2004	2008	Average 1992–2008			
Strong Democrats	85	91	94	97	97	93	95	5	3	0
Weak Democrats	63	65	82	85	82	83	79	18	8	1
Independent Democrats	68	67	72	71	86	90	77	26	21	8
Pure Independents	32	36	31	43	51	50	42	40	22	6
Independent Republicans	11	10	22	13	13	17	15	26	9	8
Weak Republicans	13	13	20	16	9	11	14	25	10	2
Strong Republicans	3	2	3	2	3	3	3	11	1	1

Source: Sapiro, Virginia, Steven J. Rosenstone, and the National Election Studies. 2005. *American National Election Studies Cumulative Data File, 1948–2004* [computer file]. The American National Election Studies (ANES; www.electionstudies.org). 2008. *The ANES 2008 Time Series Study* [data set]. Stanford University and the University of Michigan [producers].
Note: Average of annual percentages.

In 2008, 82 percent of Independent Republicans voted for John McCain. Over the period 1952–2008, on average 72 percent of Independent Democrats—but only 12 percent of Independent Republicans—voted for the Democratic presidential candidate. In sharp contrast, Pure Independents demonstrated no loyalty to either party; they have typically voted for the winner in two-party races and divided their votes three ways when a third candidate has emerged (1968, 1980, and 1992).

The same partisan behavior is found among independent leaners with regard to voting for the U.S. House of Representatives. Prior to the 1990s, leaners were on average nearly as loyal as weak partisans: three-quarters of Independent Democrats joined their kindred strong and weak partisans in voting Democratic, and two-thirds of Independent Republicans joined the Weak and Strong Republicans in voting Republican.[32] Since 1992, this relative pattern has continued. In 2008, 84 percent of Independent Democrats voted for the House Democrat, while Independent Republicans voted just as decidedly for the House Republican. Pure Independents typically did not heavily favor either party in 2008.

Myth concluded that "the [generally partisan] voting behavior of independent leaners [is] a spectacular refutation of the orthodox belief that party regularity is proportionate to strength of party identification . . . leaners do not always match or exceed weak identifiers on all measures of partisan affect, but *they are never neutral, and the extent of their affect almost invariably resembles that of weak partisans*."[33] The conclusion is as valid now as it was for the period reviewed in *Myth*.

Party Identification Remains Important as a Voting Cue

One reason scholars have taken notice of the rise in the proportion of individuals claiming to be independent is that the increase potentially undermines the well-established idea that the strength and direction of party identification underpin the voting behavior of Americans. This idea was a central tenet of *The American Voter*. Looking back 30 years later, Warren Miller found, even without classifying leaners as partisans, that party was no less relevant in the determination of how to vote in the 1980s than it had been in the 1950s.[34] Larry Bartels looked more extensively at partisanship and voting behavior through the 1996 presidential and congressional elections.[35] Classifying leaners as partisans, and estimating the impact of party identification on presidential vote propensity, he found that while partisan identification became less and less correlated with voting in presidential and congressional elections from the 1950s through the mid-1970s, the reduction in the role of party identification then reversed itself with a steady rise such that: "By 1996, this trend has produced a level of partisan voting 77% higher than in 1972—an average increase of 10 percent in each election, compounded over six election cycles—and 15 to 20 percent higher than in the supposed glory days of the 1950s that spawned *The American Voter.*[36] With respect to congressional elections, Bartels likewise found that voting according to party loyalty reached its nadir in 1978, but by 1996 was nearly back to its 1964 level.

In his discussion, Bartels suggested that the recent revival of the role of party identification stems from mass reaction to developments among the elites. The parties themselves, and their candidate standard-bearers, have taken clearer and more disparate stances on issues, so that many in the electorate see clearer differences between what they and their opponents stand for. The conversion of the always-conservative South to Republican control is often cited as a key element in the parties having more closely aligned their messages and stances with classic liberal and conservative ideologies. In Congress, the House and Senate have become more unified by party, with more party-line votes. Cable news and Internet sites unceasingly pound home these differences. Voters see this and align, or adapt, their own positions and allegiances. Some scholars have referred to the electoral portion of this phenomenon as "party sorting": as clearer differences emerge between the two parties, voters more readily sort themselves as Democrats or Republicans.[37]

Recent work by Morris Fiorina, Samuel Abrams, and Jeremy Pope and by Alan Abramowitz provides a context for looking at independents in the discussion of how parties in the electorate may have changed. In their *Culture War? The Myth of a Polarized America*, Fiorina et al. argued that while political activists, political parties, candidates, and others within the American political elites have recently become more ideologically polarized, the electorate has not.[38] While the press makes much of the current chasm between "red states" and "blue states," American citizens in both types of state are fairly moderate, and no more polarized in their political views now than two and three decades ago. Fiorina et al. reached this conclusion by looking at citizens' positions on a variety of economic and especially cultural policy issues, their evaluation of candidates and parties, and their ideological self-assessment.[39] The bulk of their analysis did not focus on differences among party identifiers, but they did observe that activists among the electorate[40] and strong party identifiers tend to be more polarized than the rest of the electorate, and that strong identifiers were somewhat more polarized in 2000 than they were a generation before. The authors pointed out, however, that polarization "fades out as partisan commitment declines"—it is not a feature of the "less strong identifiers" and notably not of political independents of any stripe. In particular, they said, "strong partisans are far more polarized than weak partisans and independent leaners" on feelings about the parties, and on ratings of liberals and conservatives.[41] In sum, Fiorina et al. argued that the population's views on almost all political matters are centrist—in the shape of a normal or "bell" curve—having mostly activists plus Strong Republicans and Strong Democrats at the tails, and the rest of the population, including the leaners, clustered in the middle.

A different take on electoral polarization has been developed by Abramowitz. In 2007, he pointed out that since Converse's observation that the U.S. electorate of the 1950s did not form ideologically based opinions of candidates or elections, the electorate has become much better educated, and political elites (including party activists and candidates) have become more ideological in the messages they convey.[42] Abramowitz saw reason to expect, following the research findings of Hetherington and others, that the electorate has become more ideological in its thinking and voting.[43] Looking at the 2006 midterm elections, he found that while most Americans identified as moderate on the liberal-conservative continuum, when the same respondents were asked their opinions on twelve current issues, the registered voters—but not the nonvoters—divided between liberal and conservative positions. Only 17 percent fell in the center of the ideology scale. The liberals on the scale voted substantially for Democratic House candidates, and the conservatives on the scale voted substantially for Republican House candidates. With regard to party identification among voters in 2006, Abramowitz found that Democratic identifiers, including leaning independents, were decidedly liberal on his issues scale, and Republican identifiers, including leaning independents, were decidedly conservative. In keeping with the tendencies we have observed for leaners, Abramowitz found that Democratic and Republican leaners were more ideological than the weak partisans, scoring almost as ideologically extreme as the strong identifiers. Pure Independents were in the center of the scale.

Given the divergent portraits of leaners that emerge from these two studies, we looked at a variety of measures that address the ideological tendencies of the partisan independents. We began by examining how the seven types of identifier placed themselves over the years on the ANES liberal-conservative scale, where 1 is most liberal, 7 is most conservative, with 4 being the midpoint.

The data in table 10-4 suggest that Americans generally prefer to identify themselves as fairly moderate. The mean score for the electorate in 2008 was near the middle—at 4.3—and few respondents placed themselves at either extreme. Nonetheless, there are variations by party identification, variations that have remained remarkably stable over the decades for each group. In 2008, Strong Democrats saw themselves a

Table 10-4. Liberal/Conservative Self-Classification and Party Identification, Average from 1964–2008

	Strong Democrats	Weak Democrats	Independent Democrats	Pure Independents	Independent Republicans	Weak Republicans	Strong Republicans
Average from 1972–1988	3.63	3.97	3.66	4.17	4.64	4.67	5.25
Average from 1990–2008	3.43	3.78	3.62	4.24	4.73	4.82	5.55

Source: The American National Election Studies (www.electionstudies.org). 2010. *Time Series Cumulative Data File* [data set]. Stanford University and the University of Michigan [producers and distributors].

Note: The numbers provided are the mean scores for each group on a scale from 1 (extremely liberal) to 7 (extremely conservative), and 4 is moderate.

little below the midpoint, at 3.4. Strong Republicans were in firm, but not extreme, conservative territory at 5.7. Weak and Independent Democrats were at the same spot to the left of center, 3.7. Likewise, Weak and Independent Republicans were close together to the right of center, at 5.1 and 4.9. Pure Independents were nearly at midpoint, at 4.1.

Table 10-4 shows little indication of increased ideological polarization over time among either Democratic or Republican identifiers. Strong Republicans' average scores have edged to the right, beginning in 1994, with all three types of Republicans scoring 4.9 or higher in 1996 and 2008. For Democrats, 2004 was a year of greater ideological focus and consistency, with Strong Democrats at 3.0, Weak Democrats at 3.6, and Independent Democrats between the two at 3.3. But the three-decade trajectory hardly supports a claim that Democrats are identifying as decidedly liberal and Republicans as decidedly conservative. Leaners have continually "sorted" with the party toward which they lean. Independent Democrats ideologically have usually fallen between Strong and Weak Democrats, while Independent Republicans have scored themselves somewhat less conservatively than Weak and Strong Republicans. Pure Independents, as expected, have stayed consistently near midpoint.

As noted, Abramowitz observed that Americans are generally disinclined to identify either as liberal or conservative. To see whether identifiers, notwithstanding their preference for a moderate label, look at issues in an ideologically consistent manner, we looked at where outright partisans, leaners, and Pure Independents placed themselves on specific economic and social issues that permit liberal and conservative stances. We created an index of four economic issues consistently asked between 1984 and 2008, where each of the four questions has a possible score of 1 for "most liberal" and 7 for "most conservative," thus yielding a scale with a most liberal score of 4 and a most conservative score of 28. In most years, Independent Democrats placed themselves between Strong Democrats and Weak Democrats, averaging 14.6. Independent Republicans averaged 18.0, which was virtually identical to the score of Weak Republicans. The average score for Pure Independents, 15.8, is close to the midpoint of 16.

All three types of Democrats scored somewhat more liberal on the economic index in 2004 and 2008 than earlier. In 2008, both Weak and Strong Republicans reported their most conservative scores, and Independent Republicans were more conservative than in any year but 2000. Pure Independents continued to place themselves in the middle of the ideological spectrum. Such increased party sorting does not imply polarity, which on our scale would be indicated by single-digit scores for those taking a solidly liberal stand, and scores in the mid-20s for those taking a solidly conservative stand. Even in 2008, where the strongest ideological differences emerged, Strong Democrats scored 12.3 and Strong Republicans 21.2, with weak partisans and leaners positioned even farther from the polar extremes.

In positing that most Americans are not ideological, Fiorina et al. were primarily considering social issues rather than economic. We looked at the four ANES questions, included in the survey since 1986, that address traditional versus "new" lifestyles.[44] While these questions do not ask respondents to take stances on specific issues of the day as the economic index did, they do provide a continuum that distinguishes between a traditional or conservative view and one that is more adaptive to nontraditional approaches to living. Table 10-5 shows the average scores over time of each type of identifier on an index of the four items, each of which was a five-point scale.

Over the years, all three types of Democratic identifier averaged scores between 12 and 13. Pure Independents averaged 13.3. Independent and Weak Republicans were both at 14.1 for the period, and Strong Republicans averaged 15.6. Strong Democrats became gradually more liberal between 1986 and 2008, and Weak Democrats became more liberal from 1998 on. Independent Democrats were the most consistent—and the most liberal—between 1986 and 1996, and they became sufficiently liberal by 2000 that their scores on the lifestyle issues index comprising the three most recent elections dropped below those of Strong Democrats. The tendency of Democratic identifiers to respond more liberally in 2004 and 2008 resembles the pattern seen earlier with economic issues. All three types of Republican identifier maintained similar ideological outlooks on lifestyle issues over the two decades but did not trend to the right. Pure Independents remained consistently in the middle.[45]

The patterns we have observed with respect to the ideological differences among the various types of identifiers are consistent with the view of Fiorina et al. that the electorate is not resolutely polarized, though some edging apart has appeared recently. However, their suggestion that the electorate is essentially a bloc of centrists is not an apt characterization, at least with respect to party identification. Abramowitz's observation that voters in 2006 were divided ideologically on issues, and that this disparity of view is reflected in their identification with party, appears to apply to the electorate at large, and has for decades. Whereas Pure Independents consistently place themselves at or near the center of the ideological spectrum, partisan independents consistently share the ideological views of outright partisans. There are clear differences between Democrats and Republicans, including leaners, on economic and social issues, as well as with respect to ideological self-identification. But these differences are not so great as to warrant the term "polarized."

Table 10-5. Lifestyle Index and Party Identification, 1986–2008

	Strong Democrats	Weak Democrats	Independent Democrats	Pure Independents	Independent Republicans	Weak Republicans	Strong Republicans
1986	13.6	13.5	13.0	13.5	14.2	13.7	14.6
1988	13.3	13.4	12.8	13.2	13.8	14.3	15.2
1990	13.3	13.4	12.9	14.0	13.6	13.7	15.1
1992	12.5	13.0	12.4	13.0	14.5	14.0	15.8
1994	13.1	13.6	12.7	13.8	14.8	14.4	16.1
1996	13.0	13.4	12.8	13.1	14.3	14.8	16.5
1998	12.1	12.9	12.9	13.4	14.9	13.6	15.5
2000	12.9	12.9	12.4	13.7	13.9	14.5	15.9
2004	11.4	11.8	11.2	12.8	13.9	13.8	15.7
2008	11.6	12.3	11.5	12.8	14.0	13.7	15.6
Average	12.7	13.0	12.5	13.3	14.2	14.1	15.6

Source: The American National Election Studies (www.electionstudies.org). 2010. *Time Series Cumulative Data File* [data set]. Stanford University and the University of Michigan [producers and distributors].

Note: The numbers provided represent the mean score for each group. The scale ranges from 4 (most liberal) to 20 (most conservative), and 12 is a neutral score. The issues used in this scale were taken from the ANES opinion section. Respondents were asked to rate their agreement, on a 5-point scale, with the following statements: "The newer lifestyles are contributing to the breakdown of our society"; "The world is always changing and we should adjust our view of moral behavior to those changes"; "This country would have many fewer problems if there were more emphasis on traditional family ties"; and "We should be more tolerant of people who choose to live according to their own moral standards, even if they are very different from our own."

Leaners Agree with Partisans about Candidates

As we observed at the outset, various scholars, pundits, and politicians who have remarked on the growing bloc of independents in the electorate have focused on the notion that, because this group has little or no allegiance to parties, candidates who play their cards right will be able to capture this sizable potential vote. At this point in the chapter—equipped with the knowledge that partisan independents prefer the party toward which they lean, and that they lean liberal and conservative ideologically—we can speculate that the two groups of leaners are unlikely to unite in their evaluations of the individuals who emerge into the political limelight.

We looked at the ANES thermometer ratings of presidential and vice-presidential candidates, U.S. House and Senate candidates, plus prominent political figures from each political party, the media, and other public forums. Partisan independents resemble their fellow partisans in their feelings about political luminaries. Like partisans, leaners rated the presidential and congressional standard-bearers from their own party positively and candidates from the other party negatively. For example, Independent and Weak Democrats had identical views of Colin Powell, Rush Limbaugh, and John McCain, and their mean scores over time are never more than 5 points apart on the 100-point scale for Bill and Hillary Clinton, Ronald Reagan, George W. Bush, and Condoleezza Rice. The mean thermometer scores of Independent Republicans were identical to those of Weak Republicans on Rush Limbaugh and Condoleezza Rice. Independent Republicans were one degree more positive about Bill Clinton, Hillary Clinton, and Ronald Reagan and were one degree less positive about John McCain and Colin Powell. The widest difference between Independent Republicans and Weak Republicans was on George W. Bush, where the difference was less than four degrees. Leaners are hardly up for grabs, then, for the same candidates.

How Independents Are Classified Does Matter

Our earlier work prompted Jody Baumgartner and Peter Francia to observe recently that "it is not necessarily the measure of party identification that is the culprit in propagating the myth of the independent voter but rather how some have used the data for this measurement."[46] We hope that, in addition to quashing the notion that there is a large bloc of unattached voters out there who are choice pickings for a clever candidate or whose size portends party dealignment, our findings will encourage analysts of the American electorate to refine their approaches so as to measure most accurately that which they are seeking to assess.

Take, for example, the research of Saunders and Abramowitz on whether the ideological views of "active partisans" differ from those of the electorate at large.[47] Party leaders, the authors submitted, should take a keen interest in satisfying such activists because they are essential to providing vital resources, they act as opinion leaders, and they are an important primary voting bloc; indeed, candidates ignore the political opinions of "active partisans" at their peril.[48] In identifying active partisans, the authors began by excluding more than one third of their sample—independents, including the leaners—and then built a measure of activism to tease out the "most active citizens" from the remaining weak and strong partisans. The authors compared the opinions of these "activists" to those of the rest of the electorate and found gaps in ideological stance. Based on the findings presented in this chapter, we would expect to see a considerable number of partisan independents who fit their definition of party activists. But the authors preemptively lumped all leaners into the comparison group of inactive citizens.

As noted, Fiorina et al. also developed an "activist" group from among strong and weak partisans—after removing the leaners. By this measure,[49] however, there are significant numbers of activists who identify as leaners—indeed, there has been a higher proportion of activists among Independent Republicans than among Weak Republicans since 1996 and a higher proportion of activists among Independent Democrats than among Weak Democrats since 2004. If Fiorina et al. had counted these activists, the comparison charts in their chapter 3 would likely have demonstrated more accurately the point they wanted to make.

Our aim here is not to call into question these two articles' claims about political activists. But one does wonder, in both cases, whether shifting the not-insubstantial subset of leaners might not have produced more accurate tests of their hypotheses, and thus produced gaps of different sizes than were found.[50] In this and other research questions, where leaners are classified can make a difference in political analysis, one that extends beyond questions relating to dealignment or viability of third-party candidacies.

Conclusion

Twenty-five years ago, we first published findings distinguishing three quite different types of independents: Independent Democrats, who have pro-Democratic views and vote predictably Democratic; Independent Republicans, who have pro-Republican views and vote predictably Republi-

can; and Pure Independents, who are not grounded in a party.[51] Contrary
to the speculation about a large and growing group of independents who
were "up for grabs," we found the proportion of Pure Independents, the
only volatile group of independents, to be a consistently small fraction
of the electorate.[52] We concluded that "independents, defined inclusively,
have little in common. They are more diverse than either Republicans or
Democrats. Most of them are not uncommitted, and they are not a bloc.
They are largely closet Democrats and Republicans."[53] That observation
remains the case today.

In *Myth*, we stopped short of adducing causes for *why* individuals in
the electorate identify as independents rather than as partisans. We noted
then that Pure Independents were more likely than other identifiers to
claim alienation from the political system, and were most likely to express disapproval of the political parties. Likewise, the leaners' slightly
less sanguine (than the partisans') view of the parties may have helped
explain their not immediately acknowledging a party identification.[54]
This chapter's review of more recent data leaves open the possibility that
independent leaners may avoid party labels because of their less positive
view of the party toward which they lean.

Since *Myth*, only a few scholars have shed light on this elusive question. In the *New American Voter*, Warren Miller and J. Merrill Shanks
argued that party identification is akin to religion—that an individual has
a visceral identity, a "sense of oneness," with the group.[55] In their view,
the group with which one identifies provides to the faithful parishioner,
or to the political party follower, "many cues for normative assessments
of the outside world," including what is good or bad, acceptable or unac-
ceptable.[56] They suggested that independents, including leaners, classify
themselves as "nonpartisan" because they reject this sense of oneness with
party and, presumably, take their cues for assessment from elsewhere.

It is encouraging to see that in recent years, some studies have looked
at survey data in order to explore other possible reasons for individuals'
calling themselves independents. For example, Steven Greene used a survey of one Midwestern county's electorate, and cited several "clear and
compelling reasons why seemingly partisan individuals choose to identify
themselves as independents":

> A greater reliance on cognition and less on affect in forming overall parti-
> san evaluations, less partisan social identity and greater independent social
> identity, negative attitudes toward the party system, and intergenerational
> transmission of independence are all key factors that determine whether an
> individual will be a true partisan or an independent leaner.[57]

More recently, Frank Liu and Laura Lucas proposed that citizens are
more likely to identify as independents when they are subject to perceived

disagreement ("cross pressure") within their personal communication networks.[58] Using findings from time-series panel data, they tentatively suggested that when a person lives among family and/or friends who support candidates from a party other than the one with which the individual identifies, it is simpler to call oneself an independent than to consider oneself as a "defector" to the other party's candidate.

While it is good to see such findings offered with caution, given the limitations of the data, we applaud the continuation of research that may give greater insight into why Americans identify as independents. It is also noteworthy that party identification has remained a central concept in the study of individual political behavior, and that the traditional method of measuring it retains value. In closing, however, we would raise an eyebrow to arguments—such as that made in *The New American Voter*—that one should "ignore the differentiation of independent leaners," and in conducting voting behavior studies, group all independents together. Miller and Shanks acknowledged that leaners can have opinions that favor one party over the other, and that they can "behave very much like partisans."[59] But they also termed such behavior on the part of leaners a phenomenon of the moment—a "coincidence."

There are undoubtedly multiple reasons for some Americans to think "independent" before thinking "party" when asked in a survey how they generally consider themselves. However, when the data show, year-in and year-out for nearly six decades, that *leaners hold opinions favoring their "leaned-toward" party*, the notion that the pattern may be due to "coincidence" has to leave one somewhat perplexed. The more appropriate way to consider the impact of the independent voter is to focus on Pure Independents, apart from leaners. As things stand today, much of the speculation about independents, and indeed some from academia, continues to perpetuate a myth.

Notes

We wish to acknowledge the exceptionally helpful research assistance provided by Case Wade. Greg Skidmore and David Lassen also assisted on this chapter.

1. For the classic explication of the concept of partisan identification, see Campbell et al. (1960), p. 121; more recently, see Miller and Shanks (1996), p. 117; Green, Palmquist, and Schickler (2002).

2. The American National Election Studies (ANES) standard opening question about partisan identification. All data, unless otherwise noted, are from the ANES. The American National Election Studies (www.electionstudies.org). 2005. *The 1948–2004 ANES Cumulative Data File* [data set]. Stanford University and the University of Michigan [producers and distributors]; The American National

Election Studies (www.electionstudies.org). 2008. *The ANES 2008 Time Series Study* [data set]. Stanford University and the University of Michigan [producers].

3. The ANES was not conducted in 2006, but other polling by Gallup and the Pew Research Center for the People and the Press consistently found that throughout 2006, the modal response to their initial partisanship question was "independent." The Pew Research Center for the People and the Press (2009).

4. Wattenberg (1986), p. 130.

5. Abramson, Aldrich, and Rohde (1983), p. 240.

6. Crotty (1984), p. 37; Kessel (1984), p. 279.

7. Ladd Jr. (1982), p. 77.

8. Campbell (1979), p. 268; Abramson, Aldrich, and Rohde (1983), p. 237. See also Gallup (1974), p. 1; Sussman (1984), p. 37.

9. Niemi (1974), pp. 215–217; Wattenberg (1987).

10. Hedrick Smith (1988), pp. 685–686.

11. Ladd Jr. (1984–1985), p. 6; Campbell and Sumners (1990), pp. 513, 520, 521; Carmines, McIver, and Stimson (1987); Schneider (1984), p. 100; Dalton, Flanagan, and Beck (1984), p. 263; Beck (1988), p. 165.

12. Sherrill and Vogler (1982), p. 282 (emphasis in original).

13. Burnham (1982), p. 244.

14. Pomper (1977), p. 41.

15. Keith et al. (1992). Two prior works on the same topic were Keith et al. (1977) and Keith et al. (1986).

16. Since 1952, the University of Michigan's Center for Election Studies has asked: "Do you usually think of yourself as a Democrat, Republican, Independent, or what?" The follow-up question for partisans is: "Would you call yourself a strong Republican/Democrat or a not very strong Republican/Democrat?" Independents are asked: "Do you think of yourself as closer to the Republican or Democratic party?"

17. Campbell et al. (1960).

18. Balz and Cohen (2007).

19. Macgillis (2007); Associated Press (2008).

20. Liasson (2007).

21. Janda, Berry, and Goldman (2009), pp. 246–247. See also, Ginsberg, Lowi, and Weir (2009), pp. 341–342; Wilson and DiIulio (2008), p. 248. Some other current texts use media polls that do not differentiate the three types of independents to examine partisanship, overlooking the critical distinctions in issue positions among independents on issues (Dautrich and Yalof 2009). However, other scholars' recent textbooks give a fuller and more accurate description of independents: Samuel Kernell and Gary Jacobson correctly state that "weaker partisans are less loyal to parties and the pure independents split their votes nearly evenly between the two major party candidates" (Kernell and Jacobson 2008). Karen O'Connor and Larry Sabato point out that "independent 'leaners' in fact vote much more like real partisans" (O'Connor and Sabato 2008, p. 473). See also Thomas Patterson (2003), p. 197.

22. Wattenberg (1998), p. ix.

23. Clarke and Stewart (1998), pp. 357–378.

24. Hershey (2009), p. 136.

25. See Nelson (1997); Donovan, Tolbert, and Smith (2009).

26. Thomas Patterson conducted weekly interviews with 1,000 Americans to tap their interest in the 2000 presidential campaign, and found that leaners were no more likely than Pure Independents (or weak partisans for that matter) to be interested in the campaign. Patterson (2003), p. 44. Patterson's findings support our own.

27. Lewis-Beck et al. (2008), p. 126.

28. Ibid.

29. Although on average turnout is lower for all categories of party identification in midterm elections, the pattern is much the same as in presidential elections. Except in 1998, when nearly as many Pure Independents went to the polls as independent and weak partisans, the turnout rate among Pure Independents has in recent years been considerably lower in off-year congressional elections than that of leaners.

30. As he did regarding interest in the campaign, Patterson found, regarding voter turnout in 2000, that leaners were closer to Pure Independents than partisans: "Independents and partisans are not the same when it comes to participation." Thus, he concluded, "The rise of the independent voter has contributed to the fall in election turnout" (Patterson 2003, p. 44).

31. Keith et al. (1992), p. 65 (emphasis in the original).

32. In most of these elections, the Democrats had majorities in the House and thus more incumbents running than the Republicans did. Given the power of incumbency in determining vote choice, the greater defection among Republican identifiers in the surveys is understandable—as is the turnabout in the Republican direction during the subsequent years in which the GOP held a majority.

33. Keith et al. (1992), pp. 67, 70 (emphasis in the original).

34. Miller (1991).

35. Bartels (2000).

36. Ibid., p. 40.

37. Levendusky (2009).

38. Fiorina, Abrams, and Pope (2006).

39. Fiorina makes the interesting observation that a 2003 Pew Research Center report titled "The 2004 Political Landscape: Evenly Divided and Increasingly Polarized" extensively surveyed citizens' views over a number of years on dozens of current issues, and an objective analysis of their findings actually produces a picture that is the reverse of the report's title; Fiorina concludes that "Pew would have done better to give its report the subtitle . . . 'An Ambivalent Majority'" (p. 41). See Fiorina, Abrams, and Pope (2006), p. 66.

40. It is noteworthy that Fiorina et al. defined "activists" as partisans who report participating in "three or more (of five possible) campaign activities," (ibid., p. 67), thereby presumptively excluding the partisan independents who met this criterion. We will return to this point later in this chapter.

41. Fiorina, Abrams, and Pope (2006), p. 68.

42. Abramowitz (2007).

43. Looking at ANES data, Marc Hetherington found that "Americans in the 1990s are more likely to think about one party positively and one negatively, less likely to feel neutral toward either party, and better able to list why they like

and dislike the parties than they were ten to thirty years ago" and that "greater ideological polarization in Congress has clarified public perceptions of party ideology, which has produced a more partisan electorate." He suggested that voters should be "much better able to make . . . ideological distinctions than in the past" (Hetherington 2001, pp. 628–629). Layman, Carsey, and Horowitz provide a review of the scholarship that has abounded recently on the topic of party polarization in the electorate (Layman, Carsey, and Horowitz 2006).

44. The questions for the lifestyle index were taken from the opinion section of ANES. Respondents are asked whether they agree strongly, agree somewhat, neither agree nor disagree, disagree somewhat, or disagree strongly with this statement. The statements used in the index are:

> "The newer lifestyles are contributing to the breakdown of our society."
>
> "The world is always changing and we should adjust our view of moral behavior to those changes."
>
> "This country would have many fewer problems if there were more emphasis on traditional family ties."
>
> "We should be more tolerant of people who choose to live according to their own moral standards, even if they are very different from our own."

45. We also looked at three recent social issues: abortion, gay marriage, and gun control. We found that leaners again resembled their respective partisans.

46. Baumgartner and Francia (2008), p. 44.

47. Saunders and Abramowitz (2004).

48. Ibid., p. 286.

49. Fiorina, Abrams, and Pope (2006), p. 67. The activist measure includes those who responded "yes" to at least three of the following questions:

> "During the campaign, did you talk to any people and try to show them why they should vote for or against one of the parties or candidates?"
>
> "Did you go to any political meetings, rallies, speeches, dinners, or things like that in support of a particular candidate?"
>
> "Did you do any other work for one of the parties or candidates?"
>
> "Did you wear a campaign button, put a campaign sticker on your car, or place a sign in your window or in front of your house?"
>
> "Did you give money to a political party during this election year? Did you give money to an individual candidate running for public office?"

50. Abramowitz made this very point in his subsequent work (2007) and in a recent Internet commentary, where he encouraged readers to take note that the views of leaners on most major issues have been very similar to those of regular partisans, as has their voting behavior: "It therefore makes no sense to view independents as a homogenous bloc of floating voters. Independents are sharply divided along party lines just like the rest of the American electorate" (Abramowitz 2009). As Baumgartner and Francia have put it, "an understanding of how leaners and Independents behave politically [has] receive[d] short shrift" (Baumgartner and Francia 2008, p. 44).

51. Keith et al. (1986).

52. Keith et al. (1992), p. 14.

53. Ibid., p. 4.
54. Ibid., pp. 199–200.
55. Miller and Shanks (1996), p. 121.
56. Ibid.
57. Greene (2000), p. 530.
58. Liu and Lucas (2008).
59. Miller and Shanks (1996), p. 127.

Part III

PARTICIPATION AND REPRESENTATION

XI

Who *Really* Votes?

Stephen Ansolabehere and Eitan Hersh

Introduction

In *Who Votes?* Raymond Wolfinger and Steven J. Rosenstone compare voters with nonvoters and find that while the two groups are demographically distinct, they share similar political views. This finding leads Wolfinger and Rosenstone to the conclusion that if more Americans voted, they would elect the same kinds of politicians who would implement the same kinds of policies as under lower turnout levels. "For the present," the authors write, "it appears that advocates of both sides of major controversial policy issues are represented among voters in proportion to their numbers in the general population."[1]

This provocative claim inspired two important lines of research in the three decades since the publication of *Who Votes?* The first line of work has focused on measuring the counterfactual of higher turnout. Employing a broad range of models and methods, scholars have tested whether higher turnout would alter election outcomes.[2] This work continues to reaffirm the original insight by Wolfinger and Rosenstone that if more people voted, electoral outcomes would not change very much.

A second line of research challenges the assumption that all voters, particularly low-information ones, understand their own self-interest.[3] Voters and nonvoters may appear to have similar political opinions, this line goes, but it is only because uninformed citizens are not able to connect their interests to the appropriate policies and politicians. However compelling, this claim of false consciousness does not conflict with the evidence that voters and nonvoters do articulate very similar opinions about politics. Whether or not less sophisticated citizens have reasonable preferences, if they all voted, it seems that little would change.

In spite of the evidence in its favor, this claim still strikes readers as unbelievable because by nearly every demographic measure, voters and nonvoters are nothing alike. According to Wolfinger and Rosenstone, college-educated citizens vote at a rate more than 30 percentage points higher than those who have no high school degree. The wealthiest citizens vote at a rate that is 40 percentage points higher than for the poorest citizens. On average, voters are considerably older than nonvoters, they are more likely to be longtime residents of their communities, and they are more likely to be white. Because voters are wealthier, more educated, and disproportionately white compared to nonvoters, scholars have for a long time posited that high turnout would indeed affect electoral outcomes, and in favor of the Democratic Party. In the same year that *Who Votes?* was published, however, DeNardo pointed out that high turnout does not favor either political party.[4] When nonvoters come to the polls, they split their vote between the parties just as regular voters do.

In this chapter, we return to the questions posed by Wolfinger and Rosenstone regarding the nature of the participatory bias in the American electorate. We ask: how are voters different from nonvoters with respect to their demographic and ideological attributes, and would election outcomes change if everyone voted? We advance this line of scholarship in three important ways. First, we employ validated rather than reported vote data. As Highton and Wolfinger, Sides, Schickler, and Citrin in this volume, and others have pointed out, survey respondents misreporting their vote record presents a serious problem for studies of political representation. Since a significant number of survey respondents misremember or lie about whether they voted, it is difficult to make a good comparison of true voters and true nonvoters. We overcome this problem by comparing survey respondents according to their validated vote histories.

Second, we propose an advancement in how participatory bias is measured. Many scholars exploring the differences between voters and nonvoters have measured bias by taking the proportion of voters with some characteristic of interest (e.g., a college degree) and dividing this by the proportion of the full population with the characteristic.[5] This measure of bias conflates two important but distinct dimensions—the proportion of voters in the population as compared to nonvoters in the population and the characteristics of voters as compared to the characteristics of nonvoters. We suggest that these concepts ought to be disentangled from each other in studies of political participation.

Third, in predicting a counterfactual vote choice for nonvoters, we match voters and nonvoters not just on demographic characteristics, as has been done by scholars in the past, but on attitudinal variables as well. We are able to include attitudinal variables because of the availability of a large-N national survey, from which we can estimate vote choice in statewide contests from the 2006 midterm election. Our advancements lead to an even stronger claim about the nature of the participatory bias in U.S. elections than has been made in the past. To the extent that voters and nonvoters seemed at all ideologically distinct in earlier scholarship, they seem even less so in our estimation. Furthermore, the large demographic differences between voters and nonvoters are found to be partially a function of misreporting bias. Not only do voters and nonvoters share a similar political perspective, but they are not all that demographically different from one another either.

We will proceed as follows. In the next section, we will explain why vote misreporting presents a problem for studies of participatory bias. Then, we introduce the vote validation study conducted as part of the 2006 Cooperative Congressional Election Study (CCES). The CCES is the first national survey to have been validated since the American National Election Studies (ANES) discontinued its validation efforts after its 1990 study. The CCES validation is a significant contribution to the field, not only because it is the first validation project in 16 years, but also because of the new validation methodology it employs. Next, we compare voters to nonvoters along key demographic and attitudinal variables, using both CCES and ANES data. Here, we show how misreporting exaggerates the differences between voters and nonvoters. At this point, we also address the problem with bias ratio measures. Finally, we simulate higher voter turnout and show that if more people voted, election results would hardly be affected at all.

The Problem of Vote Misreporting

The vote validation conducted by the American National Election Studies between 1964 and 1990 revealed that in a typical post-election survey, some 8 to 14 percent of nonvoters claim that they did vote.[6] The most common theory cited in the literature for why some respondents lie about voting is best summarized by Robert Bernstein et al.: "People who are under the most pressure to vote are the ones most likely to misrepresent their behavior when they fail to do so."[7] This explains why misreporting is especially prevalent in electoral contexts in which turnout is high and social pressure to vote is elevated.[8] Harbough conceptualizes misreporters as citizens who derive benefit for identifying as part of the voting public, perhaps because they seek praise for performing the civic act.[9] Across all validation studies, education is the most consistent predictor of misreporting. Among those respondents who did not actually vote, it is the better educated ones who claim they did vote.[10] In their recent paper comparing misreporting registration status versus misreporting vote status, Fullerton et al. show that education is the only variable that is a strong predictor of misreporting in both stages.[11]

Along with being more educated, misreporters also tend to be more partisan, more likely to claim that they were contacted by a political party ahead of the election, and as Belli et al. explain, "similar to vali-dated voters in that they see value in the political process." Misreporters are people who know and care about politics and feel that it is a civic duty to vote. Belli et al. speculate that over-reporters are probably people who vote intermittently.

These correlates of misreporting—namely, education and partisan-ship—are also key correlates of voting. It seems that the kinds of citizens who vote will say that they voted even when they have not done so. Be-cause nonvoters who claim that they voted are demographically similar to true voters, comparing reported voters with reported nonvoters will exaggerate the differences between the two groups.[12] The reported voting cohort includes a large group of citizens who are on the wealthier, better educated side of the socioeconomic spectrum but who are actually not voters. When these misreporters are counted as nonvoters, the nonvoting cohort appears much more like true voters as it does when only reported nonvoters are considered. After describing the 2006 vote validation, we will explore the degree to which participatory bias is exaggerated by the misreporters.

The Valid Vote and the 2006 CCES

The 2006 CCES is a web-based survey, administered to respondents within two weeks of the November election. Information on the sam-pling methodology can be found at the CCES website.[13] All respondents were asked in a pre-election survey whether they were registered to vote. They were asked in a post-election survey whether they had voted. The CCES was validated by Polimetrix, Inc., which used a "fuzzy matching" technique to search through electronic voter databases and match survey respondents to their voting records. Fuzzy matching involves using mul-tiple pieces of information—in this case, full name, age, and address—to match respondents to voting records.

The validation process used for the CCES is quite different from ear-lier validated studies conducted by the ANES. The ANES validations were conducted in person by interviewers who visited local election offices. Visiting the election offices in person was necessary because, during the period of the ANES validations, not all records were kept electronically and voter lists were held only by local registrars.

The centralization and digitization of voting records since the time of the ANES validations has led to an easier and more accurate validation process. However, there is still some variation across states in the quality of record-keeping. Because a validation process is only as good as the registration lists that are obtained from state agencies and private vendors, in this study we include only respondents in states that maintain the most reliable lists. In its analysis of voting records, Polimetrix assigned each state a record quality rating. Our study focuses on the 26 states for which the records are of the highest quality. In these states, the validators are sufficiently confident that those reported voters whose records were not found or whose records were marked as having not voted did in fact misreport their participation. The high-quality states include 65 percent of the U.S. population.

Summary of Validation Results

In the 26 high quality states, 18,079 U.S. citizens completed the pre-and post-election CCES survey and were asked whether or not they voted. Of the 18,035 who answered "yes" or "no," 86.7 percent claimed to have voted, but only 55.9 percent were validated as having voted. For the sake of comparison, we turn to statistics from two ANES validated surveys. We compare the CCES with the 1986 and 1990 ANES studies because these are the most recent midterm elections with validated surveys. As Cassel shows, over-reporting patterns in midterm elections are somewhat different than in presidential election years, at least in the ANES samples. Thus, it is appropriate to compare the 2006 CCES survey only with other midterm years. Here, we use the ANES cumulative file. In the 1986 ANES, 52 percent of 2,134 respondents reported having voted, while 43 percent were validated as having voted. In the 1990 ANES, 46 percent of 1,971 respondents reported having voted, while 40 percent were validated as having voted. The percentage of misreporters, then, is several times larger in the CCES sample than in the ANES sample.

Why is the rate of misreporting so much higher in the CCES sample than in the ANES samples? One reason is that the 2006 election was simply a more salient election than the midterms of 1986 and 1990, which would stimulate more misreporting. Another reason for the higher level of misreporting in the CCES is that different survey formats (e.g. Internet, in-person, telephone) are prone to differing levels of misreporting. A third reason is that the ANES misreporting rate might be artificially low due the low-tech technology it employed.

A fourth reason relates to the sample selection bias of the 2006 CCES. The 2006 CCES was one of the first attempts at a nationally representative, Internet-based political survey. In spite of a careful weighting of cases, the sample contains more older people and better educated people than expected in a random sample of Americans, a problem that has been mitigated in subsequent versions of the CCES. Since age and education are highly correlated with misreporting, we can expect a higher aggregate rate of misreporting in the 2006 CCES. Nevertheless, it turns out that the correlates of misreporting are quite similar in the CCES and ANES, as we show in the following discussion. The types of people who misreport make up a greater proportion of CCES respondents than ANES respondents, but still the same types of people misreport in both cases.

These four rationales—a more salient election, a web-based survey format, an improved validation technology, and a biased sample—probably account for the high rate of misreporting in the 2006 CCES. We will not know for certain whether these explanations are correct until we have future opportunities to validate survey responses. It must be emphasized that much about the research described here is very new: the survey format is new, the sampling methodology is new, the validation method is new, and the data at the core of the validation (i.e., statewide electronic voter registration files) are new. Vote validation, itself, has not been attempted on a national survey in nearly two decades. These novel approaches raise new and important questions. Chief among them are the sources of high misreporting in the 2006 CCES. As we work to validate the 2008 CCES (currently in progress) and future surveys, we hope to address this in greater detail.

In table 11-1, we provide basic summary statistics for each data set. Note that respondents who did not answer the reported vote question or who did not complete the post-election survey are not included in this table. We see, in table 11-1, that while the valid vote rate in the CCES is 13 to 16 percentage points higher than the valid vote rates in the ANES, the reported vote rate is 35 to 40 points higher. In all three samples, virtually all validated voters claim to have voted, as indicated by the third row of data. Perhaps the most striking difference between the CCES and

Table 11-1. Reported Vote and Validated Vote in the CCES and NES

	NES (1986)	NES (1990)	CCES (2006)
Reported vote	52%	46	87
Validated vote	43	40	56
Pr (report vote | valid vote)	99	96	100
Pr (valid vote | report vote)	82	83	64
Pr (report vote | valid not vote)	16	13	71
Pr (valid not vote | report vote)	18	17	36
N (reporting vote record)	2,134	1,971	18,035

ANES samples is in the fifth row of data. This row represents the proportion of over-reporters among nonvoters. In the CCES sample, 71 percent of nonvoters claim to have voted, whereas in the ANES samples only 13 percent and 16 percent claimed to have voted.

The Representativeness of the Electorate

If 13, 16, or 71 percent of nonvoters report in opinion polls that they voted, scholars may be led very far astray if voting behavior studies rely on the reported vote rather than the validated vote. The degree of the error depends on how much and in what ways the act of misreporting is correlated with explanatory variables of interest. To begin to identify the circumstances in which misreporting presents a problem for measuring participatory bias, we break down the survey population into three categories: true voters who report that they voted, nonvoters who report that they voted, and nonvoters who report that they did not vote. We exclude a fourth subset of respondents: true voters who claim they did not vote. A negligible number of people fall into this category—less than a half of a percent of valid voters in the CCES sample and similar percentages in ANES samples. Because virtually every person who actually votes reports as having voted, we will ignore these few under-reporters in the samples.

In table 11-2, we report the means of key variables within each of the three groups. These variables are coded according to the specifications of Rosenstone and Hansen (1993, appendix B). All variables, except age, range from zero to one. Income and education levels are divided into five categories each. Unemployed, homeowner, and party contact are indicator variables, the third designating respondents who claimed a political party contacted them prior to Election Day. Party ID is a four-category variable ranging from independent to strong partisan. Church is a four-category variable ranging from never or almost never attend church to attend at least once a week.

Table 11-2 holds two important lessons. The first lesson is that in spite of the very different levels of misreporting in the ANES and the CCES, the pattern is remarkably consistent. The types of respondents who misreported 16 and 20 years ago in an in-person survey are still misreporting in a 2006 Internet-based survey. The second lesson is that on each of these eight variables, misreporters look much more like true voters than like true nonvoters. Respondents who abstain from voting and willingly admit to it are a very different set of individuals from those who truly vote and those nonvoters who think of themselves as voters. They are younger, poorer, less well-educated, and less partisan. In the CCES

Table 11-2. Demographic Means by Type of Voter in the CCES and NES

Variable	CCES 2006			NES 1986, 1990		
	True voters	False voters	Nonvoters	True voters	False voters	Nonvoters
Income	0.53	0.52	0.37	0.53	0.50	0.41
	(8444, 0.26)	(4653, 0.27)	(2031, 0.26)	(1512, 0.27)	(324, 0.28)	(1878, 0.29)
Education	0.48	0.50	0.36	0.65	0.63	0.51
	(9547, 0.26)	(5347, 0.26)	(2242, 0.23)	(1647, 0.30)	(342, 0.29)	(2028, 0.28)
Age	46.9	44.2	37.6	50.5	44.0	39.6
	(9567, 13.2)	(5354, 13.3)	(2246, 11.9)	(1668, 16.9)	(348, 15.7)	(2052, 17.3)
Unemployed	0.03	0.03	0.07	0.02	0.04	0.07
	(9523, 0.16)	(5330, 0.17)	(2246, 0.25)	(1668, 0.15)	(349, 0.20)	(2053, 0.25)
Party ID	0.67	0.64	0.51	0.68	0.65	0.54
	(9457, 0.34)	(5288, 0.35)	(2119, 0.37)	(1662, 0.31)	(349, 0.31)	(1963, 0.33)
Church	0.39	0.37	0.26	0.64	0.59	0.46
	(9409, 0.42)	(5242, 0.42)	(2186, 0.38)	(1651, 0.41)	(346, 0.38)	(2030, 0.40)
Home owner	0.78	0.65	0.49	0.79	0.66	0.51
	(9527, 0.42)	(5317, 0.48)	(2235, 0.50)	(1664, 0.41)	(345, 0.47)	(2037, 0.50)
Party contact	0.81	0.72	0.39	0.33	0.25	0.13
	(9532, 0.40)	(5334, 0.45)	(2240, 0.49)	(1660, 0.47)	(346, 0.43)	(2039, 0.33)

Note: Parentheses: (observations, standard deviation)

sample, the group-level means for false voters are in all cases much closer to the means of the validated voters as compared to the validated non-voters. In the ANES, false voters are closer to true voters on all variables except for one (age).

Table 11-3 shows very clearly why we must take misreporting bias into account when observing differences between voters and nonvoters. Table 11-3 shows the differences in group means first between reported voters (RVs) and reported nonvoters (RNVs) and then between validated voters (VVs) and validated nonvoters (VNVs) in the CCES sample. Again, we restrict the sample of validated voters and nonvoters to only those who answered the "report vote" question one way or the other. This restriction ensures that the comparisons of valid voters and nonvoters and reported voters and nonvoters include all the same people, just categorized differently.

When the reported vote variable is used, the misreporters are grouped along with true voters and together they are compared to admitted nonvoters. As is shown in the first data column of table 11-3, differences between these two groups are large. When the validated variable is used, as in the second column of data, the misreporters join the group of admitted nonvoters. Now, the nonvoters consist of a weighted average of a smaller group of admitted nonvoters and a larger group of false voters. When this combined group is compared with true voters, the differences between voters and nonvoters are dulled. It should be noted that all of the differences in table 11-3 are statistically significant at the 0.001 level, which suggests that voters and nonvoters are truly different along these variables no matter whether reported or valid vote data are employed.

Table 11-3. Exaggerated Demographic Differences Between Voters and Nonvoters (CCES)

	Reported voters mean — Reported nonvoters mean	Valid voters mean — Valid nonvoters mean
Income	0.16	0.06
Education	0.13	0.03
Age	8.3	4.7
Unemployed	−0.04	−0.01
Party ID	0.15	0.07
Church	0.12	0.05
Home owner	0.24	0.17
Party contact	0.38	0.18

However, using validated vote data instead of reported vote data cuts these differences in half.

Tables 11-2 and 11-3 give a clear indication about when misreporting will create a problem for studies of political behavior and when it will not. Because false voters look like real voters, when these groups are combined together, as when relying on a reported vote measure, there will be no drastic bias in point estimates. That is, for any typical explanatory variable of voting, X, $Pr[X = k|RV]$ is roughly equivalent to $Pr[X = k|VV]$. As an example, consider X to be respondents' education levels, and let us look in particular at respondents with graduate degrees in the CCES sample:

$$Pr[Edu = GraduateDegree|RV] = 10.0\%$$
$$Pr[Edu = GraduateDegree|VV] = 9.5\%$$

This result, if generalizable, is quite astonishing. In the CCES sample, there are roughly 10,000 valid voters and 5,500 false voters. Whether or not this latter group is included among voters is basically inconsequential to the result here. About 10 percent of voters in the sample, measured either as reported or as validated voters, have graduate degrees. This is precisely what Sigelman had in mind when he argued that "adding [misreporters] to the ranks of the voters does not introduce major compositional changes."[14]

Oftentimes, we are interested not in $Pr[X = k|Vote]$ but in the opposite conditional probability, $Pr[Vote|X = k]$. Given different levels of education or income or some other variable of interest, what is the expected rate of voting? Under this condition, misreporting is likely to introduce significant bias in the results. As an example, consider again respondents who hold a graduate degree and let us observe data from the CCES:

$$Pr[RV|Edu = GraduateDegree] = 95.0\%$$
$$Pr[VV|Edu = GraduateDegree] = 58.3\%$$

Now, the results are drastically different depending on the vote measure used. If we were to look at only the reported vote, it would appear as if almost all respondents with advanced degrees voted. The validated vote tells us the more plausible story that those with graduate degrees all think of themselves as voters, and they say that they voted whether or not they actually did.

Demographic Differences

In the classic studies of participatory bias—such as those conducted by Wolfinger and Rosenstone (1980); Rosenstone and Hansen (1993); and

Verba, Schlozman, and Brady (1995)—researchers have studied participation using two different approaches. The first approach is regression
analysis. Similar to the second part of the graduate-level education exam-
ple earlier, scholars observe $E[Y|X]$, or the expected rate of voting given
various explanatory variables. As we showed with the education example,
this kind of analysis is quite susceptible to misreporting bias. The second
approach that these scholars have taken is the opposite relationship to
regression, $E[X|Y]$, which is analogous to the first part of the graduate-
level education example. That example suggests that the relationship of
X given Y will not be severely biased by misreporting, since misreporters
look so much like voters. However, we will show how misreporting can
be problematic in this kind of measure as well.

To explore how representative or unrepresentative the voting public is
of the public at large, Wolfinger and Rosenstone devise a ratio measure,
later called the "representation ratio" by Rosenstone and Hansen, that
is generated by first taking a variable of interest, like education, and observing how the sample population is distributed among the categories of
that variable. Then, they observe how the participant population, like the
population of reported voters, is distributed among the categories. The
ratio of participants in category i to population in category i is meant
to provide an indication of how representative the participant group is
of the population group. Verba, Schlozman, and Brady (1995) utilize
the natural log of this ratio in *Voice and Equality*, referring to it as the
"logged representation scale."

Using both ANES data and CCES data, we replicate the representation
ratios for education and income levels to determine whether including
misreporters among voters or nonvoters makes any difference to the results. The data, presented in table 11-4, reveal that the ratios are nearly
the same whether we use the reported vote variable or the validated vote
variable. This means that the proportion of reported voters in category
k is roughly equal to the proportion of validated voters in category k for
any kth category of variable X. This generalizes the result in the graduate school illustration. Whether one looks at the reported vote ratio or
the valid vote ratio, higher levels of income and education are associated
with a higher propensity to vote.

The presence of misreporters in vote studies does not disturb representation ratio measures so long as the ratios are treated as a comparison
of voters and the full population rather than a comparison of voters and
nonvoters. What can be tricky about representation ratios is that they
are not necessarily informative about how voters differ from nonvoters.
This is due to the fact that measures of participatory bias depend on two
distinct relationships that exist in the data. First, they depend on how
different voters are from nonvoters. Second, these measures depend on

Table 11-4. Replication of Representation Ratios with Validated Data

	Income				
NES	% Pop.	% rep. voters	% valid voters	Ratio (rep.)	Ratio (valid)
0–16th percentile	17	12	11	0.67	0.65
17th–33rd percentile	16	14	14	0.89	0.88
34th–67th percentile	33	34	34	1.01	1.00
68th–95th percentile	29	35	36	1.21	1.25
96th–100th percentile	4	5	5	1.25	1.19
N	3,777	1,870	1,540		
CCES	% Pop.	% rep. voters	% valid voters	Ratio (rep.)	Ratio (valid)
0–15th percentile	10	8	7	0.83	0.77
16th–43rd percentile	23	21	20	0.93	0.91
44th–69th percentile	30	31	31	1.01	1.02
70th–84th percentile	31	34	35	1.08	1.10
85th–100th percentile	6	7	7	1.10	1.06
N	15,579	14,011	9,342		

Education

NES	% Pop.	% rep. voters	% valid voters	Ratio (rep.)	Ratio (valid)
No high school	9	8	8	0.82	0.83
Some high school	13	7	8	0.51	0.58
High school degree	36	33	33	0.92	0.92
Some college	22	24	24	1.10	1.07
College degree or higher	20	28	28	1.40	1.44
N	4,099	2,034	1,682		
CCES	% Pop.	% rep. voters	% valid voters	Ratio (rep.)	Ratio (valid)
No high school degree	4	3	3	0.80	0.76
High school degree	39	37	38	0.94	0.97
Some college or two-year college	31	32	32	1.04	1.04
College degree	17	18	17	1.07	1.03
Graduate school	9	10	10	1.10	1.05
N	17,998	16,250	10,755		

the proportion of the sample made up of voters. The greater the share of voters in the sample, the less sensitive the ratio measures will be to large differences between voters and nonvoters. Representation ratios are not wrong, per se, but they can lead to faulty inferences because of the way they conflate these two different relationships.

Given that everyone in the population is either a voter or a nonvoter, it seems intuitive that the ratio of voters with some characteristic to the population with that characteristic should tell us something about nonvoters as well, but this is not necessarily the case. We cannot make inferences about the how representative voters are of nonvoters by merely looking at how voters compare with the population at large. To help explain this crucial point, consider table 11-5. Here, we have an imaginary sample of 1,000 citizens. Each citizen either does or does not have each of three attributes, X, Y, and Z, and each citizen either does or does not vote.

On all three attributes, the proportion of voters who have the attribute (20 percent) is nearly identical to the proportion of the population with that attribute (19 to 21 percent). Yet, in each case, we learn nothing about how well nonvoters are represented. A greater percentage of nonvoters than voters have X, a smaller percentage of nonvoters have Z, and Y they have in equal proportions. The marginal percentages do not change very much, of course, because nonvoters in this case make up a relatively small part of the population. As it happens, the distribution of voters and nonvoters in this imaginary sample is not far off from the true distribution of reported voters and nonvoters in the CCES sample.

Because representation ratios depend both on the characteristics of voters and nonvoters and the proportions of voters and nonvoters, in order to consider how nonvoters compare with the population at large, in table 11-6 we construct ratios for nonvoters parallel to the ones in table 11-4. We see that whether or not misreporters are included in the ranks of nonvoters drastically changes our interpretation of how representative voters are of nonvoters. In table 11-4, as one moves up through the categories of income or education, voters appear to be present in larger proportion, irregardless of the vote measure used or the data set employed.

Table 11-5. Illustration of the Problem with Representation Ratios

	Population	% with X	% with Y	% with Z
Voters	900	20	20	20
Nonvoters	100	30	20	10
Total population	1,000	21	20	19

Table 11-6. Representation Ratios for Nonvoters

Income					
CCES	% pop.	% rep. nonvoters	% valid nonvoters	Ratio (rep.)	Ratio (valid)
0–15th percentile	10	20	12	2.07	1.29
16th–43rd percentile	23	33	25	1.46	1.12
44th–69th percentile	30	29	30	0.96	0.97
70th–84th percentile	31	16	27	0.50	0.87
85th–100th percentile	6	2	6	0.39	0.92
N	15,579	1,568	6,237		

Education					
CCES	% pop.	% rep. nonvoters	% valid nonvoters	Ratio (rep.)	Ratio (valid)
No high school degree	4	9	5	2.33	1.31
High school degree	39	56	41	1.42	1.04
Some college or two-year college	31	22	29	0.72	0.95
College degree	17	9	16	0.57	0.96
Graduate school	9	3	9	0.37	0.94
N	17,998	1,748	7,243		

The groups at the lowest end of the socioeconomic status (SES) spectrum are under-represented among voters. If we look instead at the degree to which nonvoters are representative of the general population, in table 11-6, it is clear that treatment of misreporters makes a big difference to our inferences about the representativeness of voters. According to the reported vote, less educated/poorer people are over-represented among nonvoters and more educated/wealthier people are under-represented. But when we condition on validated nonvoters, and misreporters are included in the ranks of nonvoters, it appears that nonvoters are fairly representative of the full population. Across most of the income and education categories, the representation ratio hovers pretty close to exact representation of 1. When reported vote data is used, nonvoters look quite different from the population at large, but when validated vote data is used, they look much more similar.

If we are concerned about how well the voting public is representative of the nonvoting public, then, looking at the voters and the full population without also looking at the nonvoters only tells half the story. We need to look at the characteristics of nonvoters as well as voters. Once we look at nonvoters, it becomes evident that misreporting bias plagues bias calculations like these by making voters and nonvoters look more distinct than they really are. While it is true that voters seem to be better educated, wealthier, more partisan, and otherwise different from nonvoters, our analysis shows that these differences are actually rather slight.

Moving forward, we suggest that when comparing the voting behavior among different demographic groups, scholars should show how representative nonvoters are of the population in addition to showing how representative voters are of the population. Alternatively, one can reverse the relationship and examine the more typical relationship of Y given X. This would involve a probit or logit model in which voting is regressed on explanatory variables of interest. However, all of these measurement tools are vulnerable to misreporting bias, which will exaggerate the differences between voters and nonvoters.

Attitudinal Differences

We have so far shown that the severe demographic biases associated with the voting public are not quite as severe as previously thought. But still, voters and nonvoters are somewhat distinct. Therefore, we now investigate whether the remaining demographic biases lead to real consequences in the realms of policy and politics. Using validated vote data in table 11-7, we show the percentages of the nonvoting and voting cohorts who take various positions on important policy issues. Table 11-7 shows that on a range of policy issues, voters and nonvoters are distributed quite similarly.

Voters and nonvoters are most identically distributed on noneconomic issues. The areas of mild divergence are on the questions regarding union influence and minimum wage increases. In both cases, voters are slightly more conservative than nonvoters. The important question is: are these differences large enough to translate into voting and party identification biases?

In figure 11-1, we observe the distribution of voters and nonvoters in the CCES along a seven-category party identification scale. The reported voter cohort and the valid voter cohort look nearly identical to each other, but reported nonvoters and valid nonvoters are distinct. In particular, valid nonvoters look more like real voters than reported nonvoters do: they have stronger partisan leanings.

Focusing on the valid vote histograms, there are noticeably fewer Republicans among nonvoters. Forty-three percent of valid voters are on the

Table 11-7. Attitudinal Differences between Valid Voters and Nonvoters

	Nonvoters	Voters
Abortion		
Never permitted	10%	10
In extreme cases only	24	24
Only if deemed necessary	16	14
Personal choice	45	45
Other	6	7
N	7,311	10,792
Gay marriage amendment		
Strongly support	34	34
Somewhat support	10	10
Somewhat oppose	10	9
Strongly oppose	44	45
Don't know	3	3
N	3,244	5,631
Iraq invasion a mistake		
Yes	54	55
No	35	37
Not sure	11	8
N	10,842	10,798
Affirmative action		
Support	33	33
Neutral	19	17
Oppose	48	50
N	7,284	10,791
Union influence		
Want more	30	32
Want the same	35	28
Want less	35	40
N	7,122	10,536

Table 11-7. (*continued*)

	Nonvoters	Voters
Increase minimum wage to $6.25		
For	75	72
Against	19	23
Don't know	6	4
N	7,305	10,774

Note: Percentages show distribution of respondent answers and sum to 100%.

Republican side of the histogram, but only 37 percent of valid nonvoters consider themselves more Republican than not. Democrats in the electorate, on the other hand, are in proportion to Democrats among nonvoters. If we create a seven-category ordinal variable ranging from strong Republican (1) to strong Democrat (7) ("not sures" excluded), the mean for valid voters is 3.8 and for valid nonvoters 3.9, a small but statistically significant difference of means. These results are consistent with those calculated by Wolfinger and Rosenstone some thirty years ago.

The same pattern is true if we look at ideology instead of party identification. On a 100-point scale ranging from very liberal to very conservative, the average rating among validated voters is 55.4, and among validated nonvoters it is 52.8. True nonvoters appear to be slightly more Democratic and more liberal than true voters. Just as with the demographic variables, these slight differences are magnified if the reported vote is used instead.

In addition to observing the entire national sample, we might also consider state-level partisanship. Perhaps more significant differences between voters and nonvoters are lost in a national sample. Figure 11-2 shows the gap between the mean self-placement on the ideology scale for voters and nonvoters, using the validated sample and the reported sample. Fifteen states are shown. These states are those of the 26 states with high-quality voting records that have a sample size of reported nonvoters greater than 30. Because only about 15 percent of CCES respondents admitted not voting, some of the smaller states do not have sufficiently large samples of reported nonvoters to analyze here.

Consistent with similar graphs in the works of Griffin and Newman and Citrin, Schickler, and Sides, the CCES shows that reported voters in most states are more conservative than reported nonvoters.[15] Yet again, when validated vote data is used in place of reported vote data, nearly

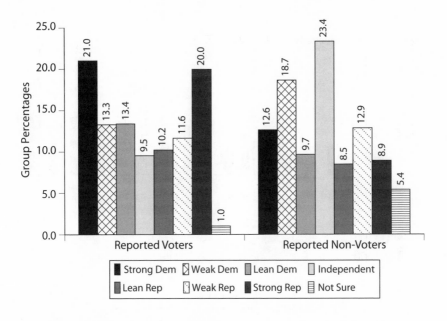

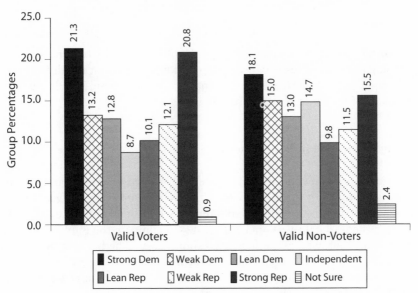

Figure 11-1
Partisan distribution of reported and valid voters and nonvoters.

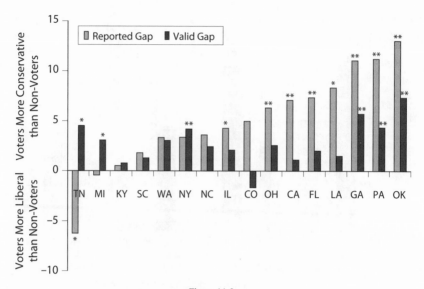

Figure 11-2
State-by-state partisan representational bias.

all of the state-level ideological gaps shrink. In sum, there appear to be ideological differences between voters and nonvoters, but the differences are quite small, and they are even smaller when the valid vote is studied in place of the more typical reported vote.

Simulations of Higher Turnout

Since true nonvoters do appear to be slightly more Democratic and liberal than true voters, it seems likely that if more nonvoters voted, Democrats might gain, but the ideological differences are so small that we would not expect them to gain very much. In order to simulate the implications of higher turnout, we will perform two simple tests. The first test estimates how election results would change if the nonvoters who were most likely to vote had gone to the polls in 2006. The second test estimates universal turnout of the CCES survey population.

In the CCES pre-election survey, respondents were asked for which House, Senate, and gubernatorial candidates they would cast their ballot. They were also given the opportunity to say that they did not intend to vote for a particular race. We assume that respondents who express a preference in the pre-election survey are those most likely to vote. After all, they recognize the names of the candidates for office and can offer a preference. One approximation of the results in a higher turnout election would be to compare the pre-election preferences of all who had a preference with the pre-election preferences of just those who ended up voting.

In table 11-8, we make these comparisons for the pooled set of House races, then Senate races, and finally gubernatorial races. Consistent with the slight ideological differences between voters and nonvoters, valid nonvoters prefer the Democrats at a slightly higher rate than valid voters. In the Senate elections, but not gubernatorial or House elections, this difference is statistically significant. If all intenders voted, Senate Democrats would be expected to increase their vote share by 1.5 percentage points, from 58.1 percent of the vote to 59.6 percent. If all the nonvoters in the survey who so much as had a preferred candidate in the pre-election poll had voted, it seems that the results would have changed hardly at all.

Although a higher turnout election would probably draw most of its increases from the pool of the more engaged citizens, students of political representation are interested in the differences in candidate preference between voters and all nonvoters, particularly the ones who do not think of themselves as voters and might not articulate a preference for a candidate in a pre-election poll. Citrin, Schickler, and Sides (2003) match vote choice in exit polls with demographic variables in the Current Population Survey (CPS) in order to estimate Senate election outcomes if everyone voted. Under their model, Democrats' vote share increases by an average of 1.5 percentage points in the simulated universal turnout condition, not nearly enough to change outcomes in most Senate races. In the 91 Senate races that Citrin, Schickler, and Sides

Table 11-8. Simulation of Partisan Outcome if All Intenders Voted

Intend Vote Dem.	Valid Voters	Valid Nonvoters	All
House	0.56	0.56	0.56
	(9,016, 0.50)	(5,738, 0.50)	(14,754, 0.50)
Senate	0.58	0.62*	0.60*
	(7,587, 0.49)	(5,207, 0.47)	(12,794, 0.49)
Governor	0.53	0.54	0.53
	(8,699, 0.50)	(6,117, 0.50)	(14,816, 0.50)

Note: Parentheses: observations, standard deviation.
Two-sample difference of means t-test. Comparison is with valid voters.
*p < .05

examine, outcomes in four would have changed under full turnout, but three of these would have changed from Democratic to Republican. (Although on average Democrats gain, in some states nonvoters are more conservative than voters.)

Citrin and his colleagues avoid the problem of misreporting by relying on exit poll data. The drawback of their analysis, however, is that they match the exit polls to data in the CPS, which does not ask citizens about their partisan preferences. The validated CCES can improve upon the estimates in this sort of universal turnout simulation because the validated vote is more reliable than the reported vote, state samples are sufficiently large for many states, and questions about partisan preferences are included in the questionnaire. Rather than pooling data from multiple data sources to estimate universal turnout, our final exercise will be to estimate universal turnout among CCES respondents. Our comparison will be between true voters and true nonvoters in 2006 Senate races. First, we build a vote choice model for validated voters in each of ten Senate races. Then, we take the coefficients from the vote choice estimates and apply them to all CCES respondents in the state.

We estimate a logit model in which an indicator for a vote for the Democratic senatorial candidate serves as the binary dependent variable. In this model, we use the the post-election survey question inquiring whom respondents actually voted for. Only validated voters who stated that they voted for either the Democrat or Republican candidate are included. The explanatory variables in the model are education, income, and age (coded as in table 11-2); party (–3 to 3 from strong Democrat to strong Republican); ideology (0 to 100); and indicators each for gender, union membership, black, hispanic, and other nonwhite races. After estimating this model for valid voters by state, we calculate predicted values for the entire state sample, for voters as well as nonvoters.

The results, shown in table 11-9, are remarkably consistent with Citrin, Schickler, and Sides' estimates. The predicted Democratic support is higher among reported nonvoters than validated voters, raising the overall predicted Democratic vote share from its level in column 2 to its level in column 3. If all participants in the CCES voted, the Democratic vote share would rise by an average of 2 percentage points in these ten Senate races. The change in votes under full turnout ranges from 0.2 percentage points more Democratic in Washington State to 4.7 percentage points more Democratic in Michigan. This model thus predicts that except in very close Senate races, universal turnout would not change election outcomes. Of these ten states, none shows a statistically significant difference between the predicted turnout among valid voters and the predicted universal turnout.

Table 11-9. Simulation of 2006 Senate Outcomes if Everyone Voted

	(1) Dem. vote share (VV)	(2) Predicted Dem. vote share (VV)	(3) Predicted Dem. vote for universal turnout	(4) Predicted difference (3)-(2)
CA	0.59	0.60	0.61	0.01
	(1,280, 0.49)	(1,142, 0.40)	(2,328, 0.40)	
FL	0.62	0.61	0.63	0.01
	(940, 0.49)	(783, 0.39)	(1,313, 0.38)	
MI	0.60	0.60	0.62	0.03
	(752, 0.49)	(681, 0.42)	(1,016, 0.41)	
MN	0.54	0.52	0.54	0.01
	(373, 0.50)	(314, 0.46)	(465, 0.46)	
MO	0.56	0.56	0.58	0.02
	(403, 0.50)	(353, 0.45)	(546, 0.44)	
NY	0.64	0.63	0.67	0.04
	(707, 0.48)	(611, 0.41)	(1,110, 0.40)	
OH	0.57	0.56	0.57	0.01
	(786, 0.50)	(676, 0.43)	(1,031, 0.43)	
PA	0.53	0.53	0.56	0.03
	(802, 0.50)	(671, 0.43)	(1,041, 0.42)	
TN	0.42	0.37	0.42	0.05
	(167, 0.49)	(134, 0.45)	(379, 0.46)	
WA	0.57	0.57	0.57	0.00
	(507, 0.50)	(436, 0.42)	(711, 0.42)	

Note: Average difference between predicted universal and predicted valid = 2 percentage points in favor of Democrats. Parentheses: (observations, standard error).
Two-sample difference of means t-test.
*p < .05

Conclusion

In this chapter, we have shown the durability of the original and provocative claims of Wolfinger and Rosenstone. While American voters tend to be wealthier, better educated, older, and in other ways, too, quite different from nonvoters, their views on politics are similar to those of nonvoters. Wolfinger and Rosenstone's insight about the ideological commonality between voters and nonvoters has been continually challenged and tested as new data and methodological tools have been introduced in the last three decades. Over time, the basic truth of their proposition has only been reinforced.

By examining data from a validated vote study, we revisited the question of representational bias from a unique angle. The results from the validated vote analysis suggest that (1) voters do not differ from nonvoters quite as much as we thought when we looked only at the reported vote record of survey respondents, and (2) while nonvoters are more liberal and more Democratic than voters, the difference is so small that it would hardly change election outcomes if every American citizen voted. Additionally, we have advanced this research agenda by showing why representation ratios should be used along with statistics describing nonvoter attributes. Observing the relationship between voters and the full population alone does not always give analysts an accurate sense of how voters differ from nonvoters.

As scholars continue to examine questions of representational bias, we suggest two promising research paths. First, simulations of higher turnout fail to take into account that nonvoters' preferences may change if they were actually to vote. While Highton and Wolfinger give us reason to doubt that nonvoters' preferences would change very much, perhaps the greatest challenge to Wolfinger and Rosenstone's initial finding comes from scholars who suggest that citizens would vote differently if they were more informed.[16] An important next step then would be to merge two related questions: how would more information (or more income, or more mobilization) affect a citizen's decision to turn out to vote, and then for whom would he or she decide to vote?

A second direction for future research is a more careful examination of reported nonvoters. In our study of the valid vote, we have shown there to be three types of voters. There are valid voters and misreporters, who share much in common in terms of participatory resources, and then there are reported nonvoters, who exist in an world apart from the others. Admitted nonvoters are unique in their lack of engagement with politics. Whereas many scholars in the past have asked who votes and who lies about voting, perhaps the literature is missing deep investigations into the behavior and psychology of those who do not vote and do not feel any desire to lie about it.

Notes

1. Wolfinger and Rosenstone (1980), p. 114.

2. Bennett and Resnick (1990); Citrin, Schickler, and Sides (2003); Highton and Wolfinger (2001); Sides, Schickler, and Citrin (2008); Verba, Schlozman, and Brady (1995).

3. For example, Bartels (1996, 2005).

4. DeNardo (1980).

5. Wolfinger and Rosenstone (1980); Hill and Leighley (1992); Rosenstone and Hansen (1993); Verba, Schlozman, and Brady (1995).

6. Belli, Traugott, and Beckmann (2001).

7. Bernstein, Chadha, and Montjoy (2001), p. 24.

8. Karp and Brockington (2005).

9. Harbough (1996).

10. Belli, Traugott, and Beckmann (2001); Bernstein, Chadha, and Montjoy (2001); Cassel (2003); Silver, Anderson, and Abramson (1986).

11. Fullerton, Dixon, and Borch (2007).

12. Bernstein, Chadha, and Montjoy (2001). Cassel (2003).

13. http://web.mit.edu/polisci/portl/cces/commoncontent.html.

14. Sigelman (1982), p. 55.

15. Griffin and Newman (2005); Citrin, Schickler, and Sides (2003).

16. For example, Bartels (1996).

XII

Who Governs if Everyone Votes?

John Sides, Eric Schickler, and Jack Citrin

DOES POLITICAL PARTICIPATION MATTER AND, if so, how? Turnout in American elections is lower than in most other advanced industrial democracies, and this fact continues to alarm many scholars, journalists, and political reformers. Although some deny a necessary connection between apathy and disaffection, a constant worry is that low turnout indicates a lack of commitment to democratic institutions, a kind of turning of one's back on the political system.[1] Beyond this essentially nonpartisan concern about civic engagement, a second complaint is that low turnout biases political outcomes, producing a kind of unequal democracy. The conventional wisdom, at least before Raymond Wolfinger launched his research on voting, was that higher turnout favors the Democrats and liberal causes more generally. Because individuals of lower socioeconomic status and members of ethnic minorities are less likely to vote than the wealthy and whites but more likely to favor Democratic candidates, it seemed to follow that a big increase in voter turnout would benefit Democrats. These newly mobilized constituents would then prod Democratic politicians to redress economic and racial inequality.[2] By moving the median voter to the left, higher turnout would change the content of policy.

Raymond Wolfinger's now classic research, however, boldly challenges this conventional wisdom. In *Who Votes?* Wolfinger and Rosenstone established elegantly and precisely the demographic and institutional bases of voter turnout in the United States.[3] These results put claims of a class bias in turnout on a much firmer empirical footing, while also providing insights into additional factors shaping turnout, such as residential mobility and registration laws. Wolfinger then turned to the crucial "so what?" question, exploring the implications of higher levels of participation for electoral outcomes and policy-making. Wolfinger and Rosenstone, as well as Highton and Wolfinger, argue that outcomes in recent American presidential elections would not have changed if everyone had voted.[4]

While prior studies had assumed that class and racial differences in turnout rates imply a substantial gap in policy preferences between voters and nonvoters, Wolfinger and Rosenstone show that the policy differences between them actually are quite modest. Highton and Wolfinger demonstrate that despite the class differences between voters and non-voters, the "grievances and aspirations" of the two groups are very similar and that nonvoters are, if anything, less class-conscious.[5] This raises doubts about whether less wealthy nonvoters would always be motivated by economic concerns and therefore consistently cast a pocketbook vote for the Democrats. Moreover, while nonvoters are a bit to the left of voters on economic issues, they are actually slightly more socially conservative and not much more focused on economic issues. By the same token, many well-off voters, particularly in the "new class" of professionals with postgraduate degrees, now lean to the left, which attenuates traditional patterns of class voting.[6]

Wolfinger's findings have been reinforced by studies of congressional, Senate, and presidential elections.[7] These studies conclude that the impact of higher turnout varies considerably across contexts but is usually small. In most cases, Democrats gain from higher turnout, and even a small gain for either party can change the result in very close elections. Nevertheless, in most American national elections, even universal turnout would not have produced a different winner.[8]

In assessing the relationship between turnout and outcomes, we focus on universal turnout. While compulsory voting is clearly not on the political horizon in the United States, it offers a potential administrative mechanism to approximate universal turnout—one that countries such as Brazil and Australia employ. Universal turnout is also the most straightforward normative benchmark for evaluating the concern that low turnout biases policy outcomes. While one could think of other possible criteria for democratizing electoral participation—such as equal turnout among different social classes or racial groups—it is not self-evident whether income, education, race, age, or some other characteristic should be the criterion. Beyond this normative concern, it requires fewer methodological assumptions to simulate universal turnout than alternative thresholds. That is, in the universal turnout or compulsory voting case, we do not have to ask which nonvoters "ought" to be added to the electorate (e.g., those from particular racial or income groups, those closest to the threshold separating nonvoting individuals from voting, etc.). Finally, the universal turnout counterfactual should provide an upper bound on the potential impact of increased turnout on outcomes. The simulation employed here thus provides a hard test for Wolfinger's earlier claims.[9]

In previous work building upon Wolfinger's analysis, we have simulated the potential impact of universal turnout on the outcome of the Senate elections of 1994, 1996, and 1998, and the presidential elections of 1992–2004. The present chapter extends these earlier results, providing estimates of the "partisan differential" between voters and nonvoters in each state for both presidential and Senate elections between 1990 and 2006.[10] The partisan differential captures the gap in the predicted probability of casting a Democratic vote for voters and nonvoters (had they voted). The inclusion of eight Senate elections and four presidential elections permits a more systematic comparison among states whose partisan differential scores consistently vary and a more comprehensive analysis of the variation in the partisan differential.

This chapter addresses three main questions. First, what is the partisan differential between voters and nonvoters? Second, which election outcomes would have changed party hands under universal turnout? This question, of course, directly addresses the substantive political implications of any partisan bias in turnout. Third, what factors lead some states and elections to have a larger partisan differential—that is, a greater gap in the electoral preferences of voters and nonvoters?

We find that, on average, nonvoters were slightly more Democratic than voters in each of these elections. However, the magnitude of the partisan differential varies across states and time. Some states, such as Texas and Colorado, have consistently large partisan differentials. Others, such as Pennsylvania and New York, typically have only modest differences between voters and nonvoters. In several other states, the magnitude of the partisan differential changes over time. But because so many Senate elections are not truly competitive, universal turnout would have changed the outcomes in only a small proportion of these contests. Indeed, under our preferred simulation of universal turnout's effects, just 8 of the 246 Senate contests likely would have had a different winner; 6 of the 8 represent Democratic gains, while 2 benefit the GOP. In our analysis of universal turnout in the presidential elections, we find that Bill Clinton likely would have won a handful of additional southern states in 1992 and 1996, thereby increasing his Electoral College margin. More strikingly, Al Gore and John Kerry likely would have been elected under universal turnout, but both the 2000 and 2004 elections still would have been extremely close.

Ultimately, although universal turnout might well tip very close elections into the Democratic column, the electoral landscape would not be transformed. This is not to deny the major policy consequences of a Gore or Kerry victory. But in terms of long-run representation in Congress, universal turnout would tilt the electorate only very slightly in a Democratic direction rather than generating an enduring liberal majority. And, of course, the impact of higher but less-than-universal turnout would depend on which voters were mobilized in a particular contest. Campaign managers presumably know this and concentrate on mobilizing their candidate's base and demobilizing the opposition rather than kowtowing to the civic norm of higher turnout.

Methods and Data

We have discussed our data and methods in greater detail elsewhere, and provide only a brief summary here.[11] First, we estimate a model of vote choice using the state-level exit polls, drawing on demographic variables as predictors (race, income, gender, and age, as well as education, marital status, and union membership, where available).[12] Thus, we allow the determinants of vote choice to vary across states—and in fact there is considerable variation (see also Gelman et al. 2008). More generally, analyzing state-level results is crucial for Senate races and, given the centrality of the Electoral College, for presidential races as well.

Second, we turn to the November Voter Supplement of the Current Population Survey (CPS), a data set whose use by political scientists Wolfinger pioneered. We use the coefficients from these exit poll models to generate a predicted probability of voting for the Democratic candidate for each CPS respondent, including both voters and nonvoters. In calculating predicted probabilities for CPS respondents, we account for the uncertainty that characterizes the coefficient estimates from the exit poll vote choice model. We did this by estimating our exit poll model using Clarify, and saving 500 sets of parameter estimates for each model in each state.[13] We then computed 500 predicted probabilities for each CPS respondent, using the parameter estimates from each replication of the model.[14]

Finally, we calculate the Democratic share among voters and nonvoters as the mean of predicted probabilities across the simulations within each state. These 500 iterations enable us to calculate bootstrapped standard errors for these estimates. We can then calculate whether voters and nonvoters differ and whether this difference is statistically distinguishable from zero. In calculating how full turnout would have affected the outcome of each state's election, these standard errors providing estimates of whether the percentage voting for, say, John Kerry, under universal turnout is statistically distinguishable from 50 percent. Moreover, we can also compute the percentage of the simulations in which each candidate is the "winner" under the full turnout scenario.

This methodology does assume that that the parameters of vote choice would be the same for voters and nonvoters, the so-called cloning assumption. One might object to this as unrealistic, as, for example, DeNardo does in arguing that "peripheral" voters are more likely than habitual voters to defect from their party identification.[15] However, there are good reasons to think that the cloning assumption is not unwarranted. The key question is how the process of mobilization affects so-called peripheral voters. One likely mechanism for mobilizing less interested citizens is the efforts of the political parties and candidates, who often focus on reinforcing voters' latent partisanship. Another is communication among friends and neighbors, who tend to be similar in social background and who, if politically active, are likely to exemplify the dominant connection between this background and party identification. One of the major findings of the campaign effects literature, dating back to Lazarsfeld et al., is that campaigns "activate" the electorate's underlying political predispositions, leading them to a vote choice consonant with those predispositions.[16] Indeed, since universal turnout would almost certainly stem from a compulsory voting law, the knowledge that one "had" to vote might in and of itself serve to activate these predispositions. DeNardo argues that peripheral voters have weaker predispositions than "core" voters a priori, and this may be correct. But research that has tracked the voting behavior of a set of citizens over multiple elections finds no simple dichotomy between core and periphery.[17] Many citizens move in and out of the electorate in a haphazard fashion, and when mobilized to vote in any given election, these peripherals may possess enduring political predispositions that lead them to mimic their counterparts among habitual voters.

In addition, the conventional wisdom is that racial and class inequalities in turnout lead to "biased" outcomes, in the sense of reducing the Democratic vote. So the assumption that nonvoters who are brought to the polls would behave similarly to their sociological clones among habitual voters furnishes the most favorable test for the hypothesis that higher turnout benefits the Democrats. For these reasons, we believe that the advantages of the proposed simulation overcome the objections of DeNardo and provide a novel way of identifying the partisan effects of increased turnout.

Computing and Comparing the "Partisan Differential" between Voters and Nonvoters

A first question is whether voters and nonvoters differ in their partisan preference—also known as the "partisan differential." To calculate this quantity, we simply subtract the mean probability of a Democratic vote choice among voters from the mean among nonvoters across the simulations in each state. Thus, positive values indicate that nonvoters were more Democratic than voters, as the conventional wisdom suggests.

Figure 12-1 presents kernel density plots of the partisan differential across the 50 states and the District of Columbia for each election, with vertical lines representing the mean value in each year from 1990 to 2006.

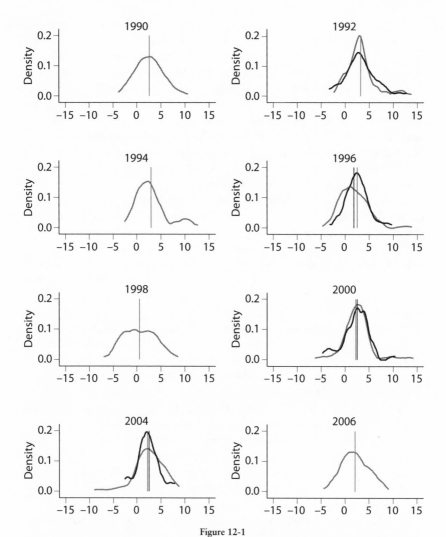

Figure 12-1

Kernel density plots of the partisan differential, by year. Note: Each figure is a kernel density plot of the partisan differential, where the unit of analysis is the state. Positive values mean that nonvoters were more Democratic than voters. Negative values mean that nonvoters were more Republican than voters were. The black lines indicate presidential races, and the gray lines indicate Senate races. The vertical black and gray lines are the mean values for each level of office.

For years with presidential elections, the plots include separate lines for the two levels of office, where the darker line indicates the partisan differential in the presidential election. Notice first that, on average, nonvoters are more Democratic in each of the elections. In figure 12-1, the mean partisan differential in the presidential elections (treating the state as the unit of analysis) ranges from a low of 1.8 percentage points in 1996 to a high of 3.2 in 1992. In the Senate elections, the mean partisan differential ranges from 0.57 in 1998 to 3.2 in 1992. Among the 450 state-year combinations for these Senate and presidential elections captured in figure 12-1, 346 (or 81%) have a positive partisan differential, and 186 of those 346 are statistically distinguishable from zero.

Second, there is considerable variation in the partisan differential—variation across years, across states, and within states over time. The mean values in figure 12-1 suggest some variation over time. While the average partisan differential is always positive, the partisan differential in each state is not always positive. In 84 of the 450 state-year combinations, the partisan differential is negative, and of these 84, 17 are statistically distinguishable from zero. In those cases, nonvoters were actually more Republican than voters.

Some of the variation across states appears to reflect chronic differences. For example, when disaggregated by state, the partisan differential in Texas appears consistently large and positive, ranging from a low of 5.7 percentage points in the 2004 presidential election to a high of 13.3 in the 2000 presidential election. In contrast, the partisan differential in Pennsylvania is consistently quite low, ranging from –0.15 points in 1994 to 2.6 in 2004. There is also variation within states over time, suggesting that the partisan differential may derive not only from fairly stable features, such as a state's demographic composition, but also from election-specific forces. In 1998, when the incumbent Democratic Party flouted tradition and actually gained congressional seats, there are a larger number of states (15) in which the partisan differential is actually negative. This suggests that Democratic voters may have been more mobilized in this election, relative to the others.

Simulating the Effects of Full Turnout on Electoral Outcomes

To estimate the effects of universal turnout on state-level outcomes, we combine our estimate of the partisan differential and the actual outcome of the Senate or presidential election in each state. The actual outcome constitutes the best available estimate of what voters did and the partisan differential constitutes the best estimate of the behavior of nonvoters. While our estimates of partisan preference in the CPS may be slightly inaccurate because of equation or sampling error, we assume that such error affects voters and nonvoters similarly, such that the *difference* between voters and nonvoters in the CPS is estimated accurately and best captures how adding in nonvoters would change the results. We weight the outcome and the partisan differential by the actual turnout in this race (expressed as a proportion of the voting-age population). Thus, the projected outcome in each state *j* equals:

$$SIM_{ij} = (outcome_j \times turnout_j) + [(outcome_j + PD_{ij}) \times (1 - turnout_j)]$$

where PD_{ij} is the partisan difference between voters and nonvoters in race *j* in the *i*th run of the simulation. The best estimate of the outcome is simply the mean of the 500 values for SIM_{ij}. To account for the uncertainty underlying this estimate, we also compute the proportion of simulations in which each candidate wins each state. The formula for *SIM* implies that full turnout is more likely to change the outcome when turnout is low, the race is close, and the partisan differential is large in absolute magnitude.[18]

Table 12-1 presents the states whose presidential election outcome would have changed under universal turnout, and table 12-2 summarizes the effects of these changes on Electoral College outcomes. Table 12-3 lists the Senate contests that would have changed hands. These tables include both the actual vote totals and the predicted vote share, averaging across the 500 simulations in each state. In 1992, universal turnout is estimated to generate Clinton victories in four states that George H.W. Bush won: Arizona, North Carolina, South Carolina, and Texas.[19] No states flipped from the GOP to Democratic column. The resulting Electoral College margin for Clinton increases from 370–168 to an even more convincing 432–106. In 1996, four states switch to the Democrats under full turnout—Colorado, Georgia, Mississippi, and Texas—thereby widening Clinton's victory in the Electoral College from 379–159 to 439–99.[20] The prevalence of Southern states on this list makes sense: in the actual campaigns, Democrats had targeted their mobilization efforts in swing states outside the South. But with a Southerner atop the ticket amid an electoral climate favorable to Democrats, these states may have been within Democratic reach given the fully mobilized electorate resulting from compulsory voting.

In 2000, our simulation suggests that universal turnout would have led to Democratic victories in four states carried by George W. Bush: Colorado, Florida, New Hampshire, and Nevada. Each of these victories is estimated to be quite narrow (see table 12-1), but they consistently emerged in a large majority of simulations—90% or better for Florida, New Hampshire, and Nevada, and 66% for Colorado. Gore therefore wins the Electoral College by a 299–239 margin. But this apparent rever-

Table 12-1. Results of Full Turnout Simulation for Presidential Elections

		Actual Outcome			Simulated Outcome		
	Type of switch	Democrat	Republican	Perot	Democrat	Republican	Perot
1992							
AZ	R→D	41.1	50.1	8.8	39.4	36.2	24.4
NC	R→D	42.7	43.5	13.3	43.9	42.9	13.2
SC	R→D	40.1	48.3	11.6	46.1	42.2	11.7
TX	R→D	37.2	40.7	22.1	42.5	34.6	22.9
1996							
CO	R→D	45.9	47.3	6.8	47.7	45.4	6.9
GA	R→D	46.2	47.4	6.4	49.3	41.9	8.8
MS	R→D	44.5	49.6	5.9	47.8	46.0	6.3
TX	R→D	44.1	49.1	6.8	51.2	42.1	6.8
2000							
CO	R→D	45.5	54.5		50.4	49.6	
FL	R→D	50.0	50.0		51.6	48.4	
NH	R→D	49.3	50.7		51.2	48.8	
NV	R→D	48.1	51.9		53.2	46.8	
2004							
CO	R→D	47.6	52.4		50.5	49.5	
IA	R→D	49.7	50.3		51.1	48.9	
NH	D→R	50.7	49.3		49.4	50.6	
NM	R→D	49.6	50.4		53.0	47.0	
NV	R→D	48.7	51.3		51.3	48.7	
OH	R→D	48.9	51.1		50.5	49.5	

Note: Cell entries under "simulated outcomes" are means of the 500 iterations of the simulation discussed in the text.

sal does not indicate any Democratic landslide: an extremely close election would still have been close under universal turnout, with the winner determined by narrow victories in only a few states.

The results for the 2004 election tell much the same story. In our preferred simulation, six states where Bush won by slim margins switch to Kerry: Colorado, Iowa, New Mexico, Nevada, and, perhaps most strikingly, Ohio. Kerry's narrow 49–51% loss in Ohio becomes, under full

Table 12-2. Actual and Simulated Electoral College Outcomes

	Actual Electoral College outcome	Simulated Electoral College outcome
1992		
Clinton	370	432
Bush	168	106
Perot	0	0
1996		
Clinton	379	439
Dole	159	99
Perot	0	0
2000		
Bush	271	231
Gore	266	307
2004		
Bush	286	245
Kerry	252[a]	293

Note: The simulated outcome is calculated taking into account the states that would have switched under full turnout, as presented in table 12-1.

[a] In 2004, one elector from Minnesota voted for John Edwards for both vice president and president. This vote is counted as Kerry's for the purposes of this table.

turnout, an even more narrow victory (50.5%–49.5%)—one that held in 82% of the simulations. In Iowa, New Mexico, and Nevada, Kerry won in the vast majority (98–100%) of the simulations; in Colorado, he won in 83% of the simulations. In contrast, New Hampshire tilts from the Kerry column to Bush in the full turnout simulation.[21] Taken together, this suggests a Kerry victory, with a 295–243 Electoral College margin. Even without Colorado, where his victory was somewhat more in question based on our simulations, Kerry still wins by a 286–252 margin—with the result dependent on a very tight Ohio contest. Once again, universal turnout tends to offer a small boost to the Democrats in some highly contested states. But much as in 2000, the 2004 race would still have hinged on a small number of votes in these battleground states.

Table 12-3 demonstrates that very few Senate election outcomes, 8 out of 246 races, would have changed under full turnout.[22] In 6 of these 8, the simulated winner was the Democratic candidate—e.g., Harold Ford in 2006. The two simulated Republican winners were Spencer Abraham in

Table 12-3. Results of Full-Turnout Simulation for Senate Elections

Year	State	Candidate	Actual outcome	Simulated outcome
1990	Oregon	Lonsdale (D)	46.2	50.5
		Hatfield (R)	53.8	49.5
1992	Georgia	Fowler (D)	49.4	58.8
		Coverdell (R)	50.6	41.2
1998	Kentucky	Baesler (D)	49.7	51.3
		Bunning (R)	50.3	48.7
2000	Michigan	Stabenow (D)	50.8	48.8
		Abraham (R)	49.2	51.2
2004	Florida	Castor (D)	49.4	50.8
		Martinez (R)	50.6	49.2
2004	Kentucky	Mongiardo (D)	49.3	50.1
		Bunning (R)	50.7	49.9
2006	Tennessee	Ford (D)	48.6	52.2
		Corker (R)	51.4	47.8
2006	Virginia	Webb (D)	50.2	49.8
		Allen (R)	49.8	50.2

Note: Cell entries under "simulated outcomes" are means of the 500 iterations of the simulation discussed in the text.

the 2000 Michigan race and George Allen in the 2006 Virginia race.[23] All of these races were quite closely decided—again indicating that full turnout will likely shift outcomes only in very competitive races. As we noted in our earlier analysis of Senate races, it is precisely the lack of competition that limits the potential impact of full turnout. In these 246 races, 78 (31%) were decided by a margin of 55–45 or less, and our simulations suggest that most races decided by an even narrower margin would still have had the same winner if everyone had voted.

Explaining the Partisan Differential

Because most of the variance in the partisan differential arises from state-level differences as opposed to differences across time, our search for the factors underlying this variation focuses on state-level factors.[24] The partisan composition of nonvoters should derive first from demographic attributes of a state's voting population. The attributes most likely to af-

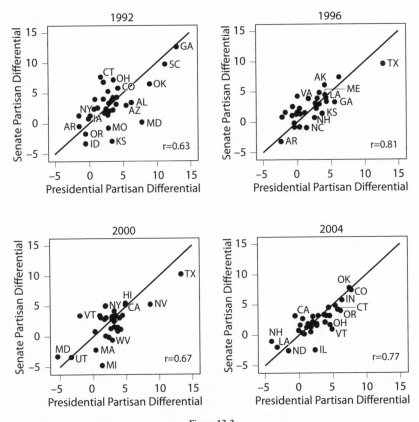

Figure 12-2
Scatterplots of the Senate and presidential partisan differentials. Note: The points are the partisan differentials for the presidential and Senate race for each state for each election year. Positive values mean that nonvoters were more Democratic than voters. Negative values mean that nonvoters were more Republican than voters. The diagonal line is a 45-degree line.

fect the partisan differential should be those correlated with both turnout and vote choice. Income and race fit both criteria.

The partisan differential may also derive from election-specific forces—notably, characteristics of the candidates, and efforts by the candidates, parties, and others to mobilize like-minded groups of voters. That these forces matter is evident in how our estimates of the "presidential" partisan differential correspond to our estimates of the partisan differential in Senate races. In figure 12-2, we provide scatterplots of these two quantities in each of the four presidential elections. The correlations between these two measures of the differential, treating states as the units of analysis, are 0.63 in 1992, 0.81 in 1996, 0.67 in 2000, and 0.77 in 2004. That these correlations are significantly greater than zero suggests that stable state attributes matter; that these correlations are far from perfect signals the relevance of election-specific forces. A simple hypothesis is that in more competitive states, get-out-the-vote efforts tend to benefit the Democratic Party more than the Republican Party. Thus, in competitive states, the partisan differential—i.e., the Democratic "bias" among nonvoters—should decrease.[25]

To examine how a state's sociodemographic composition and its level of partisan competition affect the partisan differential, we estimated a simple regression model where the partisan differential is the dependent variable. The independent variables are the level of income inequality; the proportions of the state's population comprising blacks, Latinos, and Asians; and the winning candidate's margin of victory.[26] This latter measure captures the partisan competition in the state: as the margin of victory increases, the partisan differential should also increase. With regard to the demographic measures, we expect that the partisan differential will exhibit a greater Democratic "bias" among nonvoters in states with higher levels of income inequality and in states with larger populations of nonwhites and union members.

In table 12-4, we present the results of this model, estimated separately by year. We find little role for electoral competitiveness, as the winner's margin of victory is significant only in 1992.[27] Income inequality is only weakly significant in two models. The main finding is that states with substantial Latino populations tend to have a greater partisan differential.[28] This makes sense in that Latinos tend to be Democratic and also have significantly lower turnout rates than whites or blacks. The point estimate for the impact of the percentage of Latino citizens is positive in each model, and is statistically significant in 5 of 12 cases. In the 2004 presidential race, a shift in the percentage of Latino citizens from its minimum (less than 1 percent in Alabama) to its maximum (35 percent in New Mexico) is estimated to increase the partisan differential by 6 points, or about two standard deviations, other things equal. In contrast, although African Americans are even more Democratic than Latinos, their turnout rate compares more favorably to that of whites: in the 2004 CPS, the self-reported turnout of whites and blacks was almost identical (75 percent and 72 percent, respectively). As a result, the percentage of a state's population that is African American has no consistent relationship to the partisan differential.

We can thus say with some certainty that the partisan differential depends in part on the ethnic composition of the state. This helps account for why a state such as Texas manifests a large partisan differential. It has a sizable proportion of Latinos eligible to vote—e.g., approximately 23 percent of its population, according to the 2004 CPS—and Latinos in Texas tend to favor Democratic candidates.[29] Indeed, the assumed univer-

Table 12-4. Regression Models of the Partisan Differential

	1990 Senate	1992 Senate	1992 President	1994 Senate	1996 Senate	1996 President	1998 Senate	2000 Senate	2000 President	2004 Senate	2004 President	2006 Senate
Margin of victory	-0.045 [0.035]	-0.044 [0.049]	-0.096* [0.041]	0.058 [0.068]	0.038 [0.025]	-0.046 [0.032]	-0.045 [0.045]	-0.033 [0.029]	-0.036 [0.027]	-0.023 [0.027]	0.018 [0.029]	-0.047 [0.043]
Income inequality	0.001 [0.002]	0.007 [0.007]	0.007+ [0.004]	0.015+ [0.007]	-0.003 [0.004]	0.001 [0.003]	0.003 [0.006]	0.006 [0.006]	-0.001 [0.005]	0.005 [0.007]	-0.008 [0.005]	0.006 [0.011]
% African American	-0.09 [0.073]	0.122 [0.085]	0.116* [0.044]	0.001 [0.109]	0.079 [0.047]	0.066+ [0.036]	-0.033 [0.084]	-0.018 [0.063]	0.032 [0.038]	-0.084 [0.055]	-0.032 [0.044]	-0.058 [0.115]
% Latino citizen	0.113 [0.099]	0.062 [0.198]	0.107 [0.082]	0.019 [0.100]	0.132* [0.060]	0.220** [0.051]	0.193 [0.143]	0.087 [0.088]	0.221** [0.070]	0.188+ [0.103]	0.172** [0.064]	0.087 [0.077]
% Asian American	0.011 [0.053]	0.064 [0.062]	0.025 [0.049]	0.372 [0.533]	0.475 [0.665]	-0.034 [0.044]	-0.619 [0.565]	0.078 [0.048]	0.045 [0.044]	-0.01 [0.049]	-0.082 [0.055]	0.054 [0.081]
Constant	0.041* [0.016]	-0.007 [0.032]	-0.005 [0.018]	-0.054 [0.038]	0.015 [0.021]	0.004 [0.013]	0.01 [0.027]	0.004 [0.021]	0.023 [0.017]	0.012 [0.025]	0.048** [0.017]	0.009 [0.038]
R-squared	0.17	0.21	0.28	0.28	0.31	0.35	0.1	0.21	0.24	0.2	0.24	0.12
Observations	29	33	51	26	32	51	31	33	51	33	51	29

The dependent variable is the partisan differential. Cell entries are OLS regression coefficients, with estimated standard errors in parentheses.
+$p < 0.10$; *$p < 0.05$; **$p < 0.01$ (two-tailed).

sal turnout among Latinos helps explain the simulations that put Texas in the Democratic column, even when the Republican presidential candidate was the "local" George H.W. Bush.

Conclusion

Our research is heavily indebted to Wolfinger's pioneering work on voter turnout. Methodologically, we have followed Wolfinger and Rosenstone in using the Census Current Population Surveys to study political participation. Their innovation is essential to the state-by-state analysis at the heart of this chapter and our previous work on Senate elections. Our substantive question also builds upon Wolfinger, Rosenstone, and Highton's investigations of the political implications of higher levels of turnout. We followed Wolfinger's lead in asking whether compulsory voting (or universal turnout) would consistently produce Democratic victories in American national elections and therefore result in more egalitarian public policies.

We find that just a handful of Senate elections would have changed hands under universal turnout. In 238 out of 246 Senate races from 1990–2006, our simulation indicated that the outcome would have been the same had everyone voted. Democrats would have won in 6 of the 8 simulated switches, suggesting a very small net gain. Whether this gain would have mattered for policy likely depends on the unique circumstances surrounding particular issues and Senate actions. Certainly the narrow partisan balance in the Senate during much of this period suggests that even small gains may matter. But this possibility should not overshadow a more salient generalization: the paucity of competitive Senate races drastically limits any effects of universal turnout.

Our results also generally confirm Wolfinger and Highton's conclusion that while full turnout usually would help Democratic presidential candidates, their net gain would be both variable and numerically too small to change the outcome except in very close elections (see Ansolabehere and Hersh in this volume for complementary evidence). At the same time, the unusually close presidential elections of 2000 and 2004 indicate that small changes in vote totals can at times translate into a substantial change in political outcomes. Universal turnout can be added to the long list of factors that might have tipped the 2000 election outcome to Al Gore, and it evidently would have allowed John Kerry to overcome George W. Bush's narrow 2004 victory.

Yet our results are consistent with Wolfinger's skepticism that universal turnout would lead to a dramatic, long-term shift in policy to the left or to an era of Democratic control of the White House and Congress. Al

Gore's policy agenda doubtless would have differed substantially from George W. Bush's, but the resistance to change built into the American political system and the likelihood that Gore would have faced divided party control probably would have prevented a durable shift in policy to the left.[30] Morever, had Gore triumphed in 2000, compulsory voting would not have necessarily prevented a shift toward the Republicans in 2002 or 2004: the partisan differential is typically not large enough to override the impact of election-specific factors such as the state of the economy, international events, or candidate appeal.

Although the requisite data is not yet publicly available, we suspect that the 2008 election featured a lower than usual partisan differential. That is, the combination of dispirited Republicans, an energized Democratic base, and the Obama campaign's extensive get-out-the-vote apparatus generated an electorate with a lesser Republican tilt (see, however, Abramson et al. [2009] for evidence suggesting that Republicans retained at least some of their turnout advantage). More importantly, the 2010 midterms—which, given the substantial Republican gains in the House and Senate, likely featured a partisan differential more similar to 1994 and 2002—are a reminder of how fleeting an electoral majority can prove to be in American politics, even if the policies enacted by a short-lived majority have enduring consequences.

Wolfinger opened up a domain of research where exciting prospects remain. Among the important tasks are examining how turnout levels affect the nature of the issues in campaigns and learning more about the differences in political outlook between voters and nonvoters. Perhaps universal turnout would affect party and candidate campaign strategies, which in turn could affect voters' calculus. If these strategic changes helped prime economic interests, it is plausible that universal turnout could lead to greater class voting. On the other hand, universal turnout could motivate the GOP to appeal even more to the social and cultural concerns of lower-income voters, thereby diminishing class voting. As Wolfinger and Highton show, lower-income nonvoters are often more conservative than the general public on key social issues. If the election turns on those issues, then the partisan implications of higher turnout are again not necessarily favorable to the Democratic Party. Under compulsory voting, one could envision both parties using very different appeals to win over Latinos, the demographic group that is most consistently associated with the partisan differential.

Although compulsory voting is not presently on the American agenda, there are a host of other proposals designed to increase turnout—all of which could be the subject of future research. These range from loosening registration rules to facilitating absentee voting to implementing electronic voting. Each of these measures may attract a different set of former nonvoters to the polls, with a concomitant effect on the partisan differential. In turn, beliefs about who benefits from higher levels of turnout engender partisan battles over how to monitor and regulate access to the polls. Although our research has clarified the boundaries for the impact of universal turnout, many questions remain. Still Raymond Wolfinger would probably agree that despite their public calls for more participation, politicians truly hope not that everyone votes, but rather that their partisans turn out while their rival's supporters stay home.

Appendix: Model Specification in the VNS Exit Polls

For each state in the 1992–2004 Voter News Service (VNS) exit polls, our model includes dummy variables for age (25–29, 30–39, 40–44, 45–49, 50–59, 60–64, and 65 and over, with 18–24 the excluded category); income ($15–30K, $30–50K, $50–75K, $75K, with under $15K the excluded category); race (black, Latino, Asian, and other race, with white the excluded category); and gender. Where available, we included dummy variables for education (high school diploma, some college, college graduate, advanced degree, with no high school diploma the excluded category); whether the respondent was married; and whether the respondent or someone in the respondent's family was a union member.

One obvious criticism of these models is that they are underspecified because they do not include other demographic, sociological, or political factors associated with vote choice, such as party identification. However, further analysis suggests that underspecification may have little impact on our analysis. Using the 2004 state exit polls, we estimated two models of presidential vote choice: the first, the "baseline," includes only the demographic variables noted earlier; the second, the "extended" model, includes these variables plus frequency of church attendance, an ordinal measure of political ideology, and dummy variables for Democratic and Republican party identification (with independents and others the excluded category). For each respondent, we generated a predicted probability of voting for Kerry using these two models.

The two sets of predictions correlated at $r = 0.52$, suggesting that the extended model does indeed produce somewhat different predictions. We can then ascertain whether the predictions were "correct" by comparing them to actual vote choice—assuming that anyone with a probability of 0.5 or greater (lower) is predicted to be a Kerry (Bush) voter. The baseline model correctly predicts 64% of cases, a rate significantly higher than chance alone. The extended model correctly predicts 79% of cases. This improvement is unsurprising, given the explanatory power of its additional predictors.

More surprising is that, in the aggregate, any prediction errors tend to cancel each other out, rendering the "performance" of the two models essentially equivalent. We calculate the state-level mean probability of voting for Kerry for each of the two models—i.e., Kerry's predicted proportion of the vote in each state. These state-level means correlate very highly (at $r = 0.989$). Moreover, each of these means correlates very highly with the actual proportion of exit poll respondents who voted for Kerry ($r = 0.97$ for the baseline model; $r = 0.99$ for the extended model). Given that we rely on aggregated quantities to compute the partisan differential and the simulated outcomes under full turnout, our sparsely specified models of the vote may be sufficient to model preferences.

Notes

1. Contrast Bereleson, Lazarsfeld, and McPhee (1954) and Bennett and Resnick (1990) with Lipset (1959) and Brady (1999).

2. Lijphart (1997).

3. Wolfinger and Rosenstone (1980).

4. Wolfinger and Rosenstone (1980); Highton and Wolfinger (2001), pp. 179, 192.

5. Highton and Wolfinger (2001), pp. 187–188. There is also little evidence of differences among voters and nonvoters within particular ethnic groups, though African Americans are something of an exception (Ellcessor and Leighley 2001).

6. Dalton (2008); Manza, Hout, and Brooks (1995). There has been a lively dispute over whether class voting in the United States has declined in recent decades (see, e.g., Bartels 2006; Frank 2004; Gelman et al. 2008; McCarty, Poole, and Rosenthal 2006). Ultimately, voters of low socioeconomic status do continue to vote more Democratic than their wealthier counterparts, but the strength of this relationship varies across states. Furthermore, to the extent that class voting has declined, much of this derives from high-SES individuals moving toward the Democrats because of social issues and cultural identities, rather than low-SES individuals failing to vote their pocketbooks.

7. Ansolabehere and Hersh (this volume); Brunell and DiNardo (2004); Citrin, Schickler and Sides (2003); DeNardo (1980, 1986); Martinez and Gill (2005); Nagel and McNulty (1996, 2000); Wattenberg and Brians (2002); Wuffle and Collet (1997).

8. In American municipal elections (Hajnal and Trounstine 2005) and elections in Europe (Bohrer, Pacek, and Radcliff 2000; Pacek and Radcliff 1995), higher turnout has a larger effect on election outcomes.

9. Of course, if the Democrats successfully mobilize their potential voters while Republicans do not—so that, for example, African American turnout is higher than white turnout—then Democrats would benefit more (at least in several states) than they would if everyone voted. But implicit in claims that low turnout biases outcomes against the left is the counterfactual of equal turnout

across groups, not higher turnout among the disadvantaged than among the wealthy.

10. We do not analyze the 2002 Senate election because the exit polls had substantial problems, and the resulting data file includes only small samples in most states.

11. See Sides, Schickler, and Citrin (2008).

12. In the Senate races, we ignore votes for third-party and independent candidates, although we treat Bernie Sanders of Vermont as a Democrat. (Thus, we omit the three-candidate 2006 Connecticut race, which Joe Lieberman, running as an independent candidate, won by a wide margin.) In the presidential races, we do take account of votes for Ross Perot in the 1992 and 1996 presidential elections. See Sides, Schickler, and Citrin (2008) for further details. We are limited to demographic variables because they are all that is available in the Current Population Survey, which we use to predict the vote choice of nonvoters. We discuss the consequences of this limitation in this chapter's appendix.

13. On the Clarify package, see King, Tomz, and Wittenberg (2000).

14. In Sides, Schickler, and Citrin (2008), we took the uncertainty into account by treating each coefficient estimate from the VNS model as a normally distributed random variable, with a mean equal to the point estimate and a standard deviation equal to the standard error for that point estimate. We then "drew" a value for each coefficient and calculated the predicted probability, repeating this procedure 1,000 times. The method we use now allows us to take into account the information in the variance-covariance matrix of the coefficient estimates. As it turns out, the results are virtually identical using the two simulation approaches. Citrin, Schickler, and Sides (2003) take account of underlying uncertainty in the estimates of nonvoters' preferences in a more casual fashion (see p. 84, n. 20).

15. DeNardo (1980).

16. Lazarsfeld, Berelson, and Gaudet (1948).

17. Sigelman et al. (1985); Sigelman and Jewell (1986).

18. See Citrin, Schickler, and Sides (2003) and Sides, Schickler, and Citrin (2008) for discussion of an alternative simulation and the results using this simulation.

19. Clinton wins Arizona, South Carolina, and Texas in 100 percent of our 500 simulations, and North Carolina in 81.8 percent.

20. Clinton wins Georgia and Texas in 100 percent of the simulations, and Colorado and Mississippi in 99 percent.

21. This held in 91 percent of the iterations.

22. In our earlier analysis of the 1994–1998 Senate races (Citrin, Schickler, and Sides 2003), we focused on a different method of simulating the impact of full turnout. Using this method, we reported that three other races would have flipped: the 1994 Senate races in Delaware, Washington, and Virginia. As we noted then (see n. 20, p. 84), the current method of simulation did not produce flips in Delaware and Virginia, and that continues to be true in this analysis. While we found then that the Washington race would have flipped under either method, here it does not, but the simulated outcome is very close to flipping. (The Democratic candidate garnered 44.3 percent of the vote in actuality, but 49.5 percent

in the current simulation.) Thus, our results are essentially the same as in the earlier analysis.

23. In five of these eight races, the outcome changed in the vast majority (95 percent or greater) of simulations. In three races, Oregon in 1990, Kentucky in 2004, and Virginia in 2006, the outcome changed in 74 percent, 61 percent, and 61 percent of simulations, respectively.

24. For example, if we treat the state-year as the unit of analysis and regress the partisan differential in presidential elections (N = 204) on a set of year dummies and then on a set of state dummies, the former explain much less variance than the latter (an R-squared of 0.03 versus 0.38).

25. It is of course possible, following DeNardo, that the peripheral voters attracted in high-turnout elections tend to come from the minority party in each state, which would cut against the idea that close elections are associated with a smaller partisan differential (since the Republicans are in the minority in many states).

26. The demographic measures are computed from the Current Population Surveys in each state, since these provide more up-do-date measures than the decennial Census. Income inequality is measured as the ratio between the average incomes of the 90th and 10th percentiles. We rely on income inequality rather than the mean level of income. It is not clear whether a high average income should lead to an increase or a decrease in the partisan differential within a state. In contrast, as the *gap* between rich and poor increases, there should be a stronger connection between income and vote choice. The proportion of Latinos and Asians is calculated including only those Latinos and Asians who are U.S. citizens.

27. We also investigated the possibility that the margin of victory affects the absolute value of the partisan differential, under the assumption that competitive states simply have less bias (whether Democratic or Republican) among nonvoters. There was, however, no significant relationship except in 1992. It is also worth noting that the level of turnout and the mean level of education in each state have no statistically significant relationship to the partisan differential once they are included in these models. The same is true of the percent of union members in each state. A dummy variable for the South also had no significant effects.

28. This is not directly attributable to the lower citizenship rate among Latinos. The independent variable we use is the percentage of the state's population who are Latino citizens. If we remove Texas from the analysis, the effect of the Latino population falls by approximately one-third to one-half in the 1996 Senate, 1996 presidential, and 2000 presidential elections, although it remains statistically significant in the latter two elections. In the 2004 presidential election, the effect is essentially unchanged. Thus, the effects of ethnic composition do not derive from Texas's potential status as an outlier.

29. See also Sides, Schickler, and Citrin (2008).

30. While we have not analyzed House elections, there are few House races close enough to make it likely that universal turnout in 2000 would have tipped the chamber to the Democrats.

XIII

The Effects of Registration Laws on Voter Turnout

AN UPDATED ASSESSMENT

Matthew R. Knee and Donald P. Green

SCHOLARS HAVE LONG SUSPECTED that laws regulating voter registration affect voter turnout rates. Gosnell's early work on causes of low voter turnout in the city of Chicago in 1924 brought this relationship to scholarly attention, and the nature of many Jim Crow laws suggests that policymakers were aware of this possibility as well. However, the rigorous quantitative assessment of the link between registration laws and voter turnout began with Rosenstone and Wolfinger's seminal work. Their 1978 essay argued that voter turnout rates would rise substantially if voter registration closing dates were changed so that one could register on Election Day. That article and the book that grew out of it (Wolfinger and Rosenstone 1980) also marked a turning point in the study of electoral institutions. For the first time, scholars combined behavioral models of voter turnout, which emphasized the role of factors such as education and age, with institutional explanations that focused on the costs of voting.

This new line of scholarship informed and propelled policy debates. Armed with quantitative evidence about the effects of policy innovations, students of voter turnout burst onto the political scene as advocates and advisors. Wolfinger, noting that people generally file change-of-address forms with the post office when they move, proposed facilitating voter registration by linking it to other bureaucratic settings and procedures, an intuition that ultimately led to the "Motor Voter" concept. Meanwhile, Piven and Cloward, who argued that modern voter registration obstacles continue to function "as de facto equivalents of the poll tax, literacy test and other class-and race-oriented restrictions on the suffrage of an earlier era,"[1] teamed up with certain interest groups to liberalize registration rules in ways that their scholarship suggested would encourage turnout among low-income Americans. Ultimately, a scholarly consensus emerged suggesting that the largest impact on voter turnout would result from two relatively straightforward policy innovations: loosening registration deadlines (also called "closing dates") and implementing Election

Day registration (EDR), which allows voters to register and vote simultaneously.

In the decades since Rosenstone and Wolfinger (1978), statistical research methods have evolved considerably. Rosenstone and Wolfinger analyzed a random sample of the survey of adults conducted by the Census Bureau in November of 1972 because analyzing the entire sample would have exceeded their computer capacity.[2] In its day, their statistical analysis was state-of-the-art, and their approach generated conclusions that remained authoritative for a generation. Decades of data have since accumulated, and social scientists now have access to valuable new information about the ways in which turnout rates have changed as states have changed their registration rules.

The goal of this essay is to use new data and more up-to-date statistical models to reevaluate the effects of closing date and EDR on voter turnout. We discuss alternative modeling strategies of registration deadlines and take a fresh look at the impact of closing dates and EDR during the period 1980–2006. In particular, we explore the consequences of changing the analytic focus from cross-sectional comparisons of different states at a given point in time to cross-temporal comparisons of each state over time. Our approach generates findings that qualify previous conclusions. In comparison to earlier studies, ours suggests that closing dates and Election Day registration have limited effects on turnout. The estimated effects of these variables achieve statistical significance only during presidential election years. Although our estimates are hardly the last word on the subject, they help to explain why the secular trend in favor of more liberal closing dates did not produce the surge in turnout predicted by the early statistical studies.

Evolution of Scholarship on Registration Laws and Voter Turnout

Voter registration in the United States is an individual, opt-in responsibility, rather than an automatic process as in most of Europe (Piven and Cloward 2000). Decades before economic models of political action called theoretical attention to the costs of voting (Downs 1957; Olson 1965; Riker and Ordeshook 1968), early scholars noted the way in which campaigns and laws facilitated or inhibited registration. Merriam and Gosnell (1924) described Chicago's system of voter registration, which was a one-day event featuring mobilization that paralleled Election Day itself. Key (1949) noted the demobilizing effects that restrictive registration rules and outright intimidation had on voting, particularly among blacks. The first statistical analysis of the effects of registration rules was conducted by Kelley, Ayres, and Bowen (1967), who used city-level turnout in 1960 to show that a closing date of a week before the election, instead of a month before, increases turnout 3.6 percentage points. Rosenstone and Wolfinger (1978) were the first to assess the impact of voter registration requirements on a representative national sample. Their forecasts gauged the effect of eliminating the closing date, ceasing to purge nonvoters from the rolls, instituting mail-in registration, and having regular and evening and/or Saturday office hours for registration offices. They estimated that instituting all of these reforms would increase turnout by 9.1 percentage points, with 6.1 percentage points being attributable to moving the registration closing deadline to Election Day itself (Rosenstone and Wolfinger 1978). Interestingly, Rosenstone and Wolfinger also concluded that this extra turnout would do little to alter the political composition of the electorate; the across-the-board gains in turnout would scarcely change the relative probability of voting among demographic and political subgroups (Rosenstone and Wolfinger 1978). Brians and Grofman (2001) tell a more complicated story, finding that EDR increases turnout but in a fashion that is a curvilinear function of education and income. Highton (2004), meanwhile, notes that more permissive registration deadlines should particularly affect low propensity voters who can be mobilized at the last minute by campaigns.

The key empirical finding presented by Rosenstone and Wolfinger (1978) and Wolfinger and Rosenstone (1980)—namely, that closing dates affect turnout—has been affirmed by subsequent researchers. Nagler (1991) applied similar models to a wider array of survey data and obtained similar results. Powell (1986) conducted a cross-national comparative study that measured the turnout effects of the various registration-related laws. Powell concluded that, in comparison to countries that impose no registration barriers, registration laws in the United States reduce turnout by as much as 14 percentage points. Powell's widely cited analysis was interpreted to mean that the basic mechanism of registration "costs" depressed turnout across a wide variety of electoral systems and political conditions.

As states moved to liberalize registration rules, scholars were presented with new opportunities for studying the consequences of policy change. Some states moved deadlines for registration closer to Election Day. Others instituted Election Day registration (EDR), in which voters may register at the polls on the day of the election. Several subsequent studies produced results consistent with Rosenstone and Wolfinger's (1978) findings (Fenster 1994; Mitchell and Wlezien 1995; Rhine 1996; Highton and Wolfinger 1998; Alvarez, Ansolabehere, and Wilson 2002; Ansolabehere and Konisky 2006), although the predicted size of the turnout effects of liberalizing registration laws varied by study.

One exception was an early study of Motor Voter by Knack (1995), which departed from the rest of the literature in that it used turnout rates aggregated at the state level, dummy variables controlling for the year of each election, and dummy variables controlling for each state. Additionally, Knack separated closing date and one-step voting on Election Day into two separate variables. Although Knack focused his attention on his Motor Voter result, such that closing date and EDR were controls rather than the variables of primary interest, he found little connection between either variable and voter turnout. The results presented here suggest that Knack's statistical approach and findings were prescient.

Statistical Models

In this section, we consider alternative approaches to modeling the effects of voter registration laws on voter turnout. Four models merit special attention: the cross-sectional model, the pooled aggregate model, the longitudinal model, and the dynamic time series model.

The cross-sectional model based on individual-level survey data is the model used by Wolfinger and Rosenstone (1980).[3] It can be written as follows:

$$Y_j = \beta_0 + \beta_1 X_{j1} + \beta_2 X_{j2} + \gamma_1 W_{j1} + \ldots + \gamma_K W_{jK} + \varepsilon_j \qquad (13.1)$$

where Y_j is an indicator variable for whether or not individual j voted, β_0 is an intercept, β_1 is the effect of closing date (X_{j1}), β_2 is the effect of EDR (X_{j2}), γ_1 through γ_K represent the effects of a set of K demographic or regional control variables intended to dampen heterogeneity from other factors, and ε_j is an error term. When estimating this model using regression, analysts have typically made two strong assumptions. First, they assume that registration laws are unrelated to unmeasured factors that affect turnout, such as state's electoral competitiveness or political culture. In effect, the model supposes that, once covariates such as age and education are taken into account, state registration laws are effectively assigned at random. If this assumption fails, the estimated effects of registration laws will be biased. Second, the disturbances associated with one observation are assumed to be independent of the disturbances for other observations. This assumption is almost certainly false when dealing with state-level registration rules, for even if they were assigned randomly, the assignment would be to 50 geographic clusters of individuals (as opposed to 50,000 individual assignments whereby each CPS survey respondent is assigned a registration law). Failure to take clustering into account, either by correcting the estimates that emerge from an individual level regression or by aggregating the data at the state level, results in severely biased standard errors that exaggerate the intervention's statistical significance (Arceneaux and Nickerson 2009).

One natural extension of the basic cross-sectional model is to aggregate the survey data by state, eliminating the need for clustering while at the same time augmenting the data set with additional election years:

$$Y_{it} = \beta_0 + \beta_1 X_{it1} + \beta_2 X_{it2} + \gamma_1 W_{it1} + \ldots + \gamma_K W_{itK} + \varepsilon_{it} \qquad (13.2)$$

This specification is analogous to equation (13.1) except that the dependent variable is now the voting rate in state i at time t. The control variables (W_{itk}) are now state-level attributes, such as the average level of education in a state/year.

The advantage of the model depicted in equation (13.2) is that it brings to bear additional years of state-level data. The drawback of estimating a pooled regression of this kind is that it risks bias. Pooled regressions use both within-state variability and across-state variability to estimate the effects of registration laws. Notice that equation (13.2) stipulates that all states share the same intercept. This assumption may well be false— different states may actually have different baseline rates of voting after controlling for the regressors. If these state-specific baseline rates are correlated with election laws, the pooled regression will generate biased results. For example, if states in the northern Midwest, which have more permissive registration laws, also have higher baseline rates of voter turnout, pooled regression estimates will exaggerate the causal influence of these laws. In short, pooled regression, like cross-sectional regression, presupposes that registration laws are assigned at random conditional on the W_{itk}.

A more cautious model controls for interstate differences and focuses exclusively on whether temporal variation in laws within each state predicts temporal variation in state-level turnout.

$$Y_{it} = \beta_0 + \beta_1 X_{it1} + \beta_2 X_{it2} + \gamma_1 W_{it1} + \ldots + \gamma_K W_{itK} + \\ \alpha_1 D_{1t} + \ldots + \alpha_{49} D_{49t} + \delta_1 Y_{1980i} + \ldots + \delta_{14} Y_{2006i} + \varepsilon_{it} \qquad (13.3)$$

This specification builds on equation (13.2) by including a dummy variable for each state (less one). State-level fixed effects eliminate time-invariant cross-state differences, whether they be measured variables (e.g., registration closing dates that never change in a given state) or unmeasured variables (e.g., stable aspects of the state's political culture or partisan complexion). The effect of time-varying factors such as closing dates is estimated, within each state, by tracking turnout rates over time and examining the way in which they respond to changes in closing dates. We also include year fixed effects in order to control for national trends in turnout. Introducing year fixed effects has the particular advantage of controlling for nationwide shifts in campaign tactics and registration laws during the period studied.[4]

As noted earlier, one of the most important differences between this essay and past literature is the use of state and year fixed effects. Other than Knack (1995), previous studies have relied on pooled regressions of the sort depicted in equation (13.2).[5]

Defenders of pooled regression have argued that, by utilizing both cross-sectional and cross-temporal variation, it enables the researcher to make much more statistically precise estimates of causal effects (Beck and Katz 2001). Critics, however, have noted that pooled regressions are prone to severe bias and that the gains in precision are therefore illusory (Green, Kim, and Yoon 2001). The adequacy of the pooled regression model can be assessed empirically by means of a Hausman test (Hausman 1978), which compares the estimates of β_1 and β_2 from the pooled model in equation (13.2) to the corresponding estimates from the fixed effects model in equation (13.3). Under the null hypothesis of no correlation between registration laws and omitted intercepts, both models generate consistent estimates; under the alternative hypothesis where such correlation exists, only the fixed effects model is consistent. When applied to the data analyzed here, the Hausman test decisively rejects the adequacy of the pooled model.[6]

Finally, we can incorporate a lagged dependent variable into the model to estimate the short-run effect of changes in registration laws on voter turnout:

$$Y_{it} = \beta_0 + \beta_1 X_{it1} + \beta_2 X_{it2} + \gamma_1 W_{it1} + \ldots + \gamma_K W_{itK} +$$
$$\alpha_1 D_{1t} + \ldots + \alpha_{49} D_{49t} + \delta_1 Y_{1980i} + \ldots + \delta_{14} Y_{20006i} + \rho Y_{i,\,t-1} + \varepsilon_{it} \quad (13.4)$$

This dynamic specification is analogous to equation (13.3) except that voter turnout in that state in the previous analogous election (presidential or midterm) is added to the list of independent variables. This allows us to estimate the short-run effects of changing voter registration laws (β_1 and β_2), and the estimate of ρ indicates the speed with which these increases in voting dissipate over time. The closer ρ is to 1.0, the slower the rate of decay; the closer to 0, the more rapidly a disturbance or policy shock dissipates.

Data

Our dependent variable in this essay is the state-level voter turnout rate in each federal election year from 1980–2006. Turnout rates among the voting eligible population were obtained from McDonald's ongoing voter turnout measurement project, which uses official voting returns and more detailed eligibility information (including information about disenfranchised felons) to obtain especially accurate measures of voter turnout.[7]

McDonald's turnout data date back as far as 1980.[8] In effect, our analysis picks up where Wolfinger and Rosenstone (1980) left off and provides an out-of-sample test of their empirical claims.

The primary independent variables of interest in this essay are the closing date and the presence of EDR in the form of one-step voting. EDR is coded as one if a state has one-step voting on Election Day and zero otherwise. In our coding scheme, EDR that does not include one-step voting means that both closing date and the EDR indicator variable are coded as zero. States in which voters can preregister up until a certain date as well as register at the polls will be coded as having the preregistration closing date as the closing date and be reported to have EDR.[9] We will additionally test specifications that combine closing date and EDR, as many have done in the past. In these specifications, we will set closing date to zero for all cases in which EDR is permitted, even when registration is closed for a number of days between some actual closing date and Election Day.

Closing date information is surprisingly elusive. The only remotely authoritative and centralized source of closing date data is *The Book of the States*, a (usually) biennial publication of the Council of State Governments (Council of State Governments and American Legislators' Association 1978–2006). Most studies of closing date use *The Book of the States* and then incorporate other contemporary sources such as League of Women Voters' voter guides or, during certain time periods, Human SERVE[10] to verify the data. The publication of *The Book of the States* does not always coincide with elections, and occasionally it will be wrong about closing dates that changed after the book went to press. Furthermore, *The Book of the States* typically lists only the closing date in terms of the number prescribed in black letter law. However, this date is often not the actual closing date, as the most common numbers (especially the modal 30 days) fall on a Sunday when elections are held on a Tuesday. Different states deal with this complication in different ways. Some open their election offices on Sundays; others change their closing date to Monday; still others move the closing data to the preceding Saturday. The most common solution is to move the date to Monday, but that creates a further complication, as this Monday is sometimes Columbus Day. States handle that matter differently as well, with some keeping their registration offices open for business as usual, and others moving the closing date to Tuesday. Thus, depending on the state and the year, a closing date of 30 days on the books can result in a closing date of 28, 29, 30, or 31 in practice.

In order to assemble more accurate data over a long period of time, we decided to rely on local newspaper coverage to verify the *The Book of the States* data. Generally, local newspapers print reminders on or near the last day to register, or publish stories shortly after about how registration numbers fared compared to previous years. We were able to gather about 300 relevant articles, encompassing nearly 40 percent of the observations in the data set. Because closing dates change relatively infrequently, verification via newspaper articles can be extrapolated to closing dates across runs of elections with constant black letter closing dates. We were also often able to detect consistencies in the treatment of Columbus Day from which we could extrapolate.

There remain a number of drawbacks to this method. To gather the newspaper articles, we relied on a Lexis-Nexis state newspaper search, so availability is highly correlated with the size of the largest media market in the state. The Lexis-Nexis database lacks newspapers from a handful of states (e.g., Delaware) that do not house even a single large media market. States with smaller newspapers are less likely to have long-running online archives through Lexis-Nexis or any other source. Generally, the data from 1994 and later are much more widely available than the data from before that point. Nevertheless, this method provides us with an especially large quantity of data to work with, and is far more accurate than merely using *The Book of the States*.

Figure 13-1 plots the changes in closing date, merged with EDR, from the beginning of our study (1980) to the end (2006). The 45-degree line denotes no change, with those above denoting increasingly stringent closing dates and those below denoting more permissive closing dates. Overall, the trend is toward more permissive deadlines: 20 states decreased by more than two days, 24 states either remained the same or changed by two days or less, often with closing dates around thirty days, and 6 states increased by more than two days. The most extreme increase in closing date occurred in Oregon, which went from EDR to a closing date of 21. Shortly after the repeal of EDR, Oregon instituted mail-only voting.[11] Oregon is therefore a strange case in which two policy changes occur simultaneously, but it turns out that excluding Oregon from the analysis that follows has no material effect on the results.

Results

Table 13-1 presents the results from a pooled regression analysis that includes neither state nor year fixed effects. This model, like the original Rosenstone and Wolfinger (1978) research and subsequent replications (Nagler 1991), is driven by cross-sectional comparisons of registration laws across states. And like these earlier results, table 13-1 suggests the powerful role played by closing date and EDR. Both variables have substantively large coefficients that easily surpass conventional levels of

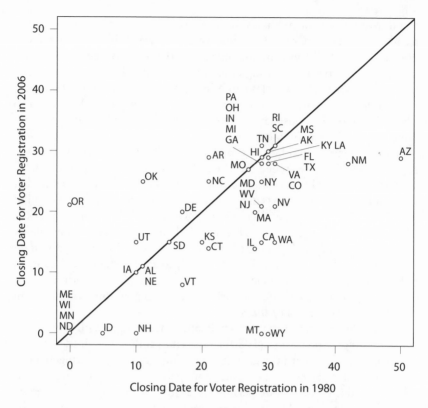

Figure 13-1

Changes in closing dates combined with EDR between 1980 and 2006. Note: "Closing date" refers to the minimum number of days prior to Election Day by which one must register to vote. States with Election Day registration are considered to have a closing date of zero.

statistical significance ($p < 0.001$). The estimates suggest that moving from a system whereby registration closed 30 days prior to the election to an at-the-polls Election Day registration system would increase turnout by more than 10 percentage points. For example, table 13-1 shows the estimated effect of closing date to be –0.224 per day and the estimated effect of EDR to be 3.436. Multiplying –0.224 × –30 days and adding 3.436 yields a 10.156 percentage-point increase in turnout.

This conclusion changes markedly when the model is expanded to include state and year fixed effects. The estimated effect of closing date is –0.066. The estimate is only one-third as large as the estimate derived from the pooled regression presented in table 13-1, and it does not achieve statistical significance. The same is true for the estimated effect of EDR, which falls to 1.586 and is also no longer statistically significant.

Table 13-1. State-Level Predictors of Voter Turnout for All Years, No Fixed Effects

Closing date	–0.224***
	(0.025)
Election Day registration	3.436***
	(0.824)
Age	–8.364**
	(3.663)
Age squared	0.094**
	(0.041)
Education	–204.488
	(158.200)
Education squared	160.850
	(112.914)
South	–6.724***
	(0.562)
Presidential election	14.870***
	(0.441)
Intercept	299.349***
	(96.273)
N	699

OLS regression estimates. Dependent variable is the percentage of eligible voters casting a vote in each state. Closing date is measured in days prior to the election. Age is in years. Education is on a zero to one scale. Data are from 1980–2006.
*$p = 0.10$; **$p = 0.05$; ***$p = 0.01$.

In light of the fact that the original work on registration laws focused on a presidential election (1972), we restrict our sample to presidential election years. Table 13-3 suggests that the effects of registration laws are stronger and more statistically robust in the context of presidential elections. Closing date and EDR are both reasonably strong and statistically significant. We find that moving from a system whereby registration closed 30 days prior to the election to an at-the-polls Election Day registration system would increase turnout by $-0.088 \times -30 + 2.137 = 4.777$ percentage points. Although considerably smaller than the estimates obtained from our initial pooled regression, this estimate remains substantively large.

Table 13-4, in contrast, shows meager effects of closing date and EDR when attention is restricted to midterm elections. Neither variable has statistically significant effects. Nevertheless, the hypothetical policy

Table 13-2. State-Level Predictors of Voter Turnout for All Years, Including State and Year Fixed Effects

Closing date	–0.066
	(0.041)
Election Day registration	1.586
	(1.277)
Age	6.022*
	(3.410)
Age squared	–0.063*
	(0.038)
Education	–8.995
	(134.169)
Education squared	33.513
	(98.880)
Intercept	–107.111
	(95.768)
N	699

OLS regression estimates. Dependent variable is the percentage of eligible voters casting a vote in each state. Closing date is measured in days prior to the election. Age is in years. Education is on a zero to one scale. Data are from 1980–2006. Fixed effects for state and year are included in the regression but not reported here.

$*p = 0.10; **p = 0.05; ***p = 0.01.$

change of shifting from a 30-day closing date to EDR is found to increase turnout slightly ($-0.059 \times -30 + 0.933 = 2.703$ percentage points) during midterm elections. Although the estimated coefficients for closing date and EDR do not vary significantly between presidential and midterm elections, it appears that registration rules have greater impact in presidential election years.

Table 13-5 returns to the full sample and shows how the results are qualified by the inclusion of a lagged dependent variable.[12] For the sample as a whole, a one-unit increase in turnout four years ago boosts current turnout by 0.391 percentage points. Extrapolating this process of geometric decay, we infer that only about 15 percent of a shock to turnout persists after eight years ($0.391^2 = 0.153$). Given the relatively weak autoregressive pattern in the data, it is not surprising that the coefficients from the dynamic specification reported in table 13-5 look similar to those from the static specification in table 13-2. The same is true when we compare the static specification for midterm elections in table 13-4 to the dynamic specification in table 13-5, as the dynamic effects reported in

Table 13-3. State-Level Predictors of Voter Turnout for Presidential Years Only, Including Fixed Effects

Closing date	−0.088**
	(0.037)
Election Day registration	2.137*
	(1.103)
Age	10.465***
	(2.874)
Age squared	−0.115***
	(0.032)
Education	83.437
	(112.180)
Education squared	−45.306
	(83.730)
Intercept	−208.359***
	(79.465)
N	350

OLS regression estimates. Dependent variable is the percentage of eligible voters casting a vote in each state. Closing date is measured in days prior to the election. Age is in years. Education is on a zero to one scale. Data are from presidential election years from 1980–2004. Fixed effects for state and year are included in the regression but not reported here.
$*p = 0.10; **p = 0.05; ***p = 0.01.$

Table 13-4. State-Level Predictors of Voter Turnout for Midterm Years Only, Including Fixed Effects

Closing date	−0.059
	(0.060)
Election Day registration	0.933
	(1.940)
Age	−3.590
	(5.318)
Age squared	0.045
	(0.060)
Education	−90.789
	(213.376)
Education squared	99.291
	(155.816)
Intercept	138.783
	(151.534)
N	349

OLS regression estimates. Dependent variable is the percentage of eligible voters casting a vote. Closing date is measured in days prior to the election. Age is in years. Education is on a zero to one scale. Data are from midterm election years from 1982–2006. Fixed effects for state and year are included in the regression but not reported here.
$*p = 0.10; **p = 0.05; ***p = 0.01.$

Table 13-5. State-Level Predictors of Voter Turnout for All Years, with Lagged Voter Turnout and Fixed Effects

	All elections	Presidential elections only	Midterm elections only
Closing date	−0.056	−0.062*	−0.074
	(0.042)	(0.037)	(0.066)
Election Day registration	0.840	1.509	−0.069
	(1.280)	(1.055)	(2.157)
Turnout lagged 4 years	0.391***	0.391***	−0.036
	(0.041)	(0.064)	(0.065)
Age	6.061	6.910**	1.975
	(3.938)	(3.195)	(6.803)
Age squared	−0.067	−0.077**	−0.017
	(0.044)	(0.035)	(0.076)
Education	39.146	62.648	31.382
	(165.189)	(132.754)	(287.506)
Education squared	−2.822	−33.695	28.113
	(119.536)	(97.127)	(206.468)
Intercept	−136.102	−145.318	−32.780
	(112.043)	(89.708)	(192.478)
N	599	300	299

OLS regression estimates. Data are from election years from 1984–2006. Fixed effects for state and year are included in the regression but not reported here.

$*p = 0.10; **p = 0.05; ***p = 0.01.$

table 13-5 are negligible in midterm election years. The only noteworthy change in results is found in presidential election years. The inclusion of a lagged dependent variable reduces the statistical significance of the estimated effects of closing date and EDR. Nevertheless, taken at face value, the estimates imply that changes in registration rules could have an important long-term impact. A permanent 30-day shift in the closing date to EDR implies a gain in turnout of $(−0.062 \times 30) / (1 − 0.391) + 1.509 / (1 −0.391) = 5.53$ percentage points.

Finally, table 13-6 reports what happens when we replace the two registration law variables with as single variable indicating the closing date. Consistent with our earlier results, we find that closing date influences turnout in a substantively and statistically significant manner only during presidential election years. Here, however, the magnitude of the implied policy effect is smaller than in table 13-3. From the static

Table 13-6. Specifications Using a Combined Closing Date and EDR Variable, with Fixed Effects

	All years	All years, with lagged turnout	Presidential years	Presidential years, with lagged turnout	Midterm years	Midterm years, with lagged turnout
Closing date with Election	−0.078**	−0.045	−0.095***	−0.060*	−0.053	−0.045
	(0.037)	(0.038)	(0.033)	(0.033)	(0.055)	(0.061)
Day registration						−0.036
						(0.065)
Turnout lagged 4 years		0.389***		0.391***		
		(0.041)		(0.064)		
Age	5.972*	6.029	10.354***	6.889**	−3.660	1.809
	(3.404)	(3.936)	(2.868)	(3.194)	(5.307)	(6.797)
Age squared	−0.063	−0.066	−0.114***	−0.077**	0.046	−0.016
	(0.038)	(0.044)	(0.032)	(0.035)	(0.059)	(0.075)
Education	−15.336	29.474	77.575	55.836	−101.722	22.988
	(133.218)	(164.101)	(111.752)	(132.467)	(211.044)	(284.431)
Education squared	39.134	4.287	−40.743	−28.954	107.775	33.768
	(98.208)	(118.710)	(83.445)	(96.923)	(154.074)	(204.008)
Intercept	−96.789	−127.974	−196.089**	−135.958	149.295	−47.039
	(94.418)	(110.728)	(78.364)	(89.447)	(149.356)	(192.307)
N	699	599	350	300	349	299

OLS regression estimates. Dependent variable is the percentage of eligible voters casting a vote. Data are from election years 1980–2006. Fixed effects are included for each state and election year but not reported here.

*p ≤ 0.10; **p ≤ 0.05; ***p ≤ 0.01.

specification reported in the third column of table 13-6, we infer that a 30-day reduction in closing date boosts turnout by $-0.095 \times -30 = 2.85$ percentage points, or $-0.060 \times -30 = 1.80$ percentage points with lagged turnout. For presidential years, the estimated long-term effect of a 30-day reduction in closing date is $(-0.060 \times -30) / (1 - 0.391) = 2.96$ percentage points. Thus, the basic substantive pattern looks the same regardless of whether we take dynamics into account. The evidence suggests that a dramatic change in closing date may increase turnout, but this increase is much smaller than previous estimates have suggested and statistically robust only for presidential elections.

Discussion and Directions for Further Research

The study of registration laws has been one of the most fruitful areas of political science investigation. A rare blend of survey research, behavioral science, and formal analysis of institutions, the resulting literature has figured prominently in policy debates and innovations. This domain is also one of the few in which political scientists conducted rigorous analysis in advance of policy interventions and subsequently had the opportunity to assess whether their predictions were borne out by events.

Some three decades after the path-breaking work of Rosenstone and Wolfinger (1978), political scientists are able to return to the fundamental research questions they posed with the benefit of hindsight and more advanced statistical methods. Rosenstone and Wolfinger concluded that registration deadlines have a powerful effect on the number of ballots cast. Our findings, based on additional data and more flexible modeling assumptions, qualify these conclusions. When the data are modeled in a manner that imposes strong assumptions about the comparability of different states, regression generates strong and significant effects of closing dates and EDR, very much in keeping with the original results that sparked interest in this topic. When these assumptions are relaxed and the causal effects of policy changes are identified by examining changes over time, the apparent effects of closing date and EDR diminish. The pattern of statistical results becomes more equivocal but suggests that the relationship between closing date and turnout is strongest during presidential election years. Apparently, during the waning days of a presidential election, states with late closing dates attract a significant number of new registrants who would not otherwise register.

This finding has interesting behavioral implications. The "costs" of registering to vote may interact with the interest generated by certain kinds of campaigns. In the absence of a presidential contest, closing dates seem to be less relevant. During the final days of a presidential campaign, on the other hand, closing dates seem to matter, arguably because a small set of eligible voters who would otherwise be insufficiently engaged by politics are stirred by campaign activity or the intrinsic importance of the pending election. By the time they become interested in the campaign, it is too late to register in states with early closing dates.

From a theoretical vantage point, the implication is that the costs of voting have behavioral significance for certain kinds of voters, within certain electoral contexts. For low and medium salience elections, closing dates are largely irrelevant; those motivated to register will do so regardless of the registration cut-off. For high salience elections, however, costs matter. And high salience elections are the ones used to compare voting rates cross-nationally. Although our results suggest that registration laws account for a much smaller portion of the turnout differential between the United States and other countries than was previously believed, registration rates remain a contributing factor.

Notes

We are grateful to Ken Scheve, who provided feedback on an earlier draft; Michael McDonald, who provided state-level voter turnout estimates; and David Nickerson, who shared Current Population Survey data. Special thanks go to Peter Aronow, who assisted in the data analysis and preparation of the manuscript. This research was supported by the Institution for Social and Policy Studies at Yale University, which bears no responsibility for the conclusions we draw.

1. *The New Leader* 1988.

2. Rosenstone and Wolfinger (1978), p. 28, n. 31.

3. We present a linear probability model in anticipation of the aggregate data models that follow in which a state's percentage turnout is the dependent variable. To their credit, Wolfinger and Rosenstone were among the first political scientists to estimate a probit model. However, the decision to use a linear or nonlinear specification does not materially affect the estimates one obtains from their data.

4. The introduction of fixed effects does not eliminate the threat of bias. The effects of closing dates will be misestimated if over-time changes in closing dates are related to over-time changes in unmeasured causes of turnout.

5. Knack (1995) used a model analogous to equation (13.3) on state-level aggregates from 1976–1992 and separated Election Day registration from closing date but used dummy variables for EDR and early closing date, rather than coding closing date in terms of days.

6. Comparing the first column of table 13-1 with the first column of table 13-2, the Hausman test rejects the adequacy of the pooled specification (chi-squared with 5 degrees of freedom, $p < 0.001$). This test statistic remains significant when we restrict the Hausman comparison to just the closing date and EDR estimates.

7. McDonald's website is http://elections.gmu.edu/voter_turnout.htm.

8. McDonald's data set lacks turnout for Louisiana in 1982. This is the only missing observation in our analysis. Our turnout measure is based on McDonald's "highest office" turnout.

9. Available data indicate that Maine may have established real, one-step-voting EDR sometime before January 2007, but as of a January 2001 source, had EDR only in certain areas, covering less than half of the state. It is unknown if or when the one-step-voting type of EDR was first implemented in parts of Maine. Because it is uncertain that Maine established true EDR statewide by 2006, and because this could not have occurred before 2002 (or 2000 if the January 2001 source was written before a policy change in the 2000 election), we code Maine as never having true EDR. We tested specifications using every possible scenario consistent with this information, including those using a 0.5 value in Maine for partial EDR, and found that the coding decision has little effect on the estimates reported in tables 13-1 through 13-5. In table 13-6, which does not distinguish between one-step-voting and EDR, this distinction is irrelevant to our results.

10. Human SERVE was an activist group that existed to advocate for the passing of the National Voter Registration Act of 1993. It is now defunct, having accomplished its objective.

11. In 1985, just before the institution of vote-by-mail, Oregon repealed EDR by initiative after a cult recruited homeless people from across the country to take over the local government of the town of Antelope (Knack 2001).

12. We also considered other specifications that tested whether registration rules have lagged effects. Perhaps due to collinearity between current and lagged rules, none of these specifications produced estimates that approached statistical significance.

XIV

Issue Preferences, Civic Engagement, and the Transformation of American Politics

Edward G. Carmines, Michael J. Ensley, and Michael W. Wagner

AMERICAN POLITICAL PARTIES HAVE undergone a fundamental transformation during the last several decades. Once seen as ideologically mixed and lacking well-defined policy positions, the modern Democratic and Republican parties have staked out clearly articulated, ideologically oriented policy positions across a wide range of issues.[1] Indeed, the growing polarization between the two major political parties is the major story of the past forty years of American party politics. While partisan polarization at the elite level is arrayed along a single ideological dimension separating liberals (on the left end of the spectrum) from conservatives (on the right end of the spectrum), the American citizenry does not organize its preferences as neatly—some citizens hold ideologically consistent opinions on most issues, while many others have more mixed, or, "heterogeneous," views, adopting liberal positions on some issues and conservative views on others.[2] Still others hold moderate views on the major policy questions of the day.[3] Thus, determining whether the increasing polarization of political elites has produced a more polarized citizenry is the subject of much discussion and debate among political scientists, political observers, and politicians themselves.[4] It turns out that the political divisions between individuals are not so easily—or accurately—summed up by calling "red state" voters conservatives and "blue state" voters liberals, and then concluding that the electorate is dangerously polarized with no one having views that are between these more extreme attitudes.

The question we address in this chapter is whether party polarization among elected officials has shaped the political engagement of American citizens. Do citizens who choose to engage in politics increasingly reflect the policy preferences of their respective party elites? And if so, where does this leave those citizens—the moderates, libertarians, and populists—who do not fit neatly into this ideological competition?

We explore these questions because one of the traditional exemplifiers of the health of American democracy is the level at which the citizenry participates in the political system. Verba and Nie embody this perspective, claiming that "the question of who participates in political decisions becomes the question of the nature of democracy in a society."[5] Indeed, several scholars have investigated questions seeking to explain who engages in political participation, finding answers that sometimes corroborate, complement, or contradict each other.[6] Regardless of what scholars find vis-à-vis the factors that influence political participation, the underlying assumption of the lion's share of research in this area is that participation is a good thing.

Morris Fiorina questions this assumption, claiming that Americans who have extreme views are the most likely people to participate in political activities, giving an unrepresentative, extremist-view-holding sample of the electorate disproportionate control over public political decision-making.[7] In Fiorina's view, this relatively small band of radicals is responsible for the mistaken perception of a public "culture war." While agreeing that those with more extreme views have increased their political participation in recent years, Alan Abramowitz[8] argues that the number of politically polarized Americans is of a significant size after all, providing evidence indicating that nearly half of all self-identified Democrats and Republicans are "active citizens." Perhaps more striking, Abramowitz lists a quarter of Republican and Democratic identifiers as "campaign activists"—people who tackle a number of political activities in an election cycle.

Concomitantly, Hibbing and Theiss-Morse argue that too much democratic participation might not be a good thing after all—not because the extremists are the chief participators—but because many Americans are not interested in politics, are quick to abandon democratic values, and do not have a realistic understanding of how politics works.[9] More generally, Theiss-Morse and Hibbing contend that we should not expect all citizens to be equally enthralled with the process of political participation because "[m]aking collective decisions in the context of heterogeneous opinions is a challenging and frustrating experience, one that many people could do without."[10]

In this chapter, we do not try to adjudicate directly between these competing claims about the normative value of political participation. Instead, we offer a new perspective on political participation that has its roots in an elite-driven theory of political behavior. We argue that as the parties have become increasingly ideologically distinct from one another, with the Republican Party's representatives in Washington maintaining[11] conservative positions on social as well as economic issues and the Democratic Party's congressmembers advocating the opposite pair of issue alternatives, there is an increased tendency for *voters* with issue preferences that match these party positions to engage in a higher level of political participation than citizens whose preferences do not reflect these party positions. Those who are "ideologically consistent"—that is, people holding the same broad issue positions offered by partisan elites (elected officials in each party)—should find participation less challenging and frustrating, recalling Theiss-Morse and Hibbing's phrasing, than those whose own preferences have no clear partisan home; as such, ideologically consistent people should be more willing to participate in political activities.

In order to investigate this hypothesis, we map voter preferences onto two broad domestic policy dimensions, one focusing on economic issues and the other on social issues. Using data from the American National Election Studies (ANES) from 1972 to 2004, we find that the consistency of voters' positions on these two issue dimensions has a significant impact on their likelihood of participating in campaign activities. People who have orthodox issue positions—consistently conservative or consistently liberal preferences on both economic and social issues—participate in more campaign activities such as displaying a yard sign, attending a rally, and trying to influence others' votes. However, Americans holding a heterodox (inconsistent) combination of preferences—a liberal position on economic issues and a conservative position on social issues or vice versa—participate in fewer activities. Further, citizens who have moderate centrist views on economic and social issues tend to participate in fewer campaign activities than liberals and conservatives. That is, we find that moderates, populists, and libertarians donate money, work for campaigns, and the like much less frequently than liberals and conservatives. On the other hand, our findings also indicate that when it comes to voter turnout, the consistency of issue preferences does not seem to be the driving force steering citizens to the polls.[12] Finally, with regard to both campaign participation and turnout, we demonstrate that ideological populists (those who prefer government intervention and regulation on both economic and social issues) are the most negatively impacted by the contemporary elite partisan divide.

It is worth pointing out that while the term "consistent" has a positive connotation and "inconsistent" has a negative one, we do not mean to make normative judgments about the intelligence or usefulness of people's issue preferences across economic and social issues. We simply use these terms to help us understand which citizens have views that are consistent with the partisan issue options offered by elected officials in Washington and which citizens have views that are not perfectly suited to either major political party.

This chapter proceeds as follows. First, we present our argument about why we believe people's issue preferences should affect their political participation. Second, we present over thirty years of evidence from the ANES to test our hypotheses about ideological consistency and political participation. Finally, we summarize our results and discuss their implications with respect to understanding both contemporary and the future of American politics.

Issue Dimensions and Political Participation

American party elites have grown increasingly polarized along a single broad ideological dimension during recent decades.[13] Today, congressional Republicans are more conservative than congressional Democrats on long-standing economic and social welfare issues related to taxing and spending as well as more recent social issues like abortion and gay rights. The ideological divide between elite partisans now spans virtually the entirety of the domestic policy agenda. Indeed, Republican elected officials prefer tax cuts, an end to legal abortion in order to protect the life of a fetus, and the protection of traditional marriage, and they oppose government-sponsored health care reform. At the same time, Democrats in high office prefer higher taxes on the wealthy, promote a woman's right to choose, support increased gay rights, and desire broad health care reform.

Even so, political conflict—from the perspective of the public—cannot be reduced to a single ideological dimension.[14] In their comprehensive analysis, Shafer and Claggett[15] show that two "deep" issue dimensions exist in the American public. The first dimension focuses on the economic and social welfare issues that dominated the domestic issue agenda during the New Deal era. These issues deal with the government's role in managing the economy and providing for the general welfare, such as taxes, spending on health care, social security, and welfare. More recently, racial issues dealing with aid to minorities and affirmative action have largely fused onto the economic dimension,[16] even though racial issues were explicitly suppressed by FDR because they cross-cut economic issues at the outset of the New Deal.[17] Regardless, the common thread linking these issues together is that they deal with regulation and distribution, focusing on the role that government should play in a market economy.[18]

The second dimension, which entered the arena of elite political debate in the late 1960s, deals with cultural, or moral, values including issues like abortion, gay rights, and prayer in public schools. These issues are bound by their common concern for the implementation of American values, values that define appropriate social behavior.[19] These two issue dimensions have become incorporated into a single broad ideological dimension for party elites, but they remain largely separate and distinct for the mass electorate.[20]

As partisan elites have become increasingly polarized over the past several decades,[21] there has been renewed interest in whether citizens are similarly divided. Hetherington[22] argues that partisans in the electorate have responded to elite polarization with polarization of their own. Fiorina (2005) disputes that claim, arguing that only a very small percentage of the electorate is strongly divided. We argue that, in a way, both Hetherington and Fiorina are correct.[23] Citizens who have issue preferences that are liberal on economic issues *and* social issues have become increasingly polarized from people who have consistently conservative issue preferences along both dimensions.[24] We call these citizens "consistent liberals" and "consistent conservatives," respectively. Voters with consistently liberal or conservative issue preferences, however, constitute only a portion of the entire American electorate. A nontrivial portion of the electorate has moderate centrist views on most political issues, even on such contentious issues as abortion and gay rights—a situation that has not changed dramatically in recent years.[25] As Fiorina observes, "reports of an American population polarized around moral and religious issues, or any other issue for that matter, are greatly exaggerated."[26] Since issue moderates find themselves wedged between an increasingly liberal Democratic Party and an increasingly conservative Republican Party, they should be less likely to have strong partisan identifications and vote straight party tickets.[27] Moreover, while they may not be less likely to vote, they should be less likely to be drawn into intense campaign activity than liberals and conservatives.

Nor should citizens, we argue, with inconsistent positions across the economic and social issue dimensions be as likely to spend their time and money supporting a candidate whose issue preferences may match those of these citizens only along one issue dimension. As party elites have increasingly polarized in a consistently liberal or conservative direction, citizens with libertarian (voters who hold conservative positions on economic and social welfare issues but liberal positions on social or cultural issues) and populist (voters who hold liberal positions on social welfare issues but conservative positions on social issues) views have become increasingly cross-pressured, preferring the Republican Party position on one issue dimension but the Democratic Party position on the other issue dimension. For example, a libertarian might hold pro-choice views on abortion (like the Democrats) but prefer lower taxes (like the Republicans). Thus, compared to people who are consistently liberal or consistently conservative, we should not expect inconsistent citizens to participate in as many political activities because the candidates they would be supporting would agree with them on only one of the two major issue dimensions. The same logic should hold true for moderates, as compared to consistent liberals and conservatives. Without strong, well-defined preferences across both major issue dimensions, moderates ought to be less interested—and thus, less motivated—to participate in political activities.

The ANES asks respondents several questions about their political involvement that we can use to help test our theory, including whether they post a yard sign for a candidate, try to influence others about the upcoming election, donate money to a candidate, or work/volunteer for a candidate. Consistent with Fiorina's view of the "dark side of civic engagement," we expect consistent liberals and conservatives to be more likely to engage in these activities than libertarians, populists, and moderates.[28] Regarding the act of voting itself, our expectations are not as neat. In general, we believe that the consistency of citizens' issue preferences should not be a determining factor in their decision to head to the polls. While those with consistent preferences should be likely to vote, libertarians and populists, all else equal, may find one issue dimension more salient than the other in general or in a particular election cycle, equally prompting them to vote.[29] Moreover, compared to campaign activities, the act of voting is less costly and demanding, and for this very reason, its exercise may depend less on the match between citizens' views on social and economic issues and elite party positions.

Miller and Schofield claim that major changes in American politics are heavily influenced by how policy-driven partisan activists and vote-seeking political elites target disaffected (and typically extreme) voters operating in a two-dimensional issue space. They argue that the end of the twentieth century saw an increase in the salience of conflict along the social issues dimension as political elites engaged in "flanking moves" to win the hearts and minds of previously disaffected voters. If they are correct, the degree of consistency between citizens' issue preferences need not be the primary driving force in their decisions about turning out to vote; simply making one of the two major dimensions "active" may be enough to encourage citizens to go to the polls.

Data, Variables, and Analyses

We analyze two aspects of participation: turnout and involvement on campaign-related activities. Turnout in the analyses reported here is simply whether the individual reported voting in the general election. To measure campaign participation (other than turnout), we aggregated a series of survey questions about political activities. In every ANES survey between 1972 and 2004, respondents were asked if they (1) attempted to influence another person's vote; (2) worked for a political campaign; (3) displayed a campaign sign, bumper sticker, etc.; (4) attended a political meeting; or (5) made a monetary campaign contribution. We added together the responses to these questions to create a six-point political action scale, where the modal category is 0 and the yearly mean ranges between 0.6 and 0.9 (with a standard deviation between 0.9 and 1). For the reader interested in our statistical techniques, our dependent variable is not technically a count variable because the number of actions is bounded from below and above (i.e., it is a proportion, or the number of activities engaged in of the five possible activities), but the skewed distribution of the dependent variable closely approximates a count variable. Thus, we chose to estimate the model using a negative binomial regression model because there is evidence of overdispersion.

To examine the relationship between issue preferences and political participation over time, we need to develop measures of our two issue dimensions. We identified any issues within each ANES survey from 1972 to 2004 that pertained to either the Social Welfare or Cultural issue dimension. This chapter's appendix provides a description of the survey questions used, the multiple imputation procedure used to handle the missing data, and the confirmatory factor analysis procedure we used to create the scores for respondents on each issue dimension. The scores are created such that higher values indicate a more conservative position. Further, the factor scores are standardized to have a mean of 0 and a standard deviation of 1.

Using the factor scores for the two issue dimensions, we can examine which citizens are most likely to participate in campaign activities and which citizens are most likely to vote. Given that we must distinguish between those individuals who have mixed positions across the two dimensions and those who have consistent positions, as well as the voters that have moderate positions, we include two additional variables in the regression models reported here. First, we multiply the Social Welfare and Cultural variables together. Since both variables are centered at zero, an individual that is either conservative or liberal on both dimensions will have high values for the interaction variable. For the heterodox citizens, who are liberal on one dimension yet conservative on the other, they will have low, negative values for the interaction variable. Thus, the interaction variable is labeled Consistency, since higher values indicate that the individual holds either more consistently liberal or more consistently conservative positions on both dimensions. We expect that there will be a positive and statistically significant relationship between the interaction variable and political participation.

Individuals who are moderate on both dimensions have values in the middle of the scale for the interaction variable described earlier. However, we also want to examine whether moderate voters are less likely to participate than cross-pressured, heterodox citizens. To determine whether individuals who are policy moderates are more or less likely to participate and vote, we include the square of the consistency variable in the regression models. If the squared term is positive and statistically significant, this demonstrates that moderate voters are the least likely to participate.

Control Variables

In addition to the issue variables, we include a set of standard attitudinal and demographic variables that have been utilized in previous studies of political participation. The attitudinal variables include three measures of political partisanship. There are two dummy variables for being a Democratic identifier and a Republican identifier (these include independent partisan leaners), where the omitted category is independent and third-party identifiers. We also include the Strength of partisan identification, which was created by folding the seven-point partisan identification scale at the midpoint. Thus, the scale ranges between 0 and 3, with higher numbers indicating a stronger identification. We expect that participation will be higher for partisan identifiers and will increase as the strength of identification increases.[30]

In addition to partisanship, we also include measures that tap individuals' perceptions of their personal financial situation. Retrospective is a scale indicating how an individual's personal financial situation has changed over the previous year, and Prospective is a scale measuring a respondent's personal financial expectations for the next year. Both of these variables are three-point scales ranging from worse (1) to better (3). It is possible that citizens' perceptions of their financial situation will influence their turnout and campaign participation. Trust in government is a summated rating scale created from four variables, and the variable has been rescaled to range between 0 and 1. We expect that increasing trust will be associated with higher levels of political participation.

The demographic control variables are Education (a seven-category variable), Income (by quintiles), and Age (in years). We include the square of the age variable as well because we expect that participation will initially increase as individuals become older but eventually the likelihood of participating may decrease (or at least, the marginal rate of participating will decrease with age). We also include dummy variables for living in the South and being Female, African American, or a member of another Minority group. Finally, for the analysis of turnout, we include an additional variable. Recent is a dummy variable indicating whether an individual has changed residences within the last four years. Individuals who have moved recently will be less likely to have registered and therefore will be less likely to be able to vote.

Multivariate Analysis of Campaign Participation

The regression analyses for campaign participation and turnout for each presidential election between 1972 and 2004 are reported in tables 14-1 and 14-2, respectively. First, consider the results for campaign participation reported in table 14-1. Not surprisingly, age, education, income, and strength of partisanship have statistically significant effects on participation across the various years. This means that individuals who have higher levels of education, are older and wealthier, and strongly identify with a political party are more likely to participate in campaigns.

For the issue variables and the interaction variables, there is significant variation across the years. For the first three elections analyzed, 1972–1980, the only coefficient that is statistically significant is for the Cultural dimension, which indicates that cultural liberals are more likely to participate, since the coefficient is negative. The other significant coefficient is the Consistency variable, which is significant in 1984 and between 1992 and 2004. Thus, there seems to be a significant change that occurred between the mid-1980s and the early 1990s, as the electorate responded to the growing polarization between party elites. Since 1992, ideologically consistent liberals and conservatives have been the most likely participants in campaign-related activities. Finally, the Consistency-squared variable is not statistically significant in any of the regressions in table 14-1; this indicates that moderates are *not* the least likely to participate, as some might suspect.

While examining the coefficients is informative, the best way to visualize the relationship between issues and political participation is to calculate predicted rates of participation for different combination of values for the Social Welfare and Cultural variables. Figure 14-1 shows the predicted rate of participation for five hypothetical citizens. A conservative (liberal) is defined as being one standard deviation above (below) the mean on both policy dimensions. A libertarian (populist) is one standard deviation above (below) the mean on the Social Welfare dimension and one standard deviation below (above) the mean on the Cultural dimension. A moderate has views that are at the mean on both policy dimensions. All of the other variables are held to their mean when calculating the predicted values.

Examining the predicted rates in figure 14-1 graphed between 1972 and 2004, we see that that there has been a change in the relative positions

Table 14-1. Negative Binomial Regression of Campaign Participation, 1972–2004

	1972 Coefficient	t	1976 Coefficient	t	1980 Coefficient	t	1984 Coefficient	t	1988 Coefficient	t
Social Welfare	-0.01	-0.34	-0.06	-1.26	0.05	1.02	0.08	1.95	-0.05	-1.09
Cultural	-0.17**	-4.01	-0.07*	-1.68	-0.09*	-1.75	-0.14**	-3.68	0.01	0.33
Consistency	0.04	0.81	0.02	0.39	0.05	0.81	0.10**	2.62	0.04	1.01
Consistency²	0.01	0.70	0.00	-0.29	0.02	1.12	0.01	0.91	0.01	0.61
Education	0.14**	6.68	0.19**	9.21	0.12**	4.42	0.17**	7.00	0.21**	8.07
Age	0.00*	-1.87	0.00	1.41	0.00	-1.04	0.00	0.57	0.01**	2.35
Female	-0.08	-1.25	-0.18**	-2.97	-0.07	-0.93	-0.18**	-2.71	-0.19**	-2.51
African American	0.07	0.60	-0.16	-1.18	-0.26	-1.67	0.11	0.92	0.19	1.34
Minority	0.02	0.13	0.21	1.61	-0.12	-0.65	-0.33**	-2.36	0.29**	2.25
South	0.03	0.48	-0.09	-1.32	-0.04	-0.46	0.02	0.32	-0.08	-1.01
Income	0.21**	6.62	0.17**	5.19	0.11**	2.82	0.04	1.08	0.21**	4.64
Retrospective	0.00	0.03	-0.09**	-2.37	-0.01	-0.31	0.02	0.53	-0.05	-1.08
Prospective	-0.01	-0.21	0.08	1.51	0.02	0.43	0.04	0.72	0.12*	1.75
Trust	0.06	0.48	-0.14	-1.02	0.03	0.16	-0.40**	-2.64	-0.21	-1.20
Strength	0.22**	5.03	0.30**	7.40	0.31**	5.97	0.32**	7.30	0.20**	4.19
Democrat	0.11	0.82	-0.17	-1.39	-0.10	-0.58	-0.03	-0.18	0.27	1.44
Republican	0.19	1.40	-0.16	-1.29	0.26	1.57	-0.10	-0.65	0.32*	1.69
Constant	-1.94**	-7.36	-1.95**	-8.60	-1.87**	-7.07	-1.93**	-7.24	-3.07**	-9.68
N	2183		1893		1398		1929		1765	
ln (alpha)	-0.74**	-5.21	-1.91**	-5.84	-1.5**	-4.84	-1.14**	-5.56	-0.70**	-4.04

*p < 0.1; **p < 0.05.

	1992 Coefficient	t	1996 Coefficient	t	2000 Coefficient	t	2004 Coefficient	t
Social Welfare	0.06	1.56	0.05	0.89	0.02	0.39	0.08**	1.88
Cultural	-0.04	-1.23	-0.03	-0.55	-0.02	-0.46	-0.09*	-1.94
Consistency	0.15**	3.59	0.21**	3.01	0.14**	2.32	0.13**	2.82
Consistency^2	0.00	-0.02	0.00	-0.24	0.00	-0.23	0.00	-0.04
Education	0.13**	6.49	0.13**	4.46	0.09**	3.33	0.06**	2.53
Age	0.00	-1.51	0.01**	3.43	0.01**	2.25	0.00	-0.74
Female	-0.19**	-3.13	-0.20**	-2.46	-0.18**	-2.28	-0.10	-1.47
African American	-0.17	-1.61	-0.08	-0.51	0.08	0.53	-0.13	-1.10
Minority	-0.08	-0.80	-0.05	-0.34	0.10	0.81	-0.02	-0.16
South	0.09	1.41	-0.01	-0.07	0.06	0.72	-0.04	-0.50
Income	0.08**	2.52	0.12**	2.61	0.13**	3.29	0.03	0.83
Retrospective	-0.02	-0.64	0.02	0.36	0.05	0.73	0.00	-0.11
Prospective	0.01	0.18	0.09	1.16	-0.06	-0.81	-0.01	-0.36
Trust	-0.29*	-1.95	0.17	0.88	0.15	0.84	-0.13	-0.79
Strength	0.17**	4.60	0.27**	5.15	0.19**	3.88	0.30**	6.91
Democrat	0.11	0.88	-0.34*	-1.69	0.10	0.52	0.05	0.33
Republican	0.03	0.26	-0.12	-0.59	0.19	0.95	-0.07	-0.43
Constant	-1.38**	-6.12	-2.61**	-7.56	-2.07**	-6.29	-0.88**	-3.86
N	2246		1532		1256		1066	
ln (alpha)	-1.25**	-6.58	-0.77**	-4.03	-1.29**	-4.76	-3.98	-1.61

*p < 0.1; **p < 0.05.

Table 14-2. Probit Regression of Turnout, 1972–2004

	1972 Coefficient	t	1976 Coefficient	t	1980 Coefficient	t	1984 Coefficient	t	1988 Coefficient	t
Social Welfare	-0.04	-0.69	0.02	0.48	0.03	0.50	0.15**	3.52	0.08	1.59
Cultural	-0.03	-0.64	0.04	0.95	0.02	0.45	-0.01	-0.33	0.00	-0.01
Consistency	0.05	0.85	0.11**	2.00	0.02	0.34	0.04	1.18	0.05	1.21
Consistency²	-0.01	-0.71	-0.02	-0.94	0.01	0.55	0.03	1.50	0.05**	2.72
Education	0.20**	7.19	0.22**	8.72	0.25**	8.63	0.22**	8.98	0.25**	9.85
Age	0.01**	4.19	0.02**	7.61	0.02**	7.82	0.02**	8.63	0.02**	8.94
Female	-0.21**	-2.68	-0.25**	-3.62	-0.05	-0.60	0.12*	1.82	0.04	0.58
African American	0.12	0.79	0.20	1.39	0.05	0.37	0.17	1.46	0.13	1.03
Minority	-0.14	-0.66	-0.24	-1.63	-0.61**	-3.53	-0.14	-1.21	0.16	1.34
South	-0.32**	-3.78	-0.26**	-3.55	-0.04	-0.52	-0.12	-1.58	-0.44**	-5.74
Income	0.16**	4.19	0.22**	5.96	0.16**	3.68	0.19**	5.43	0.25**	6.42
Retrospective	-0.02	-0.27	-0.02	-0.54	0.04	0.81	-0.02	-0.41	-0.04	-0.89
Prospective	-0.01	-0.11	0.04	0.75	-0.12**	-2.02	0.01	0.21	0.02	0.33
Trust	0.21	1.30	0.04	0.25	0.21	1.02	0.03	0.17	0.37**	2.27
Strength	0.16**	2.80	0.17**	3.33	0.14**	2.48	0.16**	3.64	0.27**	5.58
Democrat	0.33**	2.28	0.25**	1.99	0.27*	1.83	0.16	1.25	0.05	0.38
Republican	0.37**	2.47	0.26**	2.02	0.34**	2.26	0.15	1.21	0.09	0.65
Constant	-0.89**	-2.94	-1.81**	-7.41	-1.96**	-6.99	-2.03**	-7.82	-2.56**	-9.08
N	1960		1909		1407		1989		1773	

*$p < 0.1$; **$p < 0.05$.

	1992 Coefficient	t	1996 Coefficient	t	2000 Coefficient	t	2004 Coefficient	t
Social Welfare	0.10**	2.14	0.16**	2.84	0.13**	2.37	0.18**	2.79
Cultural	-0.05	-1.13	-0.04	-0.82	-0.10*	-1.92	-0.08	-1.19
Consistency	0.01	0.12	0.15**	2.08	0.08	1.34	0.07	1.10
Consistency^2	0.05**	2.24	0.00	-0.10	0.02	0.74	-0.01	-0.41
Education	0.26**	10.75	0.21**	7.27	0.23**	7.05	0.21**	5.68
Age	0.02**	8.03	0.02**	7.65	0.02**	5.99	0.01**	3.10
Female	0.05	0.71	0.03	0.33	-0.08	-0.83	0.11	1.08
African American	0.03	0.32	0.13	0.97	0.34**	2.07	0.33**	2.22
Minority	-0.33**	-3.19	-0.05	-0.44	-0.09	-0.69	-0.23*	-1.69
South	-0.28**	-3.97	-0.13	-1.47	-0.11	-1.22	-0.38**	-3.65
Income	0.20**	5.74	0.19**	4.23	0.14**	3.20	0.10**	2.28
Retrospective	-0.07*	-1.68	0.03	0.61	0.15**	2.08	0.07	1.62
Prospective	0.08	1.35	0.02	0.24	-0.03	-0.42	0.01	0.20
Trust	0.01	0.09	0.14	0.73	0.30	1.55	-0.09	-0.38
Strength	0.19**	4.50	0.30**	5.21	0.24**	3.99	0.30**	4.58
Democrat	0.24**	2.01	0.08	0.50	0.17	0.95	0.16	0.88
Republican	0.06	0.49	0.15	0.92	0.16	0.90	0.30	1.62
Constant	-2.02**	-8.15	-2.39**	-7.59	-2.28**	-6.75	-1.55**	-5.20
N	2254		1533		1249		1066	

$*p < 0.1$; $**p < 0.05$.

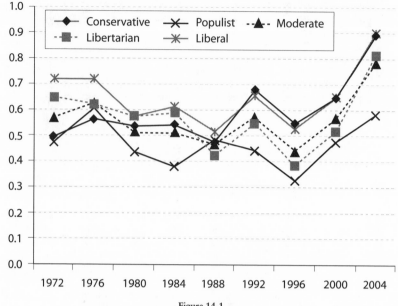

Figure 14-1
Campaign participation by ideological type, 1972–2004.

of the various types of citizens. Between 1972 and 1980, the most politically active citizens were the *cultural* liberals, i.e., liberals and libertarians. The clear pattern that emerges after 1988 is that the highest participation rate is among liberals and conservatives. The lowest participation rate is among populists. Participation rates of libertarians and moderates are located between populists and the ideologically consistent citizens. Thus, over the period analyzed here, the most notable change is that conservatives have become more involved in the political process. However, populists have remained the least participatory throughout.

Multivariate Analysis of Voter Turnout

The preceding analysis focused on forms of political participation besides voting. Given that the election results ultimately depend on who casts a vote on Election Day, it is important to analyze turnout separate from other forms of political participation. Further, voting may be subject to different psychological and sociological influences and may present a unique set of costs and benefits. Therefore, we chose to examine the link between ideological consistency and turnout separately.

Table 14-1 shows the regression model of turnout for each year. We employ the same set of independent variables used in the analysis of campaign participation. Since the dependent variable is a dichotomous variable (either someone voted or he or she did not), the regression coefficients were calculated via a probit model. Further, we calculated the predicted probability of turnout for the same five ideological types we used in calculating the participation rates in figure 14-1. The predicted probabilities of voting for the five ideological types are displayed in figure 14-2.

First, looking at the regression models reported in table 14-2, the only discernible pattern is that the Social Welfare dimension is positive and statistically significant between 1992 and 2004. This suggests that the highest participation rate is among those voters who are conservative on the Social Welfare dimension—i.e., those we label as the conservatives and libertarians. This is visible if we look at figure 14-2, which shows

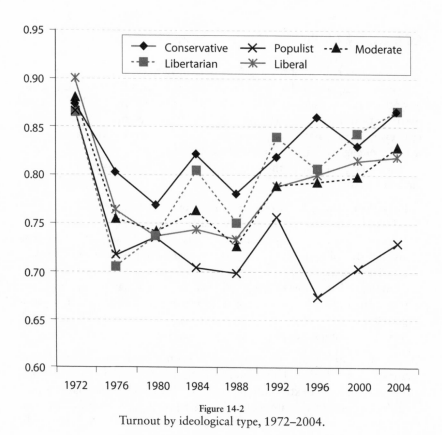

Figure 14-2
Turnout by ideological type, 1972–2004.

that the highest probability of voting belongs to the libertarians and conservatives from 1984–2004. The probability of voting for the liberals and
moderates track closely together over this time period as well, although
the probability of voting for these individuals is several percentage points
lower than probabilities for the social-welfare conservatives. Citizens'
ideological consistency across economic and cultural issue dimensions
did not lead to higher rates of turnout.

The most striking difference illustrated in figure 14-2 concerns the
populists. Across the time period analyzed, they have the lowest probability of voting. Further, the difference between the populists and the others
appears to have grown after 1992. Between 1996 and 2004, the probability that populists would vote is approximately 10 to 15 percentage points
lower than the probabilities for the other ideological types. Alternatively,
consider that the probability of voting has increased for every group since
1976 except for the populists. The probability of populist voting is approximately the same in 1976 and 2004.

Endogeneity, Ideological Consistency, and Participation

One possible critique of the argument we have made here is that we have
the causal mechanism backward—that is, it is entirely possible that we
have the story wrong. We have argued that individuals' level of political
participation responds to the package of issues presented by party elites.
However, an alternative explanation for the findings is that individuals
who are engaged and active in politics actually adjust their issue positions
to match the party elites they support. The two mechanisms are well described by Abramowitz and Saunders:

> Increased emphasis on ideological appeals by party leaders can influence the
> beliefs of active partisans through two different processes: persuasion and se-
> lective recruitment/derecruitment. In the case of persuasion, individuals who
> are already politically active may adjust their issue positions to bring them
> into line with the new positions of their party's leaders. In the case of selective
> recruitment/derecruitment, previously inactive voters may decide to become
> politically active because they agree with the new positions taken by their
> party's leaders, whereas previously active individuals who do not agree with
> these issue positions may dropout of the ranks of active partisans.[31]

Abramowitz and Saunders suggest that both selective recruitment and
persuasion are at play. This perspective seems consistent with Layman
and Carsey's conflict extension hypothesis.[32] We also believe that it is possible that some individuals may shift their positions on issues to match
party elites. However, we also want to claim that the consistency of indi-

viduals' issues positions is the dominant influence on their proclivity to participate.

If individuals are being persuaded to participate, we would expect that the relationship between ideological consistency and participation would disappear among those with high political knowledge, since these individuals will bring their issue positions in line with their partisanship. Those citizens with low political knowledge, who are also unlikely to participate in campaigns, may be unaware of the differences between the parties and thus may not adjust their issue positions. However, when we replicate the analysis presented in table 14-1 but stratify the analysis by high and low knowledge individuals, we find that the link between consistency and campaign participation is maintained, particularly among the high knowledge group. Specifically, we ran the campaign participation regression for a high and low knowledge group by splitting the sample at the mean value of knowledge.[33]

The results produced by stratifying by political knowledge confirm our expectations and add some additional insights. First, as we would expect, the average participation rates of high knowledge individuals are higher than participation rates of low knowledge individuals regardless of ideological type. More importantly from our perspective, the pattern of participation among high knowledge citizens is as we would predict. We find that by 1992, conservatives and liberals are the most likely to participate, whereas libertarians and populists have the lowest participation rates. However, when we examine participation among low knowledge individuals, we find that the pattern reflects our expectations but not until 2000. In 2000 and 2004, the pattern of participation among the ideological types is the same as for the high knowledge individuals, where liberals and conservatives are the most likely to participate. Thus, low knowledge individuals also seem to be responding to the polarization in the party system but at a slower rate than high knowledge individuals. We interpret this to mean that it takes low knowledge individuals longer to become aware of and then react to changes in the partisan divide. Overall, these results stratified by political knowledge provide strong evidence that individuals are responding to the polarization of party elites based on the ideological consistency of their issues attitudes.[34]

To further boost support for the claim that activists are being recruited to participate, we used the ANES 1992–1996 panel to examine whether previous expressions of issue attitudes can predict participation two and four years later. Panel data allows us to examine how ideological consistency affects *the same voters* over three different election periods. Thus, using the same variables and methods we used in table 14-1, we analyzed participation rates in 1994 and 1996 using individuals' issues scores in 1992 and 1994, respectively. Second, we examined participation rates in

1996 as a function of issues positions in 1992. Our expectation is that if individuals are aligning their issue positions to match party elites, then the consistency of their positions on the two issue dimensions either two or four years earlier should not be a significant predictor of participation. For in this case, elite persuasion accounts for any observed connection between citizens' issue preferences and their rate of participation. However, if individuals are responding to the package of policies presented by party elites, then the consistency of voters' previous issue preferences should have a significant effect on their current level of participation, because in this case citizens are drawn into the electoral process precisely because their issue preferences match those of party elites.

The first analysis reported in table 14-3 uses lagged values of Social Welfare, Cultural, Consistency, and Consistency-squared, which were created by using the survey data from the prior election two years earlier. Technical readers will want to know that we also used lagged values of partisan identification and strength of partisanship, as individuals' partisanship may respond to elite party polarization over this time period as well. The second analysis uses lagged values two elections prior to predict participation. The key finding is that in both regressions, the consistency variable is statistically significant and in the expected direction. Further, the magnitude of the coefficients for the consistency variable is approximately the same regardless of whether the lag is one election or two elections. The coefficients for the consistency variable are also on par with the coefficients reported in table 14-1. Thus, these results further support our claim that individuals are being mobilized, or demobilized, to participate in campaign-related activities depending on the extent to which their issue positions match those of party elites.

Conclusion

Over the past several decades, political party elites have become increasingly polarized on both social and economic issues. The Republican Party is now home to economic and social conservatives, while social and economic liberals have migrated to the Democratic Party. The analyses here suggest that citizens who have issue preferences that match those of party elites—consistently liberal or consistently conservative—are more likely to play active roles in political campaigns than citizens with heterodox or even moderate issue preferences. Even so, the differences in participation levels between these ideologically consistent voters and libertarians—and in some cases, moderates—are not as great as they would be were the analyses to wholly confirm the grim picture painted by Fiorina's discus-

Table 14-3. Negative Binomial Regression of Campaign Participation, 1992–1996 Panel

	Lagged 1 Election		Lagged 2 Elections	
	Coefficient	t value	Coefficient	t value
Lagged Social Welfare	0.14**	2.38	0.09	1.07
Lagged Cultural	0.00	0.00	0.19**	2.40
Lagged Consistency	0.12**	2.49	0.13*	1.66
Lagged Consistency^2	0.04**	2.57	0.04	1.60
Education	0.14**	4.01	0.08*	1.66
Age	0.01**	2.22	0.01**	2.08
Female	–0.06	–0.59	–0.07	–0.49
African American	0.25	1.48	0.18	0.71
Minority	–0.11	–0.53	–0.07	–0.27
South	0.10	1.06	0.05	0.34
Income	0.22**	4.35	0.29**	3.80
Retrospective	–0.03	–0.49	–0.04	–0.38
Prospective	–0.06	–0.75	–0.16	–1.24
Trust	0.00	0.33	0.00	0.52
Lagged Strength	0.15**	2.44	–0.07	–0.74
Lagged Democrat	0.13	0.56	0.79**	2.32
Lagged Republican	0.06	0.24	0.82**	2.38
1994	–0.10	–1.05		
Constant	–2.60**	–7.25	–2.76**	–5.37
N	1155		487	
ln (alpha)	–0.57**	–2.94	–0.81**	–2.46

$*p < 0.1; **p < 0.05.$

sion of the "dark side of civic engagement."[35] While ideological consistency does influence political participation, many "heterodox," or ideologically inconsistent, voters, more often than not libertarians, do not sit on the sidelines come election season.

Moreover, our results indicate that ideological consistency plays a statistically insignificant role when it comes to voting turnout, which suggests that ideological consistency has more relevance to the demanding, intense, high stakes arena represented by election campaigns than it does to the more causal and less costly act of voting.

One explanation for our findings is consistent with Miller and Schofield's account of realignment.[36] Libertarians, who are conservative on
economic issues and liberal on social issues, seem to have been activated
during the time that Miller and Schofield argue that social issues became
the "active" dimension of elite contestation. Clearly, more work needs
to be done to understand how this activation occurs, as in Miller and
Schofield's account, only one issue dimension is active, while our analysis
allows both dimensions to matter.[37]

Further, our argument and findings are consistent with Trier and Hillygus's demonstration[38] that a failure to treat individual preferences as multidimensional results in the mislabeling of heterodox voters as pure moderates, leading to biased voting predictions. In other words, it is a mistake
to assume that there are liberal voters, conservative voters, and nothing
else. Those with moderate, libertarian, or populist views are fundamentally less likely to participate in campaign activities than ideologically
consistent liberals and conservatives. Considering our results concomitantly with Trier and Hillygus's findings along with Miller and Schofield's
perspective on realignment, it is clear that treating all heterodox voters as
moderates is a mistake; indeed, future work must measure citizens' issue
preferences on both social and economic issues.

Finally, one take-away point from our turnout model is the distinct
differences between populists and all other voters. We are hard-pressed
to name a major party candidate for president who has campaigned with
a purely populist rhetorical style. While failed candidacies like that of
John Edwards's 2008 presidential campaign evoked the term "populism,"
these quixotic White House sojourns were populist on the economic issue dimension, but clearly libertarian on the social issue dimension. That
is, "populist" candidates like Edwards still provided consistently liberal
ideological cues to the public.

In sum, elite party polarization clearly provides cues to ideologically
consistent voters that encourages them to participate in election campaigns,[39] while the highlighting of particular issue dimensions by elites in
a given election cycle can systematically activate cross-pressured voters.
Thus, citizens' preferences on social and economic issues, either separately or in combination, seem to lie at the very heart of democratic political participation.

Appendix: Measurement

To test our argument, we created measures of citizens' policy preferences
on social-welfare issues and cultural issues for the ANES presidential surveys from 1972 to 2004. The ANES surveys have numerous issue ques-

tions; however, there is a significant amount of missing data when all issue questions are used simultaneously (although most individual questions have only about 10 percent of cases without a valid response). To deal with the missing data, we employ a multiple imputation technique as suggested by Schafer and Graham.[40] Specifically, we used a Markov Chain Monte Carlo (MCMC) procedure with an uninformative Jeffery's prior in SAS 9.1, where starting values were generated from an expected maximization (EM) algorithm. As in King et al.,[41] this procedure assumes that data are from a multivariate normal distribution but uses a different estimation routine than they employ.

After constructing the five imputed data sets, we performed a confirmatory factor analysis for each data set. The factor analysis specified two separate yet correlated dimensions using the survey questions for each dimension separately. Since the indicator variables are ordinal, we use weighted least-squares to estimate the parameters.[42] Based on the factor analytic results, we generated scores for both issue dimensions, and the scores were rescaled to have a mean of 0 and a standard deviation of 1, with larger values representing a more conservative orientation.

The coefficient estimates and the respective standard errors for the regression analyses reported in this chapter combine the results from the five imputed data sets. Table 14-4 presents the specific questions that were used in each year to construct the Social Welfare and the Cultural scores. It is worth noting that the correlation between these two dimensions is quite low, considering the procedure controls for measurement error. In 1996, the correlation between the two dimensions is 0.55, which was the highest correlation for any of the eight ANES surveys we used. The lowest correlation was 0.06 in 1988. The weak correlation between citizens' preferences on these two issue dimensions indicates that there are significant numbers of populist and libertarians in the electorate and that ideological conflict cannot be represented by a single measure like liberal-conservative self-identification.

Table 14-4. Items Used to Create Social Welfare and Cultural Scores

Social Welfare	1972	1976	1980	1984	1988	1992	1996	2000	2004
7-point government health insurance scale	X	X		X	X	X	X	X	X
7-point government guaranteed jobs scale	X	X	X	X	X	X	X	X	X
Does civil rights push too fast?	X	X	X	X	X	X			
Government ensure school integration	X	X				X		X	
7-point busing scale	X	X	X	X					
7-point aid to blacks scale	X	X	X	X	X	X	X	X	
Government ensure fair treatment in bobs	X				X	X	X	X	X
Change in tax rates	X	X							
Does R favor segregation?	X	X							
Government services			X						
7-point government services/spending scale				X	X	X	X	X	X
Food stamps—federal spending				X	X	X	X	X	
Social Security—federal spending				X	X	X	X	X	X
Assistance to African Americans—federal spending				X	X	X		X	
Government spending for Medicare				X					
Government spending for the unemployed				X	X	X			
Homeless—federal spending					X	X	X		
Racial preferences in hiring					X				
Racial quotas in college admissions					X	X			

Welfare programs—federal spending					X		X	X
Poor—federal spending				X	X	X	X	X
Affirmative action for hiring/promotion				X	X	X	X	
Support for affirmative action programs					X	X	X	
Child care—federal spending				X	X	X	X	X
Cultural								
7-point women's equal role scale	X	X	X	X	X	X	X	X
When should abortion be allowed?	X	X	X	X	X	X	X	X
Legalize marijuana	X	X	X					
R favor/oppose equal rights amendment		X	X					
Should prayer be allowed in schools?			X	X	X			
Protect homosexuals from discrimination				X	X	X	X	X
Gays be allowed to serve in the military				X	X		X	X
Gays/lesbians be allowed to adopt					X	X	X	X
Parental consent for abortion					X	X	X	
Government funding for abortions					X			X
Husband's consent for abortion					X			
Partial-birth abortion						X	X	X
Same-sex couples be allowed to marry						X	X	X

Notes

1. Poole and Rosenthal (1997); Jacobson (2000); Layman and Carsey (2002).
2. Carmines and Ensley (2009).
3. Fiorina, Pope, and Abrams (2005).
4. Hetherington (2001); Fiorina, Pope, and Abrams (2005); Abramowitz (2006); Jacobson (2006a); Abramowitz and Saunders (2008); Fiorina, Abrams, and Pope (2008); Claassen and Highton (2009).
5. Verba and Nie (1972), p. 1.
6. McClurg (2006); Mutz (2002); Delli Carpini and Keeter (1996); Verba, Schlozman, and Brady (1995).
7. Fiorina (1999a).
8. Abramowitz (2006).
9. Hibbing and Theiss-Morse (2002).
10. Theiss-Morse and Hibbing (2005), p. 244.
11. Petrocik (1996).
12. However, in previous work, we have found that voters with consistent positions on both the economic and social issue dimensions are less likely to cast split tickets than moderates, populists, and libertarians (Carmines and Ensley 2009).
13. Poole and Rosenthal (1997).
14. Shafer and Claggett (1995); Layman and Carsey (2002); Carsey and Layman (2006).
15. Shafer and Claggett (1995).
16. Kellstedt (2003).
17. Miller and Schofield (2003).
18. Shafer and Claggett (1995), p. 24.
19. Ibid., p. 23.
20. Layman and Carsey (2002); Fiorina, Pope, and Abrams (2005); Carmines and Ensley (2009). Levendusky (2009) demonstrates that some Americans have engaged in (primarily) party-driven "sorting" over the past few decades. In his formulation, these are the citizens who are polarized.
21. Poole and Rosenthal (1997).
22. Hetherington (2001).
23. See also Levendusky (2009).
24. Carmines, Ensley, and Wagner (2005, 2006).
25. Fiorina, Pope, and Abrams (2005).
26. Ibid., p. 33.
27. Carmines, Ensley, and Wagner (2005); Carmines and Ensley (2009).
28. Fiorina (1999).
29. Miller and Schofield (2003).
30. We have discussed elsewhere (Carmines, Ensley, and Wagner 2005) how the consistency of the ideological dimensions weakens the strength of partisan identification among individuals. Therefore, by including the strength of identification as an explanatory factor, we may be downplaying the true effect of con-

sistency on participation. If we exclude strength of identification from the models estimated here, our basic findings remain unchanged. But as we would anticipate if the strength of identification is excluded from the analysis, the effect of consistency is slightly stronger when predicting campaign participation, but the effect of consistency remains insignificant in the analysis of turnout. However, since it is possible that the strength of partisanship could affect consistency as well, we opt to keep the strength variable in the analysis.

31. Saunders and Abramowitz (2004), p. 287.

32. Layman and Carsey (2002); Carsey and Layman (2006).

33. Knowledge is measured using factual questions available in each wave of the ANES, as recommended by Mondak (1999, 2001).

34. These findings suggestively recall the importance of previous work suggesting the key role that education plays in who votes (Wolfinger and Rosenstone 1980).

35. Fiorina (1999a).

36. Miller and Schofield (2003).

37. This is consistent with the "conflict-extension," rather than "conflict displacement," theory of partisan change in American politics (see Carsey and Layman 2006; Layman and Carsey 2002).

38. Treier and Hillygus (2009).

39. See Levendusky (2009).

40. Schafer and Graham (2002).

41. King et al. (2001).

42. Schumacker and Beyerlein (2000).

References

ABC News. 2008. "Full Excerpts: Charlie Gibson Interviews GOP Vice Presidential Candidate Sarah Palin." September 13; available at http://abcnews.go.com/Politics/Vote2008/story?id=5795641, accessed October 18, 2008.

"About That Pledge of Allegiance." 1988. *The New Leader* 71(17): 12.

Abrahamson, Mark. 1965. "Cosmopolitanism, Dependence-Identification, and Geographical Mobility." *Administrative Science Quarterly* 10(1): 98–106.

Abramowitz, Alan I. 2006. "Disconnected, or Joined at the Hip?" In *Red and Blue Nation?* Vol. 1, Pietro S. Nivola and David W. Brady, eds. Washington, DC: Brookings Institution Press.

———. 2007. "Constraint, Ideology, and Polarization in the American Electorate: Evidence from the 2006 Cooperative Congressional Election Study." Paper presented at the Annual Meeting of the American Political Science Association, Chicago, IL.

———. 2009. "The Myth of the Independent Voter Revisited." In *Sabato's Crystal Ball* 8(30), August 20; available at http://www.centerforpolitics.org/crystalball/.

———. 2010. *The Disappearing Center: Engaged Citizens, Polarization, and American Democracy.* New Haven, CT: Yale University Press.

Abramowitz, Alan I., Brad Alexander, and Matthew Gunning. 2006. "Incumbency, Redistricting, and the Decline of Competition in U.S. House Elections." *Journal of Politics* 68(1): 75–88.

Abramowitz, Alan I., and Kyle L. Saunders. 1998. "Ideological Realignment in the U.S. Electorate." *The Journal of Politics* 60(3): 634–652.

———. 2005. "Why Can't We All Just Get Along? The Reality of a Polarized America." *The Forum*, 3(2): Article 1, Berkeley Electronic Press (bepress); available at http://www.bepress.com/forum.

———. 2008. "Is Polarization a Myth?" *The Journal of Politics* 70(2): 542–555.

Abramson, Paul R., John H. Aldrich, and David W. Rohde. 1983. *Change and Continuity in the 1980 Elections*, rev. ed. Washington, DC: CQ Press.

———. 2009. *Change and Continuity in the 2008 Election.* Washington, DC: CQ Press.

Achen, Christopher H., and Larry M. Bartels. 2006. "It Feels Like We're Thinking: The Rationalizing Voter and Electoral Democracy." Presented at the Annual Meeting of the American Political Science Association, Philadelphia.

Adams, Greg D. 1997. "Abortion: Evidence of an Issue Evolution." *American Journal of Political Science* 41(3): 718–737.

Adams, James, and Samuel Merrill III. 2003. "Voter Turnout and Candidate Strategies in American Elections." *Journal of Politics* 65(1): 161–189.

Aldrich, John H. 1983. "A Downsian Spatial Model with Party Activism." *American Political Science Review* 77(4): 974–990.

———. 1995. *Why Parties? The Origin and Transformation of Political Parties in America.* Chicago: University of Chicago Press.

Aldrich, John H., and Michael McGinnis. 1989. "A Model of Party Constraints on Optimal Candidate Positions." *Mathematical and Computer Modeling* 12: 437–450.

Aldrich, John H., Brittany Perry, and David W. Rohde. 2009. "House Appropriations after the Republican Revolution." Paper delivered at the 2009 Annual Meeting of the American Political Science Association, Toronto, Canada.

Aldrich, John H., and David W. Rohde. 2000. "The Consequences of Party Organization in the House: The Role of the Majority and Minority Parties in Conditional Party Government." In *Polarized Politics: Congress and the President in a Partisan Era,* Jon R. Bond and Richard Fleisher, eds. Washington, DC: CQ Press.

Aldrich, John H., David W. Rohde, and Michael Tofias. 2007. "One D Is Not Enough: Measuring Conditional Party Government, 1887–2002." In *Party, Process, and Political Change in Congress: Further New Perspectives on the History of Congress,* David Brady and Mathew D. McCubbins, eds. Stanford, CA: Stanford University Press.

Allison, Paul D. 2009. *Fixed Effects Regression Models.* Los Angeles, CA: Sage Publications.

Althaus, Scott L. 2003. *Collective Preferences in Democratic Politics.* New York: Cambridge University Press.

Alvarez, R. Michael, Stephen Ansolabehere, and Catherine H. Wilson. 2002. "Election Day Voter Registration in the United States: How One-Step Voting Can Change the Composition of the American Electorate." In *Voting Technology Project Working Papers.* Pasadena, CA/Cambridge, MA: Voting Technology Project.

American Political Science Association Committee on Parties. 1950. *Toward a More Responsible Two-Party System.* New York: Rinehart.

Anchorage Daily News. 2008. "Social Conservative: Americans Should Understand What Palin Is Offering," September 12; available at http: //www.adn .com/2008/09/12/523623/social-conservative.html, accessed July 12, 2010.

Ansolabehere, Stephen, and David M. Konisky. 2006. "The Introduction of Voter Registration and Its Effect on Turnout." *Political Analysis* 14: 83–100.

Ansolabehere, Stephen, Jonathan Rodden, and James M. Snyder. 2006. "Purple America." *Journal of Economic Perspectives* 20(2): 97–118.

———. 2008. "The Strength of Issues: Using Multiple Measures to Gauge Preference Stability, Ideological Constraint, and Issue Voting." *American Political Science Review* 102(2): 215–232.

Ansolabehere, Stephen, and James M. Snyder Jr. 2000a. "Money and Office: The Sources of the Incumbency Advantage in Congressional Campaign Finance." In *Continuity and Change in House Elections,* D. W. Brady, J. F. Cogan, and M. P. Fiorina, eds. Stanford, CA: Stanford University Press.

———. 2000b. "Soft Money, Hard Money, Strong Parties." *Columbia Law Review* 100: 598–619.

Ansolabere, Stephen, James Snyder, and Charles Stewart. 2001. "The Effects of Party and Preferences on Congressional Roll Call Voting." *Legislative Studies Quarterly* 26 (November 2001): 533–572.

Appiah, Kwame Anthony. 2006. *Cosmopolitanism: Ethics in a World of Strangers.* New York: W. W. Norton & Co.

Arceneaux, Kevin, and David W. Nickerson. 2009. "Modeling Certainty with Clustered Data: A Comparison of Methods." *Political Analysis* 17(2): 177–190.

Arnold, Douglas R. 1990. *The Logic of Congressional Action*. New Haven, CT: Yale University Press.

Aranson, Peter H., and Peter C. Ordeshook. 1972. "Spatial Strategies for Sequential Elections." In *Probability Models of Collective Decision Making*, Richard Niemi and Herbert Weisberg, eds. Columbus, OH: Merrill.

Associated Press. 2008. "John McCain Courts Swing Voters, Pledges 'Change Is Coming.'" *Chicago Sun-Times*, September 4; available at http: //www .suntimes.com/news/ elections/rnc/1145936,mccain090408.article, accessed August 5, 2009.

Bafumi, Joseph, and Robert I. Shapiro. 2009. "A New Partisan Voter." *Journal of Politics* 71 (January): 1–24.

Bai, Matt. 2006. "The Inside Agitator." *The New York Times Magazine*, October 1.

Balz, Dan, and Jon Cohen. 2007. "A Political Force with Many Philosophies." *Washington Post*, July 1; available at http: //www.washingtonpost.com/ wp-dyn/content/article/2007/06/30/AR2007063000859.html, accessed August 18, 2009.

Bartels, Larry M. 1988. *Presidential Primaries and the Dynamics of Public Choice*. Princeton, NJ: Princeton University Press.

———. 1996. "Uninformed Votes: Information Effects in Presidential Elections." *American Journal of Political Science* 40(1): 194–230.

———. 2000. "Partisanship and Voting Behavior, 1952–1996." *American Journal of Political Science* 44(1): 35–50.

———. 2002a. "Beyond the Running Tally: Partisan Bias in Political Perceptions." *Political Behavior* 24(2): 117–150.

———. 2002b. "Democracy with Attitudes." In *Electoral Democracy*, Michael MacKuen and George Rabinowitz, eds. Ann Arbor: University of Michigan Press.

———. 2005. "Homer Gets a Tax Cut: Inequality and Public Policy in the American Mind." *Perspectives on Politics* 3(1): 15–31.

———. 2006. "What's the Matter with *What's the Matter with Kansas?*" *Quarterly Journal of Political Science* 1: 201–226.

Bartels, Larry M., and John Zaller. 2001. "Presidential Vote Models: A Recount." *Political Science & Politics* 34(1): 9–20.

Baumgartner, Jody C., and Peter L. Francia. 2008. *Conventional Wisdom and American Elections: Exploding Myths, Exploring Misconceptions*. Lanham, MD: Rowman and Littlefield.

Beard, Charles A. 1928. *The American Party Battle*. New York: The Workers Education Bureau Press.

Beck, Nathaniel N., and Jonathan Katz. 2001. "Throwing Out the Baby with the Bath Water: A Comment on Green, Kim, and Yoon." *International Organization* 55: 487–495.

Beck, Paul Allen. 1988. "Incomplete Realignment: The Reagan Legacy for Parties and Elections." In *The Reagan Legacy*, C. Jones, ed. Chatham, NJ: Chatham House.

Bell, Daniel. 2000 [1960]. *The End of Ideology: On the Exhaustion of Political Ideas in the Fifties*. Cambridge, MA: Harvard University Press.

Belli, Robert F., Michael W. Traugott, and Matthew N. Beckmann. 2001. "What Leads to Voting Overreports? Contrasts of Overreporters to Validated Voters and Admitted Non-voters in the American National Election Studies." *Journal of Official Statistics* 17(4): 479–498.

Bennett, Stephen E., and David Resnick. 1990. "The Implications of Nonvoting for Democracy in the United States." *American Journal of Political Science* 34(3): 771–802.

Berelson, Bernard R., Paul F. Lazarsfeld, and William N. McPhee. 1954. *Voting: A Study of Opinion Formation in a Presidential Campaign*. Chicago: University of Chicago Press.

Bergman, Torbjörn, Wolfgang C. Müller, and Kaare Strom. 2000. "Parliamentary Democracy and the Chain of Delegation." *European Journal of Political Research* 37: 255–260.

Bergman, Torbjörn, Wolfgang C. Müller, and Kaare Strøm, eds. 2003. *Delegation and Accountability in West European Parliamentary Democracies*. Oxford, UK: Oxford University Press.

———. 2008. *Cabinets and Coalition Bargaining: The Democratic Life Cycle in Western Europe*. Oxford, UK: Oxford University Press.

Bernstein, Jonathan, and Casey B. K. Dominguez. 2003. "Candidates and Candidacies in the Expanded Party." *PS: Political Science and Politics* 36: 165–169.

Bernstein, Robert, Anita Chadha, and Robert Montjoy. 2001. "Overreporting Voting: Why It Happens and Why It Matters." *Public Opinion Quarterly* 65(1): 22–44.

Besley, Timothy, and Robin Burgess. 2001. "Political Agency, Government Responsiveness, and the Role of the Media." *European Economic Review* 45: 629–640.

———. 2002. "The Political Economy of Government Responsiveness: Theory and Evidence from India." *Quarterly Journal of Economics* 117: 1415–1451.

Binder, Sarah, Forrest Maltzman, and Lee Sigelman. 1998. "Senators' Home-State Reputations: Why Do Constituents Love a Bill Cohen So Much More Than an Al D'Amato?" *Legislative Studies Quarterly* 23 (November): 545–560.

Bishin, Benjamin G. 2000. "Constituency Influence in Congress: Does Subconstituency Matter?" *Legislative Studies Quarterly* 25 (August): 389–415.

Bishop, Bill. 2009. *The Big Sort*. New York: Mariner Books, Houghton Mifflin Harcourt.

Bohrer, Robert E., II, Alexander C. Pacek, and Benjamin Radcliff. 2000. "Electoral Participation, Ideology, and Party Politics in Post-Communist Europe." *Journal of Politics* 62(4): 1161–1172.

Bond, Jon R., and Richard Fleisher, eds. 2000. *Polarized Politics: Congress and the President in a Partisan Era*. Washington, DC: Congressional Quarterly.

Box-Steffensmeier, Janet M. 1996. "A Dynamic Analysis of the Role of War Chests in Campaign Strategy." *American Journal of Political Science* 40: 352–371.

Brady, David W., Robert D'Onofrio, and Morris P. Fiorina. 2000. "The Nationalization of Electoral Forces Revisited." In *Continuity and Change in House Elections*, D. W. Brady, J. F. Cogan, and M. P. Fiorina. eds. Stanford, CA: Stanford University Press.

Brady, Henry E. 1999. "Political Participation." In *Measures of Political Attitudes*, John P. Robinson, Philip R. Shaver, and Lawrence S. Wrightsman, eds. San Diego, CA: Academic Press.

Brady, Henry E., and Paul M. Sniderman. 1985. "Attitude Attribution: A Group Basis for Political Reasoning." *The American Political Science Review* 79(4): 1061–1078.

Brians, Craig Leonard, and Bernard Grofman. 1999. "When Registration Barriers Fall, Who Votes? An Empirical Test of a Rational Choice Model." *Public Choice* 99 (April): 161–176.

Brody, Richard. 1978. "The Puzzle of Political Participation in America." In *The New American Political System*, Anthony King, ed. Washington, DC: AEI.

Brown, Adam R., and Gary C. Jacobson. 2008. "Party, Performance, and Strategic Politicians: The Dynamics of Elections for Senator and Governor in 2006." *State Politics and Policy Quarterly* 8 (Winter): 394–409.

Brunell, Thomas L., and John DiNardo. 2004. "A Propensity Score Reweighting Approach to Estimating the Partisan Effects of Full Turnout in American Presidential Elections." *Political Analysis* 12(1): 28–45.

Bruner, Jerome S. 1957. "On Perceptual Readiness." *Psychological Review* 64: 123–152.

Burden, Barry C. 2004. "An Alternative Account of the 2004 Presidential Election." *The Forum* 2(4): Article 2.

Burden, Barry C., and David C. Kimball. 2002. *Why Americans Split Their Tickets: Campaigns, Competition, and Divided Government*. Ann Arbor: University of Michigan.

Burnham, Walter Dean. 1982. *The Current Crisis in American Politics*. New York: Oxford University Press.

Campbell, Angus, Philip E. Converse, Warren E. Miller, and Donald E. Stokes. 1960. *The American Voter*. New York: John Wiley and Sons.

Campbell, Bruce A. 1979. *The American Electorate*. New York: Holt, Rinehart, and Winston.

Campbell, Donald T. 1963. "Social Attitudes and Other Acquired Behavioral Dispositions." In *Psychology: A Study of a Science*, vol. 6, S. Koch, ed. New York: McGraw-Hill.

Campbell, James E. 2003. "The Stagnation of Congressional Elections." In *Life after Reform: When The Bipartisan Campaign Reform Act Meets Politics*, M. J. Malbin, ed. New York: Rowman and Littlefield.

Campbell, James E., and Joe A. Sumners. 1990. "Presidential Coattails in Senate Elections." *American Political Science Review* 84 (June): 513–521.

Canes-Wrone, Brandice, David W. Brady, and John F. Cogan. 2002. "Out of Step, Out of Office: Electoral Accountability and House Members' Voting." *The American Political Science Review* 96(1): 127–140.

Cann, Damon. 2008. *Sharing the Wealth: Member Contributions and the Exchange Theory of Party Influence in the U.S. House of Representatives*. Albany, NY: SUNY Press.

Carman, Raymond, Jr., Ian Farrell, and Jonathan Krasno. 2008. "Parties as Mobilizers: Party Efforts to Get Out the Vote in 2000 and 2004." Paper presented at the annual meeting of the Midwest Political Science Association, Palmer House Hotel, Hilton, Chicago.

Carmines, Edward G., and Michael J. Ensley. 2009. "Heterodox Issue Prefer-
ences, Ideologically Polarized Parties, and Split-Ticket Voting in the United
States," Working Paper, Department of Political Science, Kent State University,
Kent, OH.

Carmines, Edward G., Michael J. Ensley, and Michael W. Wagner. 2005. "Party
Polarization and Mass Partisan Identification in the United States, 1972–2000."
Presented at the 2005 Annual Meeting of the Midwest Political Science As-
sociation, Chicago.

————. 2006 "Issue Preferences and Political Participation in American Politics
1972–2004," presented at the 2006 Annual Meeting of the American Political
Science Association, Chicago.

Carmines, Edward G., John P. McIver, and James A. Stimson. 1987. "Unrealized
Partisanship: A Theory of Dealignment." *Journal of Politics* 49 (May): 376–400.

Carmines, Edward G., and James A. Stimson. 1980. "The Two Faces of Issue
Voting." *American Political Science Review* 74: 78–91.

————. 1989. *Issue Evolution: Race and the Transformation of American Politics*. Princeton, NJ: Princeton University Press.

Carsey, Thomas M., John Green, and Rick Herrera. 2003. "The New Party Professionals? An Initial Look at National Convention Delegates in 2000 and
Over Time." Prepared for delivery at the 2003 Annual Meeting of the American Political Science Association.

Carsey, Thomas M., and Geoffrey C. Layman. 2006. "Changing Sides or
Changing Minds? Party Identification and Policy Preferences in the American
Electorate." *American Journal of Political Science* 50(2): 464–477.

Cassel, Carol A. 2003. "Overreporting and Electoral Participation Research."
American Politics Research 31(1): 81–92.

Caswell, Brace E. 2009. "The Presidency, the Vote, and the Formation of New
Coalitions." *Polity* 41(3): 388–407.

Cavendish, James. 2000. "Church-Based Community Activism: A Comparison
of White and Black Catholic Congregations." *Journal for the Scientific Study
of Religion.* 39: 64–77.

Citrin, Jack, Eric Schickler, and John Sides. 2003. "What if Everyone Voted?
Simulating the Impact of Increased Turnout in Senate Elections." *American
Journal of Political Science* 47(1): 75–90.

Claassen, Ryan L., and Benjamin Highton. 2009. "Policy Polarization among
Party Elites and the Significance of Political Awareness in the Mass Public."
Political Research Quarterly 62 (September): 538–551.

Clarke, Harold D., and Marianne C. Stewart. 1998. "The Decline of Parties in
the Minds of Citizens." *American Review of Political Science* 1: 357–378.

Clinton, Joshua, Simon Jackman, and Douglas Rivers. 2004. "The Statistical
Analysis of Roll Call Data." *American Political Science Review* 98(2): 355–370.

Cohen, Jeffrey E., Jon R. Bond, Richard Fleisher, and John A. Hamman. 2000.
"State-Level Presidential Approval and Senatorial Support." *Legislative Studies Quarterly* 25 (November): 577–590.

Cohen, Marty, David Karol, Hans Noel, and John Zaller. 2008. *The Party De-
cides: Presidential Nominations before and after Reform*. Chicago: University
of Chicago Press.

Coleman, John J. 1996. "Resurgent or Just Busy? Party Organizations in Contemporary America." In *The State of the Parties: The Changing Role of Parties in American Politics*, 2nd ed., John C. Green and Daniel Shea, eds. Lanham, MD: Rowman and Littlefield.

Conover, Pamela J., and Stanley Feldman. 1980. "The Origins and Meaning of Liberal-Conservative Self Identifications." *American Journal of Political Science* 25: 617–645.

Continetti, Matthew. 2008. "Not Your Dad's Republicans." *Los Angeles Times*, March 6; available at http://www.latimes.com/news/opinion/la-op-antle-continetti6mar06,0,1215717,full.story, accessed August 2, 2010.

Converse, Philip E. 1964. "The Nature of Belief Systems in Mass Publics." In *Ideology and Discontent*, David E. Apter, ed. New York: Free Press.

———. 1970. "Attitudes and Non-Attitudes: Continuation of a Dialogue." In *The Quantitative Analysis of Social Problems*, Edward R. Tufte, ed. Reading, MA: Addison-Wesley.

Converse, Phillip E., and George Dupeux. 1962. "Politicization of the Electorate in France and the United States." *Public Opinion Quarterly*, 26: 1–23.

Corrado, Anthony, Thomas E. Mann, Daniel R. Ortiz, Trevor Potter, and Frank J. Sorauf, eds. 1997. *Campaign Finance Reform: A Sourcebook*. Washington, DC: The Brookings Institution Press.

Corrado, Anthony, Thomas E. Mann, and Trevor Potter, eds. 2003. *Campaign Finance Battle: Court Testimony on the New Reforms*. Washington, DC: Brookings.

Cotter, Cornelius P., and Bernard C. Hennessy. 1964. *Politics without Power: The National Party Committees*. New York: Atherton Press.

Council of State Governments and American Legislators' Association. *The Book of the States*. 1978–2006. Lexington, KY: Council of State Governments.

Cox, Gary W., and Jonathan N. Katz. 1996. "Why Did the Incumbency Advantage in U.S. House Elections Grow?" *American Journal of Political Science* 40(2): 478–497.

Cox, Gary W., and Mathew D. McCubbins. 1993. *Legislative Leviathan: Party Government in the House*. Berkeley: University of California Press.

Crotty, William J. 1984. *American Parties in Decline*, 2nd ed. Boston: Little, Brown.

Dalton, Russell J. 2008. *Citizen Politics*, 5th ed. Washington, DC: Congressional Quarterly Press.

Dalton, Russell J., Scott Flanagan, and Paul Allen Beck. 1984. *Electoral Change in Advanced Industrial Democracies*. Princeton, NJ: Princeton University Press.

Dautrich, Kenneth, and David Yalof. 2009. *American Government: Historical, Popular, and Global Perspectives*. Belmont, CA: Wadsworth Cengage Learning.

Davidson, Roger H., Walter J. Oleszek, and Francis E. Lee. 2009. *Congress and Its Members*, 11th ed. Washington, DC: Congressional Quarterly Press.

Delli Carpini, Michael X., and Scott Keeter. 1996. *What Americans Know about Politics and Why It Matters*. New Haven, CT: Yale University Press.

Demer, Lisa. 2008. "Abortion Opponents Give Palin High Marks." *Anchorage Daily News*, September 7; available at http://www.adn.com/2008/09/07/518512/abortion-opponents-give-palin.html, accessed August 2, 2010.

DeNardo, James. 1980. "Turnout and the Vote: The Joke's on the Democrats." *The American Political Science Review* 74(2): 406–420.

———. 1986. "Does Heavy Turnout Help Democrats in Presidential Elections?" *American Political Science Review* 80(4): 1298–1304.

Donovan, Todd, Caroline J. Tolbert, and Daniel A. Smith. 2009. "Political Engagement, Mobilization, and Direct Democracy." *Public Opinion Quarterly* 73(1): 98–118.

Downs, Anthony. 1957. *An Economic Theory of Democracy*. New York: Harper and Row.

Druckman, James N. 2001. "On the Limits of Framing Effects: Who Can Frame?" *The Journal of Politics* 63: 1041–1066.

Druckman, James N., and Arthur Lupia. 2000. "Preference Formation." *Annual Review of Political Science* 3: 1–24.

Eldersveld, Samuel J. 1964. *Political Parties: A Behavioral Analysis*. Chicago: Rand McNally.

Ellcessor, Patrick, and Jan E. Leighley. 2001. "Voters, Non-voters, and Minority Representation." In *Representation of Minority Groups in the U.S.*, Charles E. Menifield, ed. Lanham, MD: Austin & Winfield.

Ellis, Christopher R. 2010. "Why the New Deal Still Matters: Public Preferences, Elite Context, and American Mass Party Change, 1974–2006." *Journal of Elections, Public Opinion, and Parties* 20: 103–132.

Ellis, Christopher R., Joseph Daniel Ura, and Jenna Ashley-Robinson. 2006. "The Dynamic Consequences of Nonvoting." *Political Research Quarterly* 59: 227–233.

Enelow, James M., and Melvin J. Hinich. 1984. *The Spatial Theory of Voting: An Introduction*. New York: Cambridge University Press.

Enns, Peter, and Paul Kellstedt. 2008. "Policy Mood and Political Sophistication: Why Everybody Moves Mood." *British Journal of Political Science* 38: 433–454.

Epstein, Leon D. 1986. *Political Parties in the American Mold*. Madison: University of Wisconsin Press.

Erikson, Robert S. 1972. "Malapportionment, Gerrymandering, and Party Fortunes in Congressional Elections." *The American Political Science Review* 66(4): 1234–1245.

———. 1990. "Roll Calls, Reputations, and Representation in the U. S. Senate." *Legislative Studies Quarterly* 15 (November): 623–642.

Erikson, Robert S., Michael B. MacKuen, and James A. Stimson. 2002. *The Macro Polity*. Cambridge, UK: Cambridge University Press.

Fazio, Russell H. 1995. "Attitudes as Object-Evaluation Associations: Determinants, Consequences, and Correlates of Attitude Accessibility." In *Attitude Strength: Antecedents and Consequences*, Richard E. Petty and Jon A. Krosnick, eds. Mahwah, NJ: Lawrence Erlbaum.

Feldman, Stanley. 1988. "Structure and Consistency in Public Opinion: The Role of Core Beliefs and Values." *American Journal of Political Science* 32: 416–440.

Fenno, Richard F. 1973. *Congressmen in Committees*. Boston: Little, Brown.

———. 1978. *Home Style: House Members in Their Districts*. Boston: Little, Brown.

Fenster, Mark J. 1994. "The Impact of Allowing Day of Registration Voting on Turnout in U.S. Elections from 1960 to 1992." *American Politics Research* 22(1): 74–87.

Ferejohn, John A. 1977. "On the Decline of Competition in Congressional Elections." *The American Political Science Review* 71: 166–176.

Filley, Allan C., and Andrew J. Grimes. 1968. "The Bases of Power in Decision Processes." In *Promising Research Directions*, R. W. Millman and M. P. Hottenstein, eds. Bowling Green, OH: Academy of Management.

Fiorina, Morris P. 1977. *Congress: Keystone of the Washington Establishment*. New Haven, CT: Yale University Press.

———. 1999a. "A Dark Side of Civic Engagement." In *Civic Engagement in American Democracy*, Theda Skocpol and Morris Fiorina, eds. Washington, DC: Brookings Institution Press.

———. 1999b. "Whatever Happened to the Median Voter?" Paper prepared for the MIT Conference on Parties and Congress, Cambridge, MA.

Fiorina, Morris P., and Samuel J. Abrams. 2008. "Political Polarization in the American Public." *Annual Review of Political Science* 11: 563–588.

Fiorina, Morris P., Samuel J. Abrams, and Jeremy C. Pope. 2006. *Culture War? The Myth of a Polarized America*, 2nd ed. New York: Pearson Longman.

———. 2008. "Polarization in the American Public: Misconceptions and Misreadings." *The Journal of Politics* 70(2): 542–555.

Fiorina, Morris P., Jeremy C. Pope, and Samuel J. Abrams. 2005. *Culture War? The Myth of a Polarized America*. New York: Pearson Longman.

Fishbein, Martin, and Icek Ajzen. 1975. *Belief, Attitude, Intention, and Behavior: An Introduction to Theory and Research*. Reading, MA: Addison-Wesley.

Frank, Thomas. 2004. *What's the Matter with Kansas? How Conservatives Won the Heart of America*. New York: Henry Holt & Company.

Frantzich, Stephen E. 1984. "Republicanizing the Parties: The Rise of the Service-Vendor Party." Presented at the Annual Meeting of the Midwest Political Science Association, Chicago.

———. 1989. *Political Parties in the Technological Age*. New York: Longman.

Free, Lloyd A., and Hadley Cantril. 1967. *The Political Beliefs of Americans: A Study of Public Opinion*. New Brunswick, NJ: Rutgers University Press.

Fullerton, Andrew S., Jeffrey C. Dixon, and Casey Borch. 2007. "Bringing Registration into Models of Vote Overreporting." *Public Opinion Quarterly* 71(4): 649–660.

Gallup, George. 1974. "The Nation's Independents–Now a Possible Base for a New Party." *The Gallup Poll* release, November 17, p. 1.

Gelman, Andrew, David Park, Boris Shor, and Joseph Bafumi. 2008. *Rich State, Poor State, Red State, Blue State: Why Americans Vote the Way They Do*. Princeton, NJ: Princeton University Press.

Gerber, Alan S., and Donald P. Green. 2000. "The Effects of Canvassing, Telephone Calls, and Direct Mail on Voter Turnout: A Field Experiment." *American Political Science Review* 94: 653–663.

Gerber, Elisabeth R., and Arthur Lupia. 1995. "Campaign Competition and Policy Responsiveness in Direct Legislation Elections." *Political Behavior* 17: 287–306.

Gerber, Elisabeth R., Arthur Lupia, Mathew D. McCubbins, and D. Roderick Kiewiet. 2001. *Stealing the Initiative: How State Government Responds to Direct Democracy.* Upper Saddle River, NJ: Prentice-Hall.

Gibson, James L., Cornelius P. Cotter, and John F. Bibby. 1983. "Assessing Party Organizational Strength." *American Journal of Political Science* 27: 193–222.

Ginsberg, Benjamin, Theodore J. Lowi, and Margaret Weir. 2009. *We the People: An Introduction to American Politics,* 7th ed. New York: W.W. Norton & Company.

Glassman, Matthew. 2002. "Campaign Buttons as a Metric for Testing Claims about Presidential Elections." Unpublished manuscript. New Haven, CT: Yale University.

Goldenberg, Suzanne. 2008. "Meet the Barracuda: Anti-Abortion, Pro-Death Penalty, and Gun-Lover." *The Guardian,* August 30; available at http: //www .guardian.co.uk/world/2008/aug/30/johnmccain.palin2, accessed May 29, 2010.

Gould, Stephen J. 1996. *The Mismeasure of Man,* rev. ed. New York: W.W. Norton.

Gouldner, Alvin W. 1957. "Theoretical Requirements of the Applied Social Sciences." *American Sociological Review* 22(1): 92–102.

———. 1958. "Cosmopolitans and Locals: Toward an Analysis of Latent Social Roles. II." *Administrative Science Quarterly* 2(4): 444–480.

Green, Donald P., and Alan S. Gerber. 2004. *Get Out the Vote! How to Increase Voter Turnout.* Washington, DC: Congressional Quarterly.

Green, Donald P., Soo Yeon Kim, and David Yoon. 2001. "Dirty Pool." *International Organization* 55: 441–468.

Green, Donald P., Bradley Palmquist, and Eric Schickler. 2002. *Partisan Hearts and Minds: Political Parties and the Social Identities of Voters.* New Haven, CT: Yale University Press.

Green, Donald P., and Ian Shapiro. 1994. *Pathologies of Rational Choice Theory: A Critique of Applications in Political Science.* New Haven, CT: Yale University Press.

Green, John C. 2003. "A Liberal Dynamo: The Political Activism of the Unitarian-Universalist Clergy." *Journal for the Scientific Study of Religion* 42: 577–590.

Green, John C., and Paul S. Herrnson. 2002. "Party Development in the Twentieth Century: Laying the Foundations for Responsible Party Government?" In *Responsible Partisanship? The Evolution of American Political Parties Since 1950,* J. C. Green and P. S. Herrnson, eds. Lawrence: University Press of Kansas.

Greene, Steven. 2000. "The Psychological Sources of Partisan-leaning Independents." *American Politics Quarterly* 28: 511–537.

Griffin, John D., and Brian Newman. 2005. "Are Voters Better Represented?" *Journal of Politics* 67(4): 1206–1227.

Grofman, Bernard, Robert Griffin, and Amihai Glazer. 1990. "Identical Geography, Different Party: A Natural Experiment on the Magnitude of Party Differences in the U.S. Senate, 1960–84." In *Developments in Electoral Geography*, Ronald J. Johnston, Fred M. Shelley, and Peter J. Taylor, eds. London: Routledge.

Groseclose, Tim. 2001. "A Model of Candidate Location When One Candidate Has a Valence Advantage." *American Journal of Political Science* 45(4): 862–886.

Grynaviski, Jeffrey D. 2010. *Partisan Bonds: Political Reputations and Legislative Accountability*. Cambridge, UK: Cambridge University Press.

Habermas, Jürgen. 1996. *Between Facts and Norms: Contributions of a Discourse Theory of Law and Democracy*, William Rehg, trans. Cambridge, MA: The MIT Press.

Hajnal, Zoltan, and Jessica Trounstine. 2005. "Where Turnout Matters: The Consequences of Uneven Turnout in City Politics." *Journal of Politics* 67(2): 515–535.

Hamilton, Alexander, John Jay, and James Madison. 1787. "The Federalist: The Utility of the Union as a Safeguard against Domestic Faction and Insurrection (Continued)." *Daily Advertiser*, November 22.

Harbaugh, William T. 1996. "If People Vote Because They Like to, then Why Do So Many of Them Lie?" *Public Choice* 89(1): 63–76.

Hausman, Jerry A. 1978. "Specification Tests in Econometrics." *Econometrica* 46: 1251–1271.

Herrmann, Richard K., Philip E. Tetlock, and Penny S. Visser. 1999. "Mass Public Decisions to Go to War: A Cognitive-Interactionist Framework." *American Political Science Review* 93(3): 553–573.

Herrnson, Paul S. 1988. *Party Campaigning in the 1980s*. Cambridge, MA: Harvard University Press.

———. 1994. "The Revitalization of National Party Organizations." In *The Parties Respond: Changes in American Parties and Campaigns*, L. Sandy Maisel, ed. Boulder, CO: Westview Press.

———. 2000. *Congressional Elections: Campaigning at Home and in Washington*. Washington, DC: CQ Press.

Hershey, Marjorie Randon. 2009. *Party Politics in America*. New York: Pearson Longman.

Hetherington, Marc J. 2001. "Resurgent Mass Partisanship: The Role of Elite Polarization." *The American Political Science Review* 95(3): 619–631.

Hibbing, John R., and John R. Alford. 1990. "Constituency Population and Representation in the U.S. Senate." *Legislative Studies Quarterly* 15 (November): 581–598.

Hibbing, John R., and Elizabeth Theiss-Morse. 2002. *Stealth Democracy*. New York: Cambridge University Press.

Higgins, Edward T., and Gillian King. 1981. "Social Constructs: Information-Processing Consequences of Individual and Contextual Variability." In *Personality, Cognition, and Social Interaction*, Nancy Cantor and John F. Kihlstrom, eds. Hillsdale, NJ: Lawrence Erlbaum.

Highton, Benjamin. 2004. "Voter Registration and Turnout in the United States." *Perspectives on Politics* 2(3): 507–515.

Highton, Benjamin, and Raymond E. Wolfinger. 1998. "Estimating the Effects of the National Voter Registration Act of 1993." *Political Behavior* 20(2): 79–104.

———. 2001. "The Political Implications of Higher Turnout." *British Journal of Political Science* 31(1): 179–223.

Hill, Kim Quaile, and Jan E. Leighley. 1992. "The Policy Consequences of Class Bias in State Electorates." *American Journal of Political Science* 36(2): 351–365.

Hill, Kim Quaile, Jan E. Leighley, and Angela Hinton-Anderson. 1995. "Lower-Class Mobilization and Policy Linkage in the U.S. States." *American Journal of Political Science* 39(1): 75–86.

Hillygus, D. Sunshine. 2005. "Campaign Effects and the Dynamics of Turnout Intention in Election 2000." *Journal of Politics* 67(1): 50–68.

Hillygus, D. Sunshine, and T. G. Shields. 2005. "Moral Issues and Voter Decision Making in the 2004 Presidential Election." *Political Science and Politics* 38: 201–209.

———. 2008. *The Persuadable Voter: Wedge Issues in Presidential Campaigns.* Princeton, NJ: Princeton University Press.

Holbrook, Allyson L., Jon A. Krosnick, David Moore, and Roger Tourangeau. 2007. "Response Order Effects in Dichotomous Categorical Questions Presented Orally: The Impact of Question and Respondent Attributes." *Public Opinion Quarterly* 71: 325–348.

Holbrook, Thomas M., and Scott D. McClurg. 2005. "The Mobilization of Core Supporters: Campaigns, Turnout, and Electoral Composition in United States Presidential Elections." *American Journal of Political Science* 49(4): 689–703.

Holm, John D., and John P. Robinson. 1978. "Ideological Identification and the American Voter." *Public Opinion Quarterly* 42: 235–246.

Hurwitz, Jon, and Mark A. Peffley. 1987. "How Are Foreign Policy Attitudes Structured? A Hierarchical Model." *American Political Science Review* 81(4): 1099–1120.

"Interview with John Kenneth Galbraith." 1986. *California Monthly* (February): 11.

Jackman, Simon, and Lynn Vavreck. 2009. "The Cooperative Campaign Analysis Project 2007–8." Release 2.0. Palo Alto and Los Angeles.

———. 2010a. "Obama's Advantage: Race, Partisanship, and Racial Attitudes in Context." Typescript. Los Angeles: University of California.

———. 2010b. "Primary Politics: Race, Gender, and Partisanship in the 2008 Democratic Primary." *Journal of Elections, Parties, and Public Opinion* 20(2): 153–186.

Jacobson, Gary C. 1985–1986. "Party Organization and the Distribution of Campaign Resources: Republicans and Democrats in 1982." *Political Science Quarterly* 100: 603–625.

———. 1987. "Running Scared: Elections and Congressional Politics in the 1980s." In *Congress: Structure and Policy*, M. McCubbins and T. Sullivan, eds. Cambridge, UK: Cambridge University Press.

———. 2000. "The Electoral Basis of Partisan Polarization in Congress." Presented at the Annual Meeting of the American Political Science Association, Washington, DC.

———. 2004. *The Politics of Congressional Elections.* New York: Pearson Longman.

———. 2005. "Polarized Politics in the 2004 Congressional and Presidential Elections." *Political Science Quarterly* 120 (Summer): 199–218.

———. 2006a. "Disconnected, or Joined at the Hip?" In *Red and Blue Nation?*, vol. 1, Pietro S. Nivola and David W. Brady, eds. Washington, DC: Brookings Institution Press.

———. 2006b. "Polarized Opinion in the States: Partisan Differences in Approval Ratings of Governors, Senators, and George W. Bush." *Presidential Studies Quarterly* 36 (December): 732–757.

———. 2007. "Explaining the Ideological Polarization of the Congressional Parties since the 1970s." In *Process, Party and Policy Making: Further New Perspectives on the History of Congress*, David Brady and Mathew McCubbins, eds. Stanford, CA: Stanford University Press.

———. 2011. *A Divider not a Uniter: George W. Bush and the American People*, 2nd ed. New York: Pearson Longman.

Jacoby, William G. 1986. "Levels of Conceptualization and Reliance on the Liberal-Conservative Continuum." *Journal of Politics* 48: 423–432.

———. 1991. "Ideological Identification and Issue Attitudes." *American Journal of Political Science* 35: 178–205.

———. 1995. "The Structure of Ideological Thinking in the American Electorate." *American Journal of Political Science* 39: 314–335.

———. 2000. "Issue Framing and Public Opinion on Government Spending." *American Journal of Political Science* 44: 750–767.

Jamieson, Kathleen Hall. 1996. *Packaging the Presidency: A History and Criticism of Presidential Campaign Advertising.* London: Oxford University Press.

———. 2009. *Electing the President 2008: The Insiders' View.* Philadelphia: University of Pennsylvania Press.

Janda, Kenneth, Jeffrey M. Berry, and Jerry Goldman. 2009. *The Challenge of Democracy: Government in America.* Belmont, CA: Wadsworth.

Jennings, M. Kent. 1967. "Pre-Adult Orientations to Multiple Systems of Government." *Midwest Journal of Political Science* 11(3): 291–317.

———. 1992. "Ideological Thinking among Mass Publics and Political Elites." *Public Opinion Quarterly* 56: 419–441.

Karp, Jeffrey A., and David Brockington. 2005. "Social Desirability and Response Validity: A Comparative Analysis of Overreporting Voter Turnout in Five Countries." *Journal of Politics* 67(3): 825–840.

Karp, Walter. 1993. *Indispensable Enemies: The Politics of Misrule in America.* New York: Franklin Square Press.

Katz, Elihu, and Paul F. Lazarsfeld. 1955. *Personal Influence: The Part Played by People in the Flow of Mass Communications.* Glencoe, IL: Free Press.

Kaye, Randi. 2008. "Pastor: GOP May Be Downplaying Palin's Religious Beliefs." *CNN.com*, September 9; available at http: //www.cnn.com/2008/POLITICS/09/08/palin.pastor/index.html, accessed May 29, 2010.

Kedar, Orit. 2005. "When Moderate Voters Prefer Extreme Parties: Policy Balancing in Parliamentary Elections." *American Political Science Review*, 99: 185–199.

————. 2010. *Voting for Policy, Not Parties: How Voters Compensate for Power Sharing*. New York: Cambridge University Press.

Keith, Bruce E., David B. Magleby, Candice J. Nelson, Elizabeth Orr, Mark C. Westlye, and Raymond E. Wolfinger. 1977. "The Myth of the Independent Voter." Paper presented at the annual meeting of the American Political Science Association, Washington, DC.

————. 1986. "The Partisan Affinities of Independent 'Leaners.'" *British Journal of Political Science* 16 (April): 155–185.

————. 1992. *The Myth of the Independent Voter*. Berkeley: University of California Press.

Kelley, Stanley, Jr., Richard E. Ayres, and William G. Bowen. 1967. "Registration and Voting: Putting First Things First." *The American Political Science Review* 61(2): 359–379.

Kellstedt, Lyman A., and Corwin Smidt. 1991. "Measuring Fundamentalism: An Analysis of Different Operational Strategies." *Journal for the Scientific Study of Religion* 30: 259–278.

Kellstedt, Paul M. 2003. *The Mass Media and the Dynamics of American Racial Attitudes*. Cambridge, UK: Cambridge University Press.

Kenny, Lawrence W., and Babak Lotfinia. 2005. "Evidence on the Importance of Spatial Voting Models in Presidential Nominations and Elections." *Public Choice* 123(3/4): 439–462.

Kernell, Samuel, and Gary Jacobson. 2008. *The Logic of American Politics*. Washington, DC: CQ Press.

Kessel, John H. 1984. *Presidential Campaign Politics*, 2nd ed. Homewood, IL: Dorsey Press.

Key, V. O. 1984 [1949]. *Southern Politics in State and Nation*, 1st ed. New York: A. A. Knopf.

————. 1964. *Politics, Parties, and Pressure Groups*, 5th ed. New York: Ty Crowell Co.

————. 1966. *The Responsible Electorate: Rationality in Presidential Voting, 1936–1960*. Cambridge, MA: Belknap Press of Harvard University.

Kinder, Donald R., and Lynn M. Sanders. 1996. *Divided by Color: Racial Politics and Democratic Ideals*. Chicago: University of Chicago Press.

Kinder, Donald R., and David O. Sears. 1981. "Prejudice and Politics: Symbolic Racism versus Racial Threats to the Good Life." *Journal of Personality and Social Psychology* 40(3): 414–431.

King, Gary, James Honaker, Anne Joseph, and Kenneth Scheve. 2001. "Analyzing Incomplete Political Science Data: An Alternative Algorithm for Multiple Imputation." *American Political Science Review* 95: 49–69.

King, Gary, Michael Tomz, and Jason Wittenberg. 2000. "Making the Most of Statistical Analysis: Improving Interpretation and Presentation." *American Journal of Political Science* 44(2): 341–355.

Kizzia, Tom. 2006. "'Creation Science' Enters the Race: Governor Palin Is Only Candidate to Suggest It Should Be Discussed in Schools." *Anchorage Daily News*, October 27; available at http://www.adn.com/sarah-palin/background/story/217111.html, accessed July 12, 2010.

Knack, Stephen. 1995. "Does 'Motor Voter' Work? Evidence from State-Level Data." *The Journal of Politics* 57(3): 796–811.

———. 2001. "Election-day Registration: The Second Wave." *American Politics Research* 29(1): 65–78.

Knight, Kathleen. 1985. "Ideology in the 1980 Election: Ideological Sophistication Does Matter." *Journal of Politics* 47: 828–853.

Knuckey, Jonathan. 2007. "Moral Values and Vote Choice in the 2004 U.S. Presidential Election." *Politics and Policy* 35(2): 222–245.

Kolodny, Robin. 1998. *Pursuing Majorities: Congressional Campaign Committees in American Politics*. Norman: University of Oklahoma Press.

Krasno, Jonathan S. 2005. "TV or Not TV: The Decision to Advertise in House Elections." Presented at the Annual Meeting of the American Political Science Association, Washington, DC.

Krasno, Jonathan S., and Conor Dowling. 2008. "Parties and the Shrinking Field of Play in U.S. House Elections." Presented at the Annual Meeting of the Midwest Political Science Association, Chicago, IL.

Krasno, Jonathan S., and Kenneth Goldstein. 2002. "The Facts about Television Advertising and the McCain-Feingold Bill." *PS:Political Science and Politics* 35: 207–212.

Krasno, Jonathan S., and Donald P. Green. 2005. "The Trouble with Targeting: Four Reasons Why the Parties Outsmart Themselves in Congressional Elections." *Campaigns and Elections* (December/January): 61–62.

Krasno, Jonathan S., and Daniel Seltz. 2000. *Buying Time: Television Advertising in the 1998 Congressional Elections*. New York: Brennan Center for Justice.

Krasno, Jonathan S., and Frank J. Sorauf. 2003. "Evaluating the Bipartisan Campaign Reform Act." *NYU Review of Law and Social Change* 28: 121–181.

Krehbiel, Keith. 1991. *Information and Legislative Organization*. Ann Arbor: University of Michigan Press.

———. 1993. "Where's the Party?" *British Journal of Political Science* 23: 235–266.

Kuklinski, James H., and B. Peyton. 2007. "Belief Systems and Political Decision Making." In *Oxford Handbook of Political Behavior*, Russell J. Dalton and Hans-Dieter Klingemann, eds. Oxford, UK: Oxford University Press.

Kuklinski, James H., and Paul J. Quirk. 2000. "Reconsidering the Rational Public: Cognition, Heuristics, and Mass Opinion." In *Elements of Reason: Cognition, Choice, and the Bounds of Rationality*, Arthur Lupia, Matthew D. McCubbins, and Samuel L. Popkin, eds. Cambridge, UK: Cambridge University Press.

———. 2001. "Conceptual Foundations of Citizen Competence." *Political Behavior* 23(3): 285–311.

Ladd, Everett Carl, Jr. 1982. *Where Have All the Voters Gone?* 2nd ed. New York: W.W. Norton.

———. 1985. "As the Realignment Turns: A Drama in Many Acts." *Public Opinion* (December 1984–January 1985): 6.

Lakoff, George. 2004. *Don't Think of an Elephant!* White River Junction, VT: Chelsea Green Press.

Lane, Robert E. 1962. *Political Ideology: Why the American Common Man Believes What He Does.* New York: Free Press of Glencoe.

La Raja, Raymond J. 2003. "Why Soft Money Has Strengthened Parties." In *Inside the Campaign Finance Battle: Court Testimony on the New Reforms,* Anthony Corrado, Thomas Mann, and Trevor Potter, eds. Washington, DC: Brookings Insitution.

———. 2008. *Small Change: Money, Political Parties, and Campaign Finance Reform.* Ann Arbor: University of Michigan Press.

La Raja, Raymond J., and Elizabeth Jarvis-Shean. 2001. *Assessing the Impact of a Ban on Soft Money: Party Soft Money Spending in the 2000 Elections.* Berkeley, CA: Institute of Governmental Studies and Citizens' Research Foundation Policy Brief.

Lau, Richard R., and David P. Redlawsk. 2006. *How Voters Decide: Information Processing during Election Campaigns.* New York: Cambridge University Press.

Laver, Michael, and Norman Schofield. 1998. *Multiparty Government: The Politics of Government in Europe.* Ann Arbor: University of Michigan Press.

Layman, Geoffrey C., and Thomas M. Carsey. 2002. "Party Polarization and Conflict Extension in the American Electorate." *American Journal of Political Science* 46(4): 786–802.

Layman, Geoffrey C., Thomas M. Carsey, John C. Green, Richard Herrera, and Rosalyn Cooperman. 2010. "Activists and Conflict Extension in American Party Politics." *The American Political Science Review* 104(2): 324–346.

Layman, Geoffrey C., Thomas M. Carsey, and Juliana Menasce Horowitz. 2006. "Party Polarization in American Politics: Characteristics, Causes, and Consequences." *American Review of Political Science* 9: 83–110.

Lazarsfeld, Paul F., Bernard R. Berelson, and Hazel Gaudet. 1948. *The People's Choice: How the Voter Makes Up His Mind in a Presidential Campaign.* New York: Columbia University Press.

Leege, David C., and Lyman A. Kellstedt, eds. 1993. *Rediscovering the Religious Factor in American Politics.* London: M.E. Sharpe.

Levendusky, Matthew S. 2009. *The Partisan Sort: How Liberals Became Democrats and Conservatives Became Republicans.* Chicago: University of Chicago Press.

Lewis-Beck, Michael S., William G. Jacoby, Helmut Norpath, and Herbert F. Weisberg. 2008. *The American Voter Revisited.* Ann Arbor: University of Michigan Press.

Liasson, Mara. 2007. "Establishing Bipartisanship is a Big Challenge."*NPR*; available at http: //www.npr.org/templates/story/story.php?storyId=6937664, accessed August 5, 2009.

Lijphart, Arend. 1997. "Unequal Participation: Democracy's Unresolved Dilemma." *American Political Science Review* 91(1): 1–14.

Lipset, Seymour Martin. 1959. *Political Man: The Social Bases of Politics.* New York: Doubleday.

Liu, Frank C. S., and Laura Lucas. 2008. "Heterogeneity in Communications Networks and the Rejection of Party Identification." Paper presented at the Annual Meeting of the Midwest Political Science Association, Chicago.

Lodge, Milton, Patrick Stroh, and John Wahlke. 1990. "Black-Box Models of Candidate Evaluation." *Political Behavior* 12: 5–18.

Loftus, Jeni. 2001. "America's Liberalization in Attitudes toward Homosexuality, 1973 to 1998." *American Sociological Review* 66: 762–782.

Lupia, Arthur. 1994. "Shortcuts versus Encyclopedias: Information and Voting Behavior in California Insurance Reform Elections." *American Political Science Review* 88(1): 63–76.

Lupia, Arthur, Yanna Krupnikov, Adam Seth Levine, Spencer Piston, and Alexander Von Hagen-Jamar. 2010. "Why State Constitutions Differ in Their Treatment of Same-Sex Marriage." *The Journal of Politics* 72(4): 1222–1235.

Lupia, Arthur, Adam Seth Levine, Jesse O. Menning, and Gisela Sin. 2007. "Were Bush Tax Cut Supporters 'Simply Ignorant?' A Second Look at Conservatives and Liberals in 'Homer Gets a Tax Cut.'" *Perspectives on Politics* 5: 773–784.

Lupia, Arthur, and Mathew D. McCubbins. 1998. *The Democratic Dilemma: Can Citizens Learn What They Need to Know?* New York: Cambridge University Press.

———. 2000. "How Citizens Use Institutions to Help Delegation Succeed." *European Journal of Political Research* 37: 291–307.

Lupia, Arthur, Matthew D. McCubbins, and Samuel L. Popkin. 2000. *Elements of Reason: Cognition, Choice, and the Bounds of Rationality*. Cambridge, UK: Cambridge University Press.

Lupia, Arthur, and Kaare Strom. 2008. "Bargaining, Transaction Costs, and Coalition Governance." In *Cabinets and Coalition Bargaining: The Democratic Life Cycle in Western Europe*, Torbjörn Bergman, Wolfgang C. Müller, and Kaare Strøm, eds. Oxford, UK: Oxford University Press.

Macgillis, Alec. 2007. "In N.H., the Swing Voter Is Vanishing." *Washington Post*, December 18; available at http: //www.washingtonpost.com/wp-dyn/content/article/2007/12/17/ AR2007121700502.html?nav=emailpage, accessed August 5, 2009.

Magleby, David B. 2002. *The Other Campaign: Soft Money and Issue Advocacy in the 2000 Congressional Elections*. Lanham, MD: Rowman and Littlefield.

Malhotra, Neil, Jon A. Krosnick, and Randall K. Thomas. 2007. "Optimal Design of Branching Questions to Measure Bipolar Constructs." Manuscript, Stanford University.

Mann, Thomas E., and Norman J. Ornstein. 2006. *The Broken Branch: How Congress Is Failing and How to Get It Back on Track*. Oxford, UK: Oxford University Press.

Mann, Thomas E., and Raymond E. Wolfinger. 1980. "Candidates and Parties in Congressional Elections." *American Political Science Review* 74: 617–632.

Manza, Jeff, Michael Hout, and Clem Brooks. 1995. "Class Voting in Capitalist Democracies since World War II: Dealignment, Realignment, or Trendless Fluctuation?" *Annual Review of Sociology* 21: 137–162.

Marcus, George E. 2000. "Emotion in Politics." *Annual Review of Political Science*, 3: 221–250.

Martinez, Michael D. 2009. "The Resurgent American Voter, 1988–2009." Paper delivered at the 2009 Annual Meeting of the American Political Science Association, Toronto, Canada.

Martinez, Michael D., and Jeff Gill. 2005. "The Effects of Turnout on Partisan Outcomes in U.S. Presidential Elections 1960–2000." *Journal of Politics* 67(4): 1245–1274.

Mayhew, David R. 1974a. *Congress: The Electoral Connection.* New Haven, CT: Yale University Press.

———. 1974b. "Congressional Elections: The Case of the Vanishing Marginals." *Polity* 6: 295–317.

McCarty, Nolan, Keith T. Poole, and Howard Rosenthal. 1997. *Income Redistribution and the Realignment of American Politics.* Washington, DC: AEI Press.

———. 2006. *Polarized America: The Dance of Ideology and Unequal Riches.* Cambridge, MA: MIT Press.

McClurg, Scott D. 2006. "The Electoral Relevance of Political Talk: Examining the Effect of Disagreement and Expertise in Social Networks on Political Participation." *American Journal of Political Science* 50(3): 737–754.

McCubbins, Mathew D., and Thomas Schwartz. 1984. "Congressional Oversight Overlooked: Fire Alarms and Police Patrols." *American Journal of Political Science* 28: 165–179.

McDonald, Michael P. 2008. "Voter Turnout Statistics." United States Elections Project; available at http://elections.gmu.edu/.

McDonald, Michael P., and Samuel L. Popkin. 2001. "The Myth of the Vanishing Voter." *American Political Science Review* 95: 963–974.

McGhee, Eric, and John Sides. Forthcoming. "Do Campaigns Drive Partisan Turnout?" *Political Behavior.*

McGowan, John. 2007. *American Liberalism: An Interpretation for Our Time.* Chapel Hill: University of North Carolina Press.

Menefee-Libey, David. 1999. *The Triumph of Candidate-Centered Politics.* New York: Chatham House.

Merriam, Charles Edward, and Harold Foote Gosnell. 1924. *Non-Voting, Causes and Methods of Control.* Chicago: University of Chicago Press.

Merton, Robert K. 1947. "Selected Problems of Field Work in the Planned Community." *American Sociological Review* 12(3): 304–312.

———. 1957. *Social Theory and Social Structure.* Glencoe, IL: Free Press.

Milkis, Sidney M. 2003. "Parties versus Interest Groups." In *Inside the Campaign Finance Battle: Court Testimony on the New Reforms,* Anthony Corrado, Thomas Mann, and Trevor Potter, eds. Washington, DC: Brookings.

Miller, Gary, and Norman Schofield. 2003. "Activists and Partisan Realignment in the United States." *American Political Science Review* 97(2): 245–260.

Miller, Warren E. 1991. "Party Identification, Realignment, and Party Voting: Back to the Basics." *American Political Science Review* 85: 557–568.

Miller, Warren E., and J. Merrill Shanks. 1996. *The New American Voter.* Cambridge, MA: Harvard University Press.

Mitchell, Glenn E., and Christopher Wlezien. 1995. "The Impact of Legal Constraints on Voter Registration, Turnout, and the Composition of the American Electorate." *Political Behavior* 17(2): 179–202.

Mondak, Jeffery J. 1999. "Reconsidering the Measurement of Political Knowledge." *Political Analysis* 8(1): 57–82.

———. 2001. "Developing Valid Knowledge Scales." *American Journal of Political Science* 45(1): 224–238.

Moramarco, Glenn. 1999. *Regulating Electioneering: Distinguishing between 'Express Advocacy' and 'Issue Advocacy.'* New York: Brennan Center for Justice.

Mutz, Diana C. 2002. "The Consequences of Cross-Cutting Networks for Political Participation." *American Journal of Political Science*, 46(4): 838–855.

Nagel, Jack H., and John E. McNulty. 1996. "Partisan Effects of Voter Turnout in Senatorial and Gubernatorial Elections." *American Political Science Review* 90(4): 780–793.

———. 2000. "Partisan Effects of Voter Turnout in Presidential Elections." *American Politics Quarterly* 28(3): 408–429.

Nagler, Jonathan. 1991. "The Effect of Registration Laws and Education on U.S. Voter Turnout." *The American Political Science Review* 85(4): 1393–1405.

Nelson, Michael. 1997. "The Election: Turbulence and Tranquility in Contemporary American Politics." In *The Elections of 1996*, Michael Nelson, ed. Washington, DC: Congressional Quarterly.

Newton-Small, Jay. 2008. "TIME's Interview with Sarah Palin." *TIME*, August 29; available at http://www.time.com/time/printout/0,8816,1837536,00.html, accessed June 21, 2009.

New York Times. 2008. "Running Mates on the Issues." Election Guide 2008; available at http: //elections.nytimes.com/2008/president/issues/vice-presidents/index.html, accessed September 9, 2008.

Niemi, Richard G. 1974. *The Politics of Future Citizens.* San Francisco: Jossey-Bass.

O'Connor, Karen, and Larry Sabato. 2008. *American Government: Continuity and Change.* New York: Pearson Longman.

Ontheissues.org. 2008. "Sarah Palin on Civil Rights." Available at http://www.ontheissues.org/2008/Sarah_Palin_Civil_Rights.htm, accessed July 12, 2010.

Oppenheimer, Bruce I. 1996. "The Representational Experience: The Effects of State Population on Senator-Constituency Linkages." *American Journal of Political Science* 40 (November): 1280–1299.

———. 2005. "Deep Red and Blue Congressional Districts: The Causes and Consequences of Declining Party Responsiveness." In *Congress Reconsidered*, L. C. Dodd and B. I. Oppenhemer, eds. Washington, DC: CQ Press.

Pacek, Alexander, and Benjamin Radcliff. 1995. "Turnout and the Vote for Left-of-Centre Parties: A Cross-National Analysis." *British Journal of Political Science* 25(1): 137–143.

Page, Benjamin I., with Marshall M. Bouton. 2006. *The Foreign Policy Disconnect: What Americans Want from Our Leaders but Don't Get.* Chicago: University of Chicago Press.

Page, Benjamin I., and Robert Y. Shapiro. 1992. *The Rational Public: Fifty Years of Trends in Americans' Policy Preferences*. Chicago: University of Chicago Press.

Page, Benjamin I., and Tao Xie. 2010. *Living with the Dragon: How the American Public Views the Rise of China*. New York: Columbia University Press.

Pasek, Josh, and Jon A. Krosnick. 2010. "Optimizing Survey Questionnaire Design in Political Science: Insights from Psychology." In *The Oxford Handbook of American Elections and Political Behavior*, Jan E. Leighley, ed. Oxford, UK: Oxford University Press.

Patterson, Thomas E. 2003. *The Vanishing Voter: Public Involvement in an Age of Uncertainty*. New York: Knopf.

Peffley, Mark A., and Jon Hurwitz. 1985. "A Hierarchical Model of Attitude Constraint." *American Journal of Political Science* 29(4): 871–890.

Petrocik, John R. 1996. "Issue Ownership in Presidential Elections, with a 1980 Case Study." *American Journal of Political Science* 40(3): 825–850.

Plane, Dennis L., and Joseph Gershtenson. 2004. "Candidates' Ideological Locations, Abstention, and Turnout in U.S. Midterm Senate Elections." *Political Behavior* 26(1): 69–93.

Pleanants, Julian M. 2000. *Buncombe Bob: The Life and Times of Robert Rice Reynolds*. Chapel Hill: University of North Carolina Press.

Pomper, Gerald M. 1977. "The Decline of the Party in American Elections." *Political Science Quarterly* 92 (Spring): 41.

Poole, Keith T., and Howard Rosenthal. 1997. *Congress: A Political-Economic History of Roll Call Voting*. New York: Oxford University Press.

Popkin, Samuel L. 1991. *The Reasoning Voter: Communication and Persuasion in Presidential Campaigns*. Chicago: University Of Chicago Press.

Powell, G. Bingham, Jr. 1986. "American Voter Turnout in Comparative Perspective." *American Political Science Review* 80(1): 17–43.

Prior, Markus. 2007. *Post-Broadcast Democracy: How Media Choice Increases Inequality in Political Involvement and Polarizes Elections*. Cambridge, UK: Cambridge University Press.

Prior, Markus, and Arthur Lupia. 2008. "Money, Time, and Political Knowledge: Distinguishing Quick Recall from Political Learning Skills." *American Journal of Political Science* 52: 168–182.

Rakove, Milton L. 1975. *Don't Make No Waves, Don't Back No Losers*. Bloomington: Indiana University Press.

Ranney, Austin. 1954. *The Doctrine of Responsible Party Government*. Champaign-Urbana: University of Illinois Press.

Rawls, John. 1971. *A Theory of Justice*. Cambridge, MA: Belknap Press.

Reardon, Kathleen. 2005. "Should We Deep-Six the Term 'Liberal,' or Own Up to It?" *Huffington Post*, September 16.

Rhine, Staci L. 1996. "An Analysis of the Impact of Registration Factors on Turnout in 1992." *Political Behavior* 18(2): 171–185.

Riker, William H. 1965. *Democracy in the United States*. New York: Macmillan.

———. 1982. *Liberalism against Populism: A Confrontation between the Theory of Democracy and the Theory of Social Choice*. San Francisco: W.H. Freeman.

Riker, William H., and Peter C. Ordeshook. 1968. "A Theory of the Calculus of Voting." *American Political Science Review* 62(1): 25–42.

Riordan, William L. 1963. *Plunkitt of Tammany Hall: A Series of Very Plain Talks on Very Practical Politics*. New York: E.F. Dutton and Co.

Robb, Robert. 2008. "Is John McCain a Conservative?" *RealClearPolitics*, February 1; available at http: //www.realclearpolitics.com/articles/2008/02/is_john_mccain_a_conservative.html, accessed June 18, 2008.

Rohde, David W. 1991. *Parties and Leaders in the Postreform House*. Chicago: University of Chicago Press.

Rosenstone, Steven J., Roy L. Behr, and Edward H. Lazarus. 1996. *Third Parties in America*. Princeton, NJ: Princeton University Press.

Rosenstone, Steven J., and John Mark Hansen. 1993. *Mobilization, Participation, and Democracy in America*. New York: Macmillan.

Rosenstone, Steven J., and Raymond E. Wolfinger. 1978. "The Effect of Registration Laws on Voter Turnout." *American Political Science Review* 72(1): 22–45.

Rotunda, Ronald D. 1989.*The Politics of Language*. Iowa City: University of Iowa Press.

Saunders, Kyle L., and Alan I. Abramowitz. 2004. "Ideological Realignment and Active Partisans in the American Electorate," *American Politics Research* 32(3): 285–309.

Schafer, Joseph L., and John W. Graham. 2002. "Missing Data: Our View of the State of the Art." *Psychological Methods* 7(2): 147–177.

Schattschneider, E. E. 1942. *Party Government*. New York: Rinehart.

Schiffer, Adam J. 2000. "I'm Not That Liberal: Explaining Conservative Democratic Identification." *Political Behavior* 22: 293–310.

Schlesinger, Joseph A. 1994. *Political Parties and the Winning of Office*. Ann Arbor: University of Michigan Press.

Schneider, William. 1984. "Antipartisanship in America." In *Parties and Democracy in Britain and America*, Vernon Bogdanor, ed. New York: Praeger.

Schumacker, Randall L., and Susan T. Beyerlein. 2000. "Confirmatory Factor Analysis with Different Correlation Types and Estimation Models." *Structural Equation Modeling* 7(4): 629–636.

Sears, David O., and Jack Citrin. 1982. *Tax Revolt: Something for Nothing in California*. Cambridge, MA: Harvard University Press.

Sen, Amartya K. 1970. *Collective Choice and Social Welfare*. Amsterdam: North-Holland.

Shafer, Byron E., and William J. M. Claggett. 1995. *The Two Majorities: The Issue Context of Modern American Politics*. Baltimore: Johns Hopkins University Press.

Shapiro, Catherine R., David W. Brady, Richard A. Brody, and John A. Ferejohn. 1990. "Linking Constituency Opinion and Senate Voting Scores: A Hybrid Explanation." *Legislative Studies Quarterly* 15 (November): 599–621.

Sharp, Carol, and Milton Lodge. 1985. Partisan and Ideological Belief Systems: Do They Differ? *Political Behavior* 7: 147–166.

Shea, Daniel M. 1995. *Transforming Democracy: Legislative Campaign Committees and Political Parties*. Albany, NY: SUNY Press.

Shenkman, Rick. 2008. *Just How Stupid Are We? Facing the Truth about the American Voter*. New York: Basic Books.

Shepsle, Kenneth A. 1989. "The Changing Textbook Congress." In *Can the Government Govern?*, John Chubb and Paul Peterson, eds. Washington, DC: Brookings Institution.

Sherrill, Kenneth S., and David J. Vogler. 1982. *Power, Policy and Participation.* New York: Harper and Row.

Sides, John, Eric Schickler, and Jack Citrin. 2008. "If Everyone Had Voted, Would Bubba and Dubya Have Won?" *Presidential Studies Quarterly* 38(3): 521–539.

Sidlow, Edward. 2003. *Challenging the Incumbent: An Underdog's Undertaking.* Washington, DC: CQ Press.

Sigelman, Lee. 1982. "The Nonvoting Voter in Voting Research." *American Journal of Political Science* 26(1): 47–56.

Sigelman, Lee, and Malcolm E. Jewell. 1986. "From Core to Periphery: A Note on the Imagery of Concentric Electorates." *Journal of Politics* 48(2): 440–449.

Sigelman, Lee, Philip W. Roeder, Malcolm E. Jewell, and Michael A. Baer. 1985. "Voting and Nonvoting: A Multi-Election Perspective." *American Journal of Political Science* 29(4): 749–765.

Silbey, Joel H. 1994. "The Rise and Fall of American Political Parties 1790–1993". In *The Parties Respond: Changes in American Parties and Campaigns,* L. Sandy Maisel, ed. Boulder, CO: Westview Press.

Silver, Brian D., Barbara A. Anderson, and Paul R. Abramson. 1986. "Who Overreports Voting?" *American Political Science Review* 80(2): 613–624.

Sin, Gisela, and Arthur Lupia. 2010. "How the Senate and President Affect the Timing of Major Rule Changes in the U.S. House of Representatives." Manuscript, University of Michigan.

Sinclair, Barbara. 2006. *Party Wars: Polarization and the Politics of National Policy Making.* Norman: University of Oklahoma Press.

Smith, Hedrick. 1988. *The Power Game: How Washington Works.* New York: Random House.

Sniderman, Paul M., Richard A. Brody, and Philip E. Tetlock. 1991. *Reasoning and Choice: Explorations in Political Psychology.* New York: Cambridge University Press.

Sniderman, Paul M., and John Bullock. 2004. "A Consistency Theory of Public Opinion and Political Choice: The Hypothesis of Menu Dependence." In *Studies in Public Opinion,* Willem E. Saris and Paul M. Sniderman, eds. Princeton, NJ: Princeton University Press.

Sniderman, Paul M., Michael G. Hagen, Philip E. Tetlock, and Henry E. Brady. 1986. "Reasoning Chains: Causal Models of Policy Reasoning in Mass Publics." *British Journal of Political Science* 16(4): 405–430.

Snyder, James M., and Michael Ting. 2002. "An Informational Rationale for Political Parties." *American Journal of Political Science,* 46: 90–110.

Sorauf, Frank J., and Jonathan S. Krasno. 1997. "Political Party Committees and Coordinated Spending." Prepared for the Federal Election Commission for *Colorado II.*

———. 2000. Statement Prepared for *Missouri Republican Party v. Lamb.*

Srull, Thomas K., and Robert S. Wyer Jr. 1989. "Person Memory and Judgment." *Psychological Review* 96: 58–83.

Stimson, James. 1975. "Belief Systems, Constraint, Complexity, and the 1972 Election." *American Journal of Political Science* 19: 393–418.

———. 1999. *Public Opinion in America*, 2nd ed. Boulder, CO: Westview Press.

———. 2002. "The Micro Foundations of Mood." In *Thinking about Political Psychology*, James Kuklinski, ed. Cambridge, UK: Cambridge University Press.

———. 2004. *Tides of Consent*. Cambridge, UK: Cambridge University Press.

Stonecash, Jeffrey M. 2001. *Class and Party in American Politics*. Boulder, CO: Westview.

Stonecash, Jeffrey M., Mark D. Brewer, and Mack D. Mariani. 2003. *Diverging Parties: Social Change, Realignment, and Party Polarization*. Boulder, CO: Westview Press.

Sussman, Barry. 1984. "Why Anderson's Third-Party Bid May Hit Responsive Chords." *Washington Post* (national weekly ed.), May 21: 37.

Tesler, Michael, and David O. Sears. 2010. *Obama's Race: The 2008 Election and the Dream of a Post-Racial America*. Chicago: University of Chicago Press.

Theiss-Morse, Elizabeth, and John R. Hibbing. 2005. "Citizenship and Civic Engagement." *Annual Review of Political Science* 8: 227–249.

Todorov, Alexander, Anesu N. Mandisodza, Amir Goren, and Crystal C. Hall. 2005. "Inferences of Competence from Faces Predict Election Outcomes." *Science* 308: 1623–1626.

Tourangeau, Roger, Lance J. Rips, and Kenneth Rasinski. 2000. *The Psychology of Survey Response*. New York: Cambridge University Press.

Treier, Shawn, and D. Sunshine Hillygus. 2009. "The Nature of Political Ideology in the Contemporary Electorate." *Public Opinion Quarterly* 73(4): 679–703.

Tulis, Jeffrey K. 1988. *The Rhetorical Presidency*. Princeton, NJ: Princeton University Press.

Turgeon, Mathieu. 2009. "'Just Thinking': Attitude Development, Public Opinion, and Political Representation." *Political Behavior* 31(3): 353–378.

Van Houweling, Robert P., and Paul M. Sniderman. 2005. "The Political Logic of a Downsian Space." Working Paper. Institute of Governmental Studies, University of California Berkeley; available at http://repositories.cdlib.org/igs/WP2005-44.

Vavreck, Lynn, and Douglas Rivers. 2008. "The 2006 Cooperative Congressional Election Study." *Journal of Elections, Public Opinion and Parties* 18(4): 355–366.

Verba, Sidney, and Norman Nie. 1972. *Participation in American: Political Democracy and Social Equality*. New York: Harper and Row.

Verba, Sidney, Kay L. Schlozman, and Henry E. Brady. 1995. *Voice and Equality: Civic Voluntarism in American Politics*. Cambridge, MA: Harvard University Press.

Wald, Kenneth D. 2003. *Religion and Politics in the United States*. New York: Rowman and Littlefield.

Walzer, Michael. 2006. *Just and Unjust Wars*, 4th ed. New York: Basic Books.

Wattenberg, Martin P. 1986. *The Decline of American Political Parties, 1952–1984*. Cambridge, MA: Harvard University Press.

———. 1987. "The Hollow Realignment: Partisan Change in a Candidate-Centered Era." *Public Opinion Quarterly* 51 (Spring): 58–74.

———. 1992. *The Rise of Candidate-Centered Politics: Presidential Elections of the 1980s.* Cambridge, MA: Harvard University Press.

———. 1998. *The Decline of American Political Parties, 1952–1996.* Cambridge, MA: Harvard University Press.

Wattenberg, Martin, and Craig Leonard Brians. 2002. "Partisan Turnout Bias in Midterm Legislative Elections." *Legislative Studies Quarterly* 26(3): 407–421.

Weisberg, Herbert F., Jon A. Krosnick, and Bruce D. Bowen. 1996. *An Introduction to Survey Research, Polling, and Data Analysis.* Thousand Oaks, CA: Sage Publishers.

Whitby, Kenny J., and Timothy Bledsoe. 1986. "The Impact of Policy Voting on the Electoral Fortunes of Senate Incumbents." *Western Political Quarterly* 39 (December): 690–700.

Whitney, Christopher B., and David Shambaugh. 2009. *Soft Power in Asia: Results of a 2008 Multinational Survey of Public Opinion.* Chicago: Chicago Council on Global Affairs (in partnership with the East Asia Institute, South Korea).

Wilson, James Q., and John J. DiIulio, Jr. 2008. *American Government,* 11th ed. Boston: Houghton Mifflin.

Wolfinger, Raymond E., and Steven J. Rosenstone. 1980. *Who Votes?* New Haven, CT: Yale University Press.

Wood, B. Dan, and Angela Hinton Andersson. 1998. "The Dynamics of Senatorial Representation, 1952–1991." *Journal of Politics* 60 (August): 705–736.

Wright, Gerald C., Jr. 1989. "Policy Voting in the U.S. Senate: Who Is Represented?" *Legislative Studies Quarterly* 14 (November): 465–486.

Wright, Gerald C., Jr., and Michael B. Berkman. 1986. "Candidates and Policy in United States Senate Elections." *American Political Science Review* 80 (June): 567–588.

Wuffle, A., and C. Collet. 1997. "Why Democrats Shouldn't Vote." *Journal of Theoretical Politics* 9: 137–140.

Zaller, John. 1992. *The Nature and Origins of Mass Opinion.* Cambridge, MA: Cambridge University Press.

———. 1998. "Monica Lewinsky's Contribution to Political Science." *Political Science and Politics* 31(2): 182–189.

Index